From the Land of the Thunder Dragon

From the Land of the Thunder Dragon

Textile Arts of Bhutan

Diana K. Myers and Susan S. Bean, *Editors*

Diana K. Myers

with

Michael Aris

Françoise Pommaret

Susan S. Bean

Serindia Publications, London
Peabody Essex Museum, Salem

Designed and produced by Serindia Publications

ISBN 0 906026 33 4

First Published in 1994 by
Serindia Publications
10 Parkfields, London SW15 6NH, UK

and

Peabody Essex Museum
East India Square, Salem, Massachusetts 01970, USA

British Library Cataloging in Publication Data
A catalog record for this book is available from the British Library.

Library of Congress Catalog Card Number: 94-67383

Printed in Hong Kong

Contents

Her Majesty Ashi Sangay Choden Wangchuck, Queen of Bhutan

HER MAJESTY THE QUEEN

Handlooms play an important role in Bhutanese society. They are a part of our culture and are of great economic significance for many of our people. Recognizing this, the Royal Government of Bhutan has given high priority to the development of this sector with a view to providing gainful employment and enhancing the income of the rural community while preserving an important aspect of Bhutanese culture.

Our handlooms have evolved over the centuries and reflect the country's distinctive identity. Most of the designs and patterns of weaves are unique to the country. Bhutanese weavers have been very innovative in their designs while still maintaining the traditional character of the art. This is reflected in the many textiles that have well-known patterns as well as new designs adopted or created to suit both Bhutanese and international tastes.

Since our country emerged from its self-imposed isolation in 1961, many people have come to appreciate the unique culture and way of life in Bhutan. Our handlooms are an important part of this tradition.

I am happy that the Peabody Essex Museum is organizing an exhibition exclusively on Bhutanese handlooms and other textiles used in Bhutan. This display will be an important exposure of a vital part of our precious cultural heritage to the world at large. It will also be a tribute to our weaving traditions and to the thousands of weavers in our villages and towns who have kept this tradition alive.

This exhibition has been many years in the making. More than a decade ago Miss Jane Phillips and others at the Peabody Essex Museum had the vision to collect Bhutanese textiles with the goal of eventually presenting them to the American public. Both Dr. Susan Bean, Project Director, and Ms. Diana Myers, Guest Curator, have worked with great perseverance and dedication to bring this project to fruition. The exhibition is a result of their vision and untiring efforts to project an important part of the rich cultural heritage of a small but unique Himalayan country.

I would also like to take this opportunity to thank those who have supported this venture. Although it is not possible to mention them all by name, I wish to acknowledge their valuable contribution, both financial and material, to make this exhibition possible.

My personal involvement in this project and with the organizers of the exhibition has given me much pleasure and satisfaction. I wish the exhibition all success and hope that it will provide an insight into an important aspect of Bhutan's unique heritage.

Tashi Delek!

E. Wangchuk

Ashi Sangay Choden Wangchuck
Queen of Bhutan

THIS BOOK HAS BEEN MADE POSSIBLE THROUGH THE GENEROSITY OF THE FOLLOWING BENEFACTORS

The National Endowment for the Humanities

Miss Jane A. Phillips

Mrs. Stephen Phillips

Lisina and Frank Hoch

E. Rhodes and Leona B. Carpenter Foundation

Mr. Henry Lo

Ministry for Foreign Affairs, Royal Government of Bhutan

Ministry for Trade and Industry, Royal Govenment of Bhutan

Mr. Lawrence Coolidge

National Geographic Society

Inner Asia Expeditions, Ltd., San Francisco

United Nations Development Programme, Bhutan

Druk Air Corporation

LENDERS TO THE EXHIBITION

Her Majesty Queen Ashi Sangay Choden Wangchuck

Her Royal Highness Ashi Choeki Wangchuck

Barbara Adams

Avery Brundage Collection, Asian Art Museum of San Francisco

His Excellency Ugyen Tshering and Patrizia Franceschinis

The Henry Art Gallery, University of Washington, Seattle, Washington

Lisina and Frank Hoch

The Museum of International Folk Art, Santa Fe, New Mexico

Mr. Lobsang Lhalungpa and Ms. Gisela Minke

The Minneapolis Institute of Arts, Minneapolis, Minnesota

The Monk Body, Tashichö Dzong

The Museum for Textiles, Toronto, Ontario

Diana K. Myers

Mrs. Chhemey Wangmo Norbu

Mrs. Ugen Norzom Namgyel

Mrs. Chöden Namgyal and Mr. Kinley D. Dorji

Jane A. Phillips Collection, Peabody Essex Museum, Salem, Massachusetts

The Textile Museum, Washington, D.C.

The Victoria and Albert Museum, London, England

Mrs. Sonam Wangmo

Stephen and Claire Wilbur

Preface

From the Land of the Thunder Dragon marks a special juncture for the Peabody Essex Museum. The Peabody Essex is at once new and old. Created in 1992 through consolidation of the former Peabody Museum of Salem and the former Essex Institute, the Museum is just two years old, though its roots extend back to 1799. *From the Land of the Thunder Dragon* features extraordinary examples of textile art and conveys their Bhutanese significance in keeping with the Museum's new mission to blend art and culture in innovative ways.

The Peabody Essex is proud to possess the nation's most extensive collection of Bhutanese textile art. This circumstance results from the dedication and generosity of a long-time friend of Museum, Jane Phillips, who began to collect Bhutanese textiles for the Museum more than ten years ago. Fascinated by an art form hardly known in the West, Jane was particularly taken by the intricate delicacy of the woven patterns. Through her astute collecting, this catalog and the exhibition it documents are made possible. As a result of her love for the richness of Bhutanese textiles, a little known art will now be accessible to many.

Creation of the exhibition and catalog required, however, a team of people. Among them were Dr. Susan Bean, Curator of Asian, Oceanic, and African Arts and Cultures; Diana Myers, the foremost authority on Bhutanese textiles outside Bhutan; Dr. Michael Aris of Oxford University, whose publications on Bhutan are standards in the field; and Dr. Françoise Pommaret of the Centre Nationale de Recherche Scientifique whose research in Bhutan spanned a decade of residence there. Susan Bean has graciously and vigorously coordinated the project while Diana Myers has served as guest curator and principal author of the catalog.

Support for *From the Land of the Thunder Dragon* has come from many sources. Jane Phillips and her mother, Mrs. Stephen Phillips, have been most beneficent in helping make the project possible. The National Endowment for the Humanities provided essential funding to plan and carry out the project. Lisina Hoch gave wise counsel to this endaevor and, together with Frank Hoch, provided crucial early support.

Finally, it is extremely gratifying to recognize the tremendous support given by the Bhutanese. Her Majesty Ashi Sangay Choden Wangchuck, Queen of Bhutan, has been a most active patron for the exhibition since its inception. Her Majesty's Foreword to this catalog articulately conveys her deep esteem for Bhutan's textile arts and her appreciation for this endeavor. Their Excellencies Lyönpo Om Pradhan, Minister for Trade and Industry, Lyönpo Dawa Tsering, Minister for Foreign Affairs, and Ambassador Ugyen Tshering, Bhutan's Permanent Representative to the United Nations, have provided critical and invaluable support. Beyond these official ties to Bhutan, many families have lent precious heirlooms to this exhibition and shared their knowledge with us.

We are deeply indebted to these individuals and to the many members of the Museum's staff who have made the catalog and exhibition a reality. Above all, we are proud to help make the remarkable art and culture of Bhutan accessible to a wider world.

Dan L. Monroe
Executive Director

Acknowledgments

The support, energy, and assistance of many people have helped bring about the exhibition *From the Land of the Thunder Dragon* and this publication. Foremost among them is Jane A. Phillips who built the Phillips Collection at the Peabody Essex Museum, establishing a firm foundation for the exhibition.

Our deep appreciation goes to Her Majesty Queen Ashi Sangay Choden Wangchuck, who first encouraged Diana Myers in the idea of a textile exhibition in 1986, and later agreed to serve as formal adviser to *From the Land of the Thunder Dragon*. The guidance of His Excellency Lyönpo Om Pradhan, Minister for Trade and Industry, His Excellency Lyönpo Dawa Tsering, Minister for Foreign Affairs, and His Excellency Ugyen Tshering, Permanent Representative to the United Nations, fostered a genuine collaboration between the museum and the Royal Government of Bhutan.

The contributions to this volume by Dr. Michael Aris and Dr. Françoise Pommaret represent only a part of their role in the project. Their enthusiasm for an exhibition on Bhutanese textile arts was instrumental from the outset, and they generously shared their knowledge of Bhutan. Lisina Hoch, with her long ties to Bhutan and its friends in the United States, and Dr. Bruce Bunting of the World Wildlife Fund also gave their liberal support.

Diana Myers acknowledges her special gratitude to the late Lam Nado and to Dasho Shingkar Lam, who, through hours of reminiscence and conversation, introduced her to the historical and cultural importance of textiles in Bhutan and guided her work. Over many years, the Venerable Mynak Tulku Rimpoche and Am Chime Wongmo were of continuing assistance at the National Museum in Paro and in Thimphu. The generosity and friendship of Yeshe Phuntsok and his wife, Diki, who introduced Diana Myers to Bhutanese weavers in Kathmandu in 1978, were invaluable. Rajni Chavda's encouragement greatly furthered her fieldwork. Rinji Om provided a home in Thimphu and participated in excursions to remote corners of the country. Throughout Bhutan, many other people provided welcome hospitality, conversation, and stories. The lenders to the exhibition are thanked particularly. The exhibition and this book are immeasurably richer for these Bhutanese contributions.

The glossary was compiled with important assistance from Bhutanese scholars, chiefly the late Lam Nado, historian and Dzongkha Education Adviser in the Department of Education; Dasho Shingkar Lam, Secretary to the third king and former Speaker of the National Assembly; the Venerable Mynak Tulku Rimpoche, Director of the National Museum; Lopön Pemala, former Director of the National Library; Sangay Wangchuk, Undersecretary in the Council for Ecclesiastic Affairs and Acting Director of the National Library; and Dasho Sangye Dorje, Director of the Dzongkha Development Commission. Choeki Ongmo and Dorje Gyetshen confirmed loom and weaving terminology in their native Tshangla, and José Toscano verified terms against the draft Dzongkha-English Dictionary being compiled by the Dzongkha Development Commission.

Other Bhutanese were extremely helpful during the evolution of the exhibition and this publication, including Dasho Jigme Thinley, Dasho Sonam Tobgye, Cham Lopön Sigay, Am

Tshering Dem, Am Ugen Doma, Am Ugen Norzom, Ugyen Wangdi, Am Sonam Wangmo, Am Karma, and Dasho Karma Galey and his daughter Chhodön in Bhutan, and Thinley Dorji and Tashi Dorji in New York. Special thanks are due to Kunzang Norbu for his efficient services as liaison officer at the Ministry of Trade and Industry.

In the United States, Lotus Stack of the Minneapolis Institute of Arts and Mattiebelle Gittinger of the Textile Museum in Washington, D.C., were steady supporters of a Bhutan exhibition, and of Diana Myers's research, over the past decade. They shared their technical expertise on looms and weaving and, along with Dale Gluckman of the Los Angeles County Museum of Art, made available their considerable experience in developing exhibitions. Dr. Barry Bishop at the National Geographic Society helped locate and obtain archival photographs. Thanks also go to Mary Ballard, Camie Campbell, Dan Edwards, Judy Gianareles, Michal Keeley, Lobsang Lhalungpa, Julia Swetzoff, and all those who permitted their Bhutanese textiles to be studied and photographed.

At the Peabody Essex Museum, Christina Behrmann, Assistant Curator, and Michelle Tolini, Departmental Assistant in the Department of Asian, Oceanic, and African Arts and Cultures, organized the exhibits and the photography, managed the budget, and helped the project proceed smoothly. They were assisted by several volunteers and interns, including Dale Mudge, Brad Epley, and Laura Sonjara, who dedicated many hours to preparing the textiles for exhibition. Others who contributed to the project include Registrar Lucy Butler; Janet Halpin in the Development Department; Dorothy Chen-Courtin, Patti Marxsen, and Connie Wood in Public Relations; the staff of the Education Department; and the exhibition team, including Fredrick McDougall Johnson, Director of Design, and William L. Phippen, Director of Conservation and Collections Management. Our warmest thanks go to Markham Sexton for his crisp and innovative photography.

We also express our gratitude to the National Endowment for the Humanities for providing levels of planning and implementation grant support without which this project could not have achieved its full potential. Anthony Aris and Patrick Booz of Serindia Publications contributed not only their expertise as publishers, but also their considerable knowledge of the eastern Himalayas and Bhutan.

Finally, we thank our families: John and Edie Rhoads, who were always encouraging and forgiving of Susan Bean's absences from home; and Barry Sidman, who made Diana Myers's dedication of time and energy to her heart's work possible.

Diana K. Myers
Susan S. Bean

Note on Foreign Words

Bhutanese and other non-English terms are represented in simplified phonetic forms. They are all italicized on first use, where their meaning is explained; terms related to textiles are italicized thoughout. On the initial use of some important terms in Dzongkha, the national language of Bhutan, and Tibetan, orthography is shown in Roman type. For pronunciations and more information, see the Glossary.

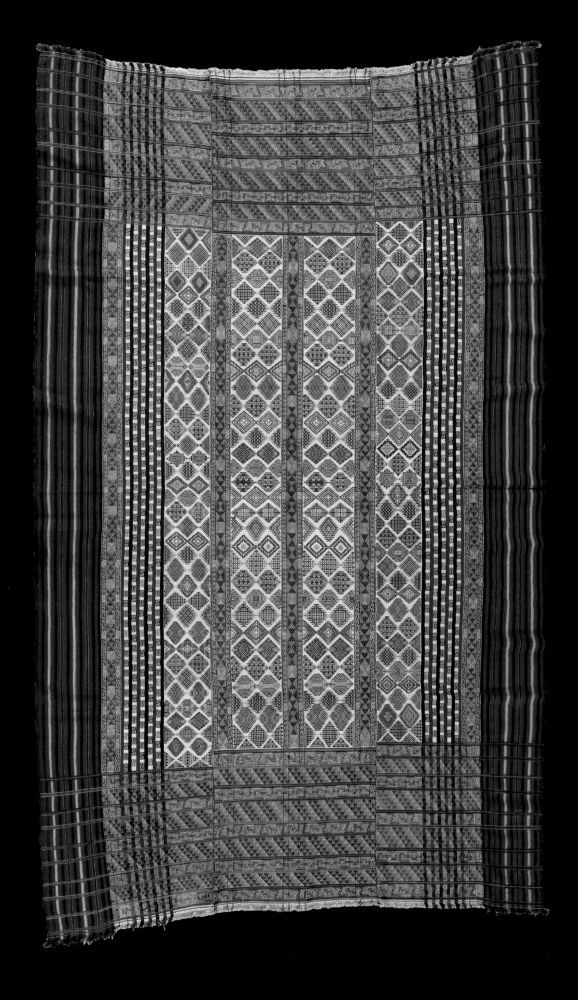

Introduction

Bhutan, Its Textiles, and the World

Textiles are a rich and complex art form deeply embedded in the culture and history of Bhutan. Weavers, always women, are esteemed as artists for their highly skilled and visually stunning mastery of color, pattern, and composition. Weavers are also creators of wealth; textiles are valuable commodities. Men, usually monks, embroider and appliqué religious images and shrine furnishings with consummate skill, remaining true to sacred prototypes and achieving sanctified magnificence. Wild silk, cotton, nettle, wool, and yak hair are the fibers basic to the region, but domesticated silk, metallic yarns, and machine-spun mercerized cotton from India and China have been available for many decades. More recently, rayon, acrylic, polyester, and wool from as far away as Hong Kong and Australia have become ubiquitous. Fine imported fabrics, especially woolen broadcloths and Chinese silks, have long been preferred for appliqués and embroideries. Textile arts in Bhutan are centuries old, vibrant, ongoing, and ever changing.

Bhutan's textiles, especially the intricate brocades and complex warp-striped patterns, are unmatched anywhere else in the world. These products of diverse regional and ethnic specializations, taken together, constitute one of the world's great textile traditions. No wonder, then, that this art, which was virtually unknown outside of the region until two decades ago, has been gathering a steadily growing, devoted following in the West and in Japan. Textiles have become Bhutan's most powerful emblem abroad.

Bhutan in the World

Bhutan has held a special place in the Western imagination as a Shangri-la, high in the Himalayas, far from the dirt and noise of modern life, surviving from a simpler time, steeped in Eastern mysteries. As the twenty-first century approaches and this image becomes ever more disconnected from actual circumstances, there are new visions emanating from Bhutan: a nation providing for the long-term protection of its environment by restricting erosion-causing activities like lumbering and setting aside extensive tracts of conservation land; a government fostering gradualism and appropriateness in social and economic change by limiting tourism and carefully managing the extent of industrial development and foreign involvement; a monarchy nurturing representational institutions through the National Assembly inaugurated in 1958 and the District Development Committees established during the reign of the present king; and a contemporary society with an artistic heritage that continues to be both relevant and evolving. But these visions are all precarious because Bhutan, like so many countries around the world, is struggling to balance the need for national unity against the realities of ethnic and linguistic diversity, and the desire for national integrity and sovereignty against the pressures of immigration, tourism, economic development, and foreign investment. For Bhutan's textile heritage, the challenges lie particularly in the cheap, easy-care, factory-made imported cloth that now competes with

FIG. I.1

In Bhutan, a woman's principal garment, the kira, *is a large rectangle of cloth, about 1.5 by 2.8 m, that is wrapped over a blouse, pinned at the shoulders, and fastened tightly at the waist. This particular woman's dress exemplifies a classic type known as* kushüthara, *that has striped edges, multiple rows of patterns creating deep end borders, and a white field into which many intricate motifs are woven. This* kushüthara *was given to its present owners by the late king and Queen (Mother) Ashi Kesang in 1955.* (see Catalog)

handloomed fabric, and in a modern educational system that keeps girls busy, away from their mothers' looms on which weaving is learned.

Until just a few decades ago Bhutan remained apart from the global community. In the West, Bhutan's detachment from the international arena was interpreted romantically as a kind of remote innocence and isolated purity. Actually, in its region Bhutan has been an active player for centuries – linked to Tibet and India by its adoption of Buddhism beginning in the eighth century, trading with its neighbors for silks from the faraway looms of China, sending yak tails for ceremonial fly whisks to the courts of Indian rajas. However, because Bhutan was never colonized, as was most of South and Southeast Asia, it remained quite unknown in the West.

Bhutan's national history began in the seventeenth century when the feudal lords who ruled its valleys were unified by the emigré Tibetan aristocrat-lama Shabdrung Ngawang Namgyel. Under the Shabdrung, Buddhism was established as the state religion and the power to rule was vested in and shared by civil and ecclesiastical heads of state. The *dzong* – the imposing fortress-monasteries strategically placed throughout the country – became the provincial centers of religion and governance. In 1627 the first Westerners, Portuguese Jesuits, visited Bhutan en route to Tibet. They met the Shabdrung and offered their services as go-betweens in relations with Tibet; their offer was declined. Until the late eighteenth century, when the government of British India in Calcutta began sending diplomatic missions to Bhutan, few other Europeans traveled there. These missions, intended to open trade through Bhutan to Tibet, met with lukewarm response from the Bhutanese who did not see much to be gained through a relationship with the British.

Despite Bhutan's formal unity in the eighteenth and nineteenth centuries under the joint rule of religious and secular leaders, there was intense competition among the armies of regionally based lords for control of large sections of the country. Eventually hostilities impinged on areas to the south that the British believed to be under their control. In the 1860s the government of British India, both annoyed by Bhutanese predations and desirous of annexing the swath of arable land in the south, went to war against the Bhutanese. They succeeded in taking the coveted territory and required Bhutan to accept British guidance in its external relations. Actually, in the decades that followed, formal contacts with British India remained minimal. Because of the desirability of having a buffer state on the edge of the Himalayas, and because it had few exploitable resources and only a sparse and scattered population that promised little as a market for British goods, Bhutan was spared much subsequent interference in its affairs from British India.

At the beginning of the twentieth century Bhutan adopted a new form of government. The dual system of religious and secular rulers had been seriously weakened by decades of civil warfare among the nobles. Ugyen Wangchuck, then *pönlop* (governor) of Tongsa in central Bhutan, emerged as the most powerful of the regional leaders–partly because he had the tacit support of the British, whom he had assisted in their 1904 treaty negotiations with Tibet [fig. 1.2]. In 1907 an assembly of leading Bhutanese selected Ugyen Wangchuck to be the first hereditary *druk gyalpo* (king) of Bhutan, establishing the supremacy of secular leadership for the first time in the country's history. During the first half of this century, under the monarchy, Bhutan was peaceful and politically stable.

In the early 1960s, however, developments in surrounding countries convinced the government of Bhutan that continued sovereignty was linked to participation in the international community. A border war between India and China emphasized Bhutan's precarious position sandwiched between two military powers. Moreover, desirable ele-

FIG. I.2

This photograph of Ugyen Wangchuck (center), the first king of Bhutan, was taken in Lhasa, Tibet, in 1904, when he was pönlop *(governor) of Tongsa and served as a mediator between envoys from British India and the Dalai Lama of Tibet. With him are members of his entourage. Ugyen Wangchuck is wearing Bhutanese boots and a robe* (go), *probably of wild silk* aikapur *(fabric with supplementary-warp-pattern bands). On his head is the "raven crown," an elaborately embroidered silk hat topped with the figure of a raven's head, a reference to the bird that guided the unifier of the country, Shabdrung Ngawang Namgyel, from Tibet to Bhutan and a fitting symbol for the leader of the people. At the time this photograph was taken, the hat was part of the regalia of the Tongsa Pönlop. It was later made the king's crown when Ugyen Wangchuck became the first* druk gyalpo *(king) in 1907. (John Claude White 1904, Courtesy Oriental and India Office Collection, the British Library)*

ments of late-twentieth-century life – communications technology, medicine, education – could only be acquired through relationships with other nations and with international organizations. In the early 1960s, with India's assistance, Bhutan's first motor roads were built. Bhutan joined the United Nations in 1971 and opened an airport in Paro, the country's largest valley, in 1983.

With a population of less than three quarters of a million in an area slightly larger than Switzerland, Bhutan is a small country bordered by giants: on the north and west by Tibet, and on the south and east by India. Its population is sustained by a subsistence economy of agriculture and herding. In recent decades a few industrial enterprises, principally matches, plywood, processed fruit, and hydroelectric power, have been established, and modern technology, including computers, video equipment, and fax machines, has been imported. Serious poverty is unknown and extremes of economic development have been avoided. Despite these great achievements, Bhutan has run headlong into many of the same conundrums that plague newly industrializing nations the world over. Economic development has been dependent on foreign aid and international loans, creating a burden of debt. The Western-rooted concept of nationhood, which stresses a common language and culture as key to political unity, has gained credence in Bhutan (despite its recent failures, even in the West). Government and popular sentiment have moved the country toward unity in language and culture: Dzongkha as the national language; Drukpa Kagyü Buddhism as the state religion; and *go* (men's robes) and *kira* (women's wrapped garments) as the national dress. This is an especially problematic course in a country where linguistic and cultural

diversity is pervasive. The national challenge, as Bhutan acquires all the accoutrements of contemporary transnational culture, is to maintain a distinct cultural identity that honors the varied traditions of all its people.

FIG. I.3
Thimphu, capital of Bhutan.
(D.K.M. 1987)

Bhutan's entrance into the global community symbolizes the worldwide end of an era; there are no longer any corners of the earth cut off from the rest. All nations and all peoples are interdependent. Acknowledging and appreciating cultural and historical diversity are an urgent need in today's interconnected world. For us in the West, knowing Bhutan is as important as knowing Italy, South Africa, or Korea. Bhutan has much to contribute to the globe's growing transnational culture: in particular, its textile arts, which are essential to the constitution of social life and to the practice of religion and which are rooted in an aesthetic that flourishes on faithfulness to traditional models while valuing creativity and innovation within a form.

Bhutan's Textiles

Textiles are Bhutan's premier art, the products of centuries of individual creativity and transmitted skills in fiber preparation, dyeing, weaving, cutting, stitching, and embroidery. Whereas in the West there is a tendency to separate art from life, to suppose that the fine arts function chiefly as vehicles of aesthetic experience, in Bhutan art and life are inextricably intertwined. Textiles are made for clothing and for various kinds of containers and covers. Textiles as garments convey the social identities of their wearers. Gifts of cloth mark important social transitions such as career promotions and marriages. Textiles are critical for the practice of Buddhist ritual, providing images of deities and markers and adornments of sacred spaces. Textiles are value, commodity, wealth, forms of payment and capital, as well as expressions of religious devotion.

Textile arts are spread unevenly through Bhutanese society. Weaving is exclusively the realm of women; complex cutting, stitching, and embroidery, as well as tailoring, are the prerogative of men. The eastern part of the country is famous for its weaving, while in the west, weaving has been of little importance. Regions, and even specific villages, are known for the special fabrics created there, such as the wool brocades (*yathra*) of central Bumthang District and the uniquely Bhutanese techniques of interworking supplementary-weft yarns with warp elements and each other (*thrima, sapma*) for which northern Lhuntshi District is renowned. Patterns originating in eastern Bhutan, which are formed by manipulating supplementary-warp yarns (*aikapur*), have been adopted nationwide and have become unofficially a national preference for the fabric of men's formal robes.

Throughout Bhutanese history textiles have played a crucial and ever-changing role. The historical depth of this relationship is indicated in language; the Dzongkha word 'cloth' (*zong*) is related to the word for trade (*tshong*), and folklore tells of the introduction of weaving by a Chinese princess in the seventh century. The Shabdrung, who unified Bhutan in the seventeenth century, is credited with introducing a special garment for men, the *go*, modified from the Tibetan man's robe (*chuba*) and made distinctively Bhutanese in form. Worn primarily by the elite in the Shabdrung's time, the *go* gradually became the attire of most Bhutanese men, and in 1989 it was proclaimed the national dress. The ubiquitous women's wrapped garment (*kira*) was also made official national dress in 1989. It has been worn in Bhutan for longer than the *go* and reveals, through weaving techniques and designs, ancient links to Southeast Asia [figs 1.1, 1.4].

Partly because the Wangchuck dynasty originated in a renowned weaving region, textile arts have flourished in the past century and a half. In the mid-nineteenth century as the Wangchucks gained influence and moved westward from north central Bhutan, eventually settling 100 years later in Thimphu, the new capital, the prestige and influence of weaving techniques and decorative styles from the royal family's home region spread throughout the country. The period from the mid-nineteenth to the mid-twentieth century was arguably the golden age of Bhutanese weaving. In the early part of this period most fibers were produced, dyed, and woven locally. Labor-intensive and complex processes of preparing fibers, spinning, dyeing, and weaving meant that the finest textiles were *hingtham*, 'heart weavings' made by women for themselves and their loved ones (if their families grew or could afford the fibers), or made in workshops maintained by elite households. Although the repertoire of dyes and fibers was much more limited than it is today, the wide distribution of skills and thorough knowledge of local materials guaranteed a supply of superbly crafted textiles.

In the twentieth century the pace of change increased enormously. Imported fibers and dyes have become widely available and weavers have adopted these with enthusiasm, altering the palette, textures, surface qualities, and hand of the cloths pro-

FIG. I.4

The man's robe (go) and the woman's wrapped dress (kira) are the principal garments of most Bhutanese. A man wears his robe with a white Bhutanese shirt underneath it, and often a button-down shirt, T-shirt, or sweatshirt as well. On his feet and lower legs he wears kneesocks with Western-style shoes. A woman wears a blouse under her kira, which is fastened with a pair of shoulder brooches and belted tightly at the waist. On top she wears a jacket, and on her feet Western-style shoes. The go and kira were decreed national dress in 1989 and must be worn in public by all Bhutanese. This dapper couple was photographed at the annual festival (tsechu) in Thimphu. (D.K.M. 1989)

duced. Inexpensive, easy-to-use chemical dyes have almost displaced natural dyes. Synthetic and factory-processed yarns have become more common than those locally produced. A frame loom, introduced from Tibet, has augmented the existing technology of backtension looms, and sparked the creative development of brocaded wool twill textiles. As money gradually replaced barter in midcentury, more Bhutanese weavers had the means to acquire a variety of imported yarns, especially the less expensive silk-like synthetics, the smoother and silkier mercerized cotton yarns, as well as the enormous variety of powder dyes which are simpler to use and have given an undreamed-of range of colors. A new world has opened to Bhutanese of more limited means.

In this contemporary scene of abundant and varied resources for weaving, fashions have changed rapidly. Members of the royal family and elite have been style leaders. The late king moved away from the practice of wearing robes of Chinese silk for formal occasions to the nearly exclusive use of Bhutanese fabrics on all occasions. Most high-ranking men now also wear *go* of Bhutanese cloth. The queens have maintained their own weaving workshops and often set the trend in color combinations and designs for *kira,* stimulating artistic creativity and innovations. Fashions now change from year to year and women must commission or buy new *kira* regularly to stay in style.

The continuing importance of textiles in Bhutanese life was demonstrated in another way in 1989 when the king decreed the *go* and *kira* national dress, to be worn virtually everywhere in public – including schools, government buildings, and temples. The edict establishes textiles and apparel as a new means for expressing contemporary Bhutanese national identity in a manner in which all citizens can (and must) participate. Because the *go* and *kira* are stylistically unique, they provide a visual means of distinguishing Bhutanese from the people of other countries. However, the decree has had two problematic effects. It has created an increased demand for *go* and *kira* fabrics that is being met by inexpensive, easy-care textiles designed expressly for the Bhutanese market and produced on powerlooms in India. These factory-made Indian exports are pushing their Bhutanese-made prototypes out of the realm of everyday wear. But the taste and aesthetics of both elite and ordinary Bhutanese, artists and patrons, still esteem handwoven cloth and prefer it, especially on formal occasions, and the demands of Buddhist practice still require embroidered and appliqué textiles.

Another consequence of the national dress edict is that it glosses over ethnic and regional diversity that exists in the country. While the *go* and *kira* have been the dominant dress throughout Bhutan, there are Bhutanese citizens, in the east in Merak Sakteng, in the north in Laya, and in the south, who do not traditionally wear these garments. Because the decree came on the heels of serious unrest in the south – when new guidelines on citizenship began to be enforced and were protested by some Bhutanese of recent Nepalese ancestry and by would-be immigrants – the national dress edict was interpreted in some quarters as directed toward the forcible assimilation of ethnically distinct Bhutanese. While the problem remains unresolved, the government, which has taken progressive positions on many conservation and development issues, must also find a way to promote national unity while maintaining its ethnic, linguistic, and cultural richness and diversity.

Bhutanese Textiles Abroad

The textiles that have come out of Bhutan and are now in museum and private collections are the most potent presence of Bhutanese culture in the outside world. Few Bhutanese live outside the country. Only a few thousand tourists from around the world visit Bhutan each

FIG. 1.5

This woman's belt (kera), *originally in the India Museum, was transferred to the South Kensington Museum (now the Victoria and Albert Museum) in 1879. First accessioned in 1855, the belt might have been acquired in or near Bhutan by one of the early nineteenth-century diplomatic missions from British India, such as that led by Capt. R.B. Pemberton in 1837-38. The belt is woven of hand-spun cotton and decorated with a few bands of red and blue wool supplementary-weft patterning. When a photograph of the belt was shown to older women in Bhutan in the 1990s, it was identified as a* matrami keré, *'a belt worth one small coin.' The belt is singular in its simplicity and narrow width; all other examples of traditional cummerbunds are densely patterned and much wider [cf. figs. 5.11, 5.12]. Although no other textiles for everyday use have been found that can confidently be assigned early-nineteenth-century dates, this example opens the possibility that in the 1800s and before, many Bhutanese textiles were made with only limited patterning. (see Catalog)*

year. To the extent that Bhutan is known abroad, it is primarily as a picturesque Buddhist kingdom, as a destination for trekking in the Himalayas, for its postage stamps, and for its distinctive and, in some instances, unique textiles. Since the early 1980s when Bhutanese textiles began to reach the West in significant numbers, the ranks of admirers of this rich and varied tradition have been growing steadily.

Before the 1980s Bhutanese textiles were virtually unknown in the West. A lone article, "Bhutanese Weaving," was published by Blanche Olschak in 1966. No other publication appeared for nearly twenty years. The few textiles in museum collections were almost all in Great Britain. These had been acquired not as textile arts but as memorabilia from diplomatic missions when the British were the only Western power to have relations with Bhutan. The British Museum, the Victoria and Albert Museum, and the Cambridge University Museum of Archaeology and Anthropology all have some textiles, originally presented to British diplomats, including Charles Bell in 1910 and Derrick Williamson in the 1930s. The Victoria and Albert Museum also has one textile originally accessioned into the collection of the East India Company's museum in 1855. This coarse and rather plain woman's belt *(kera)* may have been acquired on a British mission to Bhutan, perhaps that led by Capt. R. B. Pemberton in 1837-1838 [fig. 1.5]. The Asian Art Museum in San Francisco has two religious images *(thangka),* part of the Avery Brundage collection, that also have a British diplomatic history, probably as presents to Lt. Col. Weir in the 1930s [fig. 6.12]. All of these textiles are relatively recent, yet they are the oldest securely dated examples, at least until state and private collections in Bhutan can be more thoroughly studied.

The Peabody Essex Museum, the organizer of the exhibition that accompanies this catalog, also acquired Bhutanese objects in the early twentieth century, again from a British diplomatic mission. In 1903-04, the Younghusband Expedition to Tibet established relations between the British and the Tibetan Dalai Lama through the mediation of the Bhutanese leader Tongsa Pönlop Ugyen Wangchuck, who a few years later became Bhutan's first king. Objects acquired on the expedition were brought back to London. In 1913, through William Oldman, a well-known London dealer in ethnographic objects, the Peabody Essex Museum acquired a quiver with its arrows and a basketry-covered bamboo water container that had come back from Bhutan with a member of the expedition. The subsequent history of this collection parallels that of many others. During the next seventy years only a handful of Bhutanese objects were accessioned. Then, in 1980, Peter Fetchko, the museum's director, met a dealer who had purchased textiles in Kathmandu, Nepal. Seeing these as a fine addition to the museum's strong Asian collections, he arranged for a museum patron to view the dealer's collection. The patron, Jane A. Phillips, was captivated by the extraordinary technique and the exquisite and intricate patterns of the textiles, and she began to build the collection on which the exhibition and catalog are based.

Most Bhutanese textiles in Western collections, including the vast majority of those in this exhibition and catalog, were acquired in a similar fashion – in the 1980s, primarily from Kathmandu. During this period two major private collections were formed, published, and exhibited. Some of their contents have subsequently been dispersed to museum collections. One collection, assembled by Mark Bartholomew, was exhibited in 1978 at the Museum for Textiles in Toronto and published in 1985 as *Thunder Dragon Textiles from Bhutan.* Bartholomew first encountered Bhutanese textiles outside Bhutan, in nearby Kalimpong (India) in 1975: "a cloth merchant showed me into the back of his storage room, to pull off from the topmost shelf a weaving with colors and intricacy more splendid and unique than I'd ever seen. He said that this was the royal family of Bhutan's traditional ceremonial dress, a kushüthara ...

With that kushüthara my quest began" (Bartholomew 1985, 10). A second published private collection was brought together by Barbara Adams. In the preface to *Traditional Bhutanese Textiles,* Adams recalls how this all began. In 1979 "unexpectedly ... weavings began to appear in the shops at the Buddhist stupa at Bodhnath near Kathmandu. They were trickling in on the backs of Bhutanese pilgrims who had come to Kathmandu for a big *wang* – meaning prayer meeting – to be given by a high Lama or Buddhist priest. The *wang* was delayed for two months as the Lama fell ill, and the pilgrims began to sell a few of their cloths to finance their extra stay in Kathmandu" (Adams 1984, vii). Once a market was established, Bhutanese came to trade their old cloths for new goods, including Chinese silk brocades and Indian polyesters, and several dealers in Kathmandu became specialists in Bhutanese textiles. Kathmandu became the major source of Bhutanese textiles for Western collections.

While it seems, from this retelling, that Bhutanese textiles came into the international market quite by accident, in fact their emergence was practically inevitable. The active art market in the West, especially in the 1980s, was eager for any newly discovered genre and Western seekers of adventure and enlightenment, needing to support themselves, were frequent visitors to Kathmandu and other market towns in the Himalayas. Because most of the textiles acquired in the 1980s were purchased outside Bhutan, establishing a history of this art is particularly difficult. In nearly all cases there is no certainty of when or where the textile was made, by whom, for whom, or for what occasion. There are, however, four museum collections with portions acquired in Bhutan that are important in this regard. Chief among them is the collection at the British Museum made in 1983 by Anthony and Marie-Laure Aris, who had official sanction to travel to the major weaving centers around the country to acquire material for the museum. This collection is the most comprehensive and well documented. In Osaka, Japan, the National Museum of Ethnology also has a very large group of textiles acquired during the 1980s under Bhutanese guidance as part of its extensive ethnographic collection. The Peabody Essex Museum has a smaller but important group of textiles, fiber samples, and dyestuffs acquired in the weaving regions of Bhutan for the museum by Diana K. Myers, and the Asian Art Museum in San Francisco has a group of *kira* that were collected by Françoise Pommaret.

In preparing this catalog and the accompanying exhibition, these, and many other, collections have been examined. It has now been possible for the first time to bring together important examples of Bhutanese textile arts from many collections in the West and a few private collections in Bhutan and, through the collaboration of a team of scholars, to explore the history, technology, and significance of textiles in Bhutan. Together, the exhibition and catalog establish a firm foundation for further research, study, and new discoveries, and help garner for Bhutanese textiles a wide recognition as one of Asia's major arts.

Bhutan is a small country with a great tradition of textile arts. These are arts that speak eloquently of regional and ethnic diversity, and yet they face an uncertain future as Bhutan moves closer to the world community – as formal education takes more women from their looms and international trade brings cheaper, easy-care textiles within the reach of most Bhutanese. In the West there is a tendency to see these developments as spelling doom for handmade things, but it is unlikely that this will happen in Bhutan. Bhutan will not lose its textile arts, but they will change, and their role in Bhutanese life will change too. Indeed, as the exhibition and the catalog show, this is nothing new. Textiles in Bhutan are an evolving art and have been for centuries, changing as their role in Bhutanese life has evolved. Bhutanese textile arts are a national treasure and Bhutanese government policy, together with people's appreciation, will sustain them well into the future.

Fig. 1.6

These boys, with their motorbikes and helmets, are wearing Bhutanese robes (go). Suspended from a handlebar is a bow case and on the ground rests a quiver made of handloomed Bhutanese textiles trimmed with bright Indian cloth. In Bhutan, archery is the national sport. (Jakar, Bumthang, D.K.M. 1986)

PART ONE

Textiles in the
Cultural History
of Bhutan

Chapter One

Textiles, Text, and Context

The Cloth and Clothing of Bhutan in Historical Perspective

Tradition and Change

It is quite impossible to arrive in Bhutan without some preconceptions about this remote Himalayan country. When in 1967 my friend the late Marco Pallis arranged for me to serve as tutor to the younger children of the Bhutanese royal family, I went there with some clear ideas partly formed under his influence on several aspects of the country, not least its dress. Several but not all of these ideas I later abandoned or lost. However, my feelings of warm gratitude to him will always remain.

Although Marco had made friends with members of the Bhutanese royal family during his years in Kalimpong, the hill station located in that part of West Bengal which used to be known as "British Bhutan," he never visited Bhutan proper. However, he had often come across the highly distinctive textiles of Bhutan, either as piece goods or sewn into garments. Like everyone else, he had been immensely struck by the wonderful diversity and richness of these fabrics. For him the tradition fitted very conveniently into his wider conception of "Tradition" in general. The weaving techniques of Bhutan and the garments produced by their methods represented a static convention inherited unbroken from a distant past, a material portent whose ultimate purpose was to express an unchanging spiritual identity and meaning peculiar to the genius of the region. Traditional clothing, in his interpretation, is therefore the outer manifestation of the inner spiritual values of society passed down intact from a divine source. To alter the accepted form of such garments, or worse, to replace them with imported items, is to commit a kind of sacrilege, to desecrate those inner values which they externalize.[1]

Some may find this notion attractive, but certain practical objections can be quickly raised. It is never conceded that the clothing of a traditional society might be the product either of slow evolution or of radical change. People today are thus believed to be wearing the same clothes as their remotest ancestors. Moreover, the "spiritual values" enshrined and concretized in these garments are never clearly defined and, in this conception, never seem to take into account those crucial factors of gender, power, class, and ethnicity which have always determined who wears what in any society.

In short, what we might call the "Pallis Theory of Traditional Dress" may be appropriate to a mythical Shangri-la, but it cannot be accommodated to the real world. This is not to argue with its basic premise, that clothes tell us a great deal about matters of inner aspiration and identity. Nor indeed can one deny that the adoption of Western dress in a traditional society often coincides with the collapse or erosion of traditional values. For the authorities in Bhutan today, this is a particularly live issue.

The purpose of this essay is to situate the cloth and clothing of Bhutan in the context of history, to try to determine how traditions and attitudes of the past affect customs of the present. The overall aim is to demonstrate that, far from being static and uniform, most of

FIG. 1.0 (page 21)
*Weavers at the palace of Wangdi-chöling, principal residence of the first king of Bhutan, Ugyen Wangchuck. For this photograph, the girls put on archaic tunics (*shingkha*) that are usually worn only for rituals. (John Claude White 1905, Courtesy Anthony Aris)*

FIG. 1.1
Shabdrung Ngawang Namgyel, prince-abbot of the Drukpa Kagyü school, unified Bhutan in the seventeenth century and is credited with introducing a new, distinctively Bhutanese style of dress for men – the go *(robe). Enshrined in Punakha Dzong, this gilt clay image of the Shabdrung is believed to have been modeled by the Shabdrung himself and is specially revered by Bhutanese. When the statesman asked his likeness to represent him after his passing, the statue nodded its assent; its head remains inclined to this day. (Her Majesty Queen Ashi Sangay Choden Wangchuck 1994)*

the conventions of dress have evolved in reaction to developments both internal and external to that region. It should, however, be emphasized that the gleanings from history are relatively sparse, and that much of the evidence can only be gathered tangentially or by inference. The literary tradition of Bhutan, rich though it is, very rarely addresses itself directly to this mundane subject. Indeed, there is nothing that can really be construed as a secular literature beyond folk songs and a single genre of oral epic, and neither is of much use here. The domestic skills of weaving, as in the case of those other technical skills of agriculture, architecture, and the crafts of metalworking, cane-weaving, and the like, fall quite outside the realm of religious literature. Except on those occasions when metaphors from everyday life are sought to illustrate a particular Buddhist doctrine or viewpoint, one does not find references to any of these pursuits in the devotional or philosophical literature.[2] Although the pen and the loom meet only by accident, nevertheless a certain picture of secular life can be reconstructed. It can be further broadened by the evidence of the Bhutanese language itself and the testimonies of the earliest Western travelers. Finally, there is the witness of my own eyes and ears in Bhutan in 1967-73. However, to understand the place of textiles in the history of Bhutan, the cultural and historical setting must first be drawn in outline.

Land and Peoples

With the exception of those in religious orders, who have their own uniforms, a few scattered minorities, and the large numbers of ethnic Nepalese inhabiting the south of the country, all

FIG. 1.2
Tashichö Dzong in the Thimphu Valley was built in 1641, as one of the fort-monasteries erected to unify the administration of the country. Although portions had to be restored after fires, its imposing presence continues to dominate the valley. In the early 1960s, King Jigme Dorji Wangchuck transferred the national capital to Thimphu, and Tashichö Dzong became the seat of the central government in 1967. Much of the edifice was rebuilt to accommodate its new function; the construction employed Bhutanese joinery, which does not require nails. (D.K.M. 1987)

24

Bhutanese men and women wear a single form of garment appropriate to their gender, even though they may come from groups speaking mutually unintelligible languages. This homogeneity in respect to dress immediately tells us something about the powerful forces that have worked for national unity in Bhutan since the seventeenth century. At the same time, the survival of an extraordinary variety of generic and regional textile forms at once proclaims the many geographical, ethnic, and cultural divisions which make up the country.

The evidence for both unity and disparity provided by dress is closely mirrored by that of language. The form of speech known as Dzongkha, now officially promoted as the national language, is increasingly spoken and understood alongside a great variety of local tongues and dialects. Similarly, a national style in architecture is easily discerned, more uniform in its diffusion perhaps than any other aspect of Bhutanese life and culture, and yet, local variations of house styles can also be found. Regional folk songs also flourish together with an emerging national style of singing. All this is echoed at a more profound level in the great variety of religious techniques that are allowed to flourish within certain well-defined parameters. Indeed, the success and integrity of Bhutanese culture as a whole seem to depend primarily on a willing tolerance of diverse forms flourishing within a framework of accepted norms that are growing ever stronger under official patronage.

Certain timeless divisions affecting both the physical and human geography of the country continue to impose a fixed pattern on many aspects of the nation's life, not least on its dress. The picture is a complex one because of the way in which the major ethnic and linguistic divisions follow the lines of watersheds in a north-south direction, each occupying parallel corridors of territory descending like staircases from the high Tibetan border to the Indian plains. The steps of these corridors are formed by a great range of alpine, temperate, and tropical environments. In between these north-south corridors, and at their upper and lower limits, survive a few very small groups who seem to bear no immediate relation to their more numerous neighbors.

The people occupying the western corridor, a composite group known as Ngalops, live in the major valleys of Ha, Paro, Thimphu, Punakha, and Wangdi Phodrang as far east as the so-called Black Mountains, and in the adjacent regions to the north and south of these valleys [see Map 2, p.170]. Politically dominant since the seventeenth century, their speech, which has variants in each valley or district, comes nearer to standard Tibetan than that of any other group in Bhutan, and it has close affinities with standard Sikkimese. Other aspects of life shared between the Lepcha people of Sikkim and of western Bhutan (where 2,000 of them are still found)[3] point to the fact that in the distant past this was a single cultural area. Weaving traditions are similar, and the cult of the local village oracle, the male *pawo* and the female *nenjorm*, is found in both places. In its most polished form, the Ngalop language is referred to as *dzongkha* ('the language of the dzong [state fort-monastery]'). Some 160,000 people out of the country's 600,000 are reckoned to speak this as their mother tongue. Now recognized as the national language, Dzongkha was only committed to writing in the 1960s.[4]

The Ngalops grow rice in those central valleys which allow it, and barley and wheat higher up. The pastoral groups to the west and northwest, who are also considered to belong to this group, barter their dairy products for grain. Transhumance, that is, the seasonal migration of peoples from high and cold areas to low and hot areas, used to affect a sizable portion of the Ngalop population, as it still does other groups further east. The wealth of the Ngalops certainly depended in the past on the conversion of their agricultural surplus. Traded in Tibet, or recycled by the state as revenue, it went to build the many fine monasteries and forts of the west [fig. 1.2].

The central group, quite distinct from the Ngalops to the west, have no specific name of their own, but are distinguished by their use of an ancient language which has its center in the Bumthang region. Distinct variants of the language are also found in Tongsa, Mangdelung, Kheng, and Kurtö. All these interrelated dialects are spoken by about 90,000 people. Like Paro in the west, Bumthang has a number of ancient associations with the period of the first diffusion of Buddhism to Tibet in the seventh to ninth centuries. The broad Chökhor Valley in particular is filled with famous sites inherited not only from the distant past when the valley was a major cultural center but also from the time when the monarchy became established in the early twentieth century. Buckwheat and barley are grown as staples at this altitude, and most inhabitants migrate south with their cattle in the winter.

It was in the Chökhor Valley that the first palaces of the present dynasty were built and where the royal family introduced highly refined styles and techniques of weaving associated with the form called *kushü* (ku shud) from their original home to the east in Kurtö. As explained elsewhere in this volume, these techniques were developed and later diffused throughout the country. From an even earlier period, the region appears to have served as the source of two of the most popular textiles in Bhutan, the very names of which are synonymous with the Bumthang region, *bumthang mathra* (bum thang dmar khra) and *bumthang yathra* (bum thang ya khra). The former are finely checked woolens used by both men and women, and the latter, all-purpose thick woolens, woven in panels and sewn into

Fig. 1.3
The Bumthang area is renowned for woolen textiles with colorful motifs executed in supplementary-weft brocade on a dark (or, more rarely, white) field. Capes or raincloaks (charkab), like this one, are made of three panels of cloth sewn together. This lovely example is decorated with large, boldly rendered flowers, swastikas, stars, meander patterns, and what Bhutanese call "vases of long life" (tshebum) and pineapples (kongtsi). Across the middle, the cloak has three large diamond motifs, the two at the sides imitating a patchwork of colored triangles that often appears in ritual textiles. (see Catalog)

squares or oblongs to be used as rain capes [fig. 1.3], lap rugs, blankets, floor rugs, or, more recently, jackets. The women of the district are distinguished from their neighbors by their use of Tibetan-style striped aprons and sheepskin cloaks. The inhabitants of the Kheng region, now numbering 40,000, used to pay taxes mostly in the form of cotton and wild silk textiles for which they were famous. Traversing the country eastward, it is likely that the inhabitants of Kheng were, until recently, the first group encountered to produce all their traditional clothing requisites without relying on imports from other areas. They not only paid taxes to the government in this form, but they also exported a large quantity for profit.

The major eastern group in the country is known simply as *shachop* ('easterners'). Like their neighbors to the west, they have no specific name of their own, although they refer to their very distinct language as Tshangla. Of all the Bhutanese languages theirs is the most difficult to classify within the Tibeto-Burman family, since it has very few affinities with any other recorded language. The native speakers of Tshangla, who inhabit the regions of Mongar, Tashigang, and Tashiyangtse, number approximately 138,000. Their language is well known to some neighboring groups for whom it serves as a kind of *lingua franca*. The kinship system of these easterners is markedly different from that in the rest of the country since marriage between cousins is allowed, perhaps a vestige of the old system of clan organization which characterized their society before it was incorporated into the theocracy. Maize is the main staple, though other grain crops are also cultivated. Weaving is an absolutely integral part of the everyday life of each household in this area, more so even than in the central region of Bumthang and its adjacent districts. Indeed, if great forts and monasteries are the symbols of the west and center, it is the humble loom and its dazzling products which exemplify the culture of the east.

Just as the textiles of the far west of the country and other aspects of its ancient culture link up with those of Sikkim to reveal how the present political borders cut through ancient ties of race and language, so also does the weaving of eastern Bhutan connect directly with that in the adjoining Indian state of Arunachal Pradesh, and in particular with the corridor of territory known as the 'land of Mon' *(mon yul)*. Several groups on the fringe of the major ethnic divisions maintain their own forms of dress. The highland yak-herding pastoralists call themselves *brokpa*; they inhabit Merak Sakteng on the eastern border (population 5,000). The Laya community of pastoralists (numbering a few hundred) live in the northwest of the country; both groups are particularly distinguished by dress. The Brokpas, with their hats of yak hair, their circular mats suspended for permanent convenience from their waists, tunic-style upper garments, and cloaks of animal hide, are closely related to the Mönpa people of the adjoining Tawang District in Arunachal Pradesh, now under Indian control. They are also related by culture, lifestyle, and dress to another group known locally as *dakpa* (or *dap*), numbering 1,000. The women of the Laya people of the far northwest, who are yak herders, wear a conical hat of woven cane and long woolen coats. The southern, jungle-dwelling Mönpas of Kheng and Mangdelung (population 1,000) are among the most distinct and interesting of the minority groups. They are unrelated to the people of the same name in Tawang, the Toktops of Toktokha (numbering just a few hundred), or the Lhokpus (or Lhops/Lhups) of Taba-Dramding and Loto-Kuchu, who are known to the Nepalese as the Doyas (population 1,000). The Toktops till recently wore a garment known locally as the *pakhi* (Aris 1979, xviii), identical it seems to the *pokwi* worn by the Lhokpus (Driem 1991 ms., 21), and closely resembling the traditional dress of the Lepchas in neighboring Sikkim. We shall see later that this article, woven from the fiber of nettles and crossed over the chest and shoulders, is of great historical significance.

Some Key Terms

A clear sense of how the skills of weaving and its products are absolutely integral to the life of the region is gained by a brief consideration of language. The primary word for a woven fabric, *thag* (spelled "'thags," but the final "s" is silent), is a close cognate of the common word for rope or cord, spelled and pronounced *thag(pa)*. This is an obvious reminder of how the most basic textile is, in fact, rope, which is nothing but an assemblage of fibers, compacted by twisting or plaiting into a long flexible line. The fibers of rope, as those for cloth, are first combed or carded, then slivered and spun into yarn. The processes of making rope and cloth thus start in the same way. The close relation of these two domestic crafts is intimately reflected in the language. A similar relation is found in the almost identical words for woven piece goods *(zong)* and trade *(tshong)*. True, the word *zong* in Tibet usually has the wider sense of 'merchandise' in general, but in Bhutan it is used exclusively to refer to a collection of textile fabrics stored or displayed for sale or gift. Cloth was produced not only to dress the members of the household where it was woven; it was also a major item of barter, sale, gift, and taxation, in fact fundamental to the local economy.

The word for cotton cloth, *ré* (ras), gives rise to many compound terms for specific materials, but it also tends to lose the meaning 'cotton' and acquire the sense of 'cloth' in general.[5] Textiles woven from the fiber of nettles, for instance, are commonly called *yüra* (yul ras), literally 'country cloth.' Though the classical term "zwa cha" ('nettle thing') is also known, the more common term *yüra* reflects the view that this fabric is the humblest homespun produced by the most marginal communities. Assamese wild silk *(endi)*, imported in large quantities to Bhutan, is termed *bura* (spelled "bu ras," literally 'insect cloth'). Similarly, the word for towel, *acho tora*, is made up of an imported Mongolian word, "alcûr," and "lto ras," literally 'food cloth.' The last element in this compound originally refers to the square of cloth in which food ("lto," a word used especially for cooked rice) is often carried. That cloth has enormous prestige value throughout the area is reflected in the universal word for a gift of any sort bestowed by a superior upon an inferior. This is *söra* (gsol ras), which was in origin presumably no more than the honorific word for cloth.[6]

The word for silk, *dar*, is a homophone for 'flag,' and it also appears interestingly as the verb 'to flourish, prosper, spread.' Sericulture, which involves the killing of the silkworm, was never sanctioned in Tibet and the Buddhist Himalayas, though silk has been imported from China since early times. The recorded legends of Nyarong in eastern Tibet claim that the gift of silk was first brought to Tibet by the Chinese princess who married King Songtsen Gampo in AD 641.[7] A similar 'eulogy of silk' (dar bshad) from the Merak Sakteng region of eastern Bhutan is recited on the occasion of weddings.[8] With its soft and lustrous qualities, this material evokes ideas of wealth and prosperity, and both these sources make full use of wordplay and punning on this theme. The finest silk brocade is termed *göchen* (spelled "gos chen," literally 'the great garment'), and many grades and types are distinguished by name. Indeed, one eighteenth-century document provides a veritable mine of technical terms pertaining to silk, as we shall see.

The word for the common male garment in Bhutan is *go*, the local form of the Tibetan word *gö* (written as "gos"). In the common literary language used throughout areas of Tibetan influence, including Bhutan, and in colloquial Tibetan, the word is used to refer to all clothing in general. Thus while the Tibetans have a specific term for their national dress *(chuba)*, for the Bhutanese male, his dress is simply termed a 'garment' or 'clothing.' *Tögo* (spelled "stod gos," literally 'upper garment'), the white cotton shirt worn by men, the collar and sleeves of which are folded back over the *go*, is a term borrowed from an item of monastic dress and points to its late adoption in the evolution of the male dress. The principal woman's garment is called specifically *kira* (dkyis ras), literally a 'wrapping cloth.' It is a rectangle of cloth, normally decorated with woven designs, wrapped around the body, folded twice across the front, fastened with brooches at the shoulders, and belted at the waist.

Early Fragmentation

The area that came to be Bhutan is consistently presented in the historical sources as a kind of wild and uncivilized barbary awaiting the "taming" effect, first of refugee princes and later of Buddhist lamas from Tibet (Aris 1990, 85-101). Many Bhutanese have a picture in their minds of the earliest inhabitants wearing the skins of animals and the foliage of plants, or nothing at all (Nado 1986, 2). Even today when the Bhutanese want to adopt a humorous, self-deprecating tone, they sometimes speak of themselves as a crude, jungle-dwelling folk, deliberately overlooking the fact that most of them actually live in temperate, well-cultivated valleys rather than the inhospitable tropical forests of the south.

This derogatory self-image is balanced by the realization that for the Tibetans in the north the area was actually worth fleeing to. The luxuriant and varied vegetation of the land, the physical security of its sheltered valleys, not to speak of the sheer beauty of the landscape at every turn – all these factors served as a powerful magnet to draw prestigious figures down from the mostly barren, windswept northern plateau. It seems to have been for this reason that the conception of Bhutan as a 'hidden land' (*beyul*, sbas yul), or an area made up of several such arcadias, eventually gained currency in the literature. Here the faithful would find refuge and enlightenment during a period of future chaos. The patron saint universally adopted for the region and claimed as the originator of the 'hidden land' was the quasi-historical Padmasambhava, who had been responsible for the consecration of Tibet's first monastery at Samye in the eighth century. This tantric master from the Swat Valley in present-day Pakistan is elevated to the position of supreme cult figure in the national and religious consciousness of the Bhutanese [fig. 1.4].

The human, as opposed to the divine, history of the region really begins with the arrival of Prince Tsangma, son of King Tridé Songtsen, who ruled Tibet approximately from 800 to 815. All the earliest Tibetan sources agree on either Paro or Bumthang as the prince's place of exile, which took place in the context of a struggle that finally brought about the end of the empire. The main Bhutanese source, however, says that Tsangma finally settled in the east of the country rather than in Paro or Bumthang. It was there, among the people now called Shachops, that a network of royal clans emerged claiming him as their progenitor.

Fig. 1.4

Every year on the final day of the festival held in March at Paro Dzong, this monumental image (thongdröl) of Padmasambhava, who is credited with bringing Buddhism to Bhutan, is unfurled before dawn over a wall of the temple. For a few hours the vision of this precious teacher brings blessings to all who see it. As the sun rises, the image is lowered, to be wrapped and stored for another year. (Note how the thongdröl dwarfs the men rolling it). The Paro thongdröl, one of about twenty such images in the country, is approximately 180 years old. The image of Padmasambava and his two mystic consorts is composed of cut, pieced, and embroidered imported silks. (D.K.M. 1987)

Only their names survive today in the historical records, the whole structure of society having undergone radical change at the hands of the triumphant theocracy in the mid-seventeenth century. The power of the early clans in the east was supplanted by that of the central government in the west and by a network of local families belonging to the emerging religious nobility *(chöjé)*.

The earliest picture gained of the west of the country is entirely different from that of the east. Typically, great lamas would arrive either as refugees or as honored guests, or in some convenient combination of these roles. Having promulgated the doctrines and methods peculiar to their own spiritual lineages, the local patrons and disciples of these masters would in time found permanent religious communities dedicated to upholding these traditions. The rival fortunes of these ecclesiastical estates make up the history of western Bhutan. One of them ultimately won political supremacy over the whole of Bhutan. This was the *drukpa* or 'Thunder Dragon School,' one of the main branches of the *kagyüpa*, 'School of Oral Transmission.'

The only instance when "proto-Bhutan" served as the active source rather than recipient of major influence is seen in the depredations and ultimate defeat in Tibet of a people known as the Dung. In the mid-fourteenth century they appear in the Tibetan records as causing havoc over a large area of central Tibet. There are several indications pointing to their home being located in parts of what is now Bhutan or its frontier zones. They were tricked and bloodily defeated in 1352 by a military force of the Sakya school, which held temporal authority in Tibet in this period.[9] There is reason to suspect that the remote descendants of one of their groups are the jungle-dwelling Lhokpus and Toktops of southern Bhutan, whose traditional attire seems to have been the dominant male dress of western Bhutan.[10]

With only two exceptions, discussed below, the local tradition of weaving is never mentioned in our scattered sources for this long period. Cloth and clothing appear in them only incidentally in the form of gifts presented to a lama or received from a lama by his patrons and disciples.

Vignettes from the Thirteenth and Fifteenth Centuries

One of the earliest Tibetan lamas active in the area that is now Bhutan was Phajo Drukgom Shikpo (1208-76) of the nascent Drukpa school. His biography seems to have been put in its present form in about 1580, but it claims to be wholly based on a work written by one of the lama's sons and later "rediscovered."[11] The episode in this work which mentions weaving may be the first to appear in the literature.

The saint is still known today by his title of Phajo, which is normally reserved for certain village priests in Bhutan who are said to belong to the supposedly pre-Buddhist school of the Bönpo. However, he was not a local figure, for it is known he came south from his homeland in the eastern Tibetan province of Kham by way of Ralung, the head monastery of the Drukpa school in central Tibet. His biography is mostly taken up with an account of his struggles with the leaders of another school known as the Lhapa who were already established in western Bhutan. The relevant passage reads as follows:

> Then at dawn on the fifteenth day of the first month of autumn, having meditated in a session of *guruyoga*, he [Phajo] went on his way. On a site shaped like a demoness lying spread-eagled on the ground he danced according to his heart's desire and he sang this song to a group of five girls who were there in a weaving yard[12] across the river on a hillside opposite:

> You girls who stay there on the hillside across the river
> Stop your distracting chatter and listen to this song.
> The beggar who has come from the country of Kham
> Has arrived at the place foretold by the father, the lama.
> Do you know in what place there resides
> The single mother whose karma and aspirations match my own?
> The time has come to disclose our karmic connections.

The girl in the center of the group cast the backstrap[13] [of her loom] behind her and her sword [to beat the weft][14] to the right of her. As soon as she got up, a drum of acacia wood fell from the sky. She picked it up and sang this song:

> You ascetic beggar on your way up there
> Listen to the girl's song for a moment.
> You are either the prophesied son of a lama
> Or else a magic-working demon,
> But you seem to resemble an emanation of the Compassionate One.
> I beg you to lead me to the holy site of Bodh Gaya
> Prophesied by the Buddhas of former ages.
> (*Pha drukgom shikpai namthar* n.d. [c. 1580?], fols. 16v-17r)

Eventually the hero identifies the leader of the weavers as his destined wife and spiritual consort. Ashi Sonam Pedon bears him seven sons, three of whom turn out to be demons and are drowned. When the remaining four grow up they are deputed by their father to control various districts in western Bhutan. Each was later held to be the ancestor of a powerful family of the Drukpa ecclesiastical nobility.

There is no particular reason to doubt this evidence for weaving in the thirteenth century, but the episode with the weavers must be understood primarily in symbolic terms. The exchange of songs has a bantering tone typical of various genres, sung or declaimed, of formal repartee between the sexes. The scene opens with the hero interrupting his quest for the promised land by dancing upon a piece of ground that has the form of a recumbent demoness prostrate on her back. This is an old ritual metaphor representing the subjugation of the untamed and threatening nature of the physical world (conceived as female) to the power of religion (conceived as male). The scene changes abruptly to bring in a convincing domestic scene of girls chattering as they weave, an unambiguous image of the specific attractions of the region waiting to be tamed. The heroine, who represents the whole region because she occupies the center of the team, puts aside her weaving, the symbol of local culture, to give herself to the hero, who stands for a higher, nobler cause. The magical drum which comes to her is the confirmation of her hidden, divine nature and that of the region she personifies. The obstacles, both physical and cultural, which stand between the hero and heroine, and between the rival conceptions of the land as barbaric and sacred, are represented by the river which separates them. This is eventually crossed to bring about their union. A new, enlightened order is perpetuated in society through their progeny.

Leaving aside the world of ritual and symbolism, there survives in Thimphu a site which has authentic connections both with our hero and the issue of clothing. Phajo deputed his son Nyima to rule the villages of Chang and Gung in the Thimphu Valley, and from there

FIG. 1.5

The wall paintings at Chang Gangkha temple in Thimphu date from the thirteenth century and are the earliest firmly dated frescoes in Bhutan. The costumes on the cosmological deities depicted are of mysterious origins, without clear correspondences in later Bhutan or in the surrounding regions. (Monica von Schulthess)

he gained control of the "outer passes." At Chang he built a little hillside temple known as Chang Gangkha that became the seat of his descendants, who had the title of Gangkha Shengo. Among the complex of chapels still standing today, most of which have been refurbished at different times, is a very small one containing a unique and mysterious set of wall paintings.[15] They portray a host of cosmological deities which include the seven planets, the twenty-eight lunar asterisms, and some of the subterranean serpent spirits. The chaff embedded in the plaster beneath the paintings has been dated by the radiocarbon process to within a few years of 1270, that is, within the last seven years or so of Phajo's lifetime.[16] Of particular interest are the extraordinary costumes worn by the deities portrayed, the like of which are not seen in any other known paintings from Bhutan or any other area in the Himalayas or Tibet. Nor do they correspond to any article of clothing found in the region, though there is some resemblance to the caftans of Central Asia.

The standing figures of the seven planets are each shown wearing a long, broad-sleeved tunic, open at the front and flowing in heavy folds or pleats to the ankles [fig. 1.5]. Beneath the outer robe are layers of long undergarments, crossed over the chest and belted at the middle. Some wear their hair in a high double topknot bound with a ribbon whose ends come down on either side of the head. The lunar asterisms wear the same garments, with the sleeves of the heavy outer tunic rolled all the way back to the shoulders. All have exceptionally heavy earplugs and cloth slippers of a distinctive type. Faces are mostly shown in half-profile, with the further eye protruding sharply in a manner found in some Indian paintings of the Buddhist and Jain traditions. The details of dress are so finely executed and so consistent throughout that one is tempted to believe the artist was depicting secular garments known in the later thirteenth century. The possibility remains, however, that they are an archaic survival of a much older tradition of dress that had by then disappeared everywhere except in painted form. In either case, these clothes are unlikely to have been worn by the inhabitants of what later came to be Bhutan, for the paintings must surely be an imported tradition from the north. The mysteries of their origin and nature await further study.

The paintings that survive in temples and monasteries in such profusion throughout the modern kingdom are, with rare exception, from a much later period. Except where lay patrons are shown as donor figures supplicating, or making offerings to, the Buddhist deities or lamas portrayed, this art reveals little about the secular dress of the country that is not either very well known or highly stylized. By contrast, the wonderful attention given in the paintings to the richly brocaded vestments of the Drukpa lamas achieves a highly ornamental effect of its own.

In addition to the reference to local weaving found in the biography of Phajo Drukgom Shikpo, another is found in the autobiography of Pemalingpa (1450-1521) (Pemalingpa [n.d.] 1976, vol. *pha* [14]: fol. 26r-v, and Aris 1989b, 32). Few exceed this saint in historical importance for he not only is looked on as the chief of all the 'text-discoverers' of Bhutan but he is also counted as the ancestor of a huge network of noble families (the *chöjé* noted above) who occupy the area from his homeland in Bumthang to the eastern borders. From among them arose the present royal family of Bhutan. The Sixth Dalai Lama of Tibet, Tsangyang Gyamtso (1683-1706), was the lineal descendant of Pemalingpa's younger brother.

In the account of his early youth, Pemalingpa explains how he mastered the crafts of working metal, wood, and stone – and also weaving. Such craftsmanship is unusual, not to say unique, in the life of a Buddhist scholar or saint typically preoccupied with the study of texts, the performance of ritual, and the practice of meditation. However, the inclusion of weaving among his skills points to a trait in this saint's makeup which marks him out as a kind of holy deviant, for weaving is exclusively a female pursuit and when the odd man feels inspired to take it up he is regarded with derision, even when his products arouse great admiration and command good prices. Pemalingpa was anything but a conformist: "Apart from directly pursuing whatever fancies came to mind, I did not listen to what my parents said ... I left undone whatever anyone entrusted me to do ... The people in general called me Döndrupgyel, the False Joker. Everyone, whether close or distant, kept me out of their affections" (Aris 1989b, 34). There is no further mention of his weaving in the autobiography.

Unification and the Evolution of a National Dress

A central state was imposed on the country for the first time in the seventeenth century. Bhutan thus began to move toward unity in the century after Sikkim put a Buddhist monarch at its head and a century before Nepal was consolidated under a Hindu monarch. Although Bhutan too experimented unsuccessfully with various forms of hereditary rule, the system it finally adopted was the same one chosen more or less simultaneously in Tibet, namely, rule by a lineage of the reincarnations of the founding lama. Practical differences in the form of government developed in Bhutan and Tibet, but both depended for their legitimacy and authority on the powerful and charismatic figures of their founders.

In the year 1616 Shabdrung Ngawang Namgyel, the eighteenth hereditary prince-abbot of the Drukpa school [figs. 1.1, 1.6], came as a refugee south to Bhutan from his main seat at the Ralung monastery in central Tibet. A prolonged and bitter dispute had come to a head

Fig. 1.6
This detail of an eighteenth-century thangka *(scroll painting), in the collection of the National Museum in Paro, portrays Shabdrung Ngawang Namgyel wearing the red hat of the Drukpa sect and a monk's patchwork shawl. (Guy van Strydonck)*

between him and a rival claimant to the school's throne whose case had been favored by the Tibetan ruler of the day. It happened that the Shabdrung, the title by which he is universally known in Bhutan, had a senior disciple from a prominent local family in western Bhutan who owed allegiance to the Drukpas. It was this person who encouraged his master to take refuge in the southern Himalayan valleys. By this date the communities and families loyal to the school were so firmly implanted in western Bhutan that they could provide a power base from which the fortunes of the refugee prince-abbot might be recouped in exile. The literature, however, speaks of the arrival of the state's founder exclusively in terms of the fulfillment of sacred prophecy.

In the course of the next thirty-five years, the Shabdrung laid the basis for the new state by bringing the western valleys under his personal control. He did this largely by construct-ing a chain of imposing fort-monasteries known as dzongs across the center of the country in Paro, Thimphu, Punakha, and Wangdi Phodrang, also to the north at Gasa and to the south at Dagana. The impetus for their construction came from the need to contain the opposition posed by the rival Buddhist schools established in the west of the country. Still more pressing were the requirements of defense from foreign attack. The princes of Tsang who held nominal authority in Tibet until 1644 invaded the country three times. After the victory of the Gelukpa school in that year, the new Tibetan regime and its Mongol allies invaded on two further occasions during the Shabdrung's lifetime. Some of these attempts to destroy his growing power in the south may have been temporarily successful, but as a whole they were an unmitigated disaster.

It was not only by force of arms that the new state was created. The Shabdrung was also a clever diplomat, dispensing favors and privileges to those whose support he needed and negotiating settlements in local conflicts which left him the stronger. The ease with which he encouraged more and more groups to flock to his banner speaks loudly for his personal charisma and credibility. His reputation was constantly enhanced by the stories of his scholarship, powers of magic, and artistic skills. Much also seems to have depended on his gifts of delegation, particularly in choosing efficient commanders and administrators from among his monastic followers. The emerging government of the country was thus wholly based on the principles of monastic organization, and this was to continue throughout the duration of the theocracy. Toward the end of the Shabdrung's life, tribute missions from a growing number of regions came voluntarily to his court to make submission, and these were eventually transformed into a compulsory, seasonal requirement. After his death, which seems to have taken place in 1651, the new state quickly pushed its frontiers eastward to its present limits. This was done in the course of a single campaign, and again the territory was consolidated by the construction of dzongs. It is still not clear when the name of the Shabdrung's school *(drukpa)* was first adopted as that of the country *(drukyul)*, but in the popular historical imagination it dates from the period of his lifetime. (*Bhutan* is a late Indian misnomer derived from *bhot*, the Indian term for Tibet.) The role of the country's founder and unifier is still celebrated in countless ways, and the many legends surrounding his figure must have developed partly because of the obscurantist tendencies in his recorded biography, which fails to bring him to life as a person of flesh and blood. The Shabdrung is in fact credited in legend with instituting a great number of national traditions for which the literary records provide no evidence at all.

Among these "invented traditions" is the promulgation of a code of dress. It is said that the male *go* was the Shabdrung's own innovation, particularly brought in to raise the inhabitants of the new state from their former condition of barbarism. The *go* is essentially the same garment worn by most Tibetan males but hitched up to the knees to give greater freedom of movement to the legs, and distinguished above all else by the great variety of woven designs peculiar to Bhutan. It was therefore originally a foreign garment that was adapted to the hotter, more humid, and more mountainous environment of Bhutan, and it gave full scope to the local genius of weaving.

There is no question but that in time the *go* became an essential symbol of the nation. However, there is an authoritative source on the customs of dress current in the lifetime of the Shabdrung which points to the legendary nature of the tradition which makes him the inventor of the *go*. In 1627 two Portuguese Jesuits, Estevão Cacella and João Cabral, traveled to Bhutan and met the Shabdrung for the first time at Cheri above the Thimphu Valley. They found him in a "tent, very well decorated with silk, and he was sitting in a high place clothed with red silk embroidered in gold" (Cacella 1627, in Aris 1986, 172). The Jesuits spent eight months at the Shabdrung's court and became very well acquainted with him. Cacella's account, written in October of that year and sent to his superior in India from Cheri, is a mine of information not only on the character and personality of their host but on many aspects of the country. This is what he had to say about lay dress:

> [T]heir arms are naked and from their necks to their knees they are covered with one of these woolen cloths, having another big one as a cape; they have leather belts with plates very well made and worked as are the bracelets which they normally have on their arms and the reliquaries which they wear over their shoulders; normally they are barefoot but they also have leather boots or socks made of their cloth specially for journeys ...
>
> (Cacella 1627, in Aris 1986, 181)

Cacella's account of monastic dress is less interesting because it is exactly what one would expect: "All the lamas are dressed in oriental tunics which cover their chests well, leaving their arms uncovered, and the rest of their body down to their feet they have well covered with another large cloth, yet another being a cape, which they never take off, nor do they walk about naked" (Cacella 1627, in Aris 1986, 182).

The common garment of all laymen in Bhutan in this period was certainly not the *go*, since Cacella is quite clear that the robes he saw lacked sleeves. In fact sleeves on robes must occupy the same mental category as handles on pots: "by introducing laws where there had been no Southern laws and by fixing handles on pots where there had been no handles, he [the Shabdrung] committed many actions which established beings on the good path to beneficial happiness" (Tendzin Chögyel 1759, fol. 56r, quoted in Aris 1979, 229).[17] Here, in this late source, the allusion to handles on pots is simply a figure of speech, a metaphor for the material benefits of civilization. The notion that the Shabdrung introduced the sleeved *go* is surely no more than an expression of the same idea, but interpreted in its most literal sense.

What then was the common male dress worn in Bhutan before and during the process of unification before it became the *go*? The evidence provided by the Jesuit missionary's

Fig. 1.7
View Between Murichom and Choka, *1813 aquatint by William Daniell after a Samuel Davis watercolor, 1783. One of the men, holding a bow in his left hand, is wearing a* pakhi, *a wrapped and pinned garment that was probably common male dress in southwestern Bhutan in the eighteenth century. (Courtesy Oriental and India Office Collections, the British Library)*

account of 1627 can be combined with that found in the drawings executed by Samuel Davis some 156 years later, in 1783. Among the latter are found several figures (Aris 1982, pls. 24, 39, 41) wearing a sleeveless garment which must be identical with, or very similar to, the so-called *pakhi,* until recently still worn by the inhabitants of the Toktokha area and even today used by the Lhokpus, who know it as the *pokwi* [fig. 5.42]. It is seen clearest of all in an aquatint by the great William Daniell published in 1813 [fig. 1.7], based on an original drawing by Davis which has unfortunately not survived. Captioned "View between Murichom and Choka," the original was done precisely in that area where the memory of this garment is still alive. Here the figure wears a red-sleeved garment beneath the *pakhi,* the two halves of whose upper part are draped over the shoulders instead of being knotted or fastened with a clip or brooch as one would expect. Perhaps Daniell's reworking of the Davis original has obscured the detail. A careful look at Davis's other scenes painted in the colder valleys farther north reveals that many are wearing the same garment, though it is usually covered by shawls or jackets worn over it. However, by 1783 the whole tradition of male dress was in a state of transition, and the overall impression in these drawings is of a motley collection of garments.

It is unfortunate that not a single clear drawing of the distinctive female *kira* is to be found among Davis's drawings, or indeed anywhere else. This sleeveless garment belongs to the same generic type as the male *pakhi,* but unlike male dress, there are no accounts of the primary dress of the Bhutanese women undergoing structural change. The reason for this can surely be found in the fact that women never played a significant role in those male-dominated processes which brought about significant change in the life of the nation. On the single occasion in history, in 1697, when a woman, in the absence of a male heir, was elevated to the highest position, we are told that she had to be dressed for her enthronement "in the manner of a fake man" in order to win even a temporary, token approval. We do not know how long the ceremonial transvestism imposed on her lasted, but she died a year later.[18]

The sleeved *go* as we now find it, worn by all men, is seen in Davis's drawings, having first appeared in Tilly Kettle's oil painting, c. 1775 [fig. 1.8]. In that painting the third figure from the right wears a *go* of the standard *aikapur* design, though the model who posed for the painting has failed to pull the skirt of the robe up to form the usual pouch that hangs below the belt, nor has he turned back the sleeves of his white *tögo* underneath, in the approved manner. In fact, several of the figures are incorrectly dressed, and this points to the mock-up nature of the picture. It is thought to be an artificial reconstruction, painted in Calcutta, of George Bogle's reception at the court of the Panchen Lama at Shigatse in Tibet.

The figure on the far left is intriguing. The green silk brocade jacket, worn with a scarlet *tögo* beneath it, is separate from the white skirt below, and both are partially covered by the broad white cloth worn over the left shoulder. The shoulder cloth is in fact the *kabné* (bkab ni), compulsorily worn by all lay commoners in Bhutan on official occasions and in the dzongs. We shall turn back to consider its origins shortly. A jacket of the type seen here would normally never be worn over a *go,* and here I believe it covers the upper portion of a sleeveless *pakhi*-type garment. The white skirt of the garment in fact has pleats, which a *go* never has. Such pleats are also seen in some of Davis's drawings (Aris 1982, pls. 27, 28).

Today the only pleated white skirts used by laymen are the so-called *meyö* (smad g.yogs, literally 'lower covering') worn for the performance of the *wang zhé* and other folk dances during certain public festivities. They are also worn by the figure representing a warrior deity in the New Year Festival at Punakha. The term *meyö* is normally applied to the petticoat worn by monks beneath their robes, and its application to the pleated skirts of these male

FIG. 1.8
The Third Panchen Lama Receives George Bogle at Tashilhunpo, *oil painting attributed to Tilly Kettle, c. 1775. This is the oldest extant depiction of Bhutanese dress by a Western artist. The third figure from the right is attired in a* go *of typical* aikapur *(supplementary-warp-patterned fabric). His* go, *however, is shown in a very un-Bhutanese manner: its skirt should fall only to the knees, with much of the length pulled up over the belt to form a copious pouch; its sleeves should be turned back to make deep cuffs of the white* tögo *(shirt) underneath. Indeed, several of the figures are incorrectly dressed and it is likely that the painting is a fanciful reconstruction of George Bogle's reception. (Courtesy The Royal Collection © 1994 Her Majesty Queen Elizabeth II)*

dancers is something of a misnomer, the original name having presumably been lost. The costume still worn in the dances is presented as the archaic dress of the Thimphu Valley, revived for ceremonial purposes. It is unclear what relationship, if any, the *meyö* may once have had to the *pakhi*.

The *kabné* sash which makes its first recorded appearance in the Kettle painting, c. 1775, is full of associations for the unified state and nation. According to popular tradition, the white material worn for this garment by all laymen is an allusion to the white cotton garment worn by yogis, celebrated for instance in the name of Milarepa (mi la ras pa, 'the cotton-clad one of the Mila clan'). The layman's white *kabné* is supposed to recall the belief that all Bhutanese in the past took the minor vows of the yogin, which did not impose celibacy but served to introduce a universal moral standard in society. The closely cropped hairstyle of the Bhutanese, both men and women, is also pointed to as a symbol of the religious obligations of the laity, since it resembles the new growth of hair on the shaven heads of monks and nuns. Though neither of these assertions about the lay sash and hairstyle can be validated in the historical records, as statements of belief they point to a true sense of belonging to a single group having a common purpose and identity.

The literal meaning of *kabné* (bkab ni) is 'covering.' In eighteenth-century texts we find a garment called a *jabkab* (rgyab bkab, literally 'back cover') among the articles presented by officials to their followers, either as a reward for heroic service in war or else as one of a standard set of gifts distributed on occasions of special significance.[19] It is surely this item that we see swathing many of the figures drawn by Samuel Davis in 1783 (Aris 1982, pls. 25-29), though none of them wear it in the formal style that is now absolutely de rigueur for the *kabné*. One figure (pl. 27) in particular wears a striking white sash with a broad stripe in its center that looks like the *khamar kabné* worn by all headmen in Bhutan. It is identical to a similar sash worn by tantric priests of the older schools both in Tibet and Bhutan.

The 'red scarf' (*kabné map*, bkab ni dmarp) worn by senior government officials as their badge of office is nothing but the outer shawl (*zen*, gzan) worn by all monks, draped over the left shoulder in the same way as the layman's white *kabné*. It is a reminder of the fact that all senior officials under the theocracy were either fully ordained monks who took on secular duties or else laymen who were required to observe monastic vows for the duration of their office. Such officials are still today sometimes termed *nyikem* (gnyis bskal ma), literally 'those [who receive] a double portion [of food rations as salary-in-kind].' The monastic character of government was subjected to a gradual secularization in the eighteenth and nineteenth centuries that culminated in the secular rule of the present monarchy, but the symbols of the theocracy live on in many ways besides this. Today the king's shoulder cloth is the same yellow as that of the chief abbot; ministers wear the orange of senior monks; and there has been a steady differentiation of colors and stripes for the *kabné* appropriate to new government offices as they are created.

Notions of what is proper and seemly in dress had certainly become fixed by the eighteenth century, and probably much earlier. We can conveniently close this discussion on the evolution of national dress by quoting the passage by Samuel Turner in which he recounts the Bhutanese ruler's reactions in 1783 to English dress, which was found basically unseemly despite its obvious advantages:

> A long conversation ensued with the Raja on the dress and customs of the English. He admired, and minutely examined, every part of our clothes; nor did the pockets least of all excite his wonder and surprise, by presenting such a number of comprehensive and concealed resources. He gave due credit to the convenience of our dress, its lightness, and the liberty it left to the limbs; but I could plainly perceive he judged its structure defective, as differing from his own, in shewing too plainly the general outline of the body. Thus it is, that the less enlightened Bootea, accustomed to observe the dignity of human character exist in factitious concealment, looks for importance in exterior ornament: divest his sacred superior of the robe of state, and his pontifical insignia, and he would, no doubt, conclude all authority and religion to be entirely at an end (Turner [1800] 1971, 73).

A Source of the Mid-Eighteenth Century

The essential impetus given by the founding Shabdrung to the creation of the Bhutanese state only came to full fruition about a century after his death. While the process of unification and consolidation continued, the new country was beset with problems of succession. Who could legitimately rule in the name of the dead founder, with his full authority? It was fortunate that at the end of his life the Shabdrung had delegated his secular powers to one of his monks, Tendzin Drugye, who became the first in an unbroken line of so-called *druk desi* ('brug sde srid), known to the British as the *deb rajas*. Fifty-five of these succeeded each other from the time of the Shabdrung's death, c. 1651, to 1907 when the present monarchy was established. They were in theory the nominees of the Shabdrung's own successors, but many of the struggles at the center of the Bhutanese state revolved precisely around that fundamental question: who had the right to be installed as the Shabdrung's legitimate heir? His own son, Jampel Dorje, was incompetent to succeed, and a number of lamas came, therefore, to serve as the "representatives" of the founding Shabdrung while a final, constitutional settlement to the problem was sought.

A lasting solution was finally enunciated in the first official history of Bhutan, the *Lhoi chönjung* [*Religious History of the South*], completed in 1759. The compromise it proposed gave authorization to a political settlement that had already been worked out in practice over several decades. Thus the various incarnations of the Shabdrung, who had been discovered and installed by rival powers after the secret of his death had been revealed, were *all* declared legitimate: they were said to be, variously, the embodiments of his physical, verbal, and mental qualities dispersed in different bodies. In fact, the "physical" embodiment never became established in Bhutan, while the "verbal" assumed a subordinate position to the "mental." Thus the line of six officially recognized incarnations of the mind of the Shabdrung were accorded the role of heads of state, known to the British as the *dharma rajas*, 'the kings of religion.' None exercised anything like the power and authority of the first of their line, the founding Shabdrung.

This settlement was achieved during the long and stable reign of the thirteenth Druk Desi, Sherab Wangchuk, who ruled from 1744 to 1763. The country at this time achieved a real measure of internal cohesion among its disparate elements, and a confident relationship was developed with its neighbors on all sides. Much of the state's success in this period can be attributed to the ruler's administrative skills. These are amply reflected in the official eulogy of his material achievements contained in a work entitled *Mutig doshel [The Necklace of Pearls]* by Yönten Thayé. Detailed tax lists are reproduced in full, as well as the accounts of nine separate distributions of largesse to the public, and a full list of every temple and monastery throughout the whole country.[20] An impression is gained of how, by this date, the state was further consolidating and extending its power not so much by coercion, but by bestowing favors on its officials and subjects in a graded system of reward and inducement.

A key component of the system lay in the distribution and recycling of cloth in all its varied forms. Local weaves were extracted as tax from some communities to serve as gifts to the expanding population of government servitors. These are referred to as 'dyed cloth woven [by command of the chief local] official' (dpon thag tshos ras), and large quantities were distributed at regular intervals, for instance to the headmen of villages. These local weaves are rarely differentiated by name or type, but on three occasions they are listed by general provenance as 'eastern cloth' (shar ras), an indication of the early primacy of the eastern Bhutanese weaving traditions. Only the *khamar* (kha dmar, 'red mouth') weave of the Adhang region is specifically mentioned.[21] Otherwise the references are generally to multiple loads of 'common cloth' (ras dkyus ma), or simply to 'dyed cloth' (tshos ras) or 'woven cloth' (thag ras).

In contrast with Bhutan's domestic textile products of this period, when imported cloth is listed in this source we are faced with a cornucopia of descriptive terms applied to Indian, Chinese, and Tibetan fabrics. These luxury cloths were reserved for the higher grades of the ecclesiastical government in a descending hierarchy of quality carefully matched to individual rank and status. From India there was brought the finest muslin known as "ka shi ka" from Kashi, the ancient name of Banaras. English broadcloth (*jachen*, rgya phyings) also found its way into Bhutan along with various Indian textiles. Specifically mentioned are a silk, "a dho li shi" (or "a rdo li shi"), used for dance costumes, and a thin cotton, "bha ra ha ti" (or "bha ras ha sti"), used for lining walls before painting. Assam was a particularly important source, one of its wild silk textiles known as "arti" appearing here in the form of "a back-cover [having a] white center."[22] This sounds like the striped shoulder cloth worn by headmen in Bhutan, already discussed. However, it is not clear whether the Assamese item was produced for export to a Bhutanese design or whether the design we now recognize as Bhutanese was influenced by an Assamese model.

In 1757, an embassy from the Ahom king of Assam arrived bearing gifts of "various Assamese silks of different material, color, and design." In return a wide selection of imported Chinese fabrics were presented by the court of this Druk Desi (Yönten Thayé [n.d.] 1970, fols. 73v-74r).[23] In 1760, there is mention of a rich Kashmiri merchant called "Su ta" (or "Byar gdong") being welcomed at the Bhutanese court. His gifts included "many precious items from all regions including India, Kashmir, China and Kham." Foremost among these are listed a medley of Chinese brocades and silks, and in return, the merchant received 'many loads of textile merchandise' (zong dos mang po) including Assamese silks (fols. 77v-78r). In 1762 or shortly thereafter the Druk Desi sent down twenty or more loads of Chinese silk to the Nawab of Bengal and the Raja of Cooch Bihar as part of his attempt to persuade them to discontinue the evil practice of widow immolation *(sati)* among their subjects (Yönten Thayé [n.d.] 1970, fol. 84r). Exchanges of cloth continued between the courts of Bhutan and Cooch Bihar as an integral part of diplomacy (fol. 84r-v). The country clearly served in this period as an important entrepôt for the import and export of luxury cloths produced in many parts of Asia.

The information on Chinese silk textiles in this source is particularly rich, since the Bhutanese developed a wide descriptive vocabulary, elaborating on standard Tibetan terms and a selection of Chinese loan words. The technical study of this subject must await a competent specialist in the Chinese tradition of silk textiles with access to the wealth of surviving imports preserved in the dzongs and monasteries of Bhutan, but in the meantime some observations can be made.

The common term *dar* for silk, noted above, is found in many combinations, but the element *dzö*, "mdzod" ('treasury'), appears in a wealth of compounds applied to the richest Chinese brocades. It seems these were produced by weavers at the imperial court of China and stored in its treasury.[24] The term "mdzod gos" ('treasury clothes') appears in a Tibetan-Chinese dictionary as "ku duan" ('treasury satin'), with the definition 'a yellow silk with the design of a dragon nest' indicating that the key element 'treasury' is probably translated from a standard Chinese term. The words for other silk types are straight loans, such as "ta hung" from the Chinese "da hong," 'bright red satin,'as used in Chinese weddings, and "ling" for a particularly fine, soft silk; also "lu hang" from the Chinese "lu huang" for the 'sulphur' used for dyeing silk yellow. But the relationship of the unidentified Tibetan terms "za 'og" and "jus" to their Chinese equivalents "jin" and "jin se" is unknown.[25]

In the case of "sman rtse" (pronounced *mentsi* or *mensé*), the term universally applied to the yellow silk fabric stamped with floral patterns used as protective hangings in front of scroll paintings, we can be quite confident that this is the Chinese *mianzi*, which seems to mean nothing more than 'covering.' In our source various grades of the basic "sman rtse" are identified in compound terms.[26] Both in Tibet and in Bhutan during the eighteenth century small squares of this material were used as a low denomination of currency.[27] The term occurs in the vernacular as an element in the local names of certain Bhutanese weaves, such as *mensé mathra* (sman rtse dmar khra), and an Indian version of the material is also recognized in our source (rgya gar sman rtse). However, the Bhutanese are certainly unaware of its Chinese derivation, particularly since the spelling has been naturalized by assimilation to the Tibetan and Bhutanese words for 'medicine' (sman) and 'peak' (rtse).

Apart from the profusion of detail on various imported textiles, the importance of this key source lies in the way it helps to counter the received picture of Bhutan as a land wholly isolated even from its closest neighbors. The eighteenth century in particular saw wide and fruitful contacts on all sides, amply reflected in the story of its cloth.

FIG. 1.9

This dance, known as chözhé *('dharma song'), celebrates the opening of the route to a famous pilgrimage site at Tsari in southeastern Tibet in the twelfth century. The dancers are monks, dressed as the monastic militia of the Drukpa school of Buddhism, exemplifying the mutual dependence of spiritual and secular values. The warriors wear cloth headbands to protect them from the blows of weapons; their lower garment is of dark fabric appropriate to monks, worn with a jacket and breastplate secured with cloth straps. The senior monk (center) plays the traditional instrument known as* dramnyen. *(F.P. 1982)*

The Preservation of Archaic Traditions of Dress

The state festivals of sacred dance celebrated annually in nearly every dzong since the seventeenth century must have played a vital role in disseminating new forms and styles of dress, for these occasions are welcome opportunities for the display of finery. From the point of view of the performance, the festivals also served to preserve archaic costumes solely for ceremonial purposes because of their associations with antiquity and divinity. It is the auxiliary dances and ceremonies of the Bhutanese monks and laymen performed in the festivals alongside the main repertoire of sacred dance which are of special interest. A few of those, whose costumes have interesting associations, may be briefly described.

The dance known as *chözhé* (chos gzhas, literally 'dharma song') is performed to reenact the ancient monastic militia of the Drukpas [fig. 1.9]. It is a beautiful, slow-moving spectacle which celebrates the opening of the route to the famous site of Buddhist pilgrimage at Tsari in southeastern Tibet by an early hierarch of the school, Tsangpa Gyaré (1161-1211). In one of their performances the warrior monks are led by their senior playing the stringed instrument known as *dramnyen* (sgra snyan). On their heads they wear a circular tube of cloth that is meant to be a protection from the blows of weapons. Their lower garment is a pleated dress of the darker material appropriate to monks, worn with a jacket, the whole secured with the straps of a kind of breastplate. On the thumbs of their right hands are worn large ivory rings which are said to have been used in former times as aids to drawing a bowstring. In their other hands the monks hold ivory rosaries. The tradition as a whole exemplifies that mutual dependence of spiritual and secular values which is such a hallmark of the Drukpa theocracy.

41

During the New Year Festival celebrated at the former winter capital of Punakha, representatives of the 'eight great hosts of the Wang people' (wang tsho chen brgyad), who have the status of most-favored patrons of the Drukpa state, form their own ceremonial militia known as *pazap* (dpa' rtsal pa). They come under the control of their headmen, who are dressed as monks for the occasion, a reminder of how all such officials were under monastic vows during the theocracy. The *pazap* militia also appoint their own generals, who are magnificently attired in an array of multicolored silk scarves tightly plaited to form a kind of armor that is said to resist the stroke of a sword. The helmets they, and the common militia, wear are all inherited from a period when they had far more than a ceremonial purpose. The dark maroon of the standard *pazap* uniform is reminiscent of the color worn by monks.

Descriptions of the dress of Bhutanese soldiers in the eighteenth century can usefully be given here for the contrast afforded with the festival scenes of the present. The first is by the celebrated Scotsman George Bogle, written in 1774:

> Their warlike garb is various and not uniform. Some wear a cap quilted, or of cane and sugar-loaf shape, with a tuft of horse-hair stained; others, an iron-netted hood, or a helmet with the like ornament; under these they often put false locks to supply the want of their own hair, which among this tribe of Bhutanese is worn short. Sometimes a coat of mail is to be seen. In peace as in war, they are dressed in short trousers, like the Highland philabeg; a woolen hose, soled with leather and gartered under the knee; a jacket or tunic, and over all two or three striped blankets. Their leaders only are on horseback, and are covered with a cap, rough with red-dyed cowtails [yak tails]. They sleep in the open air, and keep themselves warm with their plaids and their whisky (Bogle, in Markham [1876] 1971, 63).

And here again is Samuel Turner writing about his visit of 1783:

> The accoutrements of a fighting man, fully equipped, are extremely cumbrous. A prodigious deal of loose clothing surrounds the body: besides the common mantle, he wears very often a blanket, or thick quilted jacket. This, as well as the helmet (which is made either of stained cane, coiled conically, or else of cotton rope, quilted between two cloths, with flaps that occasionally turn down over the ears, and a piece to cover the nose), if not absolutely proof against the stroke of a sword or arrow, must at least considerably loosen its force (Turner [1800] 1971, 118).

This fleeting sight of the rich panoply of festival costumes can do little more than point to the wide scope for a thorough treatment of the subject through further detailed research.

The Spiritual Metaphors of the Loom

If the literary sources on the art of weaving are generally thin and scattered, there survives a passage in one work where the subject is directly addressed. It is *Ashi nangsai namthar [The Biography of Nangsa Öbum]*, a Tibetan work enjoying wide diffusion throughout the Himalayan region, particularly in Bhutan where a Dzongkha version is now used in all schools.[28]

Ashi Nangsa, as she is known in Bhutan, is a quasi-legendary figure remembered as a *delog* ('das log), that is to say 'one who returned from the dead' to tell of her experiences in hell and to indicate to the common people the path to salvation. At least twelve such biographies are extant today in Tibetan, and the fact that we are dealing with more than just mythology is proved by the existence, even today, of several persons in eastern Bhutan and elsewhere who are recognized and revered as *delog*.[29] Ashi Nangsa's biography makes her a contemporary of Rechungpa (1083- 1161), one of Milarepa's chief disciples. However, her story is revealed in terms which resonate across the boundaries of time.

Ashi Nangsa's song, which celebrates the domestic technology of the backstrap loom as a symbol of the wonderful complexity and richness of the Buddhist teachings, affords a close parallel to a song attributed to Drukpa Kunley (1455-1529) rejoicing in the domestic technology of beer brewing as a symbol or metaphor for the path to enlightenment (Ardussi 1977). In her song Ashi Nangsa instructs a group of girls from her village in the Tsang Province of Tibet on how they can turn the whole process of weaving into a constant reminder of fundamental spiritual concepts. In the Dzongkha version all the songs which intersperse the prose have been left untranslated from the original Tibetan. Bhutanese have little difficulty in recognizing the various parts of the loom [fig. 1.10] referred to by their Tibetan names. The songs themselves belong to a common literary idiom that would present no particular difficulty to any Bhutanese steeped in the religious culture that transcends all Himalayan borders. In the notes to the translation which follows I have provided the Dzongkha equivalents of these names. The continuing relevance and appeal of the song to its Bhutanese audience today demonstrate how weaving is still so closely integrated into common life. It also shows the constant movement on the part of Buddhism to penetrate and absorb every aspect of life:

Obeisance to the host of lamas, meditational deities and dakinis.
Please look down with compassion on girls who lack religion.

Listen here, girls of Nanyam.
Hear me Nangsa Back-from-Dead.
Using the parts of this loom[30] as similes, I the girl
Shall sing a song to turn your minds to religion.

This square frame beam[31] dragging on the ground
Causes delight when conceived as a meditation hut for single occupancy.
This square weaving mat[32] laid out below
Causes joy when conceived as a little cushion for meditation.

I the girl Nangsa Öbum Back-from-Dead
Am joyful when conceived as someone intent on spiritual realization.
You the maidservant Jompa Kyipa
Are delighted when conceived as the assistant who carries provisions to the meditator.

The frame beams[33] implanted to the left and right at the front of the loom[34]
Cause delight when conceived as victory banners of the Buddhist teachings.
This warp beam[35] which holds the head of the cloth
Causes joy when conceived as the lama's spiritual counsels.

This thick backstrap[36] cast behind
Causes delight when conceived as the casting of *samsara* behind one.
This breast beam[37] made with its [two halves], mother and son, joined flat together
Causes joy when conceived as the coalescing of bliss and emptiness.

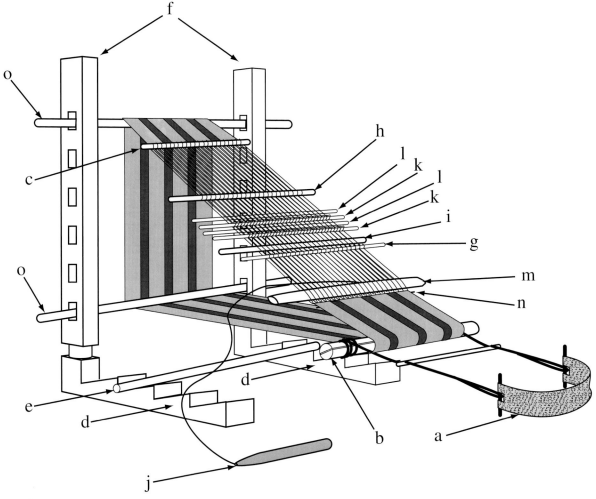

Fig. 1.10

The Backstrap Loom.

Dzongkha (Dz)/Bumthangkha (Bu)/Kurtötkha (Ku): *pangthag* (spang 'thag), 'lap loom,' Tshangla (Tsh): *dangshing*

(a) Backstrap
Dz/Bu/Ku: *kethag* (sked 'thag), Tsh: *chethag*

(b) Breast beam
Dz/Bu/Ku: *tshe, tshig* (tshig), Tsh: *khom*

(c) Closing rod
[This rod secures warp-end loops wound from opposite directions and is not always present.]
Dz: *sogshing* (srog shing), 'life wood'; *thaggi sog* ('thags gyi srog), 'loom's life', Bu: *nushing, ruishing, yamyam*, Ku: *mantan*, Tsh: *whybrung*

(d) Ground frame beam
Dz: *kangthé* (rkang theg), Bu: *kangthen*, Ku: *kangthen, kangthing*, Tsh: *bitantsham*

(e) Foot brace
Dz/Bu/Ku: *kangshing* (rkang shing), Tsh: *kangshing, bitanpang*

(f) Frame beam
Dz: *thagshing* ('thags shing), 'loom wood', Bu: *tharbang, tharwang*, Ku: *thagshing, thaling*, Tsh: *dangshing*

(g) Heddle rod (ground warp)
Dz/Tsh: *néshing* (gnas shing), Bu/Ku: *nat tseng*

(h) Leash (coil) rod
Dz: *drip* (sgrib), Bu: *griba*, Ku: *dipa*, Tsh: *nyé*

(i) Shed rod
Dz/Bu: *udung* ('u dung), *ulu* ('u lu), Ku: *ulu, oo-ih, we*, Tsh: *shogodong*

(j) Shuttle case
Dz/Bu/Ku: *pündung, pünshing* (spun dung, spun shing), Tsh: *phunpalang* (the slender wooden rod on which yarn is wound before being placed inside the shuttle is the *phunbrung*)

(k) Supplementary-warp-pattern heddle rods
Dz/Bu/Ku: *péshing* (dpe shing), Tsh: *péshing, shipibrung, sipchurung*

(l) Supplementary-warp-pattern shed rods
Dz/Bu/Ku: *péshing* (dpe shing), Tsh: *pébrung, shipi shogodong*

(m) Sword
Dz/Ku: *tham, thama* (thagm, thag ma), Bu: *thagsha, thama*, Tsh: *thagchung*

(n) Temple
[This slender stick is hardly visible because it is always inserted underneath the web.]
Dz/Bu: *tser* (tser, btsir), Ku: *tser, nitma*, Tsh: *lizi, lizu, tser*

(o) Warp beams
Dz: *théshing* (the shing), *jushing*, Bu: *thrishing, tha-eh*, Ku: *thé, thédung*, Tsh: *badi*

Loom accessories not shown:

Brush to moisten wild silk warp web
Tsh: *phrugshi*

Pattern pick
Dz: *metok thagchung* (me tog 'thag chung), Bu: *tsimbang*, Ku: *metok tsang*, Tsh: *sipchur, dungsambrung* ('making flower stick'), *zumpi* (for a porcupine quill)

This warp[38] inserted between them [the two halves of the breast beam]
Causes delight when conceived as the abiding nature of the universal basis.[39]
This cord[40] which fastens [the backstrap to] the breast beam left and right
Causes joy when conceived as the moral discipline of the Ten Virtues.[41]

This closing rod[42] which holds the life-force of the warp
Causes delight when conceived as the female consort[43] who holds the life-force.
This white warp, soft and long,
Causes joy when conceived as the white path to liberation.

This well-made heddle rod[44] which pulls upwards
Causes delight when conceived as the upper realms[45] that pull upwards.
This well-made heddle rod[46] which injures downwards
Causes joy when conceived as the kick that injures the evil destinies.[47]

This shed stick[48] which distinguishes the warp
Causes delight when conceived as the distinguishing of cause and effect.
This rapid movement of the weft[49] which makes the warp shout
Causes joy when conceived as the mind of enlightenment [generated by] 'giving and
  taking.'[50]

This shuttle[51] which offers incense to the warp
Causes delight when conceived as the purification of the Two Obscurations.[52]
This bobbin[53] which completely winds the weft
Causes joy when conceived as the completion of the Two Provisions.[54]

This temple[55] which stretches the width of the woolen cloth[56]
Causes delight when conceived as the common flavor of the Eight Worldly Concerns.[57]
This sound of weaving, the clear noise of *tak-tak*,[58]
Causes joy when conceived as a pure discourse in religious language.

This casting out and taking back of the weft
Causes delight when conceived as the equal exchange of self for other.
These 84,000[59] wefts layered upon the warps
Cause joy when conceived as the holy dharma of the sutras and tantras.

This white woolen cloth, soft and long,
Causes delight when conceived as this girl's superior aspiration.

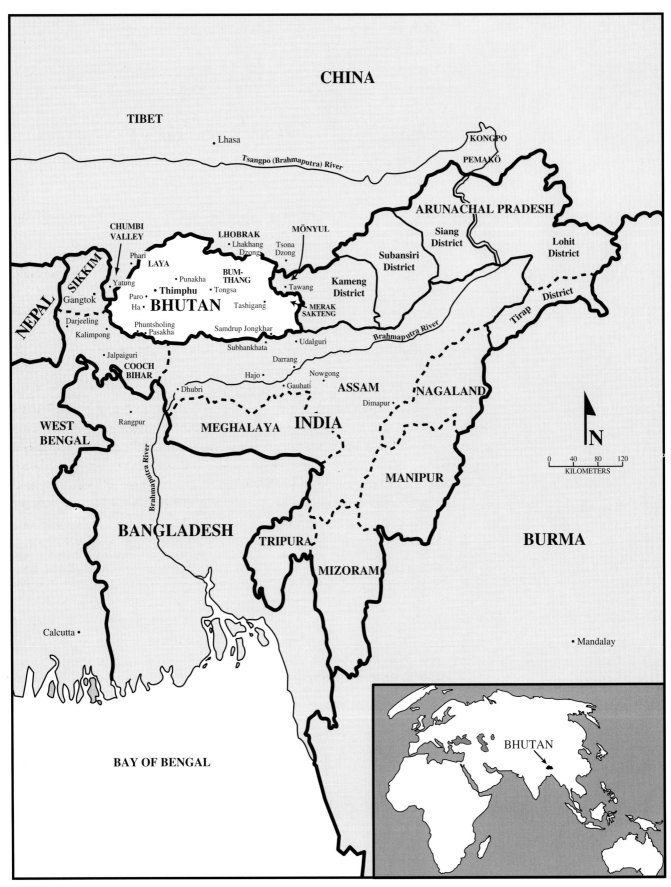

Map 1   Bhutan in its Region

46

Chapter Two

Bhutan and Its Neighbors

Links between the weaving traditions of people in Bhutan, India, Tibet, Burma, and more distant lands long predate current national identities. Some very specific textile and dress features shared by Bhutanese and immediately adjacent communities arose from common cultural histories. Textile and design influences also transcended borders through economic, political, and religious contacts between the Bhutanese and their more far-flung neighbors in present-day northeast India. Other forms and practices, many of them relating to ritual and ceremonial textiles, emanated – like Buddhism – from Tibet. Together, these influences helped create Bhutan's extraordinary, rich, and sophisticated textile heritage.

Situated near major crossroads of ancient trade and migration routes, Bhutan has enjoyed access to Tibet, China, Southeast Asia, India, and destinations far to the west. Commerce undoubtedly flourished from earliest times, although the first written evidence of trade dates only from the second century AD. The spread of Buddhism from India into the Himalayas in the seventh century further increased Bhutan's contacts, especially with Tibet. Religious teachers and devout laypeople traveled to holy sites outside the country, and later Bhutan administered Buddhist establishments as distant as Ladakh. Religious and economic activities were closely intertwined; religious devotees covered the expenses of long, arduous journeys by trading goods, and merchants on trading expeditions gained merit by visiting temples. The production and uses of textiles in Bhutan mirror these centuries of material, decorative, and technological exchanges.

Shared or related origin legends, language, rituals, and methods of cloth production and decorative techniques abound in the larger region (Map 1), stretching from the eastern Himalayas through Southeast Asia to Indonesia.[1] These connections have been noted by some authors, but no studies as yet have taken the Himalayas as a starting point for adding to a textile perspective. Bhutanese, Chinese, Indian, and Western writings, oral traditions, and the textiles themselves are rich sources for illuminating the development of Bhutanese weaving, cloth use, and design.

Common Cultural Histories

Immediately on Bhutan's borders to the east, south, and west are peoples who came originally from Bhutan or have the same ethnic origin as people in Bhutan, but who live in territory that is now divided between Bhutan and India. Their social and cultural history is intertwined with that of communities in Bhutan, and their weaving and dress styles are related because of a common past and proximity.

Before the mid-1600s, parts of eastern Bhutan and areas that now lie in India and Tibet (China) were encompassed in a single cultural and political area. The region of Mönyul, as it was known to the Tibetans, stretched from the former provincial capital of Tsona Dzong in Tibet through the religious center of Tawang south to Assam.[2] *Mön* was originally a term

Tibetans applied to non-Buddhist lands south of the Himalayas, whose inhabitants were generically called *mönpa* ('people of Mön'). Today *mönpa* is the name many Bhutanese give to remote villagers in Tongsa District considered primitive for their nettle-weaving traditions. Among Bhutanese and Indians, *mönpa* also refers to communities in the Tawang region of Kameng District (Arunachal Pradesh, India) whose inhabitants are ethnically similar to their neighbors in eastern Bhutan.

Three groups of Mönpas, all of them now Buddhist, live in Arunachal Pradesh (Aris 1980a, 10; Fürer-Haimendorf 1982, 146-71; Verma 1976 ms). History, language, religion, lifestyles, weaving, and dress bind them closely to populations that have been Bhutanese since the late 1600s. One group is made up of highland herders living in the Tawang region who are akin to the people of the adjacent Merak and Sakteng valleys in Bhutan. Communities on either side of the border speak the same language and call themselves by the same name *(brokpa)*.[3] In their general appearance and dress, the Mönpas of Tawang and the people of Merak and Sakteng cannot be distinguished. Men and women wear characteristic yak hair hats [fig. 2.1]. Men wear a red woolen jacket belted at the waist, trousers, and boots. Women wear a striped, knee-length dress of wild silk *(shingkha)*, cut like a tunic and belted, a patterned jacket [fig. 2.2], and boots. The people of Merak Sakteng have had traditional grazing rights in the Tawang region, and there has been a constant flow of people, animals, and goods between these two cross-border locations.

Bhutan's recorded history of association with Tawang began in the ninth century. At that time, a nobleman from Tibet fled to Bhutan, where he is now considered the ancestor of all the clans in the east.[4] His eldest son settled in the Tawang region (Mönyul) and became the progenitor of an important clan there. In later centuries, connections between Mönyul and what is now central and eastern Bhutan endured.[5] Recent research indicates strong affinities – in language, myth, and ritual as well as clothing – between the people of central Bhutan and those of Merak Sakteng and Tawang.[6] Common ancestry may help explain why the early Bhutanese felt an affinity with people farther east and why this intercourse between the regions persisted.

South of Tawang are other Mönpas who belong to the same ethnic group as the majority people of eastern Bhutan, the 'easterners' *(shachop)*.[7] Although their language links them to the Shachops, these Mönpas are closer to the Mönpas of Tawang and the Merak Sakteng people of Bhutan in their weaving practices and dress. Men wear a heavy robe of maroon wool that crosses over the chest and fringed, knee-length trousers made of wild silk. Women wear a knee-length tunic *(shingkha)*, woven of white wild silk and tied at the waist by a long cummerbund. This outfit is completed with a red, patterned wild silk jacket and the distinctive yak hair hat worn by women and men alike.

In the middle of the seventeenth century, the emergence of new religious and political powers in Tibet and Bhutan led to the delineation of a border in this region for the first time.[8] Eastern Bhutanese did not become isolated from their neighbors by this development. Ngawang, the monk-author of the *Logyu*, the most important Bhutanese source of the period, wrote that

FIG. 2.1

The people of Merak Sakteng are a reminder that eastern Bhutan is part of a cultural area that includes lands now in India and Tibet. Their language, dress, and lifestyle link them to communities in adjacent Tawang (Arunachal Pradesh, India), and more distant regions of southeast Tibet. Men's garments are mainly woven from the wool of local sheep; leggings and vests are made from the hides of deer and wild goats. Women wear striped red-and-white tunics – a unique style in Bhutan today – and one or two jackets made of wild silk. Their red jackets are typically patterned with stars, flowers, horses, elephants, and birds [fig. 2.2]. The felted yak hair hats worn by men and women have long, thin tentacles to channel rain away from the face. (Tashigang, D.K.M. 1987)

FIG. 2.2

Merak Sakteng women's wild silk jackets have distinctive supplementary-weft patterning, a detail of which is illustrated here. The same jackets, some of them manufactured in Bhutan, are worn by Mönpa, Sherdukpen, and Aka women in nearby districts of Arunachal Pradesh [fig. 2.6]. The jackets always show rows of star-like flowers, geometric motifs, horses, long-tailed birds, and elephants (whose curling trunks have here been stylized into heads, probably because the weaver had never seen them). Sometimes, as in this example, the horses or elephants have human figures on their backs; identical motifs are seen as far away as Indonesia. Swastikas appear in these jackets and other Bhutanese textiles as good luck symbols; their orientation to the left or right is a function of design and weaver's choice and does not have other, religious significance. (see Catalog)

people traveled quite freely in all directions and that trade flourished (n.d., fol. 23r, quoted in Aris 1986, 112). If, in later centuries, occasional friction occurred between governments, the people of Merak and Sakteng, under Bhutanese authorities, continued their traditional contacts with the Mönpas, whose homelands were administered by Tibet until 1914, and then by India.

In addition to these shared cloth traditions, barter involving cloth still links communities in eastern Bhutan with the Mönpa peoples of Arunachal Pradesh. Patterned women's jackets worn by both groups are woven in both places but exported mainly from Bhutan.[9] Eastern Bhutanese carry these jackets to India, exchanging them for rice and aluminum wares which are cheaper there than in Bhutan. The Mönpas meanwhile take handwoven cotton bags, wild silk cloth, and deerskins to eastern Bhutan to trade for men's maroon wool robes, heavy blankets, and yak hair hats. Buddhist festivals in eastern Bhutan and in Mönpa communities in India attract the faithful, with their goods to trade, from both sides of the border. Age-old commercial activities, although modest in scope, thus continue to reinforce the ethnic and historical links between these peoples.

The Sherdukpens of Arunachal Pradesh live near the Mönpas, wear similar dress, and are also Buddhists.[10] Sherdukpen weaving bears a strong likeness to weaving in Bhutan. Women use a backtension loom, and work with cotton and wild silk imported from the plains as well as with nettle. Their process for obtaining fiber from the nettle plant is the same as that used by eastern Bhutanese.

The common Sherdukpen carrying cloth *(bogré)* closely resembles Bhutanese bundle wraps *(bündri, kushü bogdri)*; both are typically made of nettle fiber. A sort of knapsack or pouch, the *bogré* is tied around the shoulders to form a fold at the back. Its central motif is always a swastika, "around which are woven variegated patterns such as the eyes of yaks or pigeons, face of a sheep, and Tibetan flags ... pictures of flowers, leaves, or trees" (Sharma 1961, 23-24). These patterns in red, black, and yellow are exactly like those on Bhutanese carrying cloths [fig. 2.3]. The names of the designs are similar, the names of the textiles are

related, and both indicate a strong connection.

Sherdukpen men and women wear yak hair hats that associate them with neighboring Mönpa groups and the people of Merak Sakteng in Bhutan. Women wear identical sleeveless, knee-length tunics and patterned, red jackets. The dress of the men, however, is quite different from the present apparel of the Mönpas or Bhutanese. It consists of a white cotton or wild silk cloth *(sapé)*, the corners of which are crossed over the chest and pinned or fastened with hooks at the shoulders. The garment is belted with a sash and hangs to the knees. A loincloth or trousers and a long-sleeved jacket reaching below the hips complete the outfit (Sharma 1961, 17). Elsewhere in the region, wearing a garment that fastens at the shoulders is a style that, for men, is reserved for special occasions; in most places, it has disappeared altogether. Farther east, wrapped clothing is now rarely seen, but to the west it is identified with the Lhops of Bhutan and the Lepchas of Bhutan and Sikkim.

Living on Bhutan's southern and western borders, the Lepchas are another group now artificially divided by political boundaries. Although the Lepchas are most often thought of as the indigenous inhabitants of Sikkim, an Indian state west of Bhutan, their settlements extended well beyond Sikkim's borders to Kalimpong and surrounding territory that was, or is now, part of southern Bhutan.[11] Lepcha dress and cloth production exhibit strong

Fig. 2.3

Textile Motifs and Common Cultural Histories.
Some of the most striking similarities between Bhutanese and northeast Indian weaving occur in designs of the Sherdukpens of Kameng District, adjacent to eastern Bhutan. Sherdukpen motifs (left) *compare closely with Bhutanese motifs* (right). *The top pair shows the Sherdukpen 'Chinese flag' and the Bhutanese double thunderbolt* (dorje jadam), *which has many variations. The next pair shows a motif known to the Sherdukpens as 'the eyes of doves,' resembling a Bhutanese motif described as 'popped barley with water eyes'* (te bomé chu mik). *The third Sherdukpen motif is identified as either a 'flower' or*

'shrine with prayer flags'; its Bhutanese counterpart is an 'areca nut tree' (guwashing). *The fourth Sherdukpen motif shows 'yak eyes,' while the Bhutanese variation is 'pigeon eyes'* (parewa mik). *At bottom are two designs whose appearance in Bhutanese and Sherdukpen textiles is identical. The upper motif is a 'coiled rope' to Sherdukpens and a 'circular rope'* (kholo thagpa) *or version of a lucky knot to Bhutanese. The meander at bottom is known to both groups as a 'Chinese wall'* (Dzongkha: janachari), *which Sherdukpens say is a fence that divides their country from China.* (Sherdukpen designs, after Elwin 1959a.)

FIG. 2.4
Supplementary-warp-patterned cloth, such as this woman is weaving, is characteristic of Lepcha communities that once extended from Sikkim into what is now southwestern Bhutan. The Lepcha backtension loom, like its Bhutanese counterpart, has two warp beams, here lashed to upright sticks in the ground. This photograph, taken in Darjeeling (India) in the early part of this century, illustrates dress styles in a region settled by several ethnic groups. Two of the women are garbed in what appear to be long, wrapped gowns and jackets of undyed, white wild silk, one style of customary Lepcha dress. Another woman standing at center is in a striped Bhutanese kira. All three women who are standing seem to be spinning yarn with drop spindles. The men seated at left and right have on Tibetan-style robes, while the man standing at right has on a Nepalese hat and probably trousers. All of the women are wearing cuffed blouses and one or more jackets, a style that was also popular in Bhutan at this time. (Photographer unknown, Peabody Essex Museum)

affinities with the traditions of nearby native peoples in southwestern Bhutan. These communities include the Lhops (Doyas) in Dorokha (Samtse District), the Toktops in Chukha District, and the Mönpas in southern Tongsa District. These groups share the same geophysical environment, live close to one another, and have retained until recently what other Bhutanese consider archaic dress and weaving practices, such as the use of nettle fiber.

The customary clothing of Lepcha men was a wrapped cloth, resembling the garment worn by Sherdukpens in Arunachal Pradesh. Until recently, the same style was common among the Lhops, Toktops, and Mönpas in Bhutan, where it is widely known as a *pakhi*. Lepcha dress was described in 1855 as:

> one cotton vestment, which is loosely thrown round the body, leaving one or both arms free; it reaches to the knee, and is gathered round the waist: its fabric is close, the ground color white, ornamented with longitudinal blue stripes, two or three fingers broad, prettily worked with red and white ... . In cold weather an upper garment with loose sleeves is added (Hooker 1855, 121).

Lepcha women's apparel was wrapped around the body like a Bhutanese woman's dress *(kira)*. Consisting of a "thick piece of home-woven striped material, fastened over one shoulder with a brooch," it was belted with a sash and reached to the knees (Gorer [1938] 1967, 52-53). In a variation of this style, "a long, linen robe [was] artistically gathered at the belt and held at the shoulders by short, sharp slivers of bamboo or a pair of huge silver pins joined by a little chain" (Nebesky-Wojkowitz 1956, 142). This dress was topped with a jacket, completing this parallel to the outfit of a Bhutanese woman.

By the mid-nineteenth century, Tibetan influence was affecting fashions in Sikkim. While the botanist J.D. Hooker observed that ordinary women (which the Lepchas were) wore long robes of "coarse silk," well-to-do Sikkimese favored the style of the Tibetan nobility: a blouse and petticoat, worn under a "sleeveless woolen cloak, of gay pattern, usually covered with crosses, and fastened in front by a girdle of silver chains" (1855, 122-23).[12] By the 1950s, many Lepcha women had adopted the styles of the more numerous Sikkimese who were of Nepalese origin, and today the traditional wrapped dress is rarely seen. Lepcha men, too, abandoned their customary wrapped garment by the mid-twentieth century – in favor of Western-style jackets and trousers (Nebesky-Wojkowitz 1956, 141-42).

In addition to the historical similarities between Lepcha and Bhutanese dress, Lepcha weaving closely resembles Bhutanese weaving. Weavers of both groups use nearly identical backstrap looms and patterning techniques to manufacture warp-striped and supplementary-warp-patterned cloth [fig. 2.4].[13] While striped cloth is ubiquitous in the Himalayas to the east and west, supplementary-warp-patterned cloth like that for which the Bhutanese are well known *(aikapur)* does not appear farther west than the Lepcha region. It seems that among the Lepchas this decorative fabric was common for festive apparel, while, as in Bhutan, everyday outfits were made of plain nettle fiber, coarse wild silk, or cotton.

Textile Influences Across Bhutan's Borders

Bhutan shares important traditions with groups in the more distant plains and hills of what is now India. South of Bhutan lie the Indian states of Assam and West Bengal, both famed as the sites of powerful, ancient kingdoms – one of which may even have encompassed Bhutan.[14] These realms were noted for their textiles and for the unusual "silk cotton" trees on which silkworms fed, as they do in Bhutan (Lahiri 1991, 97). Bhutan and Assam also share the backstrap loom, cultivation of lac (dye) insect colonies, some cloth terminology, and cloth patterns that the Bhutanese remember as Assamese.

For 600 of the past 750 years (1228-1824), Assam was ruled by a dynasty that originated in Burma and left a strong imprint on local weaving and dress styles (Gait [1905] 1967, 71-78; Milne [1910] 1970, 16-21). The Ahoms were Shans, a branch of the Tai who first reached Assam from Yunnan in the eighth century (Mackenzie [1884] 1989, 2). Excellent spinners and weavers, Ahom women produced fine silk cloths that Muslim historians compared to those of China. Cotton and silk cloth were highly valued and stored in the royal Ahom treasury for use as gifts of state (Gait [1905] 1967, 271-72).

The Shan Ahoms are credited with popularizing a style of women's dress that consists of a wrapped garment and a jacket, the traditional dress in Burma (Elwin 1959a, 84). Among the peoples of the Assam plains and the northeast Indian hills, as in Bhutan, this style is almost universal today, reflected in many distinctive costumes. Plaid and checkered cloths, like those popular in Burma, are also associated with Assam, and the Bhutanese point out that at least one pattern they use, *pangtsi,* is Assamese in origin. Further, Assamese lac, like lac from Bhutan, was both cultivated by artificial propagation and gathered in the forests, since it was in great demand as a trade item (Watt [1889] 1972, 2:399-409). For many centuries, the eastern Bhutanese must have shared the knowledge of extracting dye from this source.

Similarities in words naming cloth unmistakably link eastern Bhutanese weaving with traditions to the southeast. The southeastern terms all include the element *kapur* or *por,* which occurs in the names of patterned fabrics from eastern Bhutan *(aikapur, kapur phatsa).* Among several peoples of Arunachal Pradesh, *pore* means 'design.'[15] In Bengali, *kapur* means 'cloth,' and in Assam the word also refers to decorated textiles.[16] These linguistic commonalities point to old, close relations between the eastern Bhutanese and these neighboring regions.

The Bhutanese often note their affinities with their neighbors in the northeast Indian hills: agricultural practices such as slash-and-burn cultivation; the importance of maize in the diet; breeds of cattle *(mithun);* bamboo houses built on stilts; bamboo and wooden wares; and

| Bhutan | India | Burma | Thailand |

FIG. 2.5
Textile Influences Across Borders.
Textiles are a rich source for future study of the links between eastern Bhutan and regions farther to the east and south. Eastern Bhutanese patterning, seen on textiles such as women's belts (kera), for example, is shown at far left. Patterns from the coats woven by the Mishmis of Siang District in Arunachal Pradesh (northeastern India) are at near left. Designs from textiles of the Burmese Kachins and Chins, at near right, and from Thai weaving, at far right, complete the spectrum. (Mishmi patterns, after Elwin 1959a; Kachin and Chin patterns, after Fraser-Lu 1989, figs. 133 and 134; and Thai patterns, after Fraser-Lu 1989, fig. 142.)

weaving technologies. Recurrent fabric patterns, similar terminology applied to designs and to cloth, and related clothing styles are further expressions of these links.

Backtension looms are widespread among the peoples of Arunachal Pradesh, Nagaland, and Manipur in northeast India.[17] Among some groups, looms consisting simply of a warp secured to a beam and kept taut by the strap around a weaver's body are easily portable. In other communities, looms with a second, lower beam for the warp are braced with the help of two upright pieces of wood or a fixed wooden frame. Just as in Bhutan, wooden swords are employed for beating down the weft, hollow bamboo shuttle cases for throwing the weft, and the fabrics produced are warp-faced.

Because the northeast Indian hills are ecologically similar to Bhutan, identical or nearly identical fibers and dyestuffs are known to weavers there. The Mishmis of Arunachal Pradesh, a group particularly famous for weaving, process nettle fiber for spinning by soaking the stalks in ash water, just as the Bhutanese do (Dalton 1872, in Elwin 1959b, 337). Cotton and wool are also widely used in the region.[18] The Singphos in Lohit (eastern Arunachal Pradesh), as well as other groups, call local indigo *rom* or *ram*; one of the terms heard in Bhutan is *ram* (Dalton 1872, in Elwin 1959b, 407; Survey of India 1915, 277). Among the Mishmis, just as in Bhutan, women dyeing yarns once had to observe many taboos, including abstinence from meat.[19]

The textile designs of northeast India display striking resemblances to those of Bhutan. As in Bhutan, pattern bands of different widths – showing zigzags, triangles, fret and grid patterns, and diamonds – are woven with both supplementary-warp and supplementary-weft techniques, and serve as borders for more complex designs or as the entire pattern. The Mishmis, whose language is akin to that of the Kachins of Burma and China and of the Lepchas of Sikkim and Bhutan (Elwin 1957, 22), decorate textiles with pattern bands that are typically illustrative of these similarities with Bhutanese design [fig. 2.5]. Other groups employ wide warp-pattern bands alternating with narrow plainweave stripes, in the manner of eastern Bhutanese cloth. For example, the Adis of Siang District (Arunachal Pradesh) arrange "red and black stripes on a white ground; white and yellow stripes on a black ground; alternate bands of red and black ... ," which recall the traditional color-pattern associations in eastern Bhutan (red and black bands being a kind of *möntha*; white and yellow being *jadrima*; and so on) (Elwin 1959a, 36-38).

Naga weaving, south of Arunachal Pradesh, characteristically features stripes and pattern bands floating on the background cloth and belt details that are strikingly similar to Bhutanese patterns (Jacobs 1990, 299, plate at upper right). The Bhutanese, who mingle with Nagas in Assam's market towns, themselves have a sense of cultural affinity with the Nagas and occasionally marry Naga women. Among the Tangkhul people of nearby Manipur, the colors of shawls for men (and women) indicate status, as do ceremonial shoulder cloths for men in Bhutan. Red or white with black stripes or plain white is for commoners; black with red stripes is for the rich and elderly (Singh 1987, 154; Jacobs 1990, 282-83, plates). The red shawls with white stripes worn by Tangkhul village headmen combine the same colors as the textiles used by their counterparts in Bhutan.

Fig. 2.6

Affinities between peoples in Bhutan and those of culturally distinct communities in northeast India (Arunachal Pradesh) are evident in dress styles, textile designs, and weaving technology. Wrapped garments, such as this Aka woman is wearing, closely resemble Bhutanese styles; her patterned jacket is identical to the jackets worn by women of Merak Sakteng in Bhutan. The weaver's silver headband is an ornament once also worn in eastern Bhutan, but now used only in festivals at which Bhutanese women dress as they did long ago [fig. 5.29]. Backtension looms throughout northeast India are constructed similarly; the textiles woven often incorporate related motifs and are sometimes even called by the same names. (Nari Rustomji, c. 1960; originally appeared in Rustomji 1971, p. 65)

The Khamptis and Singphos, who migrated from Burma to Arunachal Pradesh in the early eighteenth century, are known for weaving cotton and silk fabrics decorated with checkered or plaid patterns. Early British travelers described how "they wrap[ped] themselves in plaids of thick cotton ... in the fashion of the Scotch Highlanders" (Dalton 1872, in Elwin 1959b, 406).[20] These patterns, which speak of the groups' bonds with Shan peoples in northern Burma, and connections to design legacies as far away as Indonesia, became popular in Assam. Plaid patterns are prominent in Bhutanese textiles as well.

Elements of dress in northeast India's hills show clear relationships to clothing styles in Bhutan. For example, a wrapped garment recalling that formerly worn by Bhutanese men (*pakhi*) was traditional garb for men of the Aka, Dafla, and Bugun groups in Arunachal Pradesh.[21] Further, Aka women wore dresses, sashes, and jewelry startling in their resemblance to what some Bhutanese women used to wear:

> [The] dress consists of a cloth wound round the body similar to that worn by a man, except that it reaches almost to the ankles and is often of Assamese silk. [A woman] wears a jacket of Assamese silk, rather longer than a man's jacket ... . Round her head, a well-to-do Aka woman wears a very striking and pretty fillet of silver chain-work ... made either in Assam or neighboring Tawang (Kennedy 1914, in Elwin 1959b, 446).[22]

Aka women, like those of several other groups in Arunachal Pradesh and most Bhutanese, wear their hair cropped short. The silver headbands, identical to archaic jewelry in Bhutan, were also worn by Mönpas, Buguns, Mijis, and Adis [fig. 2.6]. The Akas traded with the Assamese but kept up "constant intercourse with their Butan neighbors," from whom they obtained these silver ornaments, as well as clothing and warm blankets (Hesselmeyer 1867, in Elwin 1959b, 445).[23]

Wide cloth belts like those worn by Bhutanese women secure traditional women's dresses throughout the region. In Singpho communities in eastern Arunachal Pradesh, women's belts were "a piece of colored cloth, often in large broad horizontal bands of red and blue" (Dalton 1872, in Elwin 1959b, 406). These words recall Bhutanese cummerbunds, which were patterned in the same colors. Even the nomenclature for waistbands (*kera* in Bhutan) is similar among some northeast Indian groups, for example, *kerak* among the Boris.[24] The Bhutanese custom of wearing one or more loose, waist-length, long-sleeved jackets was also shared by women in northeast India. Bugun and Aka women wore an inner jacket of undyed wild silk and an outer jacket that was red with patterning, exactly as the women of Merak Sakteng in eastern Bhutan do today. Although fashions have changed, earlier this century central Bhutanese women favored inner and outer jackets of undyed white wild silk as well.

West of Bhutan, the hills of Nepal are populated by two dozen other ethnic groups speaking Tibeto-Burman languages, among many of whom weaving is an ancient tradition.[25] The peoples of eastern Nepal are particularly well known for weaving with nettle fiber, which they process in the same way as the Bhutanese and Mishmis. Men wore this nettle cloth as a wrapped garment crossed over their chests – like the *pakhi* worn by some southern Bhutanese. Many Nepalese use backtension looms, and most dye plants that flourish in Bhutan are found in the ecologically comparable forests of eastern Nepal. As in Bhutan and Tibet, card looms are used in Buddhist communities in northern Nepal to make narrow ties for fastening Tibetan-style boots and for binding religious books.

Tibetan Influences

In historical times, a form of Mahayana Buddhism spread from centers in Tibet into Mongolia and the Himalayas, including present-day Bhutan. With Buddhism, over the centuries, came new kinds of cloth, new ritual uses for cloth that maintains a Tibetan character even when made by Bhutanese, Tibetan-derived clothing styles for men, and, much later, the Tibetan frame loom.

Bordered by Tibet on its entire northern and most of its western frontier, Bhutan received several influxes of Tibetan settlers. Some, said to have been soldiers in an army defeated by the Bhutanese, arrived as early as the ninth century (Aris 1979, 57-9). The progenitor of the leading clan in eastern Bhutan, Prince Tsangma, the son of a Tibetan king, settled there around the same time. By the eleventh and twelfth centuries, Tibetan religious teachers (lamas) had extended considerable influence into western Bhutan. During this period, friction among competing religious schools in Tibet intensified, making Bhutan an attractive refuge and source of new patrons for some factions.

Textiles used for Buddhist ritual and ceremony in Bhutan are intimately linked to this spread of the Tibetan form of Mahayana Buddhism. The design and decoration of shrines, the making of images on cloth scrolls *(thangka)* – indeed, the entire ethic of ritual Buddhist art – are similar throughout the Buddhist Himalayas, Tibet, and Mongolia. The role of men in producing these textiles, the techniques and formats for manufacturing the textiles, the use of imported Chinese silks, even the detailed iconography of images are essentially the same. To be sure, local and regional specialties, such as Bhutan's noted appliqué work, developed over time. However, the Bhutanese use ritual textiles made in Tibet alongside examples made locally, and in most cases it is difficult to tell one from the other.[26]

Beginning in 1738, after the consolidation of Bhutan into a Buddhist state, an annual diplomatic mission traveled from the old capital of Punakha to Lhasa. These goodwill

FIG. 2.7
*Bhutanese fabrics were sent regularly
as gifts to governments and individuals in neighboring states. Large
quantities of cloth were carried to
Tibet, for example, by annual goodwill
missions that began in 1738 and
continued until the 1950s. Private
citizens on pilgrimage and trading
trips in Tibet also presented fabrics to
hosts and friends. This textile was
among many given to Kungo Chozur
Gyaltshen Tharchin of Lhalung
Zimkhang, Lhasa, the former state
oracle of Tibet, by Dasho Gyurme
Dorji, a brother of the second king, in
the 1930s. Although in Bhutan this
would be a woman's dress* (thara), *in
Tibet, patterned cottons like this were
used to cover trunks, or cut and
stitched into cushion linings, doorway
hangings, and other household
furnishings.* (see Catalog)

missions *(lochag)* presented gifts, including woven fabrics, to Tibet's Dalai Lama. The
ceremonial Bhutanese cloths *(chagsi pangkheb)*, which in 1986 still covered the pillars of the
audience hall in the Potala Palace, were undoubtedly among those offerings. One textile in
the exhibition [fig. 2.7] was similarly a gift to the former state oracle of Tibet in the late 1930s
from a Bhutanese emissary. Missions continued until China occupied Tibet in the 1950s.

Tibet shares with Bhutan the popular tradition that looms were first introduced by the
Chinese wife of King Songtsen Gampo in the seventh century. Before the Chinese occupation, two looms were widely employed for weaving cloth, the backstrap loom and the
horizontal frame loom worked with treadles.[27] The former is still used by nomads and in
subtropical areas of southeastern Tibet, while the latter was most popular in central Tibet (Ü
and Tsang provinces). Tibetans wove primarily with abundant wool from the huge flocks of
sheep and goats that grazed throughout the Tibetan plateau. As in Bhutan, those who could
afford to supplemented local supplies of wool with wool, silk, and cotton yarns imported
from China and India.[28] Many of the traditional dyestuffs in Bhutan were also used in Tibet,
and regional recipes for the most important dyes – and taboos associated with dyeing – are
similar (Myers 1984, 47-48; 1990, 10-15).

Woolen textiles had a multitude of domestic uses and were arguably Tibet's most
important manufacture and export. Though lacking the great diversity of Bhutanese textiles,
these fabrics (as well as Tibetan pile carpets) were unlike anything made in Bhutan.
Plainweave and twill cloths *(nambu)* were traded across all borders, including Bhutan's, and
better qualities were given as gifts. The most important types were: *purug*, a narrow woolen
sold in natural white, or dyed maroon or blue; *therma*, a finer-quality twill; and the finest of
all, a cloth with the silky feel of cashmere called *shema*.[29] Tibet was also known for its blankets
made of striped loom lengths stitched together. One distinctive type, with weft stripes at
wide intervals, was loosely woven and had yarns inserted in the foundation to form a long,
shaggy pile on one side *(tsugtru)*.

Compared with Bhutanese textiles, the range of designs in Tibetan cloth was limited. The most prevalent patterning was weft striping, seen in fabrics from rainbow-hued women's aprons to more soberly banded blankets. Parallels are seen especially in the woolen textiles of central Bhutan, which imported many fabrics from Tibet and produces its own varieties of striped cloth [fig. 2.8].

The elite in Bhutan also adopted some aspects of high-status Tibetan dress, creating fashions that spread throughout the country. Men's apparel and the custom of women wearing blouses are the two most important borrowings. With the unification of Bhutan under Shabdrung Ngawang Namgyel in the seventeenth century, a new type of men's dress *(go)* styled after the Tibetan robe *(chuba)* was introduced. Senior officials and monks wore boots in Tibetan style, made of thick woolen cloth and gartered under the knees with colorful ties. Just as the Tibetans favored costly silks for important occasions, so did the Bhutanese. In the late nineteenth and early twentieth centuries, Bhutanese officials as well as the kings and queens wore hats related to, if not inspired by, fashions in Tibet.

While Bhutanese women's most important garment, the wrapped dress *(kira)*, was not a style influenced by Tibet, accessory garments were. During the early twentieth century, the nobility of central Bhutan helped popularize silk blouses, styled like those Tibetan women wear. The central Bhutanese custom of wearing a striped, woolen apron likewise parallels Tibetan practices. Aprons are ubiquitous in photographs of court women and their retainers taken earlier this century in Bumthang [fig. 2.9], but, nowadays, with the emphasis on distinctively Bhutanese traditions, aprons are slowly disappearing.

In Kongpo and Pemakö (southeastern Tibet), clothing styles are very different from those in central Tibet. Women wear a woolen dress *(goshub)*, generally of dark fabric and often decorated with appliqué at the neck, much like archaic Bhutanese tunics *(shingkha)*. Appliqué may also appear at the armholes, side seams, and hem. The belts worn in this region are patterned densely (Yuthok 1990, 195-96), like a Bhutanese woman's traditional belt. Men's dress is similar to that in Merak Sakteng and among the Mönpas of Arunachal Pradesh: a

FIG. 2.8

Central Bhutan enjoyed close ties to Tibet, to which it was nominally subject before the seventeenth century, and imported many striped Tibetan textiles. On the right is a Bhutanese woman's apron illustrating Tibetan influence on fabric design, weaving technology, and fashion. The cloth is a Tibetan pattern known to the Bhutanese as hothra, *'Mongolian pattern,' woven on a horizontal frame loom. The custom of wearing aprons was common to central Bhutan and neighboring regions of Tibet.*

*On the left are two warp-striped textiles, typical of those produced on native backstrap looms in areas of northern Bhutan close to Tibet. The folded multipurpose textile (*charaki charkab)*, woven from rough, water-repellent yak hair, can serve as a raincloak, for drying grains in the sun, to wrap a bundle, or to cover a load on a pack animal. Its corners are trimmed with tufts of natural white and red-dyed yak tail. The fringed textile, a woolen covering (*yangtsep charkab)* from Tashiyangtse District in the northeast, is used to protect loads on horseback and as a tent-like shelter.*
(see Catalog)

woolen jacket, worn under a tunic-like vest made of goatskin or monkey hide, with the hair on the outside. This vest has a slit in the center so it can be slipped over the head and is belted at the waist (Trungpa 1985, 201-02; Sakya 1990, 55). The fact that Tibetans from these regions wear the hide with the fur outward reflects their environmental and cultural affinity with the southern Himalayas, because in other parts of Tibet the hide is reversed. Inhabitants of Kongpo and Pemakö say they have historical links with the Bhutanese and peoples such as the Adi groups now living in Arunachal Pradesh.[30] The migration patterns between Bhutan and these Tibetan areas have not been studied, but were surely a factor in the development of such closely related dress styles.

Trade

Over the centuries, cloth has connected Bhutan to the world beyond its borders not only through shared traditions of weaving and dress but also through trade. Networks centered in nearby Assam and Tibet radiated outward in all directions: Chinese narratives document well-established links 2,000 years ago, stretching westward as far as Afghanistan (Lahiri 1991, 134, 163-64; Liebenthal 1956).[31] Travelers in the seventh century wrote of an arduous, two-month journey – the "mountain path" via Tibet – which was the shortest way from Szechuan "to the five Indias."[32] Trade crossroads in Assam and Tibet thus provided nearby entrepôts where Bhutanese could obtain goods from distant lands.

Bhutanese frequented market centers to the south, north, east, and west of their frontiers. To the south, all along the Brahmaputra River in Assam, local traders and entrepreneurs from other parts of India bartered with hill people, who in turn traded with communities deeper in the northeastern hills. Local stick lac, madder, wild silk, raw cotton, and textiles were major trade items, along with ivory, bell metal bowls, gold dust, silver, amber, musk, spices, and slaves. In the eighteenth century, even fabrics from Europe were available in these market towns. British broadcloth was displayed beside Indian muslins, longcloths, chintzes, taffetas, colored handkerchiefs, Banaras silks, satins, and gold and silver cloths (Pemberton [1838] 1966, 74, quoted in Lahiri 1991, 135).

To the north, Tibetan routes were plied by caravans destined for far-off markets. Lhasa was visited regularly by Bhutanese, Nepalese, Kashmiris, Ladakhis, Indians, and Chinese, as well as traders from places as far away as Armenia and the Caucasus. In the 1860s, the French missionary C. H. Desgodins was impressed that British, American (?), Russian, Nepalese, Indian, Chinese, and local textiles were all sold in the city's streets (Desgodins 1872, 286, 309).

On Bhutan's eastern frontier in the seventeenth century, the major trade mart was at Tsona Dzong in Tibet. A caravan traveled yearly from Lhasa to Beijing, halting at Tsona, and provided the occasion for an annual fair, which attracted Bhutanese, Mönpas, and Assamese. Rice, wild silk cloth (*tussar*), lac, pearls, and corals from the south were exchanged for Tibetan woolens, gold dust, horses, and Chinese silks. In the early 1900s, the fair still attracted merchants from Lhasa, who bought wooden plates and bowls (for which Bhutan was famous), and rice, lac dye, and raw silk from Bhutan and Assam (Tsybikov 1993, 259).[33]

In western Bhutan, well-traveled paths through the Ha and Paro valleys led northward into Tibet's Chumbi Valley.[34] These routes were the ones on which the British focused their commercial ambitions from the 1770s, hoping to open up Tibetan markets for British products. George Bogle, the first envoy from Great Britain to Bhutan, secured an agreement for the passage of British goods northward from Bengal through Bhutan to Tibet – an arrangement that was frustrated for more than a century by polite, but firm, rebuffs from the

Tibetans. Bogle noted the central role of Bhutanese in north-south trade at the time: "The Bhutanese and the other inhabitants of the mountains, which form the southern frontier of Tibet, are enabled by their situation to supply it as well with the commodities of Bengal as with the productions of their own states" (Markham [1876] 1971, 125, 127). According to Bogle, the Bhutanese held a monopoly on goods of southern origin transiting their country to Tibet, especially the lucrative trade in Indian indigo (Markham, 185).[35]

Thwarted by the cautious Bhutanese and resistant Tibetans, the British established trade fairs along the Sikkim-Bhutan-Tibet border in the latter half of the nineteenth century, but with little success. When in 1894 the British finally obtained the right to hold an annual trade fair at Yatung in Tibet's Chumbi Valley, routes into the valley through Bhutan, Kalimpong in India, and Sikkim assumed new importance. From the fair at Yatung, British cloth, yarn,

FIG. 2.9

The attire of Ashi Phuntsok Chöden, the senior queen of the second king, reflects Tibetan influence in the court fashions of Bumthang in the 1930s. Her narrowly striped apron is made of imported Tibetan fabric and resembles the aprons worn by well-to-do women in Lhasa. Her embroidered woolen boots are a style that was popular in Tibet and came to be made in Bhutan, while the Chinese flowered silk for the queen's jacket also reached Bhutan through Tibet.

Ashi Phuntsok Chöden, now the royal grandmother, is fondly spoken of by many women recalling the days of workshop weaving in Bumthang. The attendants pictured with her were expert weavers, themselves from leading local families. They are dressed similarly to the queen, except that they are barefoot and wearing plain jackets that appear to be dark velvet. Panels of cloth for stitching a ceremonial multipurpose textile (chagsi pang-kheb) *have been draped on the fence between them, probably just for the photograph. (George Sherriff 1937, Courtesy Royal Geographical Society)*

and commercial dyestuffs flooded in and were quickly adopted by the elites of Tibet and, to a lesser extent, Bhutan.

By the early 1900s, the Chumbi Valley was far and away the most important route between India and Tibet, "equal to all others combined" in bringing goods of European manufacture into the area (Bell 1924, 78). Brisk trade in the Lhasa marketplace took on a newly cosmopolitan and European flavor. Bhutanese traders returning home could choose from a wide array of Tibetan, Kashmiri, Chinese, and European fabrics – cheap British cloth, moleskin,[36] calico, and felt (Tsybikov 1993, 114-15). The flow of textiles between Bhutan and Tibet, and the influx of European yard goods and dyes, continued unabated until the 1950s. After the Chinese occupation of Tibet, very modest intercommunity barter continued, but only in the 1980s did some Chinese and Tibetan goods again appear in the market.

Commercial routes between Bhutan and communities to the south through passes in the Himalayan foothills were also significant. As far back as the twelfth century, local kings of eastern Bhutan controlled land and collected taxes in present-day Assam.[37] Trade was also lively: an eastern Bhutanese clan history relates that around 1600, "a market was established at Bumpayer [probably in eastern Bhutan] and the Atsaras of India, the Tibetans, the Khampas, and all the people of Mönyul gathered" (Ngawang 1728, fol. 49v, quoted in Aris 1986, 71). At the

FIG. 2.10

The herders of Laya in northwest Bhutan incorporate Tibetan trade goods into their clothing, which is very different from that worn elsewhere in the country. Women's coats are stitched of striped and tie-dyed Tibetan cloth known as hothra jalo. The woman's Chinese tennis shoes were probably brought from Tibet as well. The couple's lower garments are striped blankets woven locally from yak and sheep wool. Like other Bhutanese, Laya men and women wear ceremonial shoulder cloths on special occasions. (Brent Olson 1986)

time of the Ahom kings (1228-1824), Sadiya, Udalguri, Darrang, Siliambari, and other Assamese market towns flourished at the edge of the hills along the Brahmaputra River valley. Hereditary responsibility for Assam's trade with Bhutan was vested in an official who lived at Siliambari near the Bhutan border and served as an exclusive broker of the commerce.[38] By 1729, Bhutan also posted officials to look after trade across its border with India, one in the east and one in the west.[39]

Historically, Assam was especially favored by Bhutanese traders because it contained sites of importance to local Buddhists, including Hajo, believed by some to be Kushinagara, the death place of the Buddha. The Bhutanese entering Siliambari were allowed, therefore, to take part of their goods with them to Hajo, "which they visited every winter, being a place of sacred pilgrimage" (Basu 1970, 192).[40]

After the 1860s, the Bhutanese attended periodic fairs established by the British at market towns throughout Assam. Although colonial officers tended to use the generic term "Bhutia" for many of the hill men, some of their descriptions speak specifically of "Bhutan Bhotias" doing business in these regional markets.[41] Among those who engaged in this lively trade, with a focus on Bhutan, were a group of Nepalese. Especially between the 1920s and the 1950s, the Nyishangbas carried on a brisk business in Nepal, Calcutta, Assam, and Bhutan. They brought wares from Calcutta – needles, safety pins, synthetic dyes, coral, and imitation stones – and purchased local wild silk yarn and woven cloth, wool, and natural dyes. In the late 1940s, some of these traders ventured into Bhutan as far north as Tashigang, bringing trade fabrics and dyes and seeking the sources of herbs and musk.[42]

Through this trade in Assam, several types of Bhutanese cloth reached Ladakh, 1,000 kilometers away in the western Himalayas, where they are now an integral part of local

Buddhist culture. One is the red-and-white wild silk textile that serves as the ceremonial shoulder cloth for village headmen in Bhutan *(khamar kabné)*. On special religious and secular occasions, and during folk dances, Ladakhi men and women drape these shawls over their shoulders and around their arms. During the winter, Ladakhis now travel mainly to New Delhi and Kathmandu, rather than Assam, to purchase these Bhutanese textiles as well as lengths of wild silk cloth for making men's and women's belts and lac dye that they take back to sell in Leh.[43]

Bhutan's principal market on its Assam border today is Samdrup Jongkhar, not far from the sites of the nineteenth-century trade fairs. Generations of Bhutanese have journeyed there, carrying back wares to barter in other parts of Bhutan or sell in Tibet. Older people still speak of the town as *gudama*, a reference to the vicinity's many godowns (warehouses). At the Samdrup Jongkhar border today, Bhutanese continue to purchase Assamese wild silk cocoons, yarns, and cloth, along with dyes from Armenian Street in Calcutta, toys from Hong Kong, aluminum trunks from New Delhi, and argyle socks from the United States. Samdrup Jongkhar is also an outlet for goods from eastern Bhutan, which Indian merchants transport through India to Phuntsholing, a border town to the west, where the goods are reexported to Thimphu. Some of the shopkeepers have contacts in Nepal and are an active conduit for Bhutanese textiles that reach the Kathmandu market.

In the eighteenth century, the most important Indian market for western Bhutan was Rangpur in what is now Bangladesh. A caravan from Bhutan arrived each February and left in May, carrying back coarse cotton cloths for Bhutanese and Tibetan markets and silver coins representing profits retained in cash (Turner [1800] 1971, 7-8, 143).[44] This commerce was interrupted by the Anglo-Bhutan War of 1864-65, but resumed when the relationship between British India and Bhutan improved at the end of the century.[45] At Rangpur, Pasakha (Buxa Duar), and Kalimpong, Bhutanese purchased betel nuts, salt, and textiles for sale at Paro, Punakha, and Ha, all in western Bhutan; and at Phari in Tibet. Today, Phuntsholing is the most important point of border commerce between western Bhutan and India.

Imports to Bhutan
Bhutan was ideally positioned to play a central part in the exchange of goods between Tibet and India and to supply the demands of its people at the same time. Indeed, Bhutanese merchants – who were also senior officials of the government – controlled the important India-Tibet trade route through western Bhutan from the late seventeenth to the mid-nineteenth century. Most Tibetan products that passed into Bhutan were destined for India, but some – salt, gold, silver, tea, wool, and textiles – were essential items of consumption in Bhutan. Raw materials for weaving, and cloth, were among the most important commodities changing hands.

Colored blankets and other woolen textiles from Tibet were used by all Bhutanese but were especially popular in colder regions of the country. Plain and patterned woolen fabrics for making into garments and cushion covers came in distinctive, narrow rolls, woven on a frame loom. Bhutanese remember the second king (r. 1926-52) presenting rolls of striped Tibetan cloth *(hothra)* to his junior officers to make winter robes. Officials and villagers alike wore robes of plain Tibetan cloth *(thruk)* and boots with woolen cloth uppers in the Tibetan fashion. Because of this thriving market, the Tibetans seem to have taken a Bhutanese plaid pattern *(mathra)* and copied it on their horizontal looms for export to Bhutan *(tsangthra)*.[46] Pile carpets woven in central Tibet also decorated the homes, horses, and yaks of the Bhutanese.

FIG. 2.11
Bhutan carried on lively commerce with India, Tibet, and other nearby regions for centuries. Bhutan's most important exports included red woolen blankets, yak tails used as fly whisks, madder and lac for dyeing yarns and cloth, baskets, wooden containers, and paper. From China and Tibet came brick tea, and from Assam, lengths of wild silk cloth. (see Catalog)

Bhutan's most distinctive Tibetan cloth import is a woolen fabric decorated by tie-dyeing. It is stitched by Bhutanese into women's dresses and cushion covers, sewn into long coats by the herders of Laya in northwest Bhutan [fig. 2.10], and made into belts and jackets by the hill peoples of northeast India. Bhutanese call the cloth *hothra jalo*, 'Mongolian weaving *(hothra)* with a rainbow *(ja)*.'

Chinese patterned silks, the most prized luxury textiles, were obtained through trade with Tibet.[47] As in Tibet, the Bhutanese clergy needed silk for temples and monasteries, to drape altars, clothe statues, and frame religious scrolls, and for creating religious images in appliqué and assembling ceremonial costumes and hats. Silks were also required in aristocratic homes where elaborate private chapels were maintained. Men of high rank used Chinese brocades for their most important robes; in the early 1900s, noblewomen favored the same fabrics for fancy jackets. White and colored silk scarves *(khada)*, for offering as gifts and presenting at temples, came from China through Tibet as well. British India, from the late eighteenth century, supplied other prestige textiles of British manufacture. British broadcloth, like Chinese silk, was chiefly reserved in Bhutan for making ritual textiles, especially appliqué seat covers and wall hangings.

Assamese wild silk and cotton cloth, and other Indian wares en route to Tibet, found ready markets in Bhutan. Some of the wild silk woven in Bhutan was imported from Assam as cocoons and yarn. At the residence of the Tongsa Pönlop (governor) in central Bhutan, in 1906, the diplomat John Claude White observed that "the silk [being woven locally] was in the main *tussar*, obtained from Assam and the northern hills" (White [1909] 1984, 164).[48] *Endi* (wild silk) and cotton fabrics from the plains just below the foothills were imported in the form of taxes, or through barter. The border-dwelling Kacharis in particular wove high-quality *endi* cloth, some of it specifically for the Bhutan market.[49]

Local cotton ("white longcloths") and silks also came from Bengal, as did broadcloth and later other textiles from Europe.[50] Plain and simply patterned Indian fabrics were in demand for making clothing and door curtains, lining cushions, and stitching into other useful items. Older Bhutanese recall one thick, heavy cotton imported for making men's robes *(sintha lu nambar)*,[51] a wider fabric used for lining the robes of the well-to-do *(dos pani)*, and a third variety *(markin)* used for lining commoners' robes. Another coarse cotton was sewn into sleeveless shifts worn by women under their dresses.[52]

Exports from Bhutan

Bhutan's reputation as a lush land whose forests contained many useful products is reflected in one of its early Tibetan names: 'southern Mön of medicinal herbs' *(lhomon menjong)*. In historical times, Bhutan exported medicinal herbs, rice, paper made from the *Daphne* shrub, hot peppers, bamboo wares, wooden containers, animal skins, and yak tails, as well as madder, lac, and textiles [fig. 2.11].

The first British envoy to Bhutan, George Bogle, in 1774 that Bhutan's "commodities for exportation [were] musk, horses, munjit [madder], blankets and some thin twilled cloths" (Markham [1876] 1971, 183). Ironically, two textiles listed are hard to identify. No examples of the trade blankets have been positively identified. However, Bhutanese men of that day wore plain-colored (often red) rectangular woolen textiles (Aris 1982, pls. 25, 26) – which would have looked like blankets to Europeans – either as wrapped garments or over their shoulders like shawls. It is conceivable that similar woolens were the important export mentioned so often in later British Indian records.[53] Other trade blankets were possibly Tibetan manufactures handled by the Bhutanese. Bogle's "thin twilled cloths" are also puzzling. Small quantities of woolen twill have long been woven in central Bhutan, but what Bogle saw is unknown.

Twenty years later, in 1794, a British report described textiles that eastern "Botan" supplied to Assam: "woolen blankets, cowtails [*sic*: yak tails used as fly whisks], ... Nainta, a kind of cloth, Goom Sing, an embroidered cloth, and Daroka, a silk of a mixture of green, red and yellow colours" (Welsh 1794, in Mackenzie [1884] 1989, 387). These latter fabrics are almost certainly eastern Bhutanese supplementary-warp-patterned cloths *(aikapur)*, which are still identified by their color combinations and look embroidered at first glance.

An illustrative sampling of Bhutanese exports from later British Indian records confirms the importance of cloth and dyes. The most numerous and valuable items brought to one Assamese trade fair in 1875 were blankets (5,058 pieces), bundles of madder (10,813), "Bhutia bags" (506), and over 4 metric tons of lac. In exchange, the hill people purchased 1,063 cotton cloths, 889 *eri* (= *endi*, wild silk) cloths, 1,289 pieces of *kharu* (?) cloth, and 919 pieces of *dunko lepa* (?) cloth, as well as great quantities of rice and betel nuts, some bundles of cotton yarn, and a few peacocks and parrots.[54] The brisk Bhutan-Bengal trade at Pasakha (Buxa Duar) centered on Bhutanese wild silk, woolen, and cotton textiles, and raw wool "from Bhutan, Tibet and Central Asia [Ladakh]" destined for export to England (Gruning 1911, 11:147).[55]

Bhutanese cloth and native dyestuffs – madder, and stick lac from the east – were vigorously traded across the entire Bhutan-Tibet frontier.[56] In the early eighteenth century, a Jesuit priest traveling in Tibet remarked on "silk from the tree" (wild silk) coming from Bhutan and being sold all over the country (Desideri 1932). One of these fabrics was a red-and-gold plaid *(shabthrawo)*, used in Tibet as in Bhutan for inner garments worn by lamas and by women. Other cotton and wild silk cloths exported to Tibet were for lining garments, ritual textiles, and pile carpets, and for stitching cushions and door curtains. In addition, the Bhutanese brought to Tibet indigo and silk and cotton cloths from India.[57]

Links to the Weaving Traditions of Southeast Asia

These networks joining Bhutan with the larger Asian region are indicative of ancient links to far-off cultures. In the realm of textiles, Bhutan's longest-standing bonds – suggested if not substantiated by historical records – are probably to the south and east. As far away as Thailand and Laos, similarities in looms and motifs indicate a very old and substantial connection that invites further study and understanding. These likenesses occur in the weaving of Tai peoples, who are now the majority population of Southeast Asia.[58] The Tai include populations in Vietnam and China, as well as the Shan Ahoms, who ruled northeast India (Assam) from 1228 until 1824. Parallels also appear in groups interspersed among the Tai whose languages, like Bhutan's, are Tibeto-Burman.[59]

Today, most of the Southeast Asian Tibeto-Burman groups weave exclusively on a backtension loom with a continuous warp that is similar to the Bhutanese loom. Tai-Lao groups, on the other hand, weave predominantly on a frame loom worked with foot treadles.[60] Gittinger and Lefferts have recently presented strong evidence that the Tai-Laos once used a backstrap loom and only adopted the frame loom some time after they migrated to their present homes (Gittinger and Lefferts 1992, 30-35). Thus, the predominant loom of Bhutan relates weaving traditions there to early, and current, technology in mainland Southeast Asia. Taboos related to dyeing processes are also alike: the coloring of yarns was carried out in isolation, away from pregnant or menstruating women, and never in the presence of men, especially monks (Fraser-Lu 1989, 27-28).

Bhutanese weavers shown a book on Tai-Lao textiles were able to identify most of the techniques and many of the motifs.[61] The most extraordinary decorative – and technical – parallel between Bhutanese and Tai textiles is seen in supplementary-warp-patterned blankets made by Thailand's Phu Tais in Kalasin Province. Interspersed with warp stripes, the textiles' supplementary-warp-pattern bands contain geometric designs separated by bars [fig. 2.14]. In structure and motifs, the cloth is virtually identical to fabric from eastern Bhutan [fig. 2.15]. Supplementary-warp-patterned women's skirts made by the Tai Nueas are similarly related to Bhutanese designs.[62]

FIG. 2.12
This detail of an early-twentieth-century Kachin skirt panel illustrates some of the likenesses in supplementary-weft-patterned Southeast Asian and Bhutanese textiles. Diamonds, hooked ornaments, and meander patterns at the end of the skirt panel recall the decorative horizontal registers on Bhutanese women's belts (kera) *and ceremonial textiles* (chagsi pangkheb). *The swastikas and varied floral motifs of the field have counterparts in Bhutanese weaving as well.* (see Catalog)

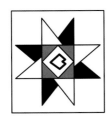

Thai: 'key design'   Kachin: 'purse' or 'star'   Bhutanese: 'butterfly' (*phenphenma*)

Thai: 'frog'   Kachin: 'poppy'   Bhutanese: 'sun rays' (*zerpa*)   'scissors'

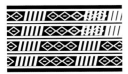

Chin   Mishmi   Bhutanese: 'lucky knot'   'eternal knot' 'thunderbolt'

FIG. 2.13
Motifs That Link Bhutan and
Southeast Asia.
*Textile motifs suggest a substantial,
ancient connection between peoples of
Bhutan and Southeast Asia. Thai,
Kachin, Chin, and Mishmi examples
are shown on the left. Their counterparts, and related designs, in
Bhutanese weaving appear on the
right. While different cultural groups
call the motifs by varying names, the
strong resemblances – in the way they
are stylized or arranged in pattern
bands – are clear. The diamond-based
designs in the third row begin with a
Chin pattern and a Mishmi lattice; the
Bhutanese employ infinite variations
of what they know as a 'lucky knot'. As
latticework (dramé), it appears in the
end borders of women's dresses. As an
eternal knot (peyab), it features in
field patterns on dresses and archaic
tunics. A related form is the thunderbolt (dorje), found in every kind of
Bhutanese textile. (Thai, Kachin, and
Chin patterns, after Fraser-Lu 1989;
Mishmi pattern, after Elwin 1959a)*

Other comparisons between design elements involve supplementary-warp patterns in Bhutanese textiles and supplementary-weft patterns in cloth made by Southeast Asian Tibeto-Burman and Tai-Lao peoples. Although supplementary-warp patterning is known among the latter, it is not widespread today. Perhaps, as frame looms were adopted in Southeast Asia, weavers preserved some patterns that had once been executed with supplementary warps in a supplementary-weft structure – a technique that allows more variability on the long warps normal to a frame loom. Thus, the Chins of western Burma produce supplementary-weft patterns, on items such as shawls, that are comparable to the patterns of eastern Bhutanese supplementary-warp-patterned cloth (*aikapur*) (Lehman 1963, 31, fig. 29; Fraser-Lu 1989, 101). Skirts and head scarves woven by Tai groups in northeastern Laos are similarly reminiscent of *aikapur*, featuring rows of primary designs separated by crosshatched bars [fig. 2.16].

Parallels with Southeast Asian weaving occur in Bhutanese supplementary-weft-pat-terned textiles as well. Like the Bhutanese, both Tai-Lao and Tibeto-Burman women use a stick, porcupine quill, or the fingers to manipulate pattern-weft yarns while cloth is still on the loom. In northern Burma, Kachin weavers produce wraparound skirts embellished with supplementary-weft designs resembling those favored by the Bhutanese: zigzags, lozenges, diamonds, stars, swastikas, and crosses. Shoulder bags and men's belts are patterned with hooked ornaments and an eight-pointed star identical in form to what Bhutanese call a 'butterfly' (*phenphenma*); it is a 'purse' or 'star' to the Kachins [figs. 2.12, 2.13]. Eastern Bhutanese and Kachins both term the same motif 'scissors' and share many other geometric designs. Among Tai peoples, one or more of the three panels that customarily make up a skirt (Thai: *phaa sin*), especially those at the garment's upper and lower edges, are often adorned

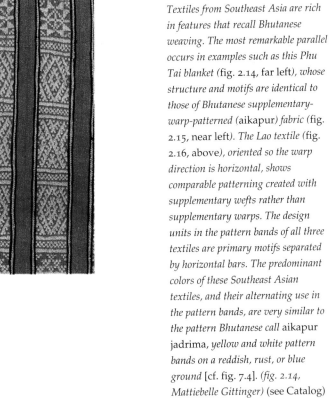

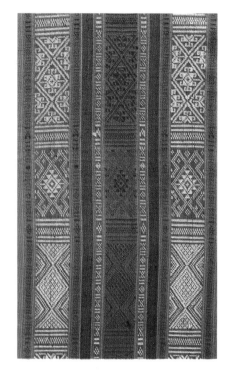

FIGS. 2.14-16
Textiles from Southeast Asia are rich in features that recall Bhutanese weaving. The most remarkable parallel occurs in examples such as this Phu Tai blanket (fig. 2.14, far left), whose structure and motifs are identical to those of Bhutanese supplementary-warp-patterned (aikapur) fabric (fig. 2.15, near left). The Lao textile (fig. 2.16, above), oriented so the warp direction is horizontal, shows comparable patterning created with supplementary wefts rather than supplementary warps. The design units in the pattern bands of all three textiles are primary motifs separated by horizontal bars. The predominant colors of these Southeast Asian textiles, and their alternating use in the pattern bands, are very similar to the pattern Bhutanese call aikapur jadrima, *yellow and white pattern bands on a reddish, rust, or blue ground* [cf. fig. 7.4]. *(fig. 2.14, Mattiebelle Gittinger)* (see Catalog)

 FIGS. 2.17-19
Animal, human, and geometric figures are striking links between Bhutanese and Southeast Asian textiles. These details show a Lao shoulder cloth (fig. 2.17, above), a Burmese Chin tunic (fig. 2.18, upper right), and a northern Lao sash (fig. 2.19, lower right). All of the textiles date to the late nineteenth or early twentieth century. In Bhutan today, similar designs are incorporated only into Merak Sakteng women's jackets [fig. 2.2], but the figures appear regularly on Bhutanese women's garments and ceremonial textiles made earlier this century [fig. 2.20]. (see Catalog)

with geometric patterns that call to mind the horizontal registers in Bhutanese women's belts and ceremonial cloths.

Many other Tai-Lao textile designs resemble Bhutanese motifs.[63] A striking correlation is seen in animal and human figures. In Bhutan, elephants, horses, and birds occur mainly in jackets worn by the women of Merak Sakteng in the east [fig. 2.2]; horses, birds, and figures on horseback also are seen on older tunic-style garments, women's dresses, women's belts, and ceremonial cloths [fig. 2.20]. In Tai contexts, the same animals are featured on temple banners, manuscript covers, and other textiles woven by the Dai (Lu) people of Sipsong Panna (Xishuang Banna) in Yunnan (China), the Lus of Thailand, and groups in Laos [figs. 2.17, 2.19]. Among Tibeto-Burman groups in Southeast Asia, figures on horseback appear on Chin garments [fig. 2.18], and on shoulder cloths, blankets, and door curtains woven by the Shans of Burma. Similar motifs are depicted in textiles from more distant Malaysia, Vietnam, and Indonesia.

FIG. 2.20
This detail of an early-twentieth-century Bhutanese ceremonial textile (chagsi pangkheb) features animal and human figures that are rarely employed in contemporary weaving, but recall designs in Southeast Asian textiles [figs. 2.17-19]. The textile, embellished with lac-dyed (red) wild silk and black cotton, is typical of eastern Bhutanese styles. (see Catalog)

Shoulder cloths from Laos [fig. 2.17] show particularly strong affinities with Bhutanese ceremonial textiles *(chagsi pangkheb)*. One end of the shoulder cloth typically features a diamond composed of concentric rows of minor patterning, spreading outward from the "eye" at the center[64] – very much like the center panel of a Bhutanese *chagsi pangkheb*. The shoulder cloth's other end is usually decorated with horizontal registers showing geometric designs arranged in the same manner as they are on *chagsi pangkheb* and on traditional Bhutanese women's belts.[65]

Checkerboard or patchwork patterns associated with Buddhism likewise link Bhutan and Southeast Asia. In Bhutan, they decorate textiles that hang over shrines or are placed on raised seats and are painted directly onto wooden altars. Among the Tai-Laos, woven or painted bamboo covers for wrapping Buddhist texts *(phaa hau khamphii)* show this same pattern (Prangwatthanakun and Cheesman 1988, 86 [lower left]; Gittinger and Lefferts 1992, figs. 3.33, 3.36). In both cultures, the colorful designs also are woven into women's garments.

Another correspondence between Bhutan and Southeast Asia exists in the format of clothing (tunics) among the Karens of Burma and Thailand and the Chins of Burma. A Karen tunic acquired in Burma in 1898 is the same style worn by Mönpa women in Arunachal Pradesh, Merak Sakteng women in eastern Bhutan, and, formerly, women in north central Bhutan. It is constructed of two loom lengths joined together, and shows red warp stripes on a white cotton ground, with simple patterning at the neck and side seams and along the hem. The placement of ornamental bobbles at the neck and below the arms recalls appliqué decoration on archaic woolen tunics *(shingkha)* from Bhutan as well. Another quite different Burmese tunic of 1898, identified as Chin, is constructed in the same way and has supplementary-weft patterning at the hem [fig. 2.18] similar to the design format of old Bhutanese *kushung* tunics. Today, unmarried Karen girls in eastern Burma and Thailand still wear an ankle-length tunic of unbleached cotton, with a slit for the head and long fringes at the hem (Fraser-Lu 1989, 94-96, fig. 122). Whether Chin women still wear tunics is unknown, but it seems that this once more widespread, regional style for women is found today only in remote areas of eastern Bhutan, southeast Tibet, Burma, and Thailand.[66]

Bhutan has been a meeting point of traditions and technologies from both Southeast Asia and the Tibetan plateau. Bhutanese ethnic groups, like the looms they use and the cloth they weave, reflect affinities with both the Tibetans close at hand and the distant Tai. The intriguing similarities between eastern Bhutanese and Burmese, Laotian, and Thai cloth and dress especially invite future attention.

Chapter Three

The Fabric of Life in Bhutan

In Bhutan, gifts of cloth are an expression of family and community networks to which an individual belongs, as well as of official popularity and favor; textile transactions also reflect larger relationships between and among families, communities, and the state. In the days when cloth was a major form of wealth, circulating throughout society like currency, woven cloth was used for payment of family and community taxes to the dzongs, for gifts to neighboring states, and for state distributions to officials and monasteries.[1] Cloth was a medium that linked villagers to church and state. The fabrics given as taxes, and as gifts, were those used in daily life. Cloth items presented as gifts today are not always useful, illustrating that emphasis is placed on the transaction rather than the actual gift.

Cloth as Wealth

Cloth is made into useful items of every sort: ordinary and formal garments, animal trappings, lamp wicks, doorway hangings, cushion covers, baby wraps, bundle carriers, tents, altar covers, religious hangings, shrine furnishings. Because cloth provides so many essentials of Bhutanese life, many families keep woven fabrics in their 'box of prosperity' (*yanggam*). Along with silver and gold jewelry and grains from the crops a family harvests, these textiles represent the resources of the home. Cloth kept in the *yanggam* usually includes one or two old articles, perhaps passed down from a grandparent, such as a ceremonial textile (*chagsi pangkheb*) or archaic tunic (*kushung*); a man's robe (*go*); a woman's dress (*kira*); and a woman's belt (*kera*). The textiles, jewelry, and food grains are three essential symbols of the family's abundance that must be blessed during annual rituals to ensure continuing household prosperity (*lochö*).[2]

Most Bhutanese believe that if a person sells something he or she has made or used, his or her 'luck' (*yang*) for being prosperous goes with it – be it a car or a piece of cloth. In order to keep this luck, the person must keep a piece of the property being sold or "wipe" a bit of the luck off it and keep that instead. In the case of a car, the seller can wipe the vehicle with a white scarf (*khada*) and keep the scarf. In the case of a textile, one keeps a thread or tiny piece of the fabric. In the past, even when well-to-do families gave presents of their own clothing to their servants, the woman of the house always saved a snippet from the fringe or inside of the garment. Some Bhutanese say that it was considered especially bad luck to sell panels of fabric received as gifts, even though the presents were not used for many years. This sentiment does not apply to commercial gift cloth sets that can now be bought in the market.

Gifts of Cloth

In Bhutan, offering gifts is essential to social life: it keeps relations harmonious, maintains friendship, softens the embarrassment of a request, places a person in the social hierarchy, and expresses personal influence. The importance of a gift is not so much the transfer of a possession but the affirmation of the relationship between donor and recipient. Often gifts received are eventually offered again as gifts to somebody else. The gift itself is of no importance unless it has strong sentimental associations or real utility.

Textiles are the most common, the most important, and the traditionally preferred gifts in Bhutan. The classic gift is a long, narrow scarf *(khada)*, whose color, fiber, quality, length, and number convey respect [fig. 3.1]. The longest and the best are presented to great lamas, high officials, and other important personages. They are usually white, a color symbolizing goodness and purity. A donor selects the quality of scarf to be given based on what he or she can afford and who the recipient is: the simplest scarves, made of coarse cotton in a very loose, gauze weave, are suitable for anyone to offer to statues of deities in a temple, but a person of means would want to purchase a silk scarf with Buddhist symbols and prayers woven into the cloth (colloquially, *ashi khada*, 'princess scarf') to present to a member of the royal family. White gift scarves, which now are also made of synthetic fibers such as silky acrylic, have always been imported from China via Tibet, and India.[3]

In Bhutan, scarves were once required on all official occasions, when they were formally exchanged by hosts and visitors. Members of the British mission of 1783 presented white, silk, fringed scarves when they first met with Bhutanese officials in Thimphu, and received the same in return (Collister 1987, 29). When the diplomat John Claude White left Bhutan after his first visit in 1905, Bhutan's Druk Desi (temporal ruler) bade him farewell saying he trusted that relations between their two countries would be "as pure as a white scarf with no blot to mar its whiteness" (White [1909] 1984, 174).[4] When scarves are exchanged between equals, each places the scarf around the other's neck. If offering a scarf to a lama, the donor bows, with the scarf, folded specially, draped over his or her outstretched hands, palms upward. The lama touches the scarf to bless it, takes it from the donor, and places it around the donor's neck. Scarves presented to a member of Bhutan's royal family are folded in such a way that the donor can release the silk cloth for display with a flourish of the hand. In Buddhist temples, important statues are often adorned with dozens of these gifts draped around their shoulders.

Many other types of cloth are offered on occasions when links between two people or two families are reaffirmed: promotions in the government, army, or ecclesiastic hierarchy, marriages, deaths, and departures [fig. 3.2]. A whole set of rules exists concerning the quality and number of fabrics and how to present them. Not abiding by these rules can lead to serious embarrassment and misunderstanding. Bhutanese have three terms for 'gift': a gift between equals *(chom)*; a gift from a superior to an inferior *(söra)*; and a gift from an inferior to a superior *(changjé)*. An item that is an appropriate gift between equals or from a superior to an inferior might be totally unsuitable from an inferior to a superior. The choice of a cloth gift is particularly difficult when it is destined for relatives, because it must take into account respective rank as well as family ties. In this case, one must be careful not to antagonize by offering fabrics that the recipient would consider below his or her rank but, at the same time, not to give fabrics of such good quality that he or she would feel patronized. The distinctions

FIG. 3.2
Bhutanese say that one becomes wealthy on only three kinds of occasions – marriage, career promotions, and death – when gifts of cloth are given in huge quantities. The army officer being honored here has just received the rank of captain. Around his neck and on the tables in front of him are white presentation scarves (khada), *the color of which symbolizes goodness and purity. The cloth panels piled in the foreground have been brought by well-wishers, as have the cylindrical bags of rice visible to the right. (F.P. 1983)*

FIG. 3.3

Supplementary-warp-patterned fabrics that originated in the east (aikapur) *are a time honored gift for many Bhutanese occasions. Their quality is distinguished by the number of crosshatches ('legs') on the horizontal bars separating the primary motifs in each warp-pattern band; the fabric here has 'nine legs'* (kang gupa). *Textiles with higher numbers of 'legs' usually have more intricate patterns and are valued most. The supplementary-warp patterning in this cloth alternates with vertical rows of supplementary-weft motifs, including stylized Chinese characters signifying long life* (tranka tshering), *flowers, and floral branches* (shinglo, 'tree leaf'). *Bhutanese examine the* shinglo *for clarity and detail, as well as the number of 'legs,' to assess the quality of a fabric. (see Catalog)*

are very subtle and, because of their diversity, textiles are perfect vectors of these social differences.

The most important occasions for giving gifts of cloth are promotions, marriages, and deaths, when textile gifts *(zong* or *zongcha)* are given in an odd-numbered set of three, five, seven, nine or more [fig. 3.1]. Even numbers are considered bad omens and must be avoided. While the quality of the fabrics bought depends on the means of the donor, the specific odd number of fabrics depends on the rank of the recipient. It would be a serious breach of etiquette, for example, to offer a set of three fabrics to somebody who is entitled to five. Supplementary-warp-patterned fabrics *(aikapur)* are often included in gift sets, and when they are, the number of 'legs' *(kang,* the crosshatches on horizontal bars in the pattern) is also important. The number of 'legs' in the design is always odd; higher numbers of 'legs' are appropriate, at least in theory, for people of rank. The number nine is said to be reserved for the king (although many Bhutanese own cloth with a 'nine-legged' pattern, or even eleven- and thirteen-legged patterns) [fig. 3.3]. It is always possible to substitute a monetary offering for a gift of cloth, but this "easy way out" is frowned upon.

Visitors to Bhutan in this century have remarked with interest how cloth-giving customs continue. When the first king received the insignia of a Knight Commander of the British Empire in 1905, "the whole [hall] ... filled up with heaps of tea, bags of rice and Indian corn, fabrics – silk, woolen and cotton – of all colors and values, with little bags of gold dust and rupees appearing on the top. ... It was amusing to watch ... the flourishes some of [the donors] gave ... as they whipped out their scarves to their full length" (White [1909] 1984, 142-43) [fig. 3.4]. At the presentation of the same award to the second king in 1932, "when the proceedings were over the spectators could hardly see over the barriers of cloth" (Collister 1987, 184). At the marriage of the third king in 1955, "fine Bhutanese weaves and Chinese brocades" were plentiful:

> The guests ... offered scarves to the wedded couple, and presented their gifts, which, again, consisted mostly of cloth. ... [The] massive rolls of cloth were hurled with utmost force onto the wooden planked floor – so that the entire assembly might be able to judge, from the resounding crash, the relative weight and value of the proffered gifts!
>
> (Rustomji 1971, 192)

At a 1992 wedding in Thimphu, which joined two very prominent families, the household shrine room where gifts were presented to the young couple was filled with piles of cloth gifts around which could be seen Western-style suitcases and other presents.[5] Weddings of ordinary Bhutanese, if celebrated at all, are much more modest events.

Cloth figures at births but is far less conspicuous. The first wrapping cloth of a baby should be soft and clean, but whatever is near at hand can be used: the mother's apron, jacket, or other cloth. In earlier days, *pöntshe* (one of the simpler tax cloths) or Indian cotton was preferred. Close friends might give a gift of *yathra* (patterned woolen cloth from central

FIG. 3.4
This fresco in the king's rooms at Tongsa Dzong depicts the celebrations at the coronation of the second king, Jigme Wangchuck, in 1926. The monarch is seated on a plinth draped with silk brocade, wearing the "raven crown" of the Bhutanese sovereign and holding a wheel of law. Barefoot officials and citizens, swathed in shoulder cloths and wearing swords, bring gifts; in the foreground are elephant tusks, red coral, tiger and leopard skins, muskets, rare fruits, religious texts, and rolls of cloth.

Most of the well-wishers are garbed in Bhutanese robes made of Chinese flowered silks that were fashionable at the time. In the crowd's midst is also an Englishman in jacket and trousers – the sole representative of the outside world. To the far right is a woman, possibly the queen, dressed as princesses were at the time [fig. 6.7], in a supplementary-warp-patterned dress, striped woolen apron, Chinese brocade jacket, and decorative boots, with a red, fringed shoulder cloth draped about her arms. (Lyönpo Om Pradhan 1994)

Bhutan), which makes a nice blanket, but there are no formalities surrounding the occasion.

Death ceremonies involve cloth gifts similar to those given at marriages and promotions, as well as other textiles. Before cremation, the body is bathed and wrapped in cloth according to the means of the family. A robe or dress is placed on the coffin or bier to indicate the gender of the deceased. At the death of a lama or king, the body is adorned lavishly in rich brocades, emulating the way that statues are dressed in temples, and befitting the person's elevated status. Guests attending the cremation bring the family white silk scarves and odd-numbered gift sets of cloth; in turn, the family offers gift cloth to the presiding lamas. A bereaved family also erects prayer flags for the soul of the deceased (see Chapter Six).

The rulers of Bhutan offered gifts, according to their own traditions, to early British emissaries with whom they developed friendships. In 1774, the first diplomat to visit Bhutan, George Bogle, received a "water tabby [silk taffeta?] gown, like what Aunt Katty used to wear, with well-plated haunches" at his initial meeting with the Druk Desi (temporal ruler) (Aris 1982, 20). Sir Charles Bell, a diplomat who made several trips to Bhutan in the early 1900s, received the following letter from the Paro Pönlop (governor) in 1915:

> When I learnt from your letter that His Majesty the King-Emperor has conferred on you the high title of C.M.G. [Commander of the Order of St. Michael and St. George], I was as glad as a peacock when it hears the noise of the thunder. I have not much to offer you. According to our Bhutanese custom we offer scarves when a chief ascends the throne, therefore I send you herewith three scarves consisting of one white silk scarf, one *mentsi* [yellow flowered silk] scarf and one red silk scarf, with a small present consisting of seven different kinds [of gifts], viz, one *pangkheb* [multipurpose cloth; see figs. 3.5, 5.44], one *khamar* [man's ceremonial shoulder cloth], one *phechung* [woven bag], one *bündri* [cloth for carrying bundles], one *kera* [belt], one *tagre* [?], and three bricks of tea, with my prayers that you may get a still higher promotion. Though the present is a small one I offer it with a pure heart and I request you to accept it, for though a flower is a small thing, yet it is offered to the gods (Bell Collection 1915a).[6]

Being given three scarves of different colors – white, *mentsi*, and red – instead of the usual single white scarf, was a mark of extreme honor because of the qualities associated with those colors and patterns. *Mentsi* is a yellow fabric, usually silk, with red and green printed flowers on it that today is reserved for use by the king and in ritual textiles such as *thangka* coverings and decorative wall hangings. Red is a hue associated with heroic virtues. The textiles given with these silk scarves are typically Bhutanese. The king of Bhutan at the same time sent Bell "a spotless silk scarf, a *than* [measure] of Bhutanese tussore [*tussar*, a wild silk cloth], one *yata* [patterned woolen cloth from central Bhutan], one *khamar* [man's ceremonial shoulder cloth], one *khati* [?], one *pangkheb* [multipurpose cloth], six squares of *liwang* [yellow] silk, four squares of red silk, one piece of *mentsi* silk, and one pony." The letter announcing these gifts was itself sent with a silk presentation scarf (Bell Collection 1915b).[7]

Today as well, fabric presentations include a variety of cotton, woolen, and silk cloth lengths [fig. 3.1]. The most prestigious textile, for example, a panel of Hong Kong brocade, is placed on top. The second quality, perhaps a set of loom lengths of wild silk *aikapur* from eastern Bhutan for a man's robe, is underneath, and the plainest cloth, which might be a striped cotton for lining cushions, is at the bottom. The lengths exchanged by Bhutanese are almost never sewn, because this suggests a textile has already been used [fig. 3.6]. Only when a used garment is presented as a token of friendship or service, or occasionally when a new garment is given to a foreigner, are the panels of cloth stitched together [fig. 3.7]. Woolen cloth is usually offered in rolls, and cotton and silk cloth are offered folded. A large number of textiles can be acquired in this way and then stored by the recipient's family, which may use them to make clothes and other useful items or present them to others.

Cloth retains its importance in gift giving, although the formats of cloth gifts are evolving. Since the 1980s, with the development of tourism, more international consultants visiting Bhutan, and more Bhutanese traveling to the West, special gift items have been manufactured locally. Many of them are made from handwoven textiles: purses, little zippered pouches, place mats, tea cozies, slippers. These have become popular gifts on nonofficial occasions and are not given in sets. For official occasions, fabrics in their traditional form are still the rule, and the protocol concerning their selection and presentation is strictly observed.

During this century, religious scroll paintings *(thangka)* also have become gift items that are much appreciated by foreigners, but they are not offered by Bhutanese to each other. Because these paintings belong to the sacred domain and are commissioned for a special purpose, it is impossible for anyone other than a lama to give a *thangka* as a gift – and a lama

FIG. 3.5
This characteristically Bhutanese textile, a chagsi pangkheb *(ceremonial multipurpose cloth), was among the gifts given to the British diplomat Sir Charles Bell on one of his several visits to Bhutan between 1905 and 1910. Bell became acquainted with Tongsa Pönlop Ugyen Wangchuck during the 1903-04 Younghusband Expedition to Tibet and made his first trip to Bhutan shortly thereafter, to present the Bhutanese leader with the insignia of a Knight Commander of the Indian Empire. The Bell textiles at the Victoria and Albert Museum, all of them diplomatic gifts, are the earliest group of Bhutanese textiles in a Western collection.* (see Catalog)

will do so as a blessing or with some other religious purpose in mind. On the other hand, Bhutanese realize that foreigners see *thangka* as objects of aesthetic value and now have them produced expressly for gift purposes. Because they are not consecrated, such *thangka* can be exchanged as purely secular items.

Nowadays, in urban areas, people who do not have weavers among their family members and do not employ weavers at home may buy commercial sets of gift fabrics, which are often not matched and have little or no obvious use. In Thimphu, as soon as a promotion or marriage is announced, the most famous Bhutanese cloth merchant sets about preparing gift sets in different numbers and patterns for his prospective customers. These fabrics are often used again as gifts on another occasion or sold back to the merchant to be reintroduced into the market.

A textile gift given to a friend or relative who is going away will be of a quality and value that suit the respective ranks of donor and recipient and their personal relationship. As in the past, it might be a dress, a belt, or a length of cloth to make a bag, but with the increasing use of traditional textiles to make items that did not exist before, one might now receive jackets, neckties, table runners, eyeglass cases, Western-style shoulder bags, or bookmarks. The recipient is expected to reciprocate by bringing back a "counter gift," which is, interestingly enough, often a piece of fabric from abroad.[8]

Social relationships are reinforced by many other transactions involving cloth. For example, cloth might be offered as a reward for a service or as a token of appreciation for somebody's work. In this case, it can only come from a superior to an inferior. Again, the quality and quantity of cloth offered – a set of wild silk loom lengths or a panel of imported silk – indicate the level of appreciation. The textile may be new, but it also has long been customary for a high-ranking person to show favor by giving an item of wearing apparel that he or she may have worn. In Thimphu, one is often proudly shown a robe that belonged to the second king and was given to a parent or grandparent. When wearing the garment at a gathering, the recipient will often mention its origin to demonstrate a relationship with the influential donor and thereby enhance the recipient's status.

Textiles also flow upward in society, from inferior to superior, in return for a favor or to accompany a request. The recipient accepts the cloth as an element of a polite petition that does not necessarily guarantee the donor a favorable answer or outcome. The fabrics offered are usually modest – belts or lengths for bags – and not too ostentatious for fear of antagonizing the recipient or creating the impression of a bribe. The official receiving the fabric knows what is expected of him by the size and quality of the gift. A poignant instance of such an "intercession with cloth" occurred in the mid-1960s. When the first eastern Bhutanese children were selected to go away to school, parents, worried at seeing precious labor taken from them, pleaded with the recruiting officials by offering them textiles.

Presenting Gifts of Cloth

Detailed etiquette surrounds not only the choice of gift cloth but also its presentation. If a gift comes from a superior, the fabric is wrapped in Bhutanese paper folded in a special way according to the rank of the donor. It may be delivered by a servant or trusted agent of the

FIG. 3.6

Whether given to a dzong as tax-in-kind or to a private recipient, cloth is generally presented – and often sold in the market – as unstitched loom lengths. This is to assure the recipient that the fabrics have not been used and allows the option of reusing the gift by passing the cloth panels on to someone else. The pair of panels shown here were given to the late Lam Nado around 1958, and presented by him to their current owner in 1987.

The panels are constituent pieces for a pangkheb, the same type of textile given to Bell [figs. 3.5, 5.44], but of a modest quality used for carrying babies and other everyday needs. The vertically patterned panel would be cut along the thin black line down its middle, and its two halves stitched to either edge of the horizontally decorated panel. After sewing, the fringe would be finished by plying and cabling the warp yarns. The prominent diamond, which is actually centered in one loom length, forms an axis of symmetry for the entire, finished textile. (see Catalog)

FIG. 3.7

The coronation of the present king, His Majesty Jigme Singye Wangchuck, in 1974, was the most recent state occasion for the presentation of cloth gifts to large numbers of guests and foreign visitors. This kira, *given to a foreign guest, has a typical pattern, rather new at that time and still popular now. Its blue ground and regular arrangement of motifs are quite modern and suitable for various occasions. The borders of a traditional woman's dress from north central Bhutan (kushüthara) have been boldly simplified into rows of meander patterning and triangular blocks of color echoing the patchwork design called* tenkheb *or* phup. *The straight diagonal spaces (between the field motifs) and evenly matched end borders are signs of quality that Bhutanese look for in a textile. (see Catalog)*

donor. If the recipient is of high rank, he or she receives the bearer of the gift with appropriate decorum and accepts the fabric in a formal manner. The protocol that both the messenger and the recipient follow is a sign of mutual honor.

Depending on the circumstances, cloth offered to a superior also may be wrapped in Bhutanese paper, but on formal occasions the presentation is elaborate and requires practice to be executed correctly. Gift cloth presentation is considered so important that it is taught as a special subject of traditional Bhutanese etiquette *(driglam namzha)*. College graduates are required to complete a course in etiquette before entering government service, and the procedure described below can often be observed at functions in the capital and elsewhere.

The details of presenting cloth vary slightly according to the rank of the person receiving the offering, but the basics are the same. The donor presents himself or herself by bowing, holding the fabrics with the left hand at knee level. The fabrics are then passed swiftly to the right hand and spread with an elegant gesture, while the left hand slips under the cloths and keeps them level to enhance this display. At last, the fabrics are laid with both hands on the floor in front of the recipient. All these movements must be smooth and perfectly coordinated, and executed if necessary while holding one's ceremonial shoulder cloth with the right hand and sometimes prostrating oneself at the same time. If the number of fabrics or their weight renders the exercise physically impossible, an attendant will take them from the donor's left hand and present them flat on the floor while the donor prostrates.

This elaborate etiquette governing the selection of the textiles and their presentation makes all Bhutanese acutely aware of their status in a community and the society at large. While innovations and alternatives are creeping into the gift-giving process, its framework and guidelines remain intact and Bhutanese take care to observe them.

Cloth Tax Payments

Cloth was once such a valued and essential commodity that villagers fulfilled their obligations to the state in part by producing annual quantities of cloth. Bhutanese say that this practice originated as the country was unified during the seventeenth century.[9] Every year, Shabdrung Ngawang Namgyel, who led this unification, received tribute missions from communities under his direct control and others seeking favorable relations (Aris 1979, 229).[10] The gifts delivered represented the products of each area: meat and butter from the colder regions, rice from the temperate valleys, and cloth from places where cotton, wild silk, and wool were plentiful. These yearly presentations became institutionalized as formal tax obligations at some point, with governors throughout the country presenting the produce of their domains to central authorities at the New Year Festival in Punakha, the capital. Taxes-in-kind were abolished between the late 1950s and late 1960s, but this practice is still reenacted during the Punakha New Year Festival.

Each dzong, which housed the district administration and monastery, set the number of fabrics that a family had to provide.[11] In southeastern Bhutan, the state first collected raw cotton in return for which villagers received rations of salt. The same cotton was then given back to villagers to be woven into tax cloth. As a class, fabrics woven for the dzong (*khé zong*, 'tax cloth') were usually rather coarse and sparsely patterned. All were intended for an eventual practical use.

The best-remembered tax cloths, which are no longer made, came from southern Bhutan. These varieties of cotton (collectively called *kamtham*) were valued according to their quality. Many of their names include the element *pön*, literally 'chief,' an allusion to the local official to whom the fabrics were tendered.[12] *Pönchu* ('little piece for the official') was a length of thin, fine, plain white cotton worth five of the smallest coins. *Pöndab*, worth ten coins, showed thin pairs of green stripes on white and was used for making lamp wicks. *Pöntshe* ('official's measure') was twice as large and twice as valuable, and could be used to line blankets, cover walls, or make lamp wicks.[13] Three panels of this fabric, sometimes patterned with red lines, were given to the lowest laborers at the dzong for making into robes or dresses (*logo pöntshe*, 'annual clothes, official's measure'). Better qualities of tax cloth included patterned cotton from Decheling in Samdrup Jongkhar District, which came to be known throughout Bhutan as *decheling kamtham*.

Other fabrics proffered to the state included multipurpose cloths (*pangkheb*, 'lap cover') [fig. 3.6] and striped cotton panels (*tharé*, 'woven cotton') and supplementary-warp-patterned cotton panels (*möntha*, 'Mön [understood as Bhutanese] weaving') given to women servants for stitching into dresses, along with woven belts.[14] Eastern Bhutan produced lengths of undecorated wild silk fabric for making men's ceremonial shoulder cloths, and supplementary-warp-patterned wild silk panels (*aikapur*) that would subsequently be given to high officers for making robes. Central Bhutan provided woolens for stitching into blankets, seat covers, and floor covers.

Cloth was also given to the dzongs as fines for various offenses. For example, if a household could not send a member to fulfill the annual labor corvée, which involved repairing dzongs and maintaining footpaths and bridges, three panels of cloth had to be given to the dzong (*zongshé*, 'absence cloth'). Annals of the late nineteenth century include many references to fines paid in cloth for other civil offenses, such as stealing horses.[15]

Cloth Collection and Distribution by the State

The collection of cloth and other taxes was managed by village headmen, who handed them over to a dzong official. At the dzong, the cloth and other revenues were kept in a storeroom supervised by a high-ranking officer (*dzöpön*, 'store master'). The government also required better-quality textiles; some of these were obtained through trade with India and Tibet, and others were bought on an ad hoc basis from people bringing cloth to sell, or ordered on commission from especially good weavers. From its storerooms, the state allocated quantities of handloomed cloth as well as silk and brocade to the dzong treasuries in every district and disbursed textiles in a variety of ways.

Officials and monks residing in the dzongs, and therefore attached to the government, were compensated partially in textiles that clothed them and helped reinforce their identity with the state they served. As early as 1783, British visitors noted that all but a handful of the most senior officers wore a prescribed uniform and had no chance to "wear fine feathers" (Collister 1987, 39). When monks and civil servants assembled every September for the festival at Tashichö Dzong (Thimphu), they received new clothes "from the public stores. ... Their dress, a scanty allowance of coarse strong cloth, with a red blanket" (Aris 1982, 53). Senior courtiers and important individuals received superior textiles and accessories. In 1750, the former Druk Desi received a full set of robes, several fine scarves, a length of *mentsi*, and three piles of mixed cloth consisting of thirteen, nine, and seven pieces each (Yönten Thayé n.d. [1970], fol. 64r). The Daga Pönlop received a hat, robe, shoes, and saddle set; his escorts received silk; and officers entitled to ride a horse received lesser gifts.[16] Even tailors at the court were given cloth of various kinds during feasts to mark the beginning, middle, and end of their projects (fol. 64v). In the 1930s, cloth for making garments was presented in the same way to court officials in Bumthang each year. The allotment included one set of woolen plaid loom lengths from Kurtö in north central Bhutan (for summer wear) and one set from Tibet (for winter robes).[17]

Eighteenth-century distributions to monastic institutions, and to the highest incarnate lamas in the land, included almost twenty types of cloth. Among them were Assamese silk, Indian cotton, Tibetan woolens, and ceremonial cloth of Bhutanese origin. Texts mention Indian silk that was used for making monastic dance costumes *(adholishi)*, thin Indian cotton for lining monastery and shrine walls prior to painting them *(bharati)*, patterned cottons from India *(kashika ré)*, and more than a dozen other textiles – all collected or imported by the state and apportioned annually (Yönten Thayé n.d.).[18] Monks transformed lengths of handloomed cloth into cushion covers, mats, ceremonial cloths, and other functional items. Panels of imported brocade, silk, wool, and cotton were put to use making *thangka*, wall hangings, floor coverings, and other essentials of a temple.

Formerly, the Bhutanese government sent cloth as gifts, and taxes, to states with which it maintained friendly relations. The columns of the audience hall of the Dalai Lamas in Lhasa's Potala Palace, for example, were covered with Bhutanese ceremonial cloths *(chagsi pangkheb)* taken to Tibet by the goodwill missions that Bhutan sent to Lhasa each year. Presents of other kinds were offered, but fabrics were very prominent because they were the specialty of Bhutan. The Bhutanese government also tendered cloth to authorities in Assam, with which it shared the revenue of certain southern borderlands. Annual payments in the mid-1700s were made up partially of striped blankets (Basu 1970, 135).[19]

Foreign officials and state guests received gifts of cloth from the government in a practice that continues today. While many of these gifts are probably lying in British attics, Tibetan cabinets, and Indian homes to this day, the exhibition includes several important examples: three textiles presented to Sir Charles Bell by the first king in 1910 [figs. 3.5, 5.5, 5.44]; a *thangka* given to a diplomat in the 1930s [fig. 6.12]; a woman's dress presented to a friend of the royal family in the 1960s; another given to a guest at the coronation of the present king in 1974 [fig. 3.7]; and a length of woolen cloth given to a visitor in 1992. Documented gift textiles – which may have been taken from a storeroom after many years – demonstrate the timelessness of gift cloth in Bhutan, and show what was considered an appropriate and fashionable selection at the time of the presentation.

In twentieth-century Bhutan, it has similarly been the custom for government offices to give gifts to a departing colleague or foreign guest as a token of friendship and appreciation – and, in a society where gift shops did not exist, the state storeroom was the only place from which government offices could obtain gifts, usually fabrics. An office representative would come to the storeroom and buy cloth in a quality and quantity appropriate to the rank of the recipient, making a careful choice because of the social meaning of the gift. The situation changed in the 1980s with the opening of the government Handicraft Emporium and private souvenir shops in urban centers. Bhutanese cloth, even in nontraditional forms, is still the preferred choice for government gifts because it is a source of national pride and a unique identity symbol.

Although Bhutan's economy is now based on currency, cloth is still an obligatory element of certain transactions in both the state and private sectors. These include constructing a house, executing works of religious art, and carrying out essential rites and prayers, activities that are critical to creating and maintaining the cultural and spiritual environment of Bhutan. The key individuals in each process are always given textiles. Thus, master carpenters who serve as architects and supervise the construction of traditional houses or public buildings are presented with sets of clothing – one for ordinary wear during work and one to wear for the important ceremonies that accompany construction of the edifice (Chime Wongmo 1985, 113).[20] Bhutanese also regularly offer textiles and other goods – butter, livestock, even land – to monasteries as a way of gaining religious merit. If the cloth is handwoven, colors appropriate to the clergy will be chosen by a weaver or donor: reds, burgundy, maroon, gold, and yellow. Silk fabrics for festival dance costumes are typically presented by the local nobility. Textiles are also presented to a lama in anticipation or appreciation of teachings or blessings received, ceremonies conducted, or rites performed.[21] Today, when a son is admitted into a monastery, parents offer textiles to the head monk and the senior monk who will look after the boy during his studies. Cash offerings have become common supplements, but fabrics are still required.

The utilitarian value of cloth, from which many essential items are made, is compounded by its symbolic value in transactions from taxes, to gifts, to payment for construction of a dwelling. Although the components of some exchanges are being modified, the favorite, if not obligatory, choices for gifts are still textiles, preferably ones that are handwoven and Bhutanese. The quality, type, and number of fabrics offered continue to reflect the structure and relationships of Bhutanese society in the late twentieth century.

PART TWO

Women
Men
and
Textiles

Chapter Four

Women and Weaving

The Origins of Weaving

Fig. 4.0 (page 81)
Men, women, and children in their best go *(men's robes) and* kira *(women's wrapped dresses), and monks in their maroon robes are among the throng at the Thimphu* tsechu *festival. The* kabné *(men's shoulder cloths) and* rachu *(women's shoulder cloths) visible on most of the adult lay participants are imperative on occasions of ceremonial importance. Men from the military wear a black sash (right foreground). (D.K.M. 1989)*

Fig. 4.1
Weaving is an ancient skill identified with women, particularly in eastern and central Bhutan. Here, a mother is helping her daughters at looms, set up in the yard of their home in the well-known weaving village of Radi (Tashigang District). The warp has just been transferred to the near loom, where mother and daughter are checking the order of the yarns before weaving begins. Both looms are warped with wild silk for making supplementary-warp-patterned (aikapur lungserma) *fabric. The second daughter has started to weave and has a supply of slender pattern-shed rods beside her. (D.K.M. 1987)*

Long ago, a woman named Böm Karma came to Bhutan as a bride. Her home was the village of Tsena in Tibet. She was married to the king of Tashigang, who lived in the fortress that used to be here long before the present one was built [in the late 1600s]. First she taught the women to weave simple designs in wool. Then she taught them how to make yarn from a "cotton tree" that grows around here. The people planted seeds from this tree and cotton crops resulted. Because the yarn made from cotton was finer than wool yarn, every year the people made different patterns. These became complicated, and spread from one village to another, and that is why there are now different designs in every village.

– A story from Tashigang District (eastern Bhutan)

Local legends such as this one present weaving as an ancient skill identified with women, especially in central and eastern Bhutan. However, few Bhutanese under forty are familiar with these oral traditions. This is not only because the legends, stories, and songs are the prerogative of older people but also because younger adults went to school instead of staying home and learning to weave; because they moved to a town from their family's village home; because they run a shop or work in an office; and because these days fewer women pass their days supervising weavers or weaving for the local nobility. As patterns of Bhutanese life are changing, once widely known lore about women and weaving is being simplified, and also forgotten.[1]

When asked how weaving began, western Bhutanese characteristically reply that it came from 'the other side of the Pelé La' *(pelé la phar ché)*, meaning the eastern part of their country.[2] Eastern Bhutanese volunteer that they have been weaving since 'lo-o-ong, long ago' *(hema-a, hema)*. Some people say the craft must have reached Bhutan from Assam and northeast India because the looms, weaving fibers, and even some patterns are so similar.

The stories heard from older Bhutanese relate how weaving was introduced from points east and north by long ago princess-goddesses, linking Bhutanese practices to traditions of cloth production in southeastern Tibet and China. The tale above about a Tibetan noblewoman has several variations. In Lhuntshi District and among the nomadic herders of Merak Sakteng, a local queen named Chöden Lhamo is remembered for the same role.[3] Early influences, personified in these noblewomen, are especially plausible when they emanate from eastern Tibet, where backstrap looms are used and weaving practices are similar.

The most beloved figure associated with weaving is a Chinese princess (Wencheng, known to Bhutanese as Ashi Jyazum) who was one of the two foreign wives of the famous seventh-century Tibetan king, Songtsen Gampo. Her biography is a favorite in Tibetan

'Heart weaving' (hingtham) defines a standard of careful work, intricate and innovative patterning, harmonious colors, and beauty. Bhutanese use the term for the most outstanding textiles, mainly women's dresses made for personal use or as commissions for the royal family, like this one. This kira *was made during the 1920s for Ashi Wangmo, daughter of the first king. It was woven in Bumthang, possibly by weavers at her home, Thinley Rabten. The princess wore it for special occasions until the 1950s.*

The format of the dress is that of a kushüthara, *but because the textile has a blue ground it is called a* ngosham. *The delicate patterning is created by supplementary wefts worked in the labor-intensive technique called* thrima, *twined and wrapped in such a way that the result looks like embroidery, including, for example, chain stitches and cross-stitches. One of the most exquisite features of this dress are the tiny horses and birds perched on trees inside some of the geometric shapes. The narrow bands of representational patterning are executed in* sapma, *where supplementary wefts are laid in with ground wefts and appear to lie flat on the surface of the cloth. These motifs include leafy trees (shinglo) alternating with clown's masks (shyauli bap) and geometric patterns. Few of the* shinglo *motifs are the same; each has tiny variations – in the number of branches, the arrangement of leaves, the presence of blossoms or a vase beside the tree – that testify to the weaver's skill and creativity.*

The end borders of the dress consist of eleven alternating rows of swastika meanders, geometric motifs, and crossed thunderbolts (dorje jadam). The center row of multicolored triangles resembles patchwork made of cut and pieced silks that covers the altars of Bhutanese shrines. The incorporation of a patchwork motif in a woman's dress border invokes long life for the wearer. (see Catalog)

Buddhist literature and contains many instructions on painting and other religious arts. What is remembered in Bhutanese oral tradition is stories not recorded in her biography. One of them describes how sad and bitter the beautiful young woman felt when her parents sent her off to be the bride of such a distant ruler. As she passed near Bhutan on her way to Lhasa, people came to know of her plight and burned incense for her, a customary way of honoring a visitor. Touched by this sympathetic welcome, she is said to have bestowed knowledge of weaving on the people of Kurtö (northern Lhuntshi District) in return.[4]

Folk songs sung by women from central Bhutan link Ashi Jyazum specifically with weaving on a backstrap loom. The lyrics tell of her trials while being escorted by a wily Tibetan minister en route from China. Although he was the king's emissary, he himself fell in love with her and sought to keep her from meeting her husband-to-be. He told the princess that the Tibetan king had no nose, and told the king that she had a terrible smell. The minister's ruses caused her to arrive in Lhasa three years after the king's other wife, a princess from Nepal. The Nepalese queen had meanwhile laid claim to most of the servants and put them to work at her horizontal frame loom, which requires two people to wind the warp. The Chinese princess ended up with only a few servants and therefore introduced weaving on a backstrap loom, whose warp can be wound by one person alone.[5] Notably, all of these oral traditions connect weaving with women and with an origin to the east.

Creators of Cloth

Designing and weaving cloth are the exclusive domain of women and the most important way in which a Bhutanese woman displays her individuality and creativity. Most other secular arts and all the religious arts are the unique realm of men. Technical skills in dyeing and weaving, and the ability to design patterns and translate them into a textile, are talents men seek in choosing wives, and, along with family and wealth, they account for a woman's prestige. In many cases today, a younger Bhutanese woman, perhaps not an expert at the loom, develops designs that are woven into cloth by weavers she employs. Bhutanese consider the most outstanding examples of women's technical ingenuity and artistry to be fine textiles made for personal use, or special commissions for the royal family and other nobility. Described as 'heart weaving' *(hingtham)* [fig. 4.2], these weavings – often women's dresses – define the standard for careful work, intricacy, and beauty.

As weavers, or as designers of textiles who work with weavers, women have great latitude in composing cloth that expresses their personal aesthetic choices, and hence their creative talents. Working within broad guidelines depending on the type of cloth, they interpret, combine, and invent designs and motifs. Social and commercial value arises from harmonious color combinations, intricacy in pattern, tightness of weave, and the introduction of innovative elements into traditional weaving formats. Weaving is quite competitive and new patterns are admired, copied, and reinterpreted in an endless process of change.

Beliefs about women and weaving suggest that a woman's reproductive nature as well as her artistry is expressed and reinforced through the activity of making cloth.[6] Admonitions associated with cloth production recall the vulnerable situation of a woman giving birth and provide the basis for interpreting weaving as a reproductive allegory.[7] For example, although spinning and weaving are activities often done in the open or in a group, the critical step of dyeing yarns is governed by various proscriptions and should be done in seclusion. In popular belief, any interference with activity at the loom has dire implications for marriage, fertility, and even life itself: if a woman steps over the warp or a pattern-shed rod for picking out designs, she will never marry or she will have a mute child.[8] If a girl is struck by the sword as a weaver is drawing it out of the warp shed, she will marry an old man. Some Bhutanese say that if a man dreams of going to a new place and sleeping with a beautiful girl, he will receive a nice piece of cloth.

Folk tales such as the following also underscore the similarity between weaving and reproduction as tasks that require focus and perseverance until completion:

At the time when Bhutan was being converted to Buddhism, there was a very powerful local demon in the east. Guru Rimpoche [Padmasambhava] assumed the fiercest of his eight forms, Dorje Drolö, and came personally to vanquish this demon.[9] When the demon learned that Guru Rimpoche was heading in his direction, he fled to a nearby house and transformed himself into an ordinary man so he would not scare the woman who lived there. Explaining that fearful enemies were pursuing him, he asked her to hide him. Giving him no more than a glance, she turned back to her loom, saying, "I'm weaving and must finish this cloth, so please don't disturb me. I can't interrupt this work until I'm done." The demon then changed his form into that of a pretty young girl and said, "Oh, if you're in a hurry, let me finish your weaving for you." The woman happily accepted and let the younger woman sit at her loom, where the cloth was finished in an instant. The woman then led the girl upstairs and hid her in a barrel in the space under the roof where grain was stored.

A short time later, Guru Rimpoche arrived and asked the woman where the demon was hiding. The woman was so terrified by his fierce appearance that she couldn't speak, but she realized immediately that she had been deceived and that this frightening form was the force of good. She pointed upstairs, where Guru Rimpoche found the demon and overwhelmed him.[10]

There are two morals for those who told this story: "Never be impatient about finishing your weaving or other work, but do it in the time it takes"; and "Don't let others do your work for you, or something bad may happen to you." Both aphorisms reflect the message that weaving, like pregnancy and giving birth, is a delicate process, taking its own time, and must not be rushed. Women and cloth, weaving and giving birth, are inextricably connected.

The identification of women with weaving is so strong that only a handful of men are remembered as weavers or dyers, or weave today.[11] Although there are no formal prohibitions against men's engaging in these arts, young boys who express an interest, or take them up, are teased and mocked. Male weavers are sometimes even referred to by feminine pronouns, reinforcing the notion that cloth production is fundamentally female work. This scorn notwithstanding, Bhutanese liken cloth woven by a man to a protective neck cord (*sunkü*) – in other words, it is as precious as a blessing given by a lama. It bestows long life on the owner or wearer and should not be sold.

The value accorded to a male weaver's work manifests the tension between women's esteemed role as weavers and their spiritual inferiority to men. The popular Buddhist view that a woman must be reborn nine times – and live out nine lives – before she has a chance to be reborn as a man shapes attitudes toward women and a young girl's perception of herself as she matures. Men and women also are thought to have fundamentally different characters, which influences the division of labor. Household and agricultural tasks may be shared by all the family members available to carry them out, but women, more than men, are constantly at work.[12] A woman is not blamed or oppressed because of her inferior position, but many Bhutanese feel that being born female foretells special hardships.[13]

Popular beliefs about cloth reflect these views about women and men. For example, many Bhutanese teach their children not to walk under clothing, especially undergarments, hung out to dry. While most people say this is a general way of observing the purity of one's body, older Bhutanese make a significant distinction: they say that men should not walk under a woman's dress or apron (lower garments) but that women can walk underneath a man's robe. The explanation is that because women are not as advanced as men, men's garments cannot defile them. Beliefs about the special powers of men's belts, and men's role as the exclusive producers of sewn textiles for ceremony and Buddhist ritual, reinforce these notions (see Chapter Six).

FIG. 4.3

The Khaling National Handloom Development Project is one of several royal government initiatives to stimulate weaving, both as a national art and as a source of livelihood for women. At Khaling, wild silk yarn imported from Assam is dyed with vegetable colors and synthetic dyes and then distributed to weavers, who produce dresses and other items at home, according to project designs. The finished textiles are then purchased for public sale through the Handicraft Emporium in Thimphu.

Khaling dresses have had a major impact on fashion since the project began ten years ago. Some of the early designs (left) reflect traditional patterns woven in new colors. Others (right) have a modern look, with just a few designs. The dress at right, called a "new-style kira," *is one of the first ones woven to order based on sample garments developed in 1985. Recent dresses (center) feature a more Bhutanese format, with color schemes that combine vegetable and synthetic tints. Khaling dresses are very popular, and Khaling silk is sought after by Thimphu women for their own weaving. (see Catalog)*

Generating Income

Today weaving is an important source of earnings for women throughout Bhutan, but the geographic distribution of weaving, the individuals who weave, and their reasons for engaging in this activity have changed in the twentieth century. In central and eastern Bhutan, weaving has long been a respected profession, and until recently almost all women worked at looms. The most skillful weavers formed a special class. Known as *thagthami* (often shortened to *tham*), they frequently served the local nobility *(chöjé)*. These weavers were mostly of low status, being from families with service obligations. In some cases the profession was hereditary – a mother who wove full time for the local noble would pass her skills on to her daughter. In other cases, a girl whose family owed labor might be singled out for service as a weaver if she demonstrated an aptitude at the loom. Many noble houses kept weavers among their permanent household staff, but they also bought from women who wove on order at their own homes. Weaving under this type of patronage was widespread when the monarchy was established in 1907, and probably had existed for at least several centuries – or as long as hereditary service defined the relationship between local elites and other Bhutanese.

In western Bhutan 100 years ago, most women did not weave, but weaving, the prestige accorded to weavers, and weavers themselves have moved west during this century. As members of what is now the royal family gained influence in the late nineteenth century, they assigned their political allies, who were, like them, from central and eastern Bhutan, to positions of administrative responsibility in the west. These administrators brought with them wives and servants who were weavers. Thimphu is home to civil servants from all over the country, and interregional marriage has helped spread weaving there and in other towns of western Bhutan.[14] Senior members of the royal government form a new political and economic elite that, like the traditional aristocracy, employs weavers who produce to order. In the past thirty-five years, with the expansion of government service, the building of roads, and increased levels of education, weaving has enjoyed true nationwide visibility.

When hereditary service was abolished in 1957, women were free to apply their weaving skills for whatever markets and clients they could find. Many central and eastern Bhutanese weavers still work on contract for local noble families. Others, married to royal bodyguards stationed in Thimphu, weave for clients in the capital. Some women are exempted from household and farming tasks to weave full time, at home or elsewhere, because of the cash income they generate. Others weave as time permits and sell their work to traders who come in the spring to purchase fabric made during the winter and take it to sell in larger towns. Whether they produce 'heart weaving' *(hingtham)* on commission for an *ashi* (princess) in Thimphu or 'commercial weaving' *(tshongtham)* for the less-discerning public market, women all over Bhutan help their households prosper by weaving.

Women of the royal family have helped stimulate weaving as an art and a source of livelihood. When the government began its move to Thimphu in the 1950s, Queen (Dowager) Ashi Pema Chöden established a palace weaving workshop there. Having a keen personal interest in weaving, she also organized weaving centers at Tashichöling (Bumthang) and in the Tashigang area (Rustomji 1971, 192). Around 1960, when the third king took up permanent residence in Thimphu, Queen (Mother) Ashi Kesang established her private weavers in a community that now resides near her palace at Dechenchöling. Today two weaving centers in eastern Bhutan, at Pemagatshel and Khaling, are managed by the National Women's Association, under the active patronage of Her Royal Highness Ashi Sonam Choden. Elsewhere in Bhutan, the National Women's Association makes weaving materials available for cash or credit and purchases woven cloth for the Handicraft Emporium in Thimphu.

The significant role of women as weavers – and income producers – is enhanced by initiatives of the royal government as well. For example, the National Handloom Development Project at Khaling in Tashigang District, which started with Swedish assistance a decade ago, has helped to revive and preserve the art of dyeing with vegetable colors. Khaling yarn is sought after by women in Thimphu, and the designs of Khaling dresses are widely admired and copied [fig. 4.3]. An Australian foreign aid project is helping to improve wool production in central Bhutan (1993), and the United Nations Development Programme is joining with the Ministry of Trade and Industry to support traditional weaving communities in Lhuntshi District.

In spite of efforts to increase women's access to credit and to provide them with marketing support, the number of women involved in cloth production is on the decline.[15]

Fig. 4.4

The most recent major development in Bhutanese fashion is the introduction in 1991-92 of Indian machine-woven fabric that copies Bhutanese designs. Sephup cloth, thus called after the home region of the Thimphu merchant who first sold the fabric, is a fraction of the cost of handwoven cloth, light-weight, comfortable, easy to wash, and quick to dry. Even well-to-do Bhutanese have embraced this practical alternative for everyday wear at home or while traveling. In light of the 1989 edict requiring Bhutanese dress in public, this cloth is welcome to many others because it is easily affordable.

These two women's dresses are möntha patterns, red-and-black or red-and-blue warp-pattern bands interspersed with colorful warp striping. The example on the left is handwoven and finished with weft twining and fringe. That on the right is machine-woven Sephup cloth, which successfully imitates the Bhutanese prototype; being cut from a bolt of cloth, it lacks weft twining and is hemmed. (see Catalog)

One reason is that more villagers are sending their daughters to school, at least for primary education. However, in weaving regions even schoolgirls may be encouraged to weave, and some schools offer weaving classes. Administrators and parents both recognize the likelihood that a girl may leave school at some point, and they know that weaving skills are a potential source of income for her. At the same time, the trend during the past twenty-five years of sending girls from well-to-do families to be educated in Kalimpong and Darjeeling (India) has had a very positive impact on weaving. While they may not have learned to work at looms, these young women are avid designers of textiles and with their husbands are part of the new economic elite that provides steady employment for weavers.

Another reason for some decline in weaving is that since 1991, Indian factory-made fabrics copying Bhutanese patterns have become popular nationwide, among all classes [fig. 4.4]. The new fabrics, called *sephup* after the home region of the Bhutanese merchant who imports them, are a fraction of the cost of handwoven cloth, and are lightweight, comfortable, easier to wash, and quicker to dry. Within two years, the availability of Sephup dresses and robes had discouraged many villagers who formerly supplemented their household income by seasonal work at the loom. The imports have also stimulated controversy in Thimphu about the feasibility of copyrighting patterns, controlling imports, or otherwise taking steps to safeguard both the character and the economic importance of traditional handloomed Bhutanese cloth. Handwoven cloth is still *de rigueur* for the well-to-do and on important occasions, so Bhutanese will continue to patronize weavers and weave for their families. But, with mixed feelings, they recognize the practicality of machine-woven cloth for everyday wear.

In spite of these recent developments, weaving is anything but a vanishing art. Skills at the loom command as much respect as ever, if not more, in the face of these challenges to the preservation of native textile traditions. Older women delight in supervising younger weavers, and all take pleasure in the female companionship that goes along with weaving [fig. 4.1]. Whenever several weavers work side by side, they entertain and amuse one another, and the girls helping them, by telling stories and singing songs. One song from south central Bhutan, sung in the fields as well as at the loom, describes each step of weaving: "This is the way I'll spin the yarn; This is the way I'll wind the warp; This is the way I'll weave the cloth," and so on.[16] Other melodies *(tsangmo* and *alo)* have lyrics sung by women in turns.[17] To pass the time, women at adjacent looms recite well-known verses and improvise new ones. Song lyrics and stories related to weaving are what a young girl hears if she grows up sitting beside her mother or an elder sister at the loom. By the time a girl is seven or eight, she will have a tiny play loom, warped with scrap yarns, set up nearby. On this, she will begin to learn the art of weaving by practicing what the eastern Bhutanese call 'designs to throw away' *(khoptang rigpa)*, 'like the peels of an onion skin.' In time, her weaving will generate both admiration and income.

Chapter Five

Warp and Weft

Garments, Coverings, and Containers

Textiles for clothing are the chief products of women's looms. The fabrics and styles worn express important aspects of Bhutanese identity. Women's main garment, a wrapped dress *(kira)*, has probably been structurally the same for many centuries, but variations in weave, colors, fibers, and decoration, as well as accessories, reflect differences in status, age, region, and wealth and also, importantly, changes in fashion. Men's tailored robes *(go)*, in contrast, are a seventeenth-century innovation that spread gradually and replaced earlier dress styles. As with women's dresses, the robe fabric itself expresses aspects of the wearer's identity. While most people today wear either the wrapped dress or a robe, other important clothing styles coexist in Bhutan, especially in remote highlands and the southern hills. In the past 100 years, a more stable political environment, the patronage of weaving by traditional and new elites, and the introduction of abundant new materials have increased the overall quality and diversity of cloth used for wearing.

Because most Bhutanese wear the same type of apparel and patterns of cloth, many outsiders do not realize the significance of fashion and etiquette. However, subtle nuances of clothing reveal the wearer's social and economic status to other Bhutanese. The quality of weaving and degree of patterning naturally vary, and Bhutanese carefully compose their outfits for each occasion, paying attention to the choice of pattern in the cloth, the fiber of which it is woven, the appropriate accessory garments, and the nature of the occasion. For example, a simple pattern may be appropriate for a formal event if it is woven in wild silk, and, in the case of a woman, worn with a silk brocade jacket. Some patterns – such as the classic plaids – are suitable almost anytime. Bhutanese place great importance on dressing properly, for either overdressing or underdressing would embarrass oneself, one's host, and other guests.

Age also affects fashion and etiquette. Until women and men are the parents of young teenagers, they may be quite clothes-conscious and attentive to fashion, wearing bright, bold patterns and fancy or luxurious clothing when the occasion warrants. As people grow older, dressing "soberly," as Bhutanese put it, is more the rule – partly because as householders they must provide for their children's education, clothing, and well-being, and partly because older people are supposed to become less worldly in their concerns. Plainer fabrics and darker colors are, therefore, more suitable.

Intimate knowledge of weaving helps a Bhutanese assess at a glance the quality of a garment, the care with which it has been arranged, and the types of accessories that have been chosen – all of which indicate whether the wearer is a villager or a civil servant. A woman's dress should be worn neatly, with the bottom edges even and the horizontal stripes nicely aligned at the right side where the inner and outer layers meet. The proper dress length corresponds to social hierarchy: villagers' *kira* (dresses) must be ankle length or higher; women of higher status or those who work in government can have their dress touch

FIG. 5.1

Festivals are welcome occasions for Bhutanese to dress in their best clothes. These women are wearing ornate wrapped dresses (kira), *which they may put on only once or twice a year. Their fancy jackets are stitched from Hong Kong silk brocade, with bright cotton or silk blouses underneath. The women casually drape their red ceremonial shoulder cloths around their necks, but the textiles are formally worn on the left shoulder. (Gangtey Gompa, D.K.M. 1986)*

"the upper part of the foot"; and women of the royal family wear *kira* that touch the ground.

The etiquette concerning ceremonial shoulder cloths and other details of men's attire is even more complex and is faithfully observed. A man's status is reflected by the neatness of his robe, the evenness of its hem (especially in back), the equal depth of the garment's folds at his back, and the whiteness of his collar and cuffs. The length of the robe and depth of the cuffs are dictated by the wearer's rank. Ordinary citizens must wear their *go* (robes) above the knee, a sign of humility; high officials may wear theirs to midknee; and the king's robe covers his knees. Similarly, the higher one's status, the deeper one's cuffs may be. These conventions are taught in courses taken by all entry-level civil servants, and are particularly carefully followed for state functions or when the head of Bhutan's religious establishment is in residence in Thimphu.

For most of the past 300 years, until earlier in this century, clothing was an even more obvious marker of status than it is today. In 1783, the British emissary Samuel Davis wrote that only two Bhutanese officials, posted in Calcutta, wore "embroidered gowns ... given them by the Rajah [of Bhutan]." They dressed in these garments in India, but sold the gowns before returning home because they could not wear them as private citizens inside Bhutan (Davis 1830, reproduced in Aris 1982, 54). Ordinary people were fined for wearing "clothes beyond their station," so they took pains to avoid exhibiting any signs of wealth and wore very humble apparel (Bell Collection 1904, 6). Among the elite, it was nevertheless common to give fine, used garments as gifts to those who served the family, from senior officials at the court to weavers retained in the household. While in the early twentieth century recipients of high rank could wear these garments on special occasions, those of lower status could not – and still may not. This is how at least some of the exquisite old *kushüthara* (brocaded wrapped dresses) have come on the market in Nepal – because their current owners could never wear them, and by now the old garments are long out of fashion. Some of these distinctions have relaxed since the 1950s, and today a villager may wear a garment with the same pattern worn by a civil servant. The status of the wearer remains discernible – at least to a Bhutanese – from the quality of the fiber and weaving, the folding and neatness of the garment, and the accessories worn with it.

A fine handwoven garment, or the set of cloth panels from which a dress or robe can be made, is literally an investment. In 1993, in Thimphu, a simple, striped cotton woman's dress cost between US $30 and $70; lengths of vegetable-dyed, plaid wool for a man's robe, if they could be found, cost from $175 to $250; a stitched man's robe of wild silk cost from $200 to $300; and a fancy woman's dress made entirely of Hong Kong silk cost $1,000 or more. While these prices are high even by Western standards, acquiring clothing was not usually a cash transaction until about thirty years ago – food, lodging, cloth, and other in-kind payments were made to weavers and tailors. Today, handloomed fabrics are so costly that it is no wonder machine-woven garments, priced under $20 for a dress or robe, are so popular.

Because Bhutanese want to stay current with fashions, even the finest clothing does not automatically become an heirloom. Instead, a woman is likely to sell her own and her husband's garments – or give them away – as they go out of vogue, in order to weave or purchase new cloth that reflects the changing tastes. Some families have cloth or garments from previous generations packed away in trunks, and now there is a new appreciation of surviving old dresses that are especially intricate in design.

FIG. 5.2

The dress of most Bhutanese women is a rectangular textile. When the garment is made of cotton, wild silk, or cultivated silk, it consists of three loom lengths woven on a backstrap loom and joined together in the warp direction. The warp stripes are oriented horizontally when the dress is worn.

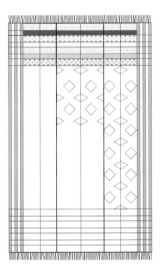

If a dress is woven of wool, it may be constructed in one of three ways. Rarely, three warp-striped panels from a backstrap loom are joined like cotton panels are. More often, woolen cloth woven on a backstrap loom is cut to an appropriate vertical length. Six or seven panels are then stitched together in the warp direction, as shown below, so that weft stripes (if present) are horizontal when the garment is worn. This type of dress has facing at the upper and lower inside edges. When a dress is stitched of narrower woolen panels woven on a horizontal frame loom, it may require twelve or thirteen vertical panels, depending on the wearer's girth.

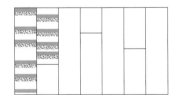

FIG. 5.3

A woman puts on her kira *over a blouse and petticoat. She positions one corner of the dress so that it comes slightly forward over her left shoulder. Holding it in position, she brings the fabric under her right arm and across her chest, and fastens it with a brooch to the corner at her left shoulder. She then makes a deep fold at the front and brings the other end of the dress around her back to her right shoulder, securing that end to the front fold with another brooch. She straightens the fold, pulls the garment up slightly so that the upper part blouses, and wraps her belt tightly. She then adjusts the dress so that its stripes or patterns are aligned nicely where the layers of fabric meet at her right hip, and so that the garment is a proper length, with its lower edges even all the way around. Her outfit is finished with a jacket, folded back into cuffs with the sleeves of her blouse. (After Bartholomew 1985)*

Women's Dress

How we girls dressed up! First I'd put on a thin, cotton dress, maybe *pangtsi* [red-and-black plaid on a white ground]. Then on top of it a wild silk *sethra* [gold plaid] dress, and on top of that, the third one would be a lovely *kushüthara*. We'd make sure that as we walked, the fringed ends would flutter in the breeze so the young men could see our beautiful dresses ... What fun it was to go to a festival!

– Am Yeshe Chöden, remembering her girlhood in Bumthang in the 1930s

A woman's dress in most of Bhutan is a large, rectangular textile *(kira)* that is wrapped around the body, folded into a wide pleat in front, and fastened at the shoulders with ornate silver and gold brooches. The dress is belted tightly and bloused about the waist to form a pouch where money, keys, and other necessities are carried. A *kira* is worn over a blouse and topped by a jacket [figs. 5.1, 5.3].

Kira made of silk, wild silk, or cotton consist of three panels *(bjang)*, joined in the warp direction and oriented horizontally [fig. 5.2, top]. These dresses are finished at each end with a neat fringe, made by twisting several warp ends together, tying a knot with two of them, and then cutting each plait to about 3 cm. *Kira* made of wool may be composed of six to fourteen panels joined lengthwise in the warp direction and oriented vertically [fig. 5.2, bottom]. The upper and lower edges of a woolen dress, and its corners, are faced with 8 cm of cotton or silk cloth (*ja*, 'rainbow'), and the ends are sometimes hemmed. Dresses of any fiber measure 150 to 180 cm by approximately 275 cm, depending on the height and girth of the owner.

There are many types of handwoven *kira*, each named for the design of the fabric. These names once indicated the fabric's place of origin or the weaver's home region. With modern transportation, development of the government infrastructure, and growth of major towns, the relationship between textiles and localities has become more complex. Patterns are still viewed as regional, but may be worn by many people, anywhere in Bhutan.

Fig. 5.4

Recently crowned as Bhutan's first king, Sir Ugyen Wangchuck (upper left) is shown here with members of his family on the steps of their residence in Tongsa in 1907. The women beside him are his sister and her two daughters, the latter both wearing patterned kushüthara *dresses for which the Wangchucks' native region is famous. A white lining – or inner jacket – is visible inside their dark outer jackets, which appear to be imported silk. As befitting an older woman with children, his sister is soberly dressed in a subdued plaid dress* (bumthang mathra), *mostly covered by her striped apron, and a jacket that is not silk. Of the three serving girls in the foreground, the one standing is in a* kushüthara, *possibly given to her by her employers, and a wide patterned cummerbund* (kera). *The servant girl in front of the king has a dress decorated like a* kushüthara, *but its field is not white and its design, which has pattern bands forming squares in the fabric, is no longer seen. The servant girls' jackets are dark cloth that appears to be imported velvet, cut much shorter than jackets are now.*

The king's robe is a typical Bhutanese plaid, resembling the fabric of his sister's dress. His Western kneesocks and shoes were a recent fashion that continues today. His nephew, standing at the far left, is outfitted in a robe with supplementary-warp patterning (aikapur), *with a sword on his right hip. (John Claude White 1907-08, Courtesy National Geographic Society)*

The most prestigious dress for women during most of the twentieth century has been the *kushüthara* [figs. 1.1, 5.5]. Identified by a white ground exuberantly patterned with intricate designs, *kushüthara* come from north central Bhutan, where a special style of discontinuous supplementary-weft patterning called *kushü* ('brocade') developed in the Kurtö region of Lhuntshi District [Map 2, p. 170]. *Kushüthara* are constructed from three cotton or silk panels.[1] Two panels show bold warp stripes that appear at the upper and lower edges of the garment when worn. Elaborate supplementary-weft patterning decorates the white field and both fringed ends of a *kushüthara*, although only one end is seen after the dress is wrapped around the wearer. The dress can be worn with either end outermost.

The development of *kushüthara* design and popularization of this type of dress throughout Bhutan are largely due to the nobility of Kurtö, where the royal family of Bhutan originated. When Sir Ugyen Wangchuck, founder of Bhutan's ruling dynasty, became the first king in 1907, his family's textile preferences and the weaving of the family's native region gained prominence throughout the country. Because the women of the royal family often wore *kushüthara* [fig. 5.4], this dress quickly acquired prestige.

During the past century, the *kushüthara* has continued to develop under the trend-setting influence of high-status women. Variants of the style include dresses with colored rather than white backgrounds: a blue field (*ngosham*, 'blue background'); a green field (*jangsham*, 'green background'); a black field (*napsham*, 'black background'); a red field (*mapsham*, 'red background') [figs. 5.6-5.10]. Lately, garments with colored fields – including hot pink, creamy yellow, and pale blue – have been more fashionable than those with white fields, although the traditional white field is making a comeback in the 1990s.

Other twentieth-century innovations are evident in the patterning of these dresses. Some dresses have undecorated areas, which are not seen when the garment is worn [fig. 5.8]. Because *kushü* patterning is created by intricate manipulation of supplementary-weft yarns, it is very time-consuming and weavers at different levels of society apparently developed this shortcut to save time as well as costly pattern yarn. Alternatively, motifs may be greatly

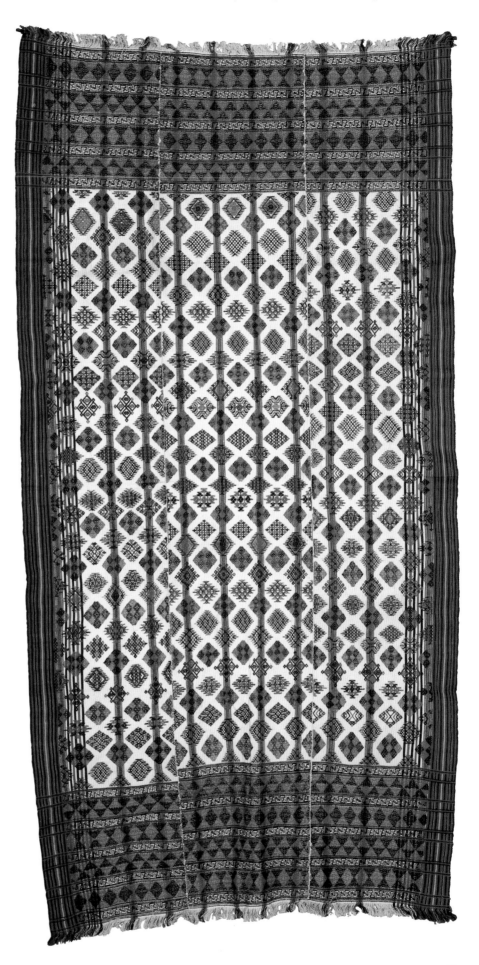

FIG. 5.5
The kushüthara *has been the most prestigious apparel for women during the twentieth century. This fine example was a gift to Sir Charles Bell from King Ugyen Wangchuck in 1910. Kushüthara have a white field patterned with dozens of distinct motifs, shaped like diamonds, or half-diamonds at the edges of the field. The patterning of these dresses exemplifies what Bhutanese call* jandha. *A dress with* jandha *has designs whose colors contrast with the field color and create a pleasing, striking impression when seen from a distance.*

This dress style originated in Kurtö, the northern part of Lhuntshi District in north central Bhutan. The techniques Kurtö weavers used to create the supplementary-weft designs are labor intensive and permit great intricacy. Similar patterning (kushü) embellishes other textiles from this region, but it is most dramatic and fully developed on the broad expanse of these women's dresses. (see Catalog)

enlarged and entire patterns may be simplified. Warp stripes at the upper and lower edges of the dress and the border patterning at each fringed end are often omitted in contemporary weaving, especially when the ground cloth is colored rather than white. A dress may be decorated with supplementary-weft designs arranged in neat rows [fig. 5.9]. *Kushüthara*-style motifs, which used to be seen on a distinct class of textiles, have been combined with bands of supplementary-warp patterning. In short, no rules limit what

a weaver can create using *kushü* and other patterning techniques. Regardless of these modifications, quality is still associated with intricate designs and with silk pattern yarns which permit a weaver to create the most delicate motifs [fig. 5.10].

Kira are also made from machine-woven fabrics imported from New Delhi, Bangkok, New York, and Paris. Bhutanese often search out plaid and striped fabrics that resemble their favorite indigenous designs. The question of copyright on Bhutanese patterns is being very hotly debated at present, because in 1991-92 an enterprising Thimphu merchant arranged to import Indian cloth that quite deliberately imitates warp-striped and supplementary-warp-patterned cloth of Bhutanese manufacture.[2] Inexpensive and much easier to care for, the machine-loomed fabrics from Ludhiana and Amritsar have achieved near universal popularity, virtually overnight.

The belt (*kera*, 'waistcloth,' not to be confused with *kira*, 'wrapped dress') that secures a woman's dress has been a focus of fashion, too. Today, two styles are seen, one among the older generation and one among the younger. The traditional *kera* is a generous length of cotton or wild silk embellished with horizontal bands of supplementary-weft patterning [fig. 5.11]. Measuring 30 to 45 cm wide and 180 to 240 cm long, the *kera* is folded over lengthwise several times and fastened around the waist by tucking in the long warp fringe

FIGS. 5.6-7

Dresses decorated with the same techniques as kushüthara *but having a blue field [fig. 4.2] or, more rarely, a white center panel flanked by two blue panels like that below (fig. 5.7), were known at the turn of the century. Although special names exist for garments with red, blue, green, or black fields, blue-and-white dresses do not have a particular name today and are seldom woven. Most often they are called* ngosham, *the name for a dress with a blue field.*

The dress below has seven pattern bands at each end, containing designs that were once conventional: a swastika meander, patchwork pattern, and, in the center, latticework called an eternal or lucky knot (dramé). The simple field patterning and use of handspun cotton in this dress suggest it was made in south central Bhutan. The vegetable dyes and long fringe, taken together, also indicate age.

Another group of blue-and-white dresses, represented above (fig. 5.6) by three panels from the loom, is not decorated with kushü *motifs, but with bands of supplementary-warp patterning (aikapur). This example shows the old-fashioned pattern that eastern Bhutanese call a design 'with little boxes' (dromchu chema). Bhutanese say these dresses, usually found today as a set of unstitched panels, were made in southeastern Bhutan and often tendered to the dzongs for distribution as a ration of 'annual clothing' (logo) to women laborers. (see Catalog)*

FIG. 5.8
Variations on the kushüthara *style are plentiful and continue to develop because Bhutanese value innovation within established formats. Weavers have great latitude in inventing new designs and color combinations. Dresses whose fields feature bands of blue, green, and red were popular in the 1960s and 1970s. The alternating-color warp panels in this dress are hardly visible in most of the garment because the field is so densely decorated with supplementary-weft patterning. Motifs in the shape of double thunderbolts extend even into the narrow warp stripes at the edges of the dress. This kind of supplementary-weft patterning (*kushü*) requires intricate manipulation of the pattern yarns and takes a long time, so weavers occasionally leave the middle part of a dress undecorated to save both time and costly silk pattern yarns. Between the bands of supplementary-weft patterning are narrow plainweave warp stripes. (see Catalog)*

FIG. 5.9
*These two dresses exhibit recent preferences for fields that lack end border patterning and have motifs arranged in orderly rows. The black dress was woven in the 1960s and features a stylized double thunderbolt motif (*dorje jadam*), repeated in different colors. The green dress illustrates the new materials of the 1980s and a pattern that became fashionable at the same time. Its bright palette is punctuated by extensive use of metallic (gold and silver) yarns. Rows of simplified* kushüthara-*like field motifs alternate with rows of diamonds arranged end to end, an element that used to appear in dress borders as the eternal knot motif (*dramé*). Instead of warp stripes at the edge of the garment, the field pattern is continued in smaller, modified form. Although the patterning in this dress is done in* kushü *style, a close look shows that the weaver has relied more on* sapma, *the simpler technique, and less on* thrima, *the more complex technique. (see Catalog)*

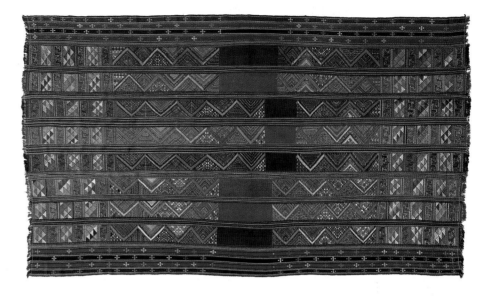

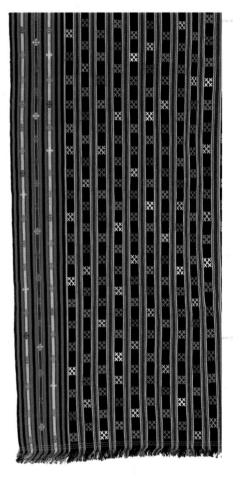

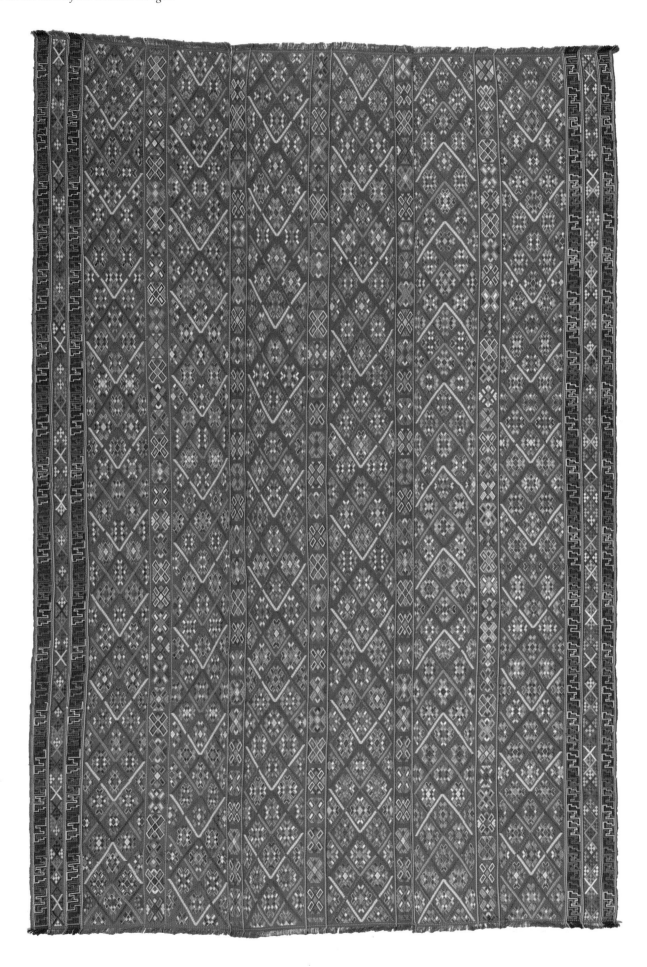

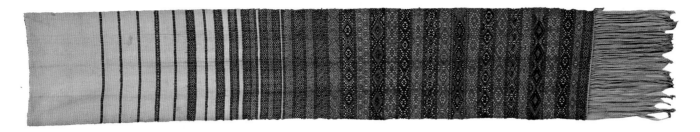

at one end. Pairs of these cummerbunds, made on backstrap looms, are sometimes woven as a single textile with elaborate patterning on the ends and a much plainer center. After weaving, this textile is cut along the weft in the middle and becomes two belts. Each has one cut end that may be turned under and hemmed and one decorated, fringed end that is seen when worn.

Traditional *kera* are decorated with two-faced patterning and have a standard format. The textiles show single-color, geometric pattern bands (Tshangla: *thangshing*), executed in red alternating with blue or black on a white ground. Every fourth pattern band combines two colors and features repeating diamonds *(thok)*.[3] In some belts, floral pattern bands *(komtsham)* also occur. Between the bands of patterning are narrow weft-wise stripes *(tsimpiring)*, formed by supplementary-weft floats whose intervals *(jhipi)* create almost identical patterns on both sides of the fabric. Some cummerbunds have a yellow or orange ground and multicolored designs, but patterns tend to adhere to the format described [fig. 5.12]. The specialized Tshangla words describing women's belt patterning point to the belts' origin in eastern Bhutan.

A mid-nineteenth century woman's belt [fig. 1.5], strikingly different from belts known today, was transferred to the Victoria and Albert Museum in London in 1879 from the East India Company Museum, also in London, which accessioned it in 1855. The textile was probably acquired by a member of a British mission to Bhutan, such as Capt. R.B. Pemberton's in 1837-38, or by an official working in British India near the Bhutanese frontier. Made of light yellow, handspun cotton, it is entirely plain except for four narrow bands of simple woolen patterning at each end. Older Bhutanese women to whom a photograph was shown called this a *matrami keré* ('belt worth one *matram*,' the smallest coin), and they said it was worn by people of very little means. This type of belt is also said to have been part of the annual gift of clothing given by noble families to their servants.

Older women, particularly in rural areas, still weave broad, patterned cummerbunds, but younger women, preferring a less bulky waistline, now use an altogether different type of belt [fig. 5.12]. Contemporary *kera* are only 5 to 8 cm wide and have shorter fringes for tucking in. Usually of cotton or wool, these belts are embellished with metallic threads and colorful silk or acrylic yarns. The patterning techniques and motifs are adapted from those in *kushüthara*, although designs on old belts are also being copied. New designs, which women take great pride in inventing, appear regularly. While the center is often plain or sparsely decorated, each fringed end of a contemporary belt is patterned and can be worn outermost. Thus, these *kera* are reversible in a way that traditional cummerbunds with only one fringed, patterned end are not.

Bhutanese women wear their dresses over a Tibetan-style *wonju*, a loose, long-sleeved blouse of silk, polyester, or lightweight cotton. Once the dress is arranged, a woman's outfit is completed with a short, wide-sleeved jacket (*tögo*, 'upper garment'). The jacket sleeves are aligned with the blouse sleeves and folded back with them into cuffs worn a little above the

FIG. 5.12

This series of women's belts (kera) illustrates fashion changes in the present century. The wide cummerbund (far left) was made in a village in Kurtö in the late 1950s. It has conventional dimensions and fibers, but its colors show transition. The diamond and chevron pattern bands, where two colors once were used, include yellow and green wild silk yarns, colored with synthetic dyes.

In contrast, the next two belts (center) show narrower widths and shorter fringe, which reduced the bulk at a woman's waistline. The patterning still conforms to early styles, but the palette has become more complex and more pattern bands have multiple colors. In the newer belt, with a yellow ground, only a few bands are woven in red or blue alone and the patterns overall are less varied. New fibers are also incorporated in the supplementary-weft patterning of both belts. The orange belt includes wild silk (maroon, probably dyed with lac), cotton (blue, a commercial Indian yarn), and bright, imported silk yarns (green, yellow, white, and pink). The yellow belt is decorated with wool-like acrylic yarns from India and its patterning is reduced to the smallest area necessary.

The two contemporary kera at right are completely different textiles. Woven on a card loom rather than a backstrap loom, they accentuate rather than conceal a woman's waist. Because of the card loom, the belts' structure has changed; supplementary-weft yarns still decorate the textiles, but the yarns are discontinuous and patterning techniques (sapma and thrima) are also different. The red belt features elements, like the eight-pointed star, that appear on older cummerbunds, but they are arranged as large, single motifs. The purple belt is embellished with motifs adapted from kushüthara dresses and created by twining and wrapping the pattern yarns (thrima). Contemporary belts are patterned on both fringed ends, so they are reversible in a way that old-style belts with only one fringed end are not. (see Catalog)

wrist. Cuffs are 7 to 10 cm deep. Everyday jackets are a solid, often dark color, while bright, patterned silk brocade is worn on fancy occasions. Pastel-hued Thai silk jackets for everyday wear have been popularized by the elite in the early 1990s. Blouses and jackets are paired so that a brighter or lighter blouse contrasts dramatically with the jacket.

Women previously wrapped their dresses over long, sleeveless shifts or 'petticoats' (*gotsum*, 'over the head'), typically made of cotton fabric imported from India.[4] Rural women still wear shifts, while urban women are more likely to wear Western-style undergarments. To protect her dress while she goes about her daily work, a woman may wear an apron or wrap a length of fabric around her lower body. In temperate areas, this is a plain cotton cloth, an old dress, or any handy fabric (*jabté*, 'back cover'), tucked in at the waist. Striped woolen aprons (*dongkheb*, 'front cover') worn in the colder valleys of central Bhutan cover the entire front of a dress below the waist and resemble Tibetan women's aprons.

The most splendid ornaments of a Bhutanese woman are her dress fasteners, one positioned at the front of each shoulder [fig. 5.13]. These are usually round brooches (*koma*), up to 9 cm in diameter, made of silver chased with floral designs and lucky symbols. Some brooches are gilded or even made of gold and have a small turquoise in the center. Other dress fasteners are shaped like stars, thunderbolts (*dorje*), or flowers [fig. 5.14].

Fig. 5.13
Bhutanese women today fasten their wrapped dresses with round silver ornaments (koma), *one positioned at each shoulder. The brooches are usually joined by a necklace of charm-like eternal knots (as here) or other auspicious Buddhist symbols. A wheel of law appears at the middle of the necklace. This woman has added cloth straps to her dress to lengthen the garment; they would ordinarily be hidden by her jacket. Her dress is made of the woolen plaid fabric called* sethra *('predominantly gold pattern'), and its facing of polka-dotted commercial cotton is visible. She wears a traditional style of earrings [fig. 5.14]. (Punakha, D.K.M. 1985)*

A pair of dress fasteners is meant to be joined by a silver necklace (*jabtha*, 'back cord').[5] Hanging to midchest, the typical necklace is a charm-like series of eternal knots *(peyab)* or thunderbolts, joined by small silver rings. Longer, old-fashioned necklaces are made of braided silver chainwork, sometimes thicker than a finger or, in eastern Bhutan, of old silver coins from China or British India. These necklaces are usually weighted with an ornament that matches the brooches and hangs almost to the waist.

Any Bhutanese woman who can afford to do so wears a pair of matching silver bracelets of the best workmanship she can buy. The bracelets (*dobchu*) are incised with foliage, dragons, and lucky symbols, and may be dipped in gold. The finest examples are produced by the silversmiths who work for the royal family and live in Dechenchöling, just north of Thimphu. Women's silver or gold earrings (*sinchu*) resemble a leaf, flower, or teardrop inlaid with a turquoise and fastened to a ring that passes through the ear.

In the past, women went barefoot in temperate areas of the country. Sturdy pieces of leather (*thebthem*) were tied to the soles for walking long distances. Women in colder climates wore, and continue to wear, leather-soled boots *(lham)* with woolen, and now polyester, uppers. Cross-stitching and simple embroidery sometimes appear on the uppers, which are secured below the knee with handwoven garters (*lhamju*). Some of these very narrow garters are woven on a backstrap loom of bright cotton, with delicate supplementary-weft motifs. Other boot ties are striped cotton or wool woven on a card loom. Today, many Bhutanese women wear Western-style sandals, tennis shoes, or high heels.

Ordinary women all over Bhutan occasionally wear head coverings made of woven bamboo to protect them from the sun and the rain. Mostly woven in Kheng, in southern Bhutan, these hats come in various shapes and are worn by men as well. Earlier in this century, central Bhutanese village women wore stiff, woolen caps modestly trimmed with embroidery, but now they tie scarves on their heads. Women of higher status do not wear these kinds of headgear.

An essential part of a woman's outfit for special occasions is her ceremonial shoulder cloth (*rachu*, 'small cloth'; or *kabné*, 'covering,' the same term that refers to a man's shoulder cloth). The traditional *rachu* is a multipurpose textile about 90 cm by 180 to 240 cm, woven of cotton or wild silk [fig. 5.15]. Carried constantly by many Bhutanese women, it secures a child or bundle on a woman's – or her husband's – back, doubles as her pillow or cover at night when traveling, or serves, quite unceremoniously, as her head scarf when she sits in the sun. Made of one loom length, or of two identical panels joined lengthwise, the textile is always red, with supplementary-weft patterning at both fringed ends. This patterning incorporates floral and diamond motifs, auspicious swastikas, and other designs seen on women's traditional belts and on ceremonial textiles (*chagsi pangkheb*). Warp stripes and tiny, scattered floral or geometric motifs may appear in the field as well.

When visiting a dzong, a temple, or a monastery, and on formal occasions, a woman must cover her left shoulder with a *rachu*. The *rachu* is folded twice lengthwise, folded again to bring the fringed ends together, and then draped with these ends in front, hanging roughly

FIG. 5.15
On all ceremonial occasions, and in the presence of senior officials and royalty, a woman must cover her left shoulder. Shoulder cloths (rachu *or* kabné) *are predominantly red, but vary widely in style. The example at left shows how a textile* (adha rachu), *originally meant for carrying a baby, is folded several times to place on the shoulder when needed. From left to right, four other examples show how, since the 1950s, the shoulder cloth has become more and more narrow, transformed into a textile just for ceremonial use. All five styles presently coexist.* (see Catalog)

FIG. 5.14 (opposite)
Originally, women's dress fasteners (thinkhab) *were long pins. The simplest were slivers of bamboo; others were of silver or silver alloys; the most elaborate were gilt with delicate carving. Necklaces attached to the large rings were worn at a woman's back to balance the weight of the* thinkhab. *In this century, round brooches* (koma) *were added to merely decorative pins* (center) *or were paired with ornamental necklaces worn on the chest. Four examples of the latter style, which is prevalent today, are shown. At lower left are a pair of dress fasteners shaped like thunderbolts and a new strap-like style that appeared in 1993. At lower right is a woman's silver-and-gilt amulet, an ornament now saved for special occasions. Nearby are gilt earrings in a current style.*

Every woman wears bracelets, customarily a pair, of the best quality she can afford. The heavy bangles set with pale coral and turquoise (top right) *are favored by the women of Merak Sakteng in the east. Above them is a similar bracelet, worn by other eastern Bhutanese; below them is a more modest pair of chased silver bracelets common elsewhere in the country. Four bangles* (top center), *made over the past fifty years, represent the finest work of silversmiths in the employ of the royal family.* (see Catalog)

level with the wearer's waist. When speaking with senior officials and receiving blessings from a lama, a woman holds these ends in front of her mouth, the idea being that humble breath should not be exhaled toward a superior. For convenience, a woman may tuck the end of the textile that falls down her back inside her belt, but this cannot be done on formal occasions. If for some reason a Bhutanese woman does not have the required cloth when it is needed, any piece of cloth or even a length of thread may be worn instead, but any person with standing in society would want to avoid this. The shoulder cloth is an integral part of Bhutanese apparel and is always carried.

When meeting an important person, Bhutanese women bow and hold the *rachu* forward with both hands in a gesture called *kabné phushé*. The higher the person's rank, the lower the *rachu* must be presented. Royal family members are allowed to wear a *rachu* like a shawl, draped over their shoulders or arms. Old photographs show noblewomen doing so as well, but Bhutanese today have different views on whether this is proper. Commoners are permitted to drape their shoulder cloths like shawls when they are prostrating in temples or in front of important lamas and royal family members, because the cloth would otherwise slip off the shoulder. Women dancing at festivals also wear their *rachu* around both shoulders, crossed over the chest and back, and tucked into their belts, to allow more freedom of movement. At archery tournaments, women dancers supporting one team wave their *rachu* to distract the other team.

Today, many women prefer a smaller, less bulky textile as their shoulder cloth [fig. 5.15]. Contemporary *rachu* measure only 15 to 30 cm wide by 180 cm long, a modified size that is more convenient for women working in government offices. This style has developed since the 1970s just for ceremonial wear. These new shoulder cloths, often of tightly woven silk or cotton, display modern as well as traditional patterns in gay silk, acrylic, and metallic yarns. In the past few years, *rachu* made of Chinese silk embellished (by men) with embroidery sometimes have been worn. Red silk *rachu* were made, for example, for the queens to wear at the public celebration of the royal wedding in 1988.

The color of a woman's shoulder cloth and the method of folding it do not change according to rank as they do for men. This is very likely because of the historical predominance of men in ecclesiastic and state positions. While women are quite visible in the private sector today, only two women in government have been promoted to the rank of *dasho* ('excellent one'), and they wear the same type of shoulder cloth as other women, as do women of the royal family who have served as ministers. It will be interesting to see whether, with the promotion of more women in government, the style and color of shoulder cloths evolve to reflect rank.

The wrapped dress *(kira)* worn by most Bhutanese women is an old style in the country and surrounding regions. Bhutanese oral traditions, eighteenth-century sketches of Bhutan by a British visitor, photographs from the early twentieth century, and surviving textiles tend to confirm that the garment has existed in some parts of Bhutan for many centuries. Bhutanese believe the wrapped dress is an indigenous style. The earliest depictions of Bhutanese women, in drawings by a British emissary in the 1770s, show them garbed in what appear to be *kira*. The first written description occurs in a British journal of 1837-38, which notes that women wore a loose garment similar to that of "Hill tribes to the Eastward of Assam" (Griffiths, in *Political Missions* 1865, 166-67). Early dresses were constructed in the same way as they are now, but often had slightly smaller dimensions because they were worn shorter. Family photographs show girls even from higher-status families with their dresses above the ankles, a style seen today only in rural areas. Dresses also had much longer fringe – on some examples made as late as the 1940s, the fringe is 10 cm long, while now it should not exceed 3 cm. Moreover, a century ago women (and men) wore more than one garment at a time, regardless of the season. This custom, preserved in the countryside and among older people, attested to the affluence of the wearer. Layered clothing also helped provide warmth in winter and served as bedding while traveling.

Another evolution that has occurred over the past 100 years is the nearly universal adoption of Tibetan-style blouses and the disappearance of the custom of wearing two jackets. Photographs from the early 1900s portray women wearing cuffs formed by an inner jacket or jacket lining rather than a blouse [fig. 5.4]. The inner jacket or lining was white cotton or wild silk, and the cuffs were much wider than now, positioned at the wrist rather than above it. Ordinary outer jackets were plain, dark cotton or wool, or black velvet, which is no longer in vogue. Fancy silk brocades with white cuff pieces were worn by the well-to-do or saved for special occasions, as they are today. Jackets were cut differently, with deeper dolman-style sleeves that began just above the waist and were often fully lined. Blouses are said by Bhutanese to have been adopted by the aristocracy of central Bhutan in the course of its contacts with the Tibetan nobility around the turn of this century, and then to have spread gradually to the general population. As blouses replaced the inner jacket, jackets

FIG. 5.16

Dress fasteners shaped like long needles with rings on the upper ends, and joined by a necklace worn at the back, are now old-fashioned. They are seen only rarely, on older women garbed in multiple, layered garments or in regions where thick woolen dresses, like the one seen here, are worn. This young woman was photographed in northern Bumthang (central Bhutan). Her dress is the pattern called tarichem, *'with tiger stripes,' unusually decorated with scattered supplementary-weft motifs showing crossed thunderbolts and flowers. She is wearing typical earrings and a woven-bamboo hat from Kheng in southern Bhutan. (D.K.M. 1987)*

were not cut as wide and narrower sleeves were introduced. White wild silk jackets remained popular until the early 1970s, were considered old-fashioned, if classic, for more than fifteen years, and then began returning to style in the late 1980s.

Major changes have taken place in women's ornaments, which in 1837-38 consisted of:

> a plate of silver fastened round the head ... , wire earrings of large dimensions, and peculiar rings fastened to a straight silver wire and worn projecting beyond the shoulder. [Women] appear to be fond of flowers and frequently decorate themselves with garlands, particularly of the scarlet rhododendron and the weeping willow (Griffiths, in *Political Missions* 1865, 166-67).

Silver headbands *(rumnang)*, worn on the forehead and made of fine chainwork with a prominent turquoise stud, are said by eastern Bhutanese to date back to the days before women converted to Buddhism and began to crop their hair short. These circlets are still kept by families in eastern and central Bhutan and worn for annual rituals when women don archaic tunics representing the everyday dress of long ago [fig. 5.29]. While it is desirable to have a traditional headband for use on these occasions, a wreath of artemisia may be substituted instead. The large wire earrings have vanished.[6]

The "straight silver wires" are a type of dress fastener that endured well into this century. Instead of relatively small round brooches at each shoulder, women wore a pair of sharp, needle-like pins, 10 to 30 cm long *(thinkhab, 'holding needle')* [fig. 5.14]. These could be made of silver, sometimes finely carved and gilded, or improvised from a sliver of wood. This style is of some age; oral traditions in Thimphu recall how, in the 1600s, a woman plunged one of her pins into a rock to release a famous local spring.[7] Large silver *thinkhab* (pins) could be quite heavy and tended to fall forward, so they were attached by rings to one or more braided silver chains worn around the back of the neck *(jabtha)*.

By the 1930s, a less cumbersome dress fastener was being worn as an alternative to the pins. Although still shaped like a needle with a ring on the upper end, this ornament *(khab-thinkhab)* had a round brooch at the lower end that actually fastened the dress. Shortly thereafter, possibly during the 1940s when wartime silver and gold prices shot up, the smaller brooches *(koma)* became standard. This development coincided with the trend toward wearing just one garment, rather than multiple dresses *(kira)* that required a long pin to fasten together. Today old-style pins are rarely seen except in regions where thick woolen dresses are worn or occasionally on a village woman [fig. 5.16].

In 1993, another style of dress fastener appeared. About 10 cm long, it consists of three round, chased silver ornaments, each one smaller than a traditional *koma*. The center roundel is decorative, while a sharp hasp on each of the other roundels secures the dress. Each fastener is thus like a "strap" at the shoulder, with a joining necklace optional. Bhutanese women like these new brooches because they are light and comfortable, and because the front of their dresses can be worn lower, which is fashionable at present.

According to their wealth, women wear various decorative necklaces. In the past, these included amulet boxes *(gau)* made of silver and gold inlaid with turquoise; multiple strands of coral; and thick silver ropes supporting a wire strung with *zi* (black agates with white patterns, which are highly prized). Today, well-to-do urban and rural woman wear fewer necklaces, even on special occasions, and these are likely to be more delicate. Women often have necklace stones restrung to keep up with jewelry fashions, and they add more stones and silver and gold ornaments to them when they can.

Finely worked boots *(lham)*, worn by elite women earlier in this century, seem to have been inspired by Tibetan styles. Much plainer but similar boots are worn in cold regions of Bhutan. Ashi Phuntsok Chöden, senior queen of the second king, and her sisters-in-law were photographed in decorated boots [fig. 6.7], and, on another occasion, in white tennis shoes in the 1930s.[8] The tennis shoes could have been purchased in India during royal visits that began in 1911 or brought to the queen and her family as gifts by British visitors. While men of rank continue to wear decorated boots on formal occasions, women prefer Western shoes.

A late-nineteenth-century fresco at Tamshing in central Bhutan shows a female patron of the temple in typical period dress for the well-to-do. She wears a *kushüthara* ('brocaded wrapped dress') fastened with long pins, a striped apron in central Bhutanese fashion, a blue jacket with tiny gold patterns, and handsome red-and-white boots resembling those worn by court women in photographs of the 1930s. A detail of the woman's outfit that points to change is her red shoulder cloth, which has gold flowers on it but shows no stripes. In the twentieth century, warp-striped shoulder cloths with tiny supplementary-weft designs have been prevalent, but this painting and some examples of the period illustrate different styles. The color red is unchanging, but sometimes the warp stripes are absent, or so fine as to be hardly visible, or clustered toward the middle of the textile. Patterning at the fringed ends of some older shoulder cloths includes animal and human figures now considered inappropriate for clothing.

A final significant innovation of the early 1990s is the "half-*kira*." This garment of machine-loomed fabric is cut and stitched to resemble the lower part of a wrapped dress, but is actually a skirt that fastens at the waist. With the half-*kira*, a woman may wear a Western-style pullover sweater or T-shirt, or the customary blouse and jacket, pinned closed in front. This outfit successfully creates the illusion of a traditional dress, but frees women from wearing a confining belt and sharp brooches and from having to retighten the belt and adjust the length and side folds of a dress at intervals during the day. Half-*kira* are acceptable attire for Thimphu women at home, but are not suitable for the office, social occasions, or even running errands in town.

Tunics

Women's garments that are very different from the wrapped dress, and rarely seen today, are the distinctive, archaic tunics from north central and eastern Bhutan. Examples survive in a number of villages from Bumthang to the eastern border, but the garments are especially identified with Kurtö in northern Lhuntshi District, Tashiyangtse District, and Bumthang District. There are two kinds of tunics, both of which natives of these regions say are old-fashioned apparel; they call them 'long-ago petticoats' *(delemé shingkha)* or 'old women's dresses' *(ganmo atsa,* for cotton or nettle tunics). Beyond the immediate area, some eastern Bhutanese recognize the style or know the tunics by names synonymous with 'petticoat,' meaning any garment that, like a woman's undergarment, slips over the head. Farther away, people do not recognize the tunics and even say they are not Bhutanese. Most tunics preserved in temples and villages, and in collections outside Bhutan, appear to be of considerable age.[9]

The *kushung* tunic is composed of two panels of unbleached cotton or nettle cloth joined in the warp direction and oriented vertically in the finished garment [figs. 5.17, 5.19, 5.20]. A neckhole is left in the center seam, and the edges of this slit are sometimes turned back and hemmed. The joined panels are folded over at the shoulder line before being stitched together along the outer selvedges, leaving armholes. Woven tunics are embellished with

Fig. 5.17
Supplementary-weft-patterned tunics (kushung) are an archaic woman's dress style from Kurtö in northern Lhuntshi District, now worn only for special rituals and used to attire ancestor figures in local temples. They are made from two loom lengths joined in the warp direction, folded over at the shoulder, and stitched at the sides, leaving neck- and armholes. Their patterning (kushü) is characteristic of the region and also seen on other textiles such as women's wrapped dresses (kushüthara). The horizontal patterning at the garments' hem includes unusual raised pattern bands not found in other Bhutanese textiles. Neck openings are sometimes decorated, as this example shows, with appliqué and tassels of cut cotton, woolen, and silk cloth and with embroidery.

The intricacy of the wild silk patterning on this cotton tunic is exceptional. The field of the garment is filled with delicate motifs; to the left of the middle seam, the first row below the shoulder shows what Bhutanese call sculpted butter offerings (torma) with flames issuing from them. The second row consists of diamonds formed of many crossed thunderbolts (dorje). Successive rows below that show variations on this thunderbolt motif that represent charm boxes or amulets. Tiny, flowering trees descend along the left edge of the tunic. Just above the hem patterning are images of a three-tiered building [fig. 5.18], said to represent Zangtopelri, the paradisiacal palace of Padmasambhava, the saint who introduced Buddhism to Bhutan in the eighth century. (see Catalog)

the supplementary-weft patterning characteristic of other textiles from the region, notably wrapped women's dresses (*kushüthara*). Designs are arranged so they spill down the front and back of the garment from an axis of symmetry that is usually along the shoulders. Very narrow warp stripes (*reth*) at intervals in the field helped the weaver to position individual motifs. The neck opening may be plain or ornamented with appliqué, couching, embroidery, and ribbons. In ceremonies today, the dress is worn both belted and unbelted.

Designs on most *kushung* tunics are taken from the same inventory as those on *kushüthara* dresses, but often include human and animal figures like those occurring on earlier women's dresses, belts, and shoulder cloths [cf. figs. 2.20, 5.21]. The handful of known nettle-cloth tunics are simply patterned with swastikas, diamonds, animals, and geometric designs. Many cotton tunics also are modestly decorated and show extensive wear, consistent with their former use as ordinary dress [fig. 5.19]. Other *kushung* tunics have such elaborate decoration that they would have been too costly for daily wear [figs. 5.17, 5.20].

A long warp fringe is retained along the tunic's lower edge, which is bordered with continuous supplementary-weft patterning. This border, which is sometimes 45 cm deep, has unusual, raised pattern bands (*taksing thrima, khodang*) formed by multiple supplementary wefts of dyed wool or undyed nettle fiber. A raised effect is achieved when several of these yarns, which are slightly thicker than the ground wefts, are used in a given shed. Patterns are created by passing the varicolored supplementary wefts over and under warp yarns at staggered intervals; individual pattern wefts within a single shed often show these differing float spans. This type of patterning is not found in any other known Bhutanese textile.

The long fringe on *kushung* tunics, which older Bhutanese say kept flies away while women were working in the fields, links the garments to other, and earlier, styles in the region. In Sherdukpen communities in adjacent Arunachal Pradesh, leggings are worn for the same purpose, and the ends of woven shoulder cloths, jackets, and belts are finished with a long fringe (Sharma 1961, 19). Untailored garments formerly worn by the Lepchas who once lived in Bhutan and Sikkim also have very long warp fringes at each end. Women's dresses from the same areas of north central and eastern Bhutan where tunics are found were formerly finished with up to 15 cm of warp fringe.

Political events apparently caused the indigenous *kushung* tunics of north central Bhutan to be abandoned as everyday wear and influenced the development of a new style of woman's dress. The new style was the *kushüthara*, which is the standard, rectangular, wrapped dress (*kira*) decorated with *kushü*, the supplementary-weft patterning used on *kushung* tunics. This transition, like the adoption of robes as men's national dress, paralleled the region's religious and political incorporation into the emergent Buddhist nation of Bhutan, a process that began under Shabdrung Ngawang Namgyel in the seventeenth century and accelerated in the eighteenth century. The similarity between the terms *kushung* and *kushü*, and between the patterning seen on these garments and other textiles from Kurtö,

FIG. 5.18
This detail of a nineteenth-century tunic from north central Bhutan shows the distinctive techniques of supplementary-weft patterning developed by weavers in Kurtö. The image of a temple is created by the technique called thrima, *where pattern yarns are interworked with each other and twined around warp yarns so that the resulting design is raised above the ground cloth, like chain-stitch embroidery. The birds and trees are created by* sapma, *where pattern yarns are laid in with ground wefts and appear to lie flat on the surface of the cloth. Wild silk pattern wefts are not visible at all on the reverse side of the tight, warp-faced ground weave.*

In some of the horizontal pattern bands below the temple, a raised effect is achieved by using as many as eight fine pattern wefts in successive, single

FIG. 5.19

Several features of this tunic support the belief in northeastern Bhutan that some of these garments were once ordinary women's dress. Its design is less ornate, consistent with a garment worn every day. Most of the patterning is created with sapma, *rather than with the more complex technique of* thrima *[see fig. 5.18].*

A notable feature of this kushung *tunic is its appliqué neck finishing. Pieced triangles of silk (locally called 'rats' teeth') outline the colored panels of woolen cloth, and clusters of silk cloth ribbons are attached nearby. This finishing obscures portions of the decorated fabric underneath, suggesting it was added some time after the garment was woven. Appliqué and ribbon work may, therefore, be associated with the tunics' conversion to ritual wear, probably in the nineteenth century.* (see Catalog)

FIG. 5.20

*This elegant tunic features animal motifs that characterize earlier decorative styles in central and eastern Bhutan. To either side of the neck are tiny figures on horseback; above the hem are horses with sculpted butter offerings (*torma*) on their backs; and long-tailed birds appear throughout. In contemporary Bhutanese textiles, similar motifs are seen only on the jackets worn by women in Merak Sakteng [fig. 2.2].*

Like the tunic in fig. 5.17, this tunic shows designs that resemble shoulder cloths to each side of the neckhole [see fig. 5.21]. The two panels of the garment are somewhat lacking in symmetry, but the diamond-shaped motifs are intricate and the neck ornamentation is outstanding. (see Catalog)

sheds. In bands showing several colors, the colored yarns are usually wool and the undyed (white) yarns are bast fiber. (see Catalog)

points to a pivotal, early connection between the two.

Most, if not all, cotton and nettle-cloth tunics were made in Kurtö villages still famed for weaving similarly decorated wraparound dresses *(kushüthara)*. Older natives recall hearing that *kushung* tunics were worn occasionally as ordinary dress in their grandparents' time (mid-nineteenth century). The derivation of the word *kushung* is unknown, but local people link it to *kushü*, the name of the patterning technique identified with Kurtö. There is also a strong identification with nettle fiber (locally, *ki* or *kui*) and tunics (also called *kishung, kibu, kigu,* or *kigo,* the latter meaning 'nettle garment'). Bhutanese say the earliest tunics were often made of nettle and rarely patterned but that few examples survive because they were converted to other uses when worn out. Although the majority of surviving *kushung* are woven of cotton, local people also hasten to point out that wrapped women's dresses *(kushüthara)* are never made of nettle.

The influence of the Drukpa state seems to have triggered, or at least hastened, the change from tunics to wraparound garments, which already were worn in western Bhutan and much of the east. In eastern Bhutan, the simplest, plainweave wrapped dresses are known as *thara* (Tshangla), which refers to their pattern [fig. 2.7] but is also the local equivalent of *kira* (Dzongkha). *Thara* show broad bands of warp striping at the upper and lower edges of the garment and narrower warp stripes in the field; that is, these textiles exhibit the colorful ground weave of *kushüthara* but lack supplementary-weft patterns. Women in Kurtö apparently adopted these wrapped dresses alongside their own tunics at some point and began to embellish them. Numerous dresses show warp-striped fields with supplementary-weft patterning only at the fringed ends [fig. 5.22]; others, even relatively recently woven, have sparse field designs [fig. 5.23]. These examples illustrate the local transformation of the striped, eastern Bhutanese wrapped dress *(thara)* through application of patterning *(kushü)* used on Kurtö tunics and other textiles. The relationship between the *kushung* tunic and *kushüthara* dress is also obvious in the arrangement of patterns on each textile. The singular end borders of a wraparound dress, for example, preserve the traditional hem patterns of a tunic, but along the sides, rather than the lower edge, of the garment. By the mid-nineteenth century, a regional sense of identity with the nation, and the local nobility's influential role in national affairs, seem to have led to the disappearance of the everyday tunic in favor of the new, majority style.

There is every reason to believe that weaving in Kurtö was flourishing when the first influences of the new Drukpa state were felt in the seventeenth century – and that local noblewomen commissioned more and more elaborately decorated wrapped dresses *(kushüthara)*, until these became a distinctive regional fashion. The nobility's fondness for excellence in weaving certainly encouraged the elegant detail in some relatively late tunics [figs. 5.17, 5.20], and the nobility no doubt welcomed an expansion of the fabric area treated in this manner: the fully patterned *kushüthara*. Even now, elite tastes favor densely embellished textiles that demonstrate weavers' skill in executing delicate designs.

Elite households were responsible for preserving old *kushung* tunics and also for producing exquisite new tunics – which continued to be used, as they are today, in local rituals observed long before the advent of the Drukpa school of Mahayana Buddhism.

FIG. 5.21
This detail of the tunic in fig. 5.20 shows a section of patterning on the left shoulder. The rectangular panels that resemble stylized shoulder cloths are seen clearly. The diamond-shaped motif at lower center shows the edging known as 'fly's wings,' formed by supplementary wefts laid in with the ground wefts (sapma), while the diagonals inside the motif are formed by thrima (wrapping and twining). The smaller, off-center motif above it is edged with 'rooster's combs.' The identical half-diamonds to either side, facing one another, represent fruit trees. (see Catalog)

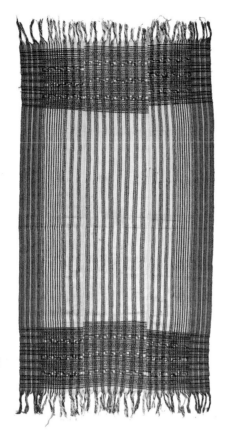

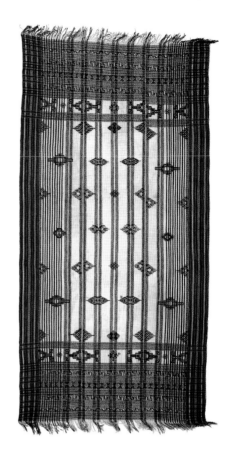

FIGS. 5.22-25

These examples show the relationship between the striped, eastern Bhutanese wrapped dress (thara) *[fig. 2.7] and the supplementary-weft patterned dresses* (kushüthara) *that developed in north central Bhutan (Kurtö). Sometime between the seventeenth and nineteenth centuries, as tunics became old-fashioned and wrapped dresses more prevalent, Kurtö weavers began embellishing the new garments with the same type of patterning seen on* kushung *tunics. This new style was quickly copied and interpreted by weavers throughout central and eastern Bhutan. Some dresses show the traditional striped ground with only end borders added in the Kurtö style (upper left). Other dresses are adorned with diamond-shaped motifs across some, or all, of the field.*

The end borders of these four dresses exhibit similar, odd-numbered pattern bands. Alternating pattern bands show diamonds and chevrons, and a swastika meander. Ordinary dresses generally have seven pattern bands, whereas more intricate examples show nine or eleven. Sometimes, the diamonds and chevrons are transformed into colored triangles, a patchwork design that invokes the blessing of long life. Because women's dresses are woven as three separate loom lengths, it is difficult to match precisely where the end borders begin when the panels are stitched together (upper left). Alignments that are perfect, or nearly so, are highly valued by Bhutanese. (see Catalog)

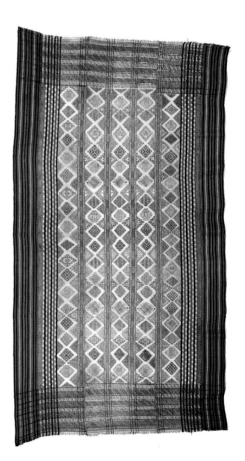

Appliqué at the neck of a *kushung* tunic usually covers patterning woven into the cloth, suggesting that the addition of the appliqué may have signaled the garment's conversion to strictly ritual wear. Further, a number of finely decorated cotton tunics with appliqué at the neck have very small armholes, perhaps because those examples were made later, specially for young girls to wear in rituals, whereas armholes on nettle-cloth and cotton tunics without appliqué are often much larger, which would be consistent with their original use as everyday dress.

Animal and human figures seen on *kushung* tunics exemplify earlier decorative styles in north central and eastern Bhutan. Although Bhutanese admire the artistry of the motifs, most people today consider such images inappropriate for use on clothing [fig. 5.26], and almost the only currently made textiles that show similar designs are jackets worn by women in Merak Sakteng farther east [fig. 2.2]. The appearance in tunics of Buddhist motifs such as reliquaries, temples, and horses carrying flaming gems is more difficult to explain. Motifs that seem not to have been used on secular textiles elsewhere in Bhutan may have been incorporated in Kurtö tunics for several reasons. Local patterning techniques can achieve unusually intricate detail, pictorial figures were already part of the Kurtö design inventory, and native weaving was dynamic when Drukpa influence reached the area. The decoration of lay garments with Buddhist motifs, therefore, may be no more than a very lively – if in a contemporary Bhutanese context, unconventional – local expression of this meeting of two vital traditions.

More recent political events also help explain why the *kushung* remains a little-known regional garment while the *kushüthara* is popular throughout Bhutan. During the second half of the nineteenth century, the influence of Kurtö nobility extended mainly to Bumthang and neighboring regions. When one nobleman acquired new national status as Bhutan's monarch in 1907, the *kushüthara* was well established as the regional fashion and was soon elevated as the most prestigious style of woman's wraparound dress. The earlier *kushung* tunics were packed away by this time and never gained national visibility.

The woolen tunic known as *shingkha* [figs. 5.27, 5.28] is constructed differently from a cotton or nettle tunic, and its origins are more obscure. In Bumthang, the garment is usually described rather fancifully as an 'angel's dress' (*kandomé atsa*), while a cotton or nettle tunic is called an 'old woman's dress' (*ganmo atsa*). This distinction reflects the woolen tunic's exclusive use in ritual in recent memory, in contrast to the fading recollections of cotton and nettle tunics as everyday wear. Made of local or Tibetan twill or imported broadcloth, the woolen tunic has seams at the shoulders and sides, and always features appliqué and ribbon work (locally called 'rat's teeth') around the neck opening, whereas such trim is optional on *kushung* tunics. The garment also has elaborate inserts at each side seam that taper to a point under the armholes. Colorful silk ribbons are often attached to these panels, which show geometric designs and animals, cut and pieced from little bits of Chinese silk, English broadcloth, and local fabric. When worn, the woolen tunic (*shingkha*) is arranged so the appliqué panels hang along the thighs, and then is secured tightly with an ordinary woman's belt [fig. 5.29]. Silver chainwork headbands (*rumnang*), associated with the days before Buddhism reached the area, are worn with the tunic.

FIG. 5.26

Textiles other than tunics also show animal and human figures, as well as special Buddhist symbols and ritual objects that most Bhutanese now consider inappropriate for use on garments. This detail of a mid-twentieth-century weaving shows numerous imaginative figures: horses with manes and tails, horned mountain goats, deer, several kinds of birds, a monkey in a tree, a little girl in a dress, a man holding two birds, and others. The Buddhist images include a stupa or reliquary (upper left, in yellow), butter lamps (for example, to the right of the stupa, also in yellow), differently shaped vases, conch shells (both among the eight lucky symbols), ritual bells, and pairs of pointed elephant tusks (a precious offering). Although the textile looks like a kira, Bhutanese say that because of the Buddhist stupa on it, it would never have been worn as a dress and was probably made to offer to a temple for use as a canopy. (see Catalog)

FIG. 5.27

Woolen tunics with appliqué patterning (shingkha), *from the same area of north central Bhutan as cotton tunics, are known only as ritual textiles. The style may be related to different tunics (also called* shingkha) *worn by the women of Merak Sakteng and by groups farther east in remote areas of Arunachal Pradesh and Tibet. Sometimes made of fabric that was imported from Tibet or woolen broadcloth from British India, the Bhutanese garments have splendid appliqué panels at the neck and in two tapering insets under the armholes. Pieced together of Chinese silk, British broadcloth, and local fabrics, the appliqué is decorated with silk ribbons. Shingkha are always made of blue or red woolen cloth.*

This tunic, called a ngaushingkha *because it is blue, has four appliqué shoulder panels showing curvilinear foliage. The colors of the appliqué are inverted on either side of the neck slit. The panels are outlined by rows of tiny triangles of pieced silk. Below the neck are a row of chevrons and a 'Chinese wall' meander* (janachari). *The inset panels at the sides show a standard arrangement of horizontal compartments. The uppermost, tapering section usually contains geometric figures, as in this example, and is symmetrical in color on both sides. The compartments lower down have the same style as the neck ornamentation and the same inverted colors, showing rows of lotus flowers, rows of stylized flaming gems on top of another 'Chinese wall,' and swastika meanders. The panels at the lower edge of the garment are striped, Tibetan cloth known as* hothra, *covering areas of appliqué that have deteriorated. (see Catalog)*

FIG. 5.28

This red tunic (leushingkha) *shows a different style of neck ornamentation, but is otherwise very similar to fig. 5.27. The two appliqué panels flanking the neck slit contain rows of trefoil shapes – the same silhouettes as are seen in the cloud collars worn by monks performing sacred dances [fig. 6.5], and known from China through Central Asia. Another row of trefoils appears below the neck slit. The outer neck panels are decorated with rows of stylized flaming gems. The rows of triangular silk piecework outlining the appliqué areas are clearly seen here. Designs throughout the garment are couched with tightly twisted, white wool yarn.*

The tapered panels at the sides have six compartments. The first section under the arms contains a geometric figure, here a simple oblong; the next, three flaming gems whose round contours are emphasized by couching; then, a lotus blossom, a flowering branch, a graceful deer in flight, and an auspicious swastika. (see Catalog)

Like the *kushung* tunic, the woolen *shingkha* points to ancient links among the peoples of north central and eastern Bhutan, the inhabitants of adjacent areas in Tibet, and communities to the east in Arunachal Pradesh. Bhutanese woolen tunics, said still to be made occasionally in Kurtö, closely resemble belted tunics *(goshub)* worn by women in Kongpo and Pemakö (southeast Tibet), whose languages are related to those spoken in central and eastern Bhutan. *Shingkha* is also the name of another belted tunic, worn by the women of Merak Sakteng, the high-altitude region of Tashigang District on Bhutan's eastern border. This dress, generally of maroon wild silk with blue-and-white warp stripes, is shared by some communities in Tawang (Arunachal Pradesh), where it is likewise called *shingkha*.[10] The terms for woolen tunics – *ngaushingkha*, when made of blue woolen cloth, and *leushingkha*, when of red fabric – may one day offer clues to the garments' origins. The form *ngau* is similar to words for blue in the major language of Kurtö, while *leu* (red) is unique to the language (Dzalakha) of the most important weaving villages there. The same language is spoken in Tashiyangtse

FIG. 5.29

Woolen and cotton tunics have a role in festivals that reaffirm the relationship between communities in north central Bhutan (Kurtö) and the mountain deity who is the locality's chief spirit. These rites are very old and have aspects that are distinctly not Buddhist. This photograph shows one such ceremony, where the women are wearing woolen tunics and silver headbands said to be the dress of long ago. The men are garbed in contemporary robes, but wear silver amulets, tubes of cloth around their heads, and colored scarves and jackets that transform them into soldiers of the seventeenth century. For three days, women and men from important families in the community dance to appease the mountain deity. Woolen tunics are essential for a woman to participate, so the garments have been handed down from mother to daughter for many generations. (Rawabi Gompa, photographer unknown 1983)

District, just to the east. Whether the term *leu* is found farther east or north, in Arunachal Pradesh or in Tibet, is unknown. The strong regional association between tunic-style dress and the word *shingkha*, however, supports other linguistic evidence suggesting that some peoples of Bhutan, Arunachal Pradesh, and nearby Tibet had a common origin (see Chapter Two).[11]

Bhutanese tunics – both *kushung* and *shingkha* – are preserved in ways that indicate their deep significance to the communities where they survive and to the families that own the garments. In many villages of north central and eastern Bhutan, local temples contain statues of a man and a woman who represent ancestral figures. Often one or both figures are garbed in clothing made of nettle fiber, and the woman sometimes wears a tunic instead of a wraparound dress. Offerings are made to these figures during annual festivals.[12] In the same region, families owning tunics keep them most of the year in the 'treasure box' *(yanggam)* that contains objects representing the family's prosperity. If it is made of cotton or nettle fiber, the tunic is taken out for annual household rituals to ensure good luck and long life, during which it is blessed, along with token food and jewelry; a circle of grain is drawn around the garment-offering, but it is not worn at this time.

The most important use of both tunics is in festivals *(pcha)* celebrated in a dozen villages in Kurtö.[13] These ceremonies reflect and reinforce relationships within the community and between the community and the chief spirit of the locality. Their origin is explained as follows: When Padmasambhava, the saint who introduced Buddhism to Bhutan in the eighth century, was constructing Samye Monastery in Tibet, his work was plagued by a spirit who repeatedly tore down at night what had been built by day. To distract and appeal to this demon-god, Padmasambhava danced, a tactic by which he succeeded in winning over the demon to assist in building the monastery. In return for this cooperation, Padmasambhava promised the deity that Buddhist believers would regularly perform these dances to honor local spirits. These dance rituals survive to this day in parts of Bhutan, and failure to perform them is said to result in hailstorms and other catastrophes.

While details vary from site to site, elements of the festival in Tangmachu village illustrate how the tunics, and other unusual dress, figure in them and aspects of the rites that are distinctly non-Buddhist.[14] The ceremony revolves around the spirit of the local god, who descends from the mountain to be with the villagers at this time. He is represented by a man from one of the local noble families. Both the "god" and villagers who dance for him wear clothing that local people point out is not their everyday dress. The god wears yak hair pants and a red-and-white shirt, which he weaves and stitches himself. The girls who dance wear woolen tunics, while the men who dance with them dress as "warriors in the Shabdrung's time." The men twist two women's belts around their heads, put on short jackets over their robes, and tie bright lengths of cloth across their chests [fig. 5.29].

Participants in this celebration observe special rituals other than their dress. During the two weeks preceding and during this celebration, no villager tends the Buddhist altar in his or her home. Unusual food taboos are observed. As the villagers go to meet the god coming from the mountain, a bird and a fish are taken along as offerings. Villagers point out that these requirements, like the man who represents the god weaving his own clothes, are contrary to the ordinary routines of twentieth-century Bhutanese life.

Ownership of a tunic is a sign of a family's status in the village and enables the family to play a role in these annual ceremonies that maintain the community's relationship with the powerful local spirit. As one man said, laughing, the "girls" offered to the local god can actually be old women – but they must wear their family's tunic. In this village, only noble families are permitted to have and wear these garments, which are always inherited by a daughter from her mother. Those of lower status cannot touch the garments.

All the woolen tunics preserved in Tangmachu are said to have been passed down for at least five generations (between 100 and 150 years). Villagers say new tunics can be made, even though this has not been done recently. In Tangmachu, one must seek the mountain god's permission to make a tunic by seeking approval from the villager who represents the god. In a trance, the villager-god then addresses the mountain and gives an answer by throwing a food basket *(bangchung)* out of a window: if it lands right side up, the garment can be made.

In Bumthang, *shingkha* are preserved in the homes of families who originally came from Kurtö, but the ceremonies in which they figure have been modified and their importance in ritual is diminishing. Some Bhutanese in this area explain that woolen tunics were worn, especially on the first day of a festival, because their colors – a rich red or dark blue – are pleasing to the mountain god. On subsequent days, people say lighter-colored dress – traditionally a cotton tunic – may be worn because only lesser spirits are present. Many tunics have suffered from poor storage or reached the collectors' market of Kathmandu, so nowadays the *kushung, kushüthara,* or even ordinary women's dresses are worn instead of the once mandatory woolen tunic.

In the village of Ura, the central figure of the ceremony where tunics are worn is identified as the 'lord of death' *(chögi gyep)* who judges souls. On the first day, he takes the form of a demon; on the second, that of a man; and on the third, that of a lama. The five "goddesses" who offer themselves to him by performing dances formerly wore *shingkha* tunics, but now do so only on the last day. The association of woolen tunics with Kurtö through the nobility who migrated to Bumthang is clear to many people in Ura.[15]

Cotton and nettle tunics *(kushung)* are occasionally integrated into Buddhist festivals in Bumthang. In Buli (Chumé Valley), a *kushung* tunic kept in the temple is worn annually by a joker, played by a man sporting a woman's mask who shakes a stick hung with bells at the spectators and cavorts to amuse them. In Ngang Lhakhang (upper Chökhor Valley), the same joker, in a tunic and black wooden mask, parodies an important Buddhist goddess. These examples demonstrate not only how fundamentally the tunics are identified with women but also how the garments symbolize anomaly when they are used in contexts other than those that explicitly recall a non-Buddhist past.

Women of Ethnic Minorities
Although most Bhutanese women today wear the wrapped garment *(kira)* and accessories described above, Bhutan's ethnic diversity is expressed in the distinctive dress of several groups. Women in the remote herding communities of Laya in the northwest wear blouses and woolen gowns secured with a woven belt [fig. 2.10]. For warmth, a striped blanket is wrapped around the lower body and held in place by the same belt. Over their dress, these women wear a long-sleeved, knee-length coat, and turn its sleeves back into cuffs with the sleeves of the blouse. The coat is stitched of narrow panels of plain and patterned woolen fabric, often from Tibet. Some women prefer a waist-length, black wool jacket. Women's

FIG. 5.30
Like this mother and her daughter, many southern Bhutanese of Nepalese ethnic origins have adopted the national style of wrapped dress (kira). *The little girl's forehead ornament and her mother's gold earrings and nose ornament, like the Indian-influenced custom of wearing a shawl, are southern Bhutanese. The woman's dress is made from machine-woven Indian fabric that imitates a Bhutanese pattern called* möntha. *(D.K.M. 1994)*

knee boots are black and green or blue felted wool with hide soles, in the Tibetan style. Their conical bamboo hats are obtained through trade from Kheng in southern Bhutan. Laya women are famous for wearing heavy necklaces of coral, turquoise, and *zi* (black-and-white agate), and sometimes they pin their coats with the silver brooches used to fasten *kira*.

The dress of women in Merak Sakteng in the east is of special interest because it preserves stylistic elements once more widely seen in Bhutan [fig. 2.1]. The basic garment of these semi-nomadic herders is a sleeveless, knee-length tunic (*shingkha*). Made of wild silk, the dress is either plain white or red with white-and-blue or -black warp stripes, oriented vertically; sometimes two tunics are worn together. No other Bhutanese wear tunics as ordinary dress today. As was earlier true elsewhere in Bhutan, Merak Sakteng women wear multiple garments for warmth and as a sign of status. Over the tunic, they have a pair of hip-length jackets made of cotton or wild silk, different in cut, color, and patterning from the jacket worn with a *kira*. One jacket (*töthung*), generally worn outermost, shows a standard pattern of animal figures on a red ground [fig. 2.2]. The other handloomed jacket is white without decoration, a style that is now less fashionable in the rest of Bhutan. In winter, women wear a black wool jacket trimmed with bright piping. The maroon woolen shawl (*themba*) covering a woman's upper back fastens in front with woolen or leather laces.

A Merak Sakteng woman wears a black woolen cloth (*tenga kema*) like an apron in back, secured by the belt that cinches her dress. A round black cushion (*kobtin*), about 15 cm in diameter and made of thick, felted yak hair, dangles from a woolen tie in back and serves as a pad to sit on. Felted-wool knee boots (*bidar*), a woven belt (*kichin*), and a felted yak hair hat (*shamu*) complete a woman's outfit. On one hip, women like to wear a penknife, hanging on a chain of silver coins. Cowrie shells and small bells on leather tassels and a leather coin purse are sometimes suspended beside it. Necklaces and earrings of silver, coral, *zi*, and turquoise are favorite ornaments. Heavy silver bracelets, studded with semiprecious stones, are characteristic. It is also fashionable for women to stick bits of colored adhesive on their temples and below their cheekbones.[16]

In southern Bhutan among women of Nepalese descent, customary dress has been influenced by Nepalese and Indian styles and uses cloth imported from India, rather than handloomed in Bhutan. Some women favor an Indian sari, while others prefer a generous length of fabric arranged around the lower body with pleats in front (*phariya*), a shorter wrapped cloth (*lungi*), or even a sari whose outer end is tucked in at the waist rather than worn over the chest and shoulder. With these wrapped lower garments, women wear the short-sleeved, close-fitting blouse (*cholo*) associated with a sari, or a long-sleeved garment that crosses over the chest and ties at the shoulder and waist (*chaubundi cholo*). Cardigan sweaters and T-shirts are also popular. Many southern Bhutanese women have adopted the *kira* (wrapped dress) [fig. 5.30].

Western-style dress has been a status symbol among Bhutanese women during the twentieth century, from the white tennis shoes worn by court women in the 1930s to designer jeans from New York or Paris in the 1990s. Before the edict of 1989 requiring people to wear *kira* and *go* in public, fashion-conscious young women could be seen driving in Thimphu in the latest European and American styles, although they would not stroll around or attend functions in these outfits. Women of means may still relax at home in slacks, but when they go out in public now only their accessories – mainly shoes and handbags – will be Western. Schoolgirls often wear pants and T-shirts at home, and shopkeepers and village women commonly wear T-shirts and cardigan sweaters under their *kira*.

Men's Dress

> This beautiful *adha mathra* [colorful warp-striped fabric]
> should be worn as a robe.
> It should be worn once where a crowd of people gather.
> If it isn't worn once in front of a lot of people
> Alas, it will just rot away in a trunk.
>
> This beautiful blade is a noble sword.
> It should be carried once where a crowd of people gather.
> If it isn't displayed once in front of a lot of people
> Alas, it will just go to ruin hanging on a hook.
>
> This beautiful *adha khamar* [red-and-white textile] should be
> a ceremonial shouldercloth.
> It should be worn once where a crowd of people gather.
> If it isn't worn once in front of a lot of people
> Alas, it will just go to waste draped on a hook.
>
> I have a beautiful song of three words
> It should be sung once where a crowd of people gather.
> If it isn't sung once in front of a lot of people
> Alas, it will just be silenced inside of me.
>
> *– Bhutanese folk song*

This song expresses a Bhutanese man's pride in his unique dress – the locally woven pattern of his robe, his distinctive sword, and his ceremonial shoulder cloth. Some Bhutanese say the articles of apparel can also be interpreted as metaphors for the innate spiritual potential within every living being. The song's more profound message can thus be understood as a call to attend to one's personal spiritual development and religious practice, an opportunity open only during a human lifetime.[17]

A man's *go* ('garment') is a full-length robe that overlaps in front and fastens with ties at each side. It is folded into two wide pleats from the hips toward the back and bloused above a narrow belt so that the hem hangs to the knees [figs. 5.31, 5.32]. A wooden bowl and cup, silver boxes of betel nuts and lime, and a dagger traditionally are carried in this exaggerated pouch [fig. 5.36]. Whereas women's dresses are fashioned by sewing alone, men's robes are made by cutting, piecing, and then joining the cloth. When a robe is made of cotton, silk, or wild silk, it requires three panels *(bjang)* of fabric and sometimes a slightly smaller fourth

Fig. 5.31
Archery is the sport of choice for Bhutanese men, who participate in impromptu matches after work and in organized tournaments on holidays. Both traditional bamboo longbows and compound tension bows imported from the United States (seen here) are used. These men are civil servants with their friends in Bumthang, celebrating a colleague's promotion. The men are attired in everyday dress, the wrapped robe (go) that is the national style for men. Under their go, men wear a loose white shirt whose sleeves are turned back into long cuffs. The depth of the cuffs and length of the robe both correspond to status, with high-ranking men permitted deeper cuffs and longer robes. Western-style shoes and kneesocks are popular, although the argyles seen in this 1985 photograph have gone of out fashion in the past few years. (D.K.M. 1985)

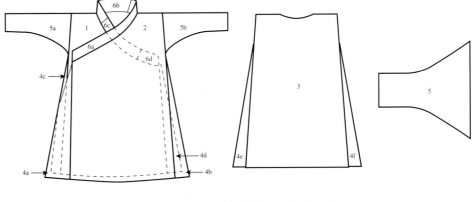

FIG. 5.32

A man puts on his go, *which is quite voluminous, over a loose shirt, the sleeves of which are cuffed over the sleeves of the robe. After lining up the seams at each side, he grips the cloth firmly and raises the garment so the lower edge is at his knees. He then folds one side back to form a deep pleat in the back; he makes a second pleat with the other side. Before wrapping his tight belt, he checks the folds, smoothing the fabric down so that the folds are of equal depth and the lower edges are all even. Once the belt is wrapped, he blouses the front of the garment to form a pouch and pulls the back down over the belt, once again straightening the pleats, if necessary. He finishes by adjusting the depth of his shirt cuffs and making sure that his white shirt collar shows just enough, but not too much, outside the robe.*

Three or four backstrap-loom lengths, or two long rolls of narrow cloth woven on a horizontal frame loom, are required to make a man's robe. Male tailors, who also assemble women's dresses and other garments, cut and stitch the robe pieces as indicated. The inside lower edge of the robe, as well as the collar, is faced with contrasting silk or cotton fabric. Robes, especially for winter wear, may be fully lined. Two narrow cloth ties (not shown) under the right arm secure the front panel of the robe when the garment is worn. (After Bartholomew 1985)

1. Inner Front Panel
2. Outer Front Panel
3. Rear Panel
4. Side Inset Panels (a-f)
5. Sleeves (a-b)
6. Collar (a-d)

panel (*zurtsi*). Robes are also stitched from woolen panels woven on backstrap and horizontal frame looms. They are always assembled by men; there are no women tailors in Bhutan.

Robes, especially for winter, are generally lined with a lightweight fabric. The lining (*nashab*) is customarily a solid-color cotton, formerly the rough Indian cotton used to sew women's petticoats or similar trade fabric. A man's robe is always faced at the cuffs and hem with an 8-cm band of cotton (*ja*, 'rainbow') and similarly edged around the collar (*goshab*). In warm weather, men wore loose cotton shorts beneath their robes, but now many choose Western-style undergarments. In the past, in cold weather, men wore semifitted trousers of wild silk or cotton (*domtha*), now often replaced by long johns tucked into kneesocks. Villagers and laborers commonly wear Western trousers under their robes, but this is not considered proper dress.

Men's robes are made from almost all the same fabrics as women's dresses. The major exceptions are *thara* (fabric with a white ground and multicolored warp stripes), *möntha* (fabric with blue or black supplementary-warp-pattern bands), and cloth decorated with *kushü* (the intricate supplementary-weft patterning from north central Bhutan). These are considered "female" cloth, too decorative or otherwise inappropriate for men. With most other fabrics, the major difference is that when stripes appear in a pattern, they are oriented vertically in a man's garment and horizontally in a woman's. The nationalization of once regional patterns applies to men's clothing as much as women's. With the increased mobility of the population, clothing is no longer a reliable indicator of a man's (or his wife's) origin. Fabrics from abroad are also as popular for men's wear as for women's, although the range of suitable patterns has been more limited: cotton or synthetic-wool blends in sober gray, blue, brown, or black and narrowly striped woolens are typical. The new, machine-made Indian imports that imitate Bhutanese patterns have expanded men's options. As with women's dress, status is revealed in the quality of the store-bought cloth, or the weaving, fiber, and patterning of the handwoven fabric.

Today, the cloth of choice for men's dress is a function of fashion no less than it is among women. If there is a classic fabric pattern for men's dress comparable to the *kushüthara* ('brocaded wrapped dress') for women, it is one of the supplementary-warp patterns *(aikapur)* from eastern Bhutan [fig. 5.33, top and bottom]. Although *aikapur* cloth is not as definitive a choice for men, partly because it is also worn by women, robes of *aikapur* have been favored for several centuries. One appears in the oil painting of 1775 attributed to Tilly Kettle [fig. 1.8]; and the fabrics are among the exports of eastern Bhutan described, albeit with frustrating lack of detail, by Captain Welsh in 1794. In turn-of-the-century photographs, the first king, his officers, and his attendants are often seen in *aikapur*. The precise type of *aikapur* cannot be determined, since the photographs are not in color, but the basic pattern is the same as that depicted and described more than a century earlier – and still seen today.

An innovation, possibly of the late nineteenth century, is the addition of supplementary-weft patterning in between the bands of supplementary-warp patterning on both men's robes and women's dresses. The patterning features trees of life *(shinglo)*, stylized masks *(shyauli bap)*, Chinese coins *(tranka)*, and other symbols of long life [figs. 5.34, 3.3]. This decoration is especially associated with the first and second kings, who frequently presented loyal officers with robes of this kind. Many of these gifts are kept in well-to-do homes in Thimphu and proudly shown to visitors. Today, newly made robes combining supplementary-warp and supplementary-weft patterning are appropriate for wear at festivals and on special occasions, an indication of their enduring popularity [fig. 5.35]. During celebrations at his coronation in 1974 and his public wedding in 1988, His Majesty King Jigme Singye Wangchuck wore robes of this fabric *(aikapur shinglo)*.

Aikapur (supplementary-warp-patterned cloth) is traditionally made of wild or cultivated silk and only occasionally of cotton, reinforcing its association with men of rank. One reason why the new machine-woven fabrics from India are so popular may be that they successfully copy these patterns in textiles now universally affordable. *Kushüthara*, on the other hand, are often woven of cotton and can be embellished with acrylic yarn or cotton as easily as wild or cultivated silk, so they have always been within the means of many Bhutanese women.

FIG. 5.33
Bhutanese men's robes are a seventeenth-century innovation, introduced from Tibet by Shabdrung Ngawang Namgyel, the remarkable statesman who unified Bhutan. When laid out in this manner, the go does resemble the Tibetan chuba, *but the style of wearing the garment – raised to the knees – is quite different.*

Supplementary-warp patterns called aikapur *from eastern Bhutan (top and bottom) are classic choices for special occasions. The example at the top of the photograph is* mensé

Fig. 5.34
This outfit was commissioned by Her Majesty Queen Ashi Sangay Choden for her eldest child, His Royal Highness Dasho Khamsum Singye Wangchuck, to wear on his third birthday in 1988. The robe is woven entirely of silk, its pattern a version of mensé mathra with seven 'legs' [cf. the red-and-gold robe in fig. 5.33], decorated with emblems called 'coins' that invoke both prosperity and long life. The robe's ties, made of patterned red silk from Hong Kong, are visible under the arm. The prince's belt is identical to belts worn by all Bhutanese men, made of wool and woven on a card loom. The little boots, a style for formal attire, have leather soles, while the uppers and lining are made of brocade and other patterned silk. The orange, fringed boot ties, made on a backstrap loom, are decorated with embroidery. The young prince is pictured in a similar outfit in fig. 5.35. (see Catalog)

mathra, *woven of mulberry silk from Hong Kong. The robe at the bottom is* lungserma, *woven of wild silk from Assam. These fabrics are also used for women's dresses, but in men's robes the patterns are oriented so that the stripes are vertical rather than horizontal. The middle* go, *also wild silk, is a plaid pattern* (pangtsi) *that originated in Assam. (see Catalog)*

A notable difference between men's and women's dress is that elite men have worn robes of imported Chinese damask and brocade for several centuries. In the 1770s, a British emissary was presented with a "water tabby gown" (Aris 1982, 20), probably of silk with a shiny finish like taffeta, and, in 1837, "among the higher orders the robe [was] generally made of Chinese flowered silks, the favorite colours being red and yellow," hues associated with royalty and the clergy (Pemberton [1839] 1976, quoted in Collister 1987, 66). The first king and senior government officers were often photographed wearing robes of Chinese brocade (*göchen*, 'great silk,' 'great garment'), sometimes boldly patterned with flowers, pheasants, cloud patterns, and Chinese characters. Because this imported fabric was so costly and rare, it was an unmistakable sign of prestige to wear it.

The same silks from China via Tibet were used for women's jackets among the elite [fig. 6.9], but never worn as wrapped dresses. Women say that bolts of fabric were sometimes kept for many years and sewn into robes or jackets decades later. Bhutanese also recall that the first two kings sometimes gave their old brocade robes to their daughters and female relatives, who made them over into jackets. On some occasions pieces of silk salvaged from worn-out robes could likewise be stitched into clothing for statues in temples, an act of religious merit for the robe's owner.

During the time of Jigme Dorji Wangchuck, Bhutan's third king (r. 1952-72), the fashion changed. The third king was known for identifying very strongly with his people, and while he occasionally did wear a brocade robe, he more often wore a garment woven locally. Moreover, because by the 1950s silk brocades from Tibet had become affordable to more people, some of the cachet they had enjoyed earlier was lost.[18] Then, with the closing of Tibet's borders in 1959, the availability of brocades from their traditional source diminished sharply. Silk from Hong Kong continues to be used in men's robes (*go*), but was of minor importance by the 1980s. Heirloom robes of old Chinese silk are still worn by the king on special occasions.

A *go* is fastened at the waist by a belt (*kera*) measuring about 5 cm wide and 180 cm long, and made by card weaving. The best belts are wool, but many are woven of cotton. The 15-cm warp fringe on each end is finished by plying sets of yarns together. Men's *kera* typically show warp stripes in red, blue, white, green, brown, and yellow. Bhutanese say that men's belts have always been striped and in the old days were sometimes decorated with a row of tiny patterns down the middle. Because men's robes are bloused so generously at the waist, belts are hardly visible. Men's belts are viewed as having intrinsic protective powers and are likened to sacred threads.

Under their robes, men wear a loose, waist-length shirt with no fastenings *(tögo)*. The shirt's collar shows at the neck of the robe, and its cuffs are folded back over the robe's sleeves about 15 cm. An innovation seen nowadays in Thimphu among ordinary people is the use of white cotton cuff and collar pieces that simulate a traditional shirt but can be changed and washed easily. Despite its practicality, this shortcut is seen as poor form.

Men of means often wear a gold or silver ring set with a turquoise or coral. Formerly, especially when traveling or going into battle, men wore amulets or charm boxes *(gau)*, fastened to cloth or leather straps and positioned over the chest or at the middle of the back. Small packets of thread, written prayers, herbal pills, and other tiny objects blessed by a lama were kept inside. These items are still carried by men and women in Bhutan, but they are kept in a small pouch or purse rather than worn in the traditional manner.

Formerly, even noblemen often went bare legged and barefoot. While traveling, men wore rawhide sandals *(thebthem)* or leather-soled boots *(lham)* with cloth leggings secured by handwoven ties. The boots were padded with long, fragrant pine needles for comfort and warmth. On formal occasions the elite wore special boots *(tsholham)* with silk damask and brocade or decorated felt uppers, whose color indicated a man's rank.

FIG. 5.35

Robes of supplementary-warp-patterned cloth whose design originated in eastern Bhutan have been a popular choice for special occasions since at least the eighteenth century. They have been worn by all the kings and are selected by many men of means for events such as weddings and promotions. His Royal Highness Dasho Khamsum Singye Wangchuck is seen here in a silk go of contemporary design, combining yellow and red pattern bands with stripes of black plainweave decorated with stylized Chinese long-life characters (tranka tshering). (Dasho Ugyen Tshechup 1993)

Today, Western shoes and ankle boots are common daily wear, but traditional Bhutanese boots are still seen with formal dress. With Western footgear, which reached the court by the early 1900s, kneesocks are worn. Argyles, first imported from England and in the 1980s brought from the United States, have been the most popular style. Now they are "out" among fashion-conscious Bhutanese, while solid-color and subtly patterned socks are "in." Nike Airs and Reeboks are popular casual footwear, as are athletic shoes from India and Hong Kong and canvas shoes of Chinese manufacture.

Bhutanese say that a man is not a man without a knife. Ordinary people carry a dagger *(dozum)* or other knife about 40 cm long, with a wooden handle and sheath made of plain or leather-covered wood. Knives, distinguished by the shape of their iron blade, are useful tools for chopping bamboo, husking and slicing betel nuts, clearing a path of weeds, cutting grass for a horse, and other common tasks. While office workers and taxi drivers do not carry knives, most other men still keep a sheathed knife in the pouch of their robe, or wear it hanging from a special, narrow card-woven belt.

Swords *(pata)* with decorative silver hilts and embossed scabbards, often showing gilt details, are associated with the upper ranks of service to the state [fig. 5.36]. Like knives, there are several styles of swords whose names indicate their places of origin in Bhutan or Tibet. In the 1770s, swords and daggers were lent to most officials from the storeroom of a dzong for the length of their government service (Davis 1830, in Aris 1982, 53). The right to wear a sword is restricted today to men who hold the rank of *dasho* or higher, honors bestowed by the king. Swords are now mostly family heirlooms, presented to a grandfather or uncle by the first king. A man wears his sword suspended on his right hip from a belt made of woolen or leather panels decorated with carved silver plates. On his left hip is a narrow textile *(pata losé)* about 30 cm long. If it is woven, this decorative item shows trees of life and other auspicious symbols. The other important insignia of rank, worn with the sword, is a man's shoulder cloth.

All Bhutanese laymen are required to wear a shoulder cloth on formal occasions, in monasteries, and in or near dzongs where monks are in residence. The cloth *(kabné,* 'covering'), usually of wild silk and occasionally of cotton, is about 90 by 300 cm, with very long warp fringes at each end. Depending on its color, a shoulder cloth consists of one or three panels, joined lengthwise. The textile, while it can be used for carrying a bundle or child on a man's back if no other cloth is available, is primarily ceremonial; its color denotes a man's rank, and it plays an important role in expressions of traditional etiquette.

FIG. 5.36

In the pouch of their garment, Bhutanese men (and women) carry small cups made of wood or ivory, sometimes lined with silver, in which they are served tea when visiting homes or on tour. Robe pouches are also likely to conceal a rectangular silver box such as the one shown, containing a supply of betel nuts and leaves that are wrapped into a chew savored by many Bhutanese. The round silver box stores lime to smear on the leaf. Swords are carried by men of senior rank – dasho (red scarf officer) and higher – in the government service. Traditional sword belts have two rings, one for the sword and one for a decorative cloth strap that secures the sword at a man's back for ease of movement. This sword, of the type called kongdi maja *from Tibet, belonged to Chimi Dorji, the Jakar Dzongpön (governor of Bumthang) who signed the oath of allegiance to King Ugyen Wangchuck at his 1907 coronation. Its scabbard is silver and wood, partially wrapped in red and green leather.* (see Catalog)

The code of etiquette *(driglam namzha)* spells out precisely how shoulder cloths are used, starting with the way an ordinary man puts the textile on. First, he holds it in front of his body, gripping the cloth so it is divided roughly in thirds. He swings the right end over his left shoulder and brings it around the right side of his body from behind. He keeps his left arm extended, covered by the other end of the textile. He places the fringe of the right end over his left arm at the elbow. Then he tosses the left end back over his left shoulder so that it hangs down the left side of his back. The right end of the cloth is enclosed in the resulting fold, positioned just below the armpit. A civil servant must turn several strands of this fringe – three, five, or seven, depending on his rank – back into the fold of the *kabné* as a sign of allegiance to the king, the country, and the people. Finally, a man carefully adjusts his shoulder cloth so that it drapes to about a palm's width above the hem of his robe. The king and full ministers wear shoulder cloths arranged in folds like the shoulder cloth of a monk.

When meeting the king or his family, or entering the office of a senior official, a man must partially unfold his *kabné* in a ceremonial gesture *(kabné phabshé)*. Holding the left end of the cloth with his left hand, he bows and sweeps the right end in front of him with his right hand. The higher the position of the person receiving the greeting, the lower the textile is brandished. Depending on the circumstances, the cloth may be kept "open" in this manner or put back in place after the salutation.[19] If a man is sitting on a chair, his *kabné* must cover his knees and be kept unfolded, unless he is ordered otherwise. If a man is sitting cross-legged on the floor, the cloth must envelop both knees and be slightly stretched across them. When a man performs prostrations to images in temples, to religious authorities, or to the king and the queens, he holds both ends of his *kabné* in front of him, with his hands pressed together in a gesture of prayer.

Bhutanese protocol even specifies how a shoulder cloth should be carried when not in use – folded and draped over the right forearm. When meeting a high official on the road, a man must place the folded cloth under his armpit in order to perform the traditional greeting properly. He bows forward with both arms extended, palms upward. In fact, many men carry their folded *kabné* in a much less formal manner, draped over a shoulder – or placed on the dashboard of a car.

The color of the *kabné* indicates a man's rank, unbleached white being for commoners. Village headmen wear a textile whose white center panel is flanked by panels of deep red *(khamar*, 'red mouth') [fig. 5.37]. Recently, white shoulder cloths with narrow red warp stripes and red sashes with white warp stripes have been introduced for officials of intermediate grade. Shoulder cloths for higher officials are routinely made of wild silk and hemmed rather than fringed. Solid maroon shoulder cloths *(buramap*, 'red wild silk') are awarded with the title *dasho* to senior officials and others whom the king wishes to recognize. Blue *kabné* are worn by members of the Royal Advisory Council. Orange shoulder cloths are worn by deputy ministers and ministers, but the former arrange the cloth in the ordinary fashion and the latter fold it with five pleats on the shoulder. On occasions when they wear a shoulder cloth, officers with the rank of director and above also wear their swords, with the tip visible below the drape of the *kabné*. Yellow shoulder cloths are reserved for the king and the chief abbot. The king wears his shoulder cloth with nine pleats on the shoulder and draped just below the hem of his robe [fig. 5.38].[20]

The *kabné* is one of the most distinctive features of Bhutanese men's dress, which is otherwise similar to the Tibetan style. The textile is related to the shoulder cloth or shawl worn by Buddhist monks *(zen)* [fig. 5.39].[21] When religious and civil authority first emanated from the dzongs, senior lay officials took certain monastic vows, and some even received

FIG. 5.37
A man's outfit is not complete without his kabné, *a ceremonial textile worn on the left shoulder for formal occasions. Its colors, fringe, and arrangement all reflect the wearer's rank. Plain white shoulder cloths are for commoners, while this red-and-white example, called a* khamar kabné *('red-mouth covering') or* adha khamar *('covering from Adhang'), is worn by village headmen and some lay priests. Woven of wild silk, its red panels are dyed with lac. Textiles resembling the* khamar kabné *were multipurpose wraps in eighteenth-century Bhutan, but the use of shoulder cloths is now governed by an elaborate protocol that is strictly observed. (see Catalog)*

FIG. 5.38
*His Majesty Jigme Singye
Wangchuck, King of Bhutan, wears a
yellow silk shoulder cloth, its color
reserved for the monarch and the chief
abbot* (je khenpo). *The close
relationship between temporal and
spiritual authorities is symbolized both
by the shoulder cloth's color and by the
way it is arranged, in the same fashion
as similar textiles worn by monks.*

FIG. 5.39
Men's shoulder cloths (kabné) *are
related to the shawls* (zen) *worn by
monks. Bhutanese credit Shabdrung
Ngawang Namgyel, who unified the
country in the seventeenth century,
with introducing the* kabné *for
laymen. Lay officials who worked in
the dzongs, which are also religious
establishments housing monks, were
required to wear shoulder cloths in
deference to these surroundings.*

*This photograph, taken around
1908, purports to show the family of
the Thimphu Dzongpön (governor).
The white shoulder cloths of the
laymen can be compared with the dark
shawl of the monk at center. Bhutanese
identified the child the monk is holding
as the Gangtey Tulku, a reincarnate
lama born into the governor's family
earlier this century whose important
lineage continues today. (John Claude
White c. 1908, Courtesy National
Geographic Society)*

religious names when they assumed their positions. Monastic rules were strictly observed on the dzong premises, where even today women are forbidden to remain after dusk. Out of deference to their surroundings, officials living in proximity to the monks, as well as citizens visiting the dzong on business, were required to wear shoulder cloths. Bhutanese say that the wild silk textiles also provided protection against swords and knives during the frequent battles of that era and doubled as blanketing at night. Watercolors of the 1780s show that textiles similar to the shoulder cloths were universally worn.

In the eighteenth century, shoulder cloths also had special purposes among the elite. For example, Bhutanese scholars say that the *tshoré khamar* mentioned in contemporary texts was a wild silk textile used by noblemen – and later the kings – to cover their feet and knees when sitting.[22] It had a white center panel flanked by narrower red panels, resembling the shoulder cloth today worn by village headmen *(khamar kabné)*. In formal settings, a seated headman or commoner must politely cover his knees by spreading his shoulder cloth over them. Thus, the multipurpose wraps have evolved into a particular element of dress governed by a code of etiquette that is vigorously taught and strictly observed.

According to Bhutanese tradition, both men's robes *(go)* and shoulder cloths were introduced by Shabdrung Ngawang Namgyel, the most important figure in the country's history. He unified the region into a more or less cohesive state for the first time, promulgated a code of law that still guides aspects of the government, and established a system of political and religious administration that endured from the seventeenth until the early twentieth century. Some Bhutanese say the Shabdrung's association with the *go* is apocryphal, but others credit him with literally inventing the style to reinforce Bhutan's new national identity and to distinguish Bhutan from Tibet, whence so much Drukpa influence emanated. Certainly the robe was initially an elite dress, popularized by officers in the Shabdrung's service, that spread from western Bhutan toward the east during the 1700s and 1800s, along

FIG. 5.40
Men performing this dance from Nubi village in Tongsa District at the Thimphu Tsechu wear attire described as dress dating to the time of the Shabdrung's arrival in the seventeenth century. (F.P. 1987)

with their administration. Uniformity of dress among officials of all ranks was encouraged by the fact that the state itself distributed cloth used for their clothing.

Unlike women's dress, which is truly indigenous and has remained structurally the same for many centuries, men's apparel changed significantly in the seventeenth century and continued to evolve for two centuries more. Samuel Davis's sketches of 1783 show some men in a long-sleeved, knee-length robe, like a *go*, worn over short trousers. Others, however, are wearing a sleeveless, knee-length tunic over a shirt with a belt at the waist, or a cloth crossed over the chest and fastened at the shoulders as a woman's dress is today [fig. 1.7]. These garments are both full below the waist. Their upper portions are often obscured by jackets and by shoulder cloths and blankets draped around the neck and shoulders.

The garment crossed over the chest (*pakhi*) is best known now as the traditional dress of the Lhops ('southerners'), the Toktops, and the Mönpas, groups native to the southwestern hills where Davis was sketching. It is also customary apparel among the Lepchas, who populated this region and areas to the west, and among the Sherdukpens and others east of Bhutan in Arunachal Pradesh. The *pakhi* is sometimes described as having been "widespread" in Bhutan before the arrival of the Shabdrung in 1607, but it is not clear what groups, if any, outside the southwestern part of the country wore this garment (see Chapter Two). Being made of cotton or nettle cloth, the garment was probably restricted to the temperate southern hills.

In Bhutan today, the *pakhi* is seen chiefly in festival dances. At the Punakha New Year Festival, for example, a similar garment is worn by laymen performing a dance that commemorates a Bhutanese victory over the Tibetans at the time of the Shabdrung. Until the 1950s, a garment crossed over the chest and fastened at the shoulders was also worn by male dancers who distracted the archers and amused onlookers at archery tournaments.[23] Dancers' garments were made of plain white cotton or patterned fabric typically reserved for women (*möntha, thara*). The Bhutanese *pakhi* was once secured with bamboo slivers (*khab*, 'needle'); today it is fastened with a safety pin or tied at the shoulders.

Other archaic forms of men's dress, recalling the styles in Davis's watercolors, are preserved in dances incorporated into annual festivals throughout Bhutan. These dances (*zhé*) with accompanying songs are peculiar to each district. They are said to have been inspired by the arrival of the Shabdrung in each region for the first time and were performed to welcome him. Such dances are still extant in Thimphu, Uchu village in Paro, the upper Chökhor Valley in Bumthang, Nubi village in Tongsa District, the far north, and other areas. In the Nubi *zhé*, for example, men wear red woolen robes with short jackets on top, circular tubes of cloth around their heads, red-and-white shoulder cloths draped over their left shoulders and knotted on the right hip, and decorative woolen knee boots [fig. 5.40]. Men perform other *zhé* in robes (*go*), wearing over them a full, knee-length skirt made of plain white or orange plaid cotton, and a shoulder cloth wrapped around the neck so that its fringed ends hang down on either side of the dancer's chest. In north central Bhutan, at ceremonies where women dance in archaic tunics, their partners are attired as soldiers of the Shabdrung's army, wearing robes with the same skirt-like lower garments, colored cloth headbands, ribbons across their chests, and large silver reliquaries to protect them [fig. 5.29].

Virtually nothing is known about men's dress before 1800 in eastern Bhutan. A text of the first half of the eighteenth century mentions "local articles of dress" associated with a king from the east imprisoned at Punakha in the west (Ngawang n.d., fol. 18v, quoted in Aris 1986). This suggests that easterners had identifiable garment styles or at least specialized textiles at that time. Perhaps the phrase refers to *aikapur*, the distinctive local fabric that was noted in a contemporary British account and appears in the Tilly Kettle painting of 1775.

By the first part of the nineteenth century, most Bhutanese men were attired much as they are today. The diary of Captain Pemberton in 1837-38 includes this description:

> The garments of the upper classes consist of a long loose robe which wraps round the body and is secured in its position by a leather belt ... Over the robe in the winter a large shawl of black satin or silk is generally thrown, and when seated, the person wearing it wraps it round the knees and feet so effectively as to conceal them from view. A legging of red broadcloth is attached to a shoe made of buffalo hide; and no Bootea ever travels during the winter without protecting his legs and feet by putting these boots on and they are secured by a garter under the knee. A cap of fur or coarse broadcloth, or blanket, completes the habiliment; and the only variation observable is the substitution of a cloth for a woolen robe during the summer (Pemberton [1839] 1976, in Collister 1987, 66-67).

In photographs of Bhutanese taken in Darjeeling in the 1860s and in Bhutan and Tibet in the early 1900s, all the men are wearing *go* (robes).[24] The array of fabrics is more diverse than in Davis's watercolors, partly because most of these photographs document the environment of the court and were taken in central Bhutan where well-developed weaving traditions existed. Wool, cotton, and wild silk yarns were available, as were silk yarns in noble households, and trade with Tibet was a source of other textiles.

The most notable changes in men's fashion in the past 100 years are the disappearance of plain, nettle-cloth garments and in recent decades the growing preference for Bhutanese cloth over Chinese silk among the elite. When the state stopped distributing cloth for making garments and abolished serfdom in the 1950s, the choices of clothing fabrics available to many Bhutanese men increased. At the start of the century, robes for the "lower classes [were] cotton or blanketing," and those of the "upper classes" were made of "*tussah* silk"

(*North and northeast frontier tribes* [1907] 1983, 115). Tussah (*tussar*) is one type of wild silk from Assam, but the term seems to have been used by the British for any wild silk seen in Bhutan; here it could refer to undecorated, plaid, and *aikapur* fabrics. Plain-colored, thick Tibetan woolens (*thruk*) were popular especially during the reign of the second king (1926-52). In cold areas, robes were lined with lambskin, as they sometimes are today. Another favorite for men's robes in this century has been *adha mathra*, a cotton or wild silk plainweave with blue, green, red, and yellow warp stripes, whose special appeal as "the dress of the Wangchuck king" is mentioned in a Bhutanese folk song.[25] Striped and plaid patterns woven of wild silk in the east, of wool in central Bhutan, and of cotton in the south are enduring styles [fig. 5.41].

In the early twentieth century, wearing multiple garments for warmth and prestige was a universal convention, now continued only by older men. One Bhutanese, who was a local governor (*pönlop*) near Thimphu until the 1950s, commented that back then, "I'd feel shy to go out in just one robe – people would talk!" His innermost robe was typically made of a striped woolen from Tibet (*hothra*); the middle robe was a thick cotton from India; and the outermost robe was a patterned wild silk. The popular explanation for why multiple garments were originally worn is very practical: thick, layered clothing protected a man from arrows and knives (if not from bullets) during the constant civil strife of the 1700s and 1800s. Quilted robes of wild silk were believed to be particularly efficacious in resisting the stroke of a sword.[26]

Older Bhutanese say wearing a shirt (*tögo*) with the robe was a well-to-do style that spread among ordinary citizens in the nineteenth century. Although shirts are now white, red or maroon shirts were worn by officers with the rank of *dasho* or higher until the abolition of most intermediate administrative ranks in the 1950s. Today, red shirts are seen only on lay priests (*gomchen*) associated especially with the Nyingma school of Buddhism.

FIG. 5.41

These four patterns, illustrated by narrow panels of wild silk from men's go sets, are favorites for men's apparel. At left is adha mathra, *immortalized in a Bhutanese folk song as the 'dress of the Wangchuck king.' This pattern takes its name from the village of Adhang in Wangdi Phodrang District, and is one of the very few textiles associated so directly with western Bhutan. The red-and-black plaid on a white ground is* pangtsi, *which Bhutanese believe was adopted long ago from Assam and is now woven throughout the country. The rainbow-striped fabric is* yütham, *or 'country cloth,' whose popularity in eastern Bhutan was recorded in the 1860s and continues today. The yellow plaid on a reddish ground* (sethra) *is of eastern origin, but has also been woven of wool for the past fifty years. All the fabrics illustrated are made from imported Assamese wild silk yarn, dyed and woven in Radi Dukpiling, Tashigang District, by eighteen-year-old Dorje Chözom.* (see Catalog)

Fig. 5.42

This young Lhop (Doya) boy is wearing the traditional garment for men in his community. Once woven of nettle fiber and now made of Indian cotton fabric, the pakhi *is a rectangular cloth knotted behind the neck, folded into two pleats in the back, and bloused over a belt. The same length of fabric, knotted at the shoulders, belted, and worn ankle-length, can serve as a Lhop woman's customary dress. (D.K.M. 1994)*

Men of Ethnic Minorities

While the belted robe *(go)* is the dominant men's attire in Bhutan, other important styles coexist. In Lhop and other villages in southwest Bhutan, men routinely wore a traditional wrapped garment *(pakhi)* until quite recently [fig. 5.42]. They now wear *go* except on special local occasions. In the high-altitude, pastoral communities of Laya in northwestern Bhutan and Merak Sakteng in the east, everyday male dress is also different [figs. 2.1, 2.10]. The men of Merak Sakteng wear three-quarter-length leather leggings *(pishup)* made of wild goat, deer, or calf hide, secured with thongs at the waist.[27] Over these, they wear loose, thick white woolen pants that end at midthigh *(kanggo,* 'leg garment'). The pants are open at the sides and fasten like the leggings with thongs at the waist.

Merak Sakteng men's upper garments are generously cut, long-sleeved woolen tunics *(chuba)*. Sleeveless hide vests *(paktsa)*, sewn together only at the shoulders, are worn over these. The vests, usually goatskin, are worn with the hide outermost during the rain. The tunics and vests are bloused and secured with a yak hair cord, leather belt, or woven wild silk cummerbund *(kichin, kera)*. The latter are similar to women's belts: they are about 15 to 20 cm wide and 240 cm long, dyed maroon, and patterned sparsely at the ends. Footgear consists of leather-soled boots with red woolen uppers that are tied at the knee and padded with tufts of sheep wool and pine needles. Nowadays, herders often wear Western-style pants with their traditional upper garments, and rubber rain boots are more common than handmade footgear. Like Merak Sakteng women, men wear distinctive yak hair hats and jewelry. A few pieces of coral, turquoise, or *zi* (agate) may be strung around the neck, and a turquoise on a string commonly hangs from one or both ears. Both men and women use multipurpose, striped bags woven of yak hair. While herding, men also carry smaller leather bags decorated with cowrie shells. They keep corn flour or other snacks inside and strike the bag with their palm to call their animals.

Styles for southern Bhutanese men of Nepalese ethnic origins have been strongly influenced by the region's proximity to India and access to Western clothing. Until recently, these men generally wore European-style shirts and pants. Today, many of them have adopted the more prevalent style of robe *(go)*.

Elements of Western dress appeal to men all over Bhutan, regardless of their customary clothing. Argyle kneesocks, worn by the elite since European shoes were introduced in the late 1800s, became all the rage in towns in the 1970s. Villagers and shopkeepers also began wearing trousers under their robes, and sometimes zippered winter jackets over them, several decades ago. More recently, young men who have studied in Berkeley or London, or traveled to Bangkok, have sported Nike's latest athletic shoes, brand-name sweatsuits, designer jeans, and army surplus fatigue jackets. Before the 1989 edict requiring Bhutanese dress in public, men were freer than women to wear this sort of casual dress to the Sunday market in Thimphu or around town. Young boys and men, particularly, still wear Western dress at home. Suits or sports jackets and ties formerly were office attire for some southern

Bhutanese, but otherwise formal Western wear has not been widespread. Today, men from all walks of life wear Western-style shoes and socks, from rubber flip-flops to Reeboks to leather dress shoes, and some continue to wear sweatshirts or T-shirts and trousers under their robes. As for women, however, their main garment will be Bhutanese.

Coverings and Containers

Besides garments, women weavers create textiles for a wide variety of uses as coverings – for cushions, beds, doorways, loads on pack animals, and outdoor shelters – and as containers for foodstuffs, belongings, and bundled goods.

A *pangkheb* ('lap cover') is a long, rectangular textile with fringed ends. Men and women use *pangkheb* to carry babies [fig. 5.43] and shoulder bundles. In homes, they serve as aprons to protect women's dresses, are spread on low tables, cover textiles not in use, hang in doorways,[28] decorate the household altar, and wrap religious scroll paintings *(thangka)*. In the past, when the servants of well-to-do families in central Bhutan went off to see a festival, the lady of the house piled several folded *pangkheb* on their shoulders as evidence of the family's prosperity.[29] Every household once kept a supply of these cloths, or loom lengths for stitching into *pangkheb*, for its own use or as gifts for close friends or monks. Bhutanese say that sparsely patterned loom lengths for making into *pangkheb* are common gifts at cremation ceremonies.

A single *pangkheb* panel that has never been sewn into a finished textile, or whose fringe is unplied, might have served as a gift or originally been a tax payment [fig. 5.44]. The state used *pangkheb* for furnishing dzong chapels and living quarters and distributed the balance to monasteries, lamas, and other individuals. Today, in dzongs and monasteries, one often sees custom-made covers for drums and other ritual instruments stitched from *pangkheb* dating from the days of cloth tax payments.

Pangkheb and *pangkheb* panels are always woven on a backstrap loom and come in varying qualities: ordinary *(pangkheb)*, better grade *(pangkheb matram chungma*, 'cloth worth ten coins'), and superior *(chagsi pangkheb)*. The simplest panels are 30 to 80 cm wide and made of modestly patterned, unbleached white cotton. If sewn into a finished textile, this type of panel will be joined along one selvedge to another, identical panel. The panels are woven in such a way that the finished textile has an axis of symmetry along its center seam. *Pangkheb* are cotton or wild silk patterned with supplementary-weft and/or supplementary-warp designs in red and blue or red and black. Usually they have a diamond motif in the center and stripes, stars, and other simple geometric designs scattered in the field. Warp ends are finished into fringe by twisting three or four yarns together and then cabling together two or three of those strands.

Some finished *pangkheb* show two seams and three panels, rather than just one center seam where two panels are joined. These examples are also made from two loom lengths of equal size, but the panels are patterned differently [fig. 5.49]. The center panel always

Fig. 5.43
Multipurpose textiles called pangkheb *('lap cover') are often used to carry babies and bundles. This woman is attired in a* mensé mathra *(red ground with gold supplementary-warp-pattern bands)* kira *and a wide, old-style cummerbund. Her infant is cushioned at her back with a woolen blanket* (yathra) *from central Bhutan. (Gangtey Gompa, D.K.M. 1986)*

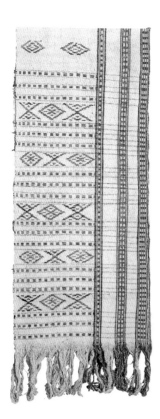

FIG. 5.44
Unstitched panels for making into pangkheb *exemplify the most utilitarian Bhutanese cloth. Finished* pangkheb *are made from two panels like the one above, so that the vertical supplementary-warp patterning appears at the outer edges of the textile. The fringe is finished by plying.* Pangkheb *serve as aprons, hang in doorways, decorate household altars – and fill many other needs.* Pangkheb *were also among the fabrics that served as taxes-in-kind, distributed by the state to dzongs and monasteries for lining cushions and wrapping ritual objects, and use as bed covers and rough toweling. Households kept a supply of these panels on hand for their own use and to give as gifts.* Pangkheb *are mentioned in letters itemizing gifts sent to Sir Charles Bell by the king of Bhutan and the Paro Pönlop in 1915. This example, now in the Victoria and Albert Museum, was presented to Bell in Bhutan in 1910. (see Catalog)*

features a diamond design flanked by horizontal rows of supplementary-weft patterning. The second panel shows supplementary-warp patterning along both selvedges. This panel is cut in two along the warp, and its two halves are stitched to the selvedges of the first panel, forming a frame of two identical, narrower panels. Better-grade textiles show finer weaving and more patterning. The finer the weaving, the more likely the *pangkheb* is to have three panels rather than two.

Pangkheb with a yellow ground were chiefly for monks to use as mattress or bed covers, as wraps and towels when bathing, and as lap covers at meals. In the 1990s, however, newly made bright yellow and orange *pangkheb* are popular in Thimphu for carrying babies. *Pangkheb* that formerly served as rain cloaks for lamas were known as *churé* ('rain cloth') *pangkheb*, but were not characterized by any special features.

The finest examples of the general type called *pangkheb* are the elaborately decorated *chagsi pangkheb* ('hand wash lap cover') [figs. 3.5, 5.45-5.48]. Although the name of these textiles refers to their occasional function as napkins, the honorific character of the Bhutanese phrase indicates that use was restricted to the lay and religious elites. Covered with patterning from end to end, *chagsi pangkheb* are impractical for everyday use at home.

Finished *chagsi pangkheb* have three panels. The center panel is embellished densely with two-faced patterning similar to that on traditional women's cummerbunds *(kera)*. The fabric shows rows of supplementary-weft pattern bands, usually executed in two colors. At the center of the panel is a large diamond composed of concentric bands of repeating geometric patterns. This motif is the axis of symmetry for the entire textile. The second panel, equal in size, has narrow bands of warp stripes and two-faced supplementary-warp patterning, flanking bands of supplementary-weft patterning. This length is cut in half along the warp after weaving, and the halves are then joined in the warp direction to the two selvedges of the main panel. End fringes of the *chagsi pangkheb* are plied together and left 15 to 20 cm long.

The most typical color scheme in these textiles is red and blue on an undyed white ground. A number of striking examples show yellow, gold, green, and blue patterning on a maroon or red ground [fig. 5.47]. These were sometimes intended for ecclesiastic use, as reds and golds are the colors of the Buddhist clergy. There are also *chagsi pangkheb* with blue grounds and green grounds [figs. 5.45, 5.46]. Regardless of the color scheme, patterns show similar designs arranged in a standard format.

Chagsi pangkheb once had functions that signified status and helped to create a lavish environment for the clergy and the nobility. Traditionally, they were among the accoutrements carried by attendants of senior officials and the king in formal processions and while on tour. The first personal attendant preceding the king had a folded *chagsi pangkheb* over his left shoulder and carried a silver water vessel or teapot, either resting on top of the cloth or held in his right hand. Ranking officials had a similar attendant who carried the textile over his left forearm, or on his shoulder if the official was the most senior personage present. The textile was folded three times in the warp direction when it was carried. When an entourage halted for a meal, the cloth could cover the lap of the official, who sat cross-legged on a low cushion. It could also drape the back of a chair or hang on a wall to enhance the sumptuousness of the surroundings or decorate a room for a ceremony [fig. 5.50].

While these conventions were observed up until the coronation of the present king (1974), they are no longer routinely followed. Today, officials of deputy minister level and above have the right to have their *chagsi pangkheb* carried by an attendant during formal processions. A 'red scarf officer' *(dasho)* who becomes a district governor *(dzongda)* may be accompanied by such an attendant on ceremonial occasions in his own district but not in

FIGS. 5.45-47

Densely patterned from end to end, these three examples typify the superior grade of pangkheb, *given the honorific name* chagsi pangkheb *('hand wash lap cover'). The name relates to their function as a napkin, carried by an attendant who would offer his master this cloth to dry his hands or cover his lap during a meal.* Chagsi pangkheb *were also hung on walls and draped on tables to enhance the setting for a ceremony, a religious rite, or, later, a formal photograph [e.g., fig. 5.50]. These textiles were reserved for use by the lay and religious elites, and were kept in homes for occasions such as visits from a high official or lama.*

All pangkheb *of this type include a diamond (khorlo) in the center of the textile. One example (fig. 5.45, far left), woven of wild silk, represents a class of weavings that incorporate animals and human figures. Another (fig. 5.46, near left) features floral, geometric, and diamond pattern bands similar to those on old-style eastern Bhutanese women's belts (kera). Woven of handspun cotton with wild silk supplementary-wefts, all vegetable-dyed, it was probably made in southeastern Bhutan. Some textiles with maroon or orange grounds, such as the* chagsi pangkheb *in fig. 5.47 at right, were meant for ecclesiastic use, because red and gold are the colors of the Buddhist clergy. This beautiful example is notable also because its field is almost filled with stars and geometric motifs rather than horizontal patterns. In between the supplementary-warp-pattern bands at each edge are zigzags known as 'water mountain' designs (churi). The textile is woven entirely of wild silk. (see Catalog)*

FIG. 5.48
This chagsi pangkheb *(far left)
incorporates many designs that
Bhutanese say are very old. The
concentric pattern rows forming the
diamonds in the field are composed of
small outlines containing a vertical
stripe, and a design called a 'bundle of
rice' (chamé chachu), 'spool' (tranti),
or 'hand drum' that is rarely used
today. The vertical supplementary-
warp-pattern bands flanking the field
have the format of* aikapur *fabric used
for clothing: primary motifs, separated
by horizontal bars, some of which are
crosshatched. Many of the primary
motifs are mysterious to Bhutanese.
Between the warp-pattern bands is
unusual red-and-blue zigzagging,
whose slightly curving contours
contrast agreeably with the angularity
of the rest of the textile. Woven in the
classic color scheme of red and blue on
white, this* chagsi pangkheb *was
probably made in the Pemagatshel
region of southeastern Bhutan not
later than the early twentieth century.
(see Catalog)*

FIG. 5.49
The pangkheb *at near left, like all of
those which are similarly decorated, is
woven as two loom lengths. One panel
from the loom shows the diamond,
flanked by horizontal rows of eight-
pointed stars. The second panel,
combining small supplementary-weft
designs with vertical bands of supplementary-warp patterning, is cut
along the warp, and its two halves are
stitched to the edges of the first panel
[see fig. 3.6]. (see Catalog)*

Thimphu or Punakha, the former capital. The ways in which the textile is folded and carried continue to reflect the rank of the officer.[30]

Ordinary people usually own these textiles, but may not have them carried in public. Sometimes a villager will use a *chagsi pangkheb* as a shawl at a festival, but the textiles are most commonly kept in homes for occasions when important visitors are received or when lamas are called to conduct ceremonies. At these times, one textile may be hung on the wall behind the lama's seat and another offered to cover his lap. High lamas also use these for covering their beds, and when they go to bathe, an attendant will hold this cloth around the lama's lower body like a towel. Today, old *chagsi pangkheb* are sometimes used as door curtains or draped on sofa backs in wealthy houses because they are beautiful and decorative.

Bags for carrying loads or personal items (*phechung*, 'small bag') are made of durable wool, heavy cotton, or tough nettle fiber [fig. 5.52]. Fabric for a bag is woven on a backstrap loom as one continuous length, up to 38 cm wide and 215 to 240 cm long. This length is cut along the weft into two panels of equal size, which are then joined along one selvedge and folded in half. The outer selvedges are stitched to make a squarish pouch. Cotton, woolen, or leather straps are attached to the sides of the bag, which is closed by folding the open end (mouth) over to one side or tying it with a cord. Auspicious swastikas flanked by linear and geometric pattern bands appear on each face of the pouch. Traditional color schemes are red and blue or black on an undyed cotton or nettle-fiber ground. Kurtö in north central Bhutan is famous for bags and wrapping cloths embellished with the same patterning techniques as *kushüthara* (brocaded women's dresses).

These bags figure in ceremonial escorts for the king and high officials. Traditionally, four attendants (*chashumi*), two walking on each side of the king's horse, carried *phechung*; the strap was worn over the left shoulder and passed under the right arm, with the bag positioned at the attendant's back. In these ornate pouches were the king's teacups, official seals, and sundries. Today, senior officials still have the privilege of retaining one or two attendants who carry *phechung*. Ordinary Bhutanese use the bags to carry schoolbooks, loads of oranges bound for market, grain, food for a picnic, or belongings taken along while traveling [fig. 5.51]. Striped woolen bags of similar dimensions are made of sheep wool or yak hair in cold regions of Bhutan.

Flat textiles (*bündi*, 'round, collected') for wrapping and carrying large bundles are also made from one loom length decorated with supplementary-weft patterning. The length is cut along the weft into three equal panels that are sewn together in the warp direction to form a textile 60 to 180 cm square [fig. 5.53]. The center panel invariably shows a large swastika, with geometric pattern bands and diamond-shaped motifs on the side panels. Cotton, woolen, or leather straps are sewn to corners of the *bündri* for tying up the packed bundle of clothing, bedding, grain, or other goods. Ritual cymbals and other religious instruments or objects may be stored wrapped in small *bündri*. In cold regions, such as Laya and Bumthang, sturdy *bündri* are also made from panels woven of black yak hair, sometimes showing narrow white stripes and decorated with bits of yak tail dyed red at each corner. These textiles are used for spreading grain out to dry in the sun as well as for wrapping bundles.

FIG. 5.51
These Bhutanese are laden with vegetables to sell, all carried in patterned, home-woven bags. The woman on the right has secured her bag to her back with a red, striped pangkheb. (Tashigang, D.K.M. 1992)

All Bhutanese carry a square white cotton cloth in the pouch of their dress or robe. This textile is used as a "plate" on which to receive rice (*tora*, 'food [rice] cloth'). A person grasps the far edge of the cloth in the left hand and holds it partially up, to hide the rice from view and thereby show good manners, while eating with the right hand. A small cup made from a wood burl, ivory, or silver, which is also carried at all times, is set on the ground to hold vegetable or meat dishes, or tea.

Cloth "plates" were especially convenient during the days when noblemen traveled with many attendants who had to be fed. Whether servants prepared meals or a village provided them, the whole company could be seated on the ground and served their rations. High-ranking officers, or the noble's family, would be seated inside a tent or home and served food in polished wooden bowls or shallow baskets woven of bamboo with fitted basketry lids. The food cloths are still used today at functions such as weddings and cremation ceremonies, where the hosts or sponsors customarily feed dozens or even hundreds of guests, some of whom may be seated outdoors on the ground. When these events are hosted by the

FIG. 5.52
Square bags are typically embellished with supplementary-weft designs. This phechung *has patterning in the style of north central Bhutan (kushü), but may have been made in nearby central Bhutan because the pattern yarns are wool rather than wild silk. It is stitched together from one loom length, cut into two panels with lucky swastikas in the center. When the joined panels are folded to make the finished textile, the swastikas appear at the bottom of the bag. A woven strap allows the bag to be carried on a shoulder, or it can be positioned on the forehead like a tumpline. Bags are woven of nettle, like this one, or of cotton; examples for use by the well-to-do are patterned in fine cotton and wild silk. (see Catalog)*

Fig. 5.53

An auspicious swastika decorates this bündri *for wrapping bundles. The textile is woven as a long panel cut into three equal lengths joined together in the warp direction; the ends are hemmed and cloth ties attached at the corners. This style of wrapping cloth, cotton with wild silk patterning, originated in Kurtö in north central Bhutan. Because its ground is embellished with diamond-shaped* kushü *motifs such as those decorating women's* kushüthara *dresses and* kushung *tunics from the same region, it is sometimes called a* kushü bündri. *Notice how the half-diamond motifs are carefully aligned to meet at the seams of the panels. A local repair shows in one arm of the swastika. (see Catalog)*

government, civil servants and members of the public must have a food cloth with them or they will not be served.

Even this simple textile reflects social hierarchy. For example, the king alone carries a food cloth *(tora)* made of wild silk, dyed red. Alternatively, it may be *mentsi*, the yellow silk patterned with red-and-green floral designs that was traditionally imported from China and Tibet for stitching into *thangka* covers and other religious textiles. Bhutan's most senior officials – the chief abbot, the four *lopön*, the four masters of discipline, the master of the choir, the Shabdrung's chamberlain, the ministers, and the red scarf officers – carry red rice cloths, too, but they are made of cotton.

Denkheb ('seat or mattress cover') are flat textiles to cover the firm rectangular cushions or low box-frame "couches" placed against the walls of a room for sitting and sleeping. Their size matches that of the cushions: 90 cm wide and 150 to 180 cm long. The textiles are sat upon during the day and rearranged as bedding at night, and they are taken on travels and picnics for the same purposes. They also may be spread directly on the floor, like a rug, for sitting on. When old and threadbare, these textiles are cut up and used as saddle padding. One style of *denkheb* is a rectangular panel of wild silk or cotton fabric, edged with wide borders of red broadcloth. The center panel is sometimes salvaged from a garment. One woman recalled ruefully how her mother gave a "beautiful *kira*" to a servant, who wore it to pieces and then cut it up to make into a *denkheb*. In unusual examples, the center panel is animal hide or a snow leopard pelt.

Another style of seat cover is made of patterned woolen cloth from central Bhutan *(yathra)* [fig. 5.55]. A single length of fabric woven on a frame loom is cut in half along the weft and joined in the warp direction. The ends and sides of the textile are turned under or bound. The woolen fabric is typically patterned with horizontal rows of flowers *(metok)*, stars *(karma)*, long-life vases *(tshebum)*, and other motifs, alternating with bands of narrow weft stripes. A variation, developed especially for fabric to be stitched into a *denkheb*, is woven to emulate a Tibetan pile rug, with a lattice pattern in the field and a meander border. Older Bhutanese remember seeing these for the first time during the reign of the second king (1926-52).[31]

FIG. 5.54
This raincloak is stitched of typically patterned woolen cloth (yathra) from central Bhutan. Its three panels were woven as one loom length. Each panel displays characteristic auspicious diamonds flanked by meander patterns. The diamonds at left and right are executed in a color scheme called tenkheb *because it imitates silk patchwork by the use of multi-hued triangles. The diamond in the center resembles that of a* chagsi pangkheb *design [cf. fig. 3.5]. (see Catalog)*

FIG. 5.55
Cushion covers or blankets are often sewn from two panels of yathra. *Here, the loom length was woven so that its two halves would form a larger design when cut and joined. The pattern, imitating a Tibetan pile rug with a meander border, was an innovation that appeared during the reign of the second king (1926-52). The framed motifs include eight-pointed stars, vases, trees, and crossed thunderbolts, all of which decorate other woolens from central Bhutan. (see Catalog)*

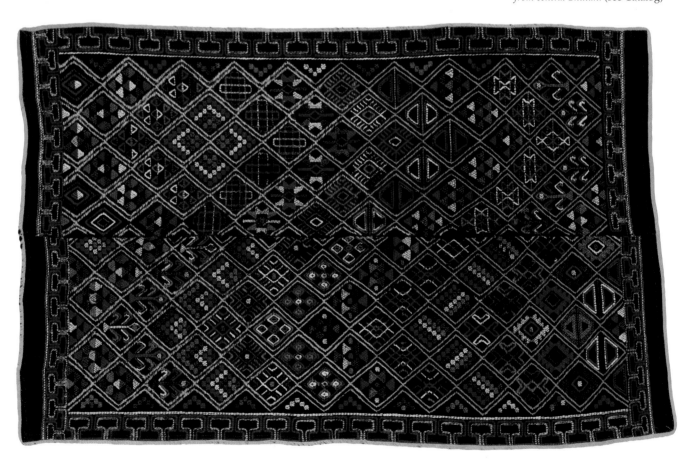

Fig. 5.56
Today, only older people, like this shepherd in Bumthang, wear woven raincloaks. Other Bhutanese may use the textiles as blankets. His white garment shows colorful, but sparse, floral designs and bands of weft striping. Woolens with a white ground like this one are traditionally associated with the Ura Valley of Bumthang. (D.K.M. 1986)

Coarser blankets of sheep wool and yak hair are used for seat and floor coverings in Bumthang and other high-altitude regions. They are plain black or brown with narrow white stripes, or they have wider stripes in two or three alternating colors. Like square carrying cloths, their corners may be ornamented with tufts of yak tail dyed red.

Raincloaks (*charkab*, 'rain covering') are fashioned from some of the same fabrics as seat covers. Although the term can refer to any handy cloth that protects one against rain or cold, these textiles are commonly made of *yathra* [figs. 1.3, 5.54]. A loom length is cut along the weft into three panels of equal size. These are joined together lengthwise, and the sides and ends of the textile may be hemmed or trimmed with piping. The cloak is draped around the shoulders and secured in front with cloth ties or a pin [fig. 5.56]. If it is made of *yathra*, the center panel of a raincloak traditionally features an auspicious diamond. The diamond is made up of colored triangles or squares, a pattern known as *tenkheb* ('cover for religious offerings') or *thrikheb* ('throne cover'), which is also seen on silk patchwork textiles for ritual use and painted on the fronts of altars in monasteries. Rendered in fabric or in the border patterning of *kushüthara* (where it is called *phup*), this patchwork is believed to bring long life to the wearer or user of the textile. Weavers from Kurtö say that a woman desiring safe delivery of a healthy child often invokes this blessing by stitching a patchwork of old scraps, thus giving them new life, or by incorporating the design into a fabric she is weaving.

Recent *yathra* raincloaks show a proliferation of designs and color, or greatly simplified patterns, and looser weave than older textiles. Earlier twentieth-century examples have fewer rows of patterning, more restrained color schemes, and very tight weaves [figs. 1.3, 5.57]. It was in part this tight twill, which forms a diamond pattern of its own in the weft-striped ground, that helped make the woolen fabric water resistant, if not quite waterproof. Cloaks of yak hair are truly water repellent. Today plastic sheets and raincoats are available even in the hills, and woolen cloaks are worn mainly by the older generation.

Living environments are also made from textiles, particularly among the pastoralists of eastern Bhutan (Merak Sakteng) and western Bhutan (Laya Lingshi). The people of Laya, for example, migrate to different grazing grounds with their flocks during the warmer months, and visit lower valleys such as Punakha to barter their yak products in the winter. They are well known for their black tents (*gur*) made of yak hair, which may be erected over a shallow, open stone basement. These low but spacious shelters are circular or oblong and supported by half a dozen poles. Yak hair bags filled with rice, dried cheese, or dried yak meat are stacked in the corners, and yak hair blankets are spread on the ground for sitting and sleeping. Similar tents accommodated the attendants of a nobleman's entourage while on tour [fig. 5.58].

Villagers may still walk for several days to attend a festival, and Bhutanese in all parts of the country often hold picnics and ceremonies outdoors when the weather permits. Tents serve as temporary lodgings at the site of a ceremony and as the setting for meals and for watching archery and dancing. In rural areas, the simplest tent is a canopy formed by a

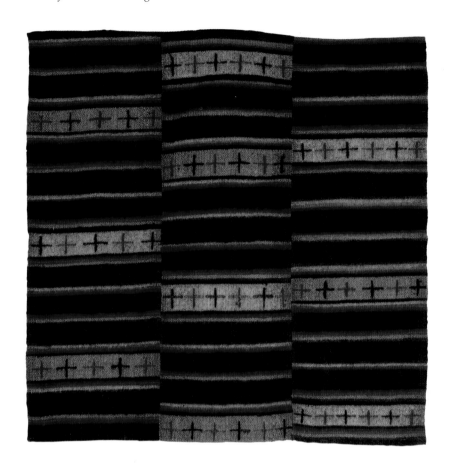

FIG. 5.57
This unusual charkab (left) *is a Bhutanese interpretation of an imported Tibetan fabric decorated with weft stripes and tie-dyed crosses* (hothra jalo)*. Here, the crosses are formed by thick, woolen supplementary-weft yarns. The ground is a tight diamond twill that Bhutanese call 'little bird's eye,' and the dyes are natural.* (see Catalog)

length of plain white cotton stretched between four sticks or tree trunks. Panels of fabric may also form walls for this shelter. These simple, home-woven tents are entirely different from tents decorated with appliqué that were traditionally used by the nobility (see Chapter Six).

FIG. 5.58
Bhutanese utilize a variety of woven tents. Black yak hair shelters are a part of everyday life for pastoral and seminomadic communities, and were once used, as this photograph shows, to house the entourage of an official on tour. The white tent would have accommodated the official. Its walls and peaked roof are features of tents used by Bhutanese for wedding banquets, archery contests, and other outdoor functions [cf. fig. 6.24]. The roof of the tent shown here displays patterning (kushü) characteristic of north central Bhutan, which does not decorate tents made today. This type of tent, sometimes having patterned sides as well, was used by the court until the 1950s. (John Claude White c. 1907, Courtesy National Geographic Society)

Chapter Six

Cut and Stitched

Textiles Made by Men

Men, Cloth, and Buddhism

FIG. 6.1

This seat cover exemplifies the textile artistry of men, who cut, stitch, embroider, and appliqué furnishings for the interiors of dzongs and temples and the living quarters of the lay and ecclesiastic elites. Square seat covers such as this one are placed on cushions in temples where high lamas sit, and on seats in audience halls, living quarters, and sitting rooms used by important people [fig. 6.2]. Because these textiles exalt a seat, they are loosely known as 'throne covers' (thrikheb), though now rarely used.

The central whirling emblem (norbu gongkhil) is associated with the primordial sound from which the universe originated. The emblem is framed by lotus petals like those that surround the pedestal of Buddhist statues, encircled by multicolored pearls and small drums used in ritual practice. In the field are four phoenixes, symbols of long life, perched gracefully on lotus fronds. At the cardinal points are mountain, cloud, and wave motifs; clusters of flaming gems, tied with flowing scarves, arise from the waters. On either side of the gems are diamond-shaped "king's earrings" or stylized cloud heads, likewise tied with scarves and borrowed from Chinese iconography. Scrolling foliage anchors the corners of the field. The seat cover is edged with wild silk fringe in five colors, creating the auspicious impression of a rainbow. A backing of plaid wild silk cloth (sethra) protects the textile when it is laid on the ground. (see Catalog)

I looked towards India and there I saw three sisters weaving cloth.
Where the oldest sister was weaving, there the youngest sister was weaving.
The cloth woven by the oldest sister was a lama's patchwork shawl.
The cloth woven by the youngest sister was a lama's woolen skirt.
The middle sister didn't know how to weave a lama's clothing,
But if she could weave a belt for my lama,
There would be a radiant light in the loom-room.

– Poem from western Bhutan[1]

This passage affirms the popular association of women with weaving and hints at the extraordinary spiritual power of the belt *(kera)* worn by men, including monks. In most of Bhutan, men are uniquely associated with the world of religion and government. This is because, according to Buddhist principles, men are superior to women in the hierarchy of life forms. They are born in this life as males because of good deeds in previous lives; they have more "spiritual merit" than women. A man's *kera* (belt) is likened to a protection cord *(sunkii)* blessed by a lama. Boys are, therefore, taught to hang their belts on a nail when undressing and not just drop them on the floor. If a boy *does* throw his belt casually aside and finds a knot in it when he picks it up, he should wear the belt that way for three days, just as if it were a knotted protection cord. Like a protection cord, a man's belt is a guardian *(sungma)* with powerful properties. Folding a man's belt in three and putting it under one's pillow or over one's blanket will bring a peaceful night's sleep. Because of these properties, belts are never washed, and women should never step over them.

Bhutanese men's principal garment – the belted robe *(go)* – like the country's religion, was derived from Tibetan models, reinforcing men's identification with elements of popular culture that relate to the source of Bhutanese Buddhism. A man's ceremonial shoulder cloth *(kabné)* symbolizes his superior spiritual status because it is the same as the shawl that a monk wears *(zen)* and explicitly represents a man's lay or ecclesiastic rank. Men's close connection to Buddhism is also reflected in their role as producers of ceremonial textiles.

Bhutanese men create marvelous textiles, but as a rule they do not weave; they cut already woven cloth and stitch it into finished forms. Many of these men are trained monks and skilled laymen who manufacture textiles by sewing appliqué *(lhemdru)*, assembling patchwork, and embroidering *(tshemdru,* 'sewing'). Unlike women, who traditionally used local dyes and fibers, men have always worked mainly with imported goods – woolen broadcloth and silk brocade from India, China, and Tibet, which by virtue of their origin or fiber are relatively costly and special. Moreover, the textiles men make are predominantly for use in dzongs, temples, monasteries, and elite homes. In production, appearance, and function, these textiles differ entirely from the cloth women weave for everyday use. Finished articles include throne covers, saddle covers, and ceremonial cloths patterned with appliqué or Buddhist motifs: altar covers, temple hangings, ceiling canopies, and shrine furnishings made of patchwork or joined brocades and silks; religious scrolls executed in embroidery, appliqué, or both; embroidered and patchwork accessories like hats and bags; and tents decorated with appliqué under which outdoor functions and rituals take place.

By their nature, these refined and highly decorative textiles are not owned by most people nor integrated into everyday secular life. They are made for the settings where religious activities and government business take place and where men rather than women preside. These cloths traditionally are used only by senior lamas, monks, ranking civil officials, the nobility and their families, and the kings [fig. 6.2]. Tents and seat covers also are used by people of means holding weddings, receptions to celebrate a promotion, and cremation ceremonies.

Some monks become skilled in carving, sculpting, or painting; others are instructed in tailoring, embroidery, and appliqué work. In a monastery attached to a dzong, novices start by working as assistants to an older monk who is a master tailor (*tshempön*). Working in groups, the monks are kept busy stitching the shrine furnishings for their chapels and producing textiles for the government or well-to-do clients. This tradition still flourishes largely because of the patronage of the royal family, which commissions many ritual textiles for temples and monasteries throughout the country.

Silk fabric (*göchen*) and yarn are preferred because they are the most beautiful and most expensive. From the Bhutanese perspective, religious textiles (and sculpture or painting) deserve the best efforts and raw materials available because they reflect on the piety of the patron and because making the textiles is a deed of faith that brings merit and blessings for this life and the next. In the past, silk was imported from India and from China through Tibet. After the closing of the Tibetan border in 1959, Chinese silk was very hard to come by, but the development of air travel in the past decade now ensures a reliable supply of fabrics from Hong Kong. This, added to general economic prosperity and active royal patronage, has led to the making of new sacred dance costumes, large appliqué banners, and shrine textiles in many villages and temples.

Some laymen and tailors (*tshemdru thumi*) who stitch garments such as men's robes and women's jackets also make textiles for use either by monks or by families in their private chapels and sitting rooms. Because these textiles are not produced by monks for the exclusive use of monks, they are, strictly speaking, not religious. However, the tailors are often monks who have left the order, and the methods and materials for producing the textiles are the same. There are no women tailors anywhere in Bhutan. Even in southern Bhutanese

FIG. 6.2

The last Druk Desi (temporal ruler) of Bhutan, Yeshe Ngudup, is seen here in his sitting room replete with textiles of the kinds made by men. In the foreground is a fringed, appliqué seat cover similar to that in fig. 6.1. On the wall behind him is an embroidered image (thangka) mounted in a surround of silk brocade. Similar Chinese silks have been stitched into an ornamental tassel – like neckties lying on top of one another – attached to his ritual drum, and into a cloth covering the table before him. The rich, patterned silk wrap folded on his left shoulder, and the hat at left, are signs of his office. (John Claude White 1907, Courtesy National Geographic Society)

communities that are partially Hindu, tailoring is a male occupation, traditionally linked to caste. The textiles laymen make include many of the items monks produce, especially woolen seat covers, cotton tents decorated with appliqué, patchwork altar covers, and other silk hangings to furnish shrines.

Monks and laymen who make these textiles participate in a long tradition of producing Buddhist religious art. The textiles, modeled on Tibetan prototypes, resemble examples produced throughout the Buddhist Himalayas. The goal is to recreate ritual icons in cloth, faithfully reproducing their colors, composition, and assembly. Because of the conservatism of the artistic traditions within Buddhism, the style, content, and functions of these textiles have changed little, if at all, in centuries. When assembling some textiles, like tents and cushion covers that are not solely for religious use, men can make choices about the symbols and colors to use, but the presentation of motifs is conventional. The textiles men produce, in contrast to fabrics made by women, are admired not for their creativity or innovation but for how closely they approximate a standard or ideal form.

Although apparent in scroll paintings, sculpture, and metalwork, regional styles in most ritual textiles are hard to discern for several reasons. Provenance is often obscured because the fabrics used to make them are the same throughout the Buddhist Himalayas. Chinese silks and imported woolen broadcloth are ubiquitous, and cloth woven in Bhutan, for example, may form the backing of an altar cover that was made in Lhasa and is now used in Ladakh. Relative degrees of detail or "sophistication" in an appliqué may suggest origin at a large religious establishment or in a town – but they cannot easily be associated with a particular country. The only characteristics of a textile that may – in combination with other information – suggest a provenance are emblems such as the Tibetan snow lions or, to a lesser extent, the Bhutanese double thunderbolt *(dorje jadam)* [fig. 6.20], which in the twentieth century have both been invested with national significance. The appearance of snow lions or double thunderbolts in an appliqué cannot alone be taken as evidence of origin, however, because both belong to a Himalayan vocabulary of religious art motifs.[2]

Thread and Color in Religion and Ritual

In religious contexts and rituals, thread and cloth take on special meaning and can be invested with protective powers. As one Bhutanese put it, thread is part of many rituals because it "keeps demons and gods at bay and appeases them at the same time."[3] The most common form of blessing from a lama, for example, is a thin cord of silk, silk-like acrylic, or cotton with a knot in it that recipients tie around their necks. Usually red or yellow, the thread should be worn for three days and then burned or worn until it falls off of its own accord. Sometimes lamas will knot a silk cord into an intricate amulet that a person carries as a form of protection. In Bhutan, as in all of the Himalayan Buddhist world, shrines made of wood and thread are seen outside many homes. The shrines consist of a wooden wand stuck in the earth, with one or more crosspieces at the top end, wound with colored yarns that look like a spider web. Bhutanese say these wand shrines *(dö)* are erected to ward off evil spirits, to maintain good relationships with the spirits, or to help heal someone who is ill. A lama provides instructions about what colors and format to use. These depend on the desired outcome, the locality, and the horoscope of the householder.

The color of the threads used for the *dö* and other rituals is very important – even more so than the fiber used – because color is an aspect of a person's identity or essence. Silk yarn is preferred, but cotton, wool, or even nettle fiber can be used as long as it is of the proper colors. A horoscope reveals which color(s) will be most efficacious. The five primary colors

FIG. 6.3

The colors of these banners, and the prayers printed on them, give power to these flags. Colors have special significance in thread and cloth used for ritual purposes because they correspond to the elements, to calendar years, to deities, to directions of the compass, and to emotions. These banners show a generally felicitous array of hues: the five primary colors – blue, white, red, green, and yellow – that are associated with the five elements – water, iron, fire, wood, and earth. Today made of Indian cotton onto which men have printed prayers with woodblocks, prayer flags are blessed by a lama before being flown. As the banners move in the wind, the prayers on them are repeated into the air. Flags are erected on specific days during the lunar year, for general merit, for the benefit of the souls of deceased family members and friends, and to decorate construction sites and the roofs of houses. (D.K.M. 1992)

(green, blue, red, white, and yellow) correspond to the five elements (wood, water, fire, iron, and earth), which in turn correlate with calendar years and the astrological setting at birth. Among high-status Bhutanese, the color of garments worn on an occasion such as marriage is selected in consultation with a lama, who assesses what color is most auspicious.

Thread and cloth of special colors are also central to activities like house construction. Bhutanese say that sometimes a thread or string literally fences a plot of land, demarcating it so it can be ritually protected. After the earth deity's blessing has been requested, a construction site is decorated with banners and flags (Chime Wongmo 1985, 111, figs. 3, 4). Four wooden poles are commonly erected at the cardinal points. Each is associated with one of Buddhism's four guardian deities, symbolized by a colored ribbon: white to the east, blue to the south, red to the west, and yellow to the north. At other critical stages in construction, colored or white banners are also raised. A prayer flag is installed on the roof.[4]

Bhutan's landscape is dotted with clusters of long, narrow prayer flags *(darpa)* that flutter on hillsides, on prominent points of land, and near temples and homes [fig. 6.3]. On the flags are woodblock-printed prayers that are wafted into the air, endlessly repeated, each time the fabric stirs in the wind. Like the written prayers contained in a hand- or water-turned prayer wheel, the message and power of the printed words are invoked with each motion, thereby enhancing the effect of the prayer and the merit accruing to the flags' donor. Although they were sometimes made of fine white wool in the past, flags today are made of inexpensive Indian cotton about 38 to 45 cm wide. Trained laymen or monks utilize square woodblocks to print the prayers on the fabric. Flags are sold in the market in white, red, blue, green, and yellow lengths, with prayers already printed on them. Panels are measured and cut according to the desired number of woodblocks, which depends on the length of the flagpole and individual preference. The length, color, and number of flags raised also varies, depending on the occasion. Donors may have narrow ribbons of colored cloth stitched at intervals to the fluttering edge of a flag, or they may commission flags that are printed with a particular prayer. Flags are taken to a lama to be blessed before being flown. After the death of a member, a family often erects 108 prayer flags, an extremely potent and auspicious number to Buddhists, for the benefit of the soul of the deceased.

Colors have special associations or qualities that determine their use in prayer flags and sometimes in other cloth. The colors of the Bhutanese clergy – red, maroon, orange, and yellow – dominate textiles for ecclesiastic use and monastic apparel. More generally, red is identified with heroic virtues, so senior officials with the title of *dasho* wear red shoulder cloths and carry swords. Yellow is a color of authority and majesty, reserved for the shoulder cloths of the king and chief abbot *(je khenpo)*. White, the "mother" color, denotes purity, goodness, and nobility, so the scarves offered to lamas and used on ceremonial occasions are white. The field color of the most prestigious woman's dress *(kushüthara)* is white, as are the shoulder cloths worn by the majority of men in Bhutan. In ritual and ritual art, colors are further associated with the four directions, with the four kinds of deeds, with different qualities and emotions, with the five Buddhas of Wisdom, and with other deities (Lauf 1976, 130; Mynak R. Tulku Rinpoche and Pommaret 1989, 7-9).

Monastic Apparel[5]

The dress code for Drukpa Kagyü monks in Bhutan was set out by Shabdrung Ngawang Namgyel when he organized the ecclesiastic community at the beginning of the seventeenth century. He closely followed the guidelines in Buddhist texts on discipline, whose precepts on vestments are common to all the schools of Tibetan Buddhism, although he made minor modifications in order to establish a Bhutanese Drukpa Kagyü convention that was distinct from its Tibetan counterpart [fig. 6.4].

In the culture of Buddhism, monks' clothes have symbolic meaning: inner garments represent the secret teachings and their realization, and outer garments, the discipline of monkhood and religious practice. In each of the Mahayana Buddhist schools, monks' apparel features slightly different ways of folding the essential garments and includes other particular elements as well. Bhutanese Drukpa Kagyü monks wear seven garments, three of which correspond to the essential garments of classical texts, the *chögo namsum* ('three types of religious garments').[6] These three sacred textiles are worn folded or draped and always

FIG. 6.4
Bhutanese Drukpa Kagyü monks dress according to guidelines laid out by Shabdrung Ngawang Namgyel in the seventeenth century. Their garments differ in only minor respects from the apparel of monks in other parts of the Buddhist Himalayas. Their clothing is mostly red, purple, and maroon, colors associated with the clergy. These young monks, who are husking betel nuts to chew, have draped their red shoulder cloths (zen) on their laps. Their vests are customary, but their wrapped lower garments are unusual because they are blue, one of several innovations that have since been forbidden by Bhutan's chief abbot. (Wangdi Phodrang, D.K.M. 1985)

should be with a monk at night.

The first of the three is a patchwork shawl (*chögo namjar*) of orange cotton for ceremonial occasions. In a pattern that several Bhutanese described as "resembling paddy fields," it has seven vertical sections, each composed of three panels sewn together so they overlap. A trident-like motif (*bja jé,* 'bird's foot') stitched on these panels is said to remind monks how to orient the shawl (the 'bird's feet' should point downward). The name *chögo namjar* ('religious garment pieced together') refers to the ancient Buddhist custom of making monks' clothing from scraps, in accordance with the vow of poverty that monks take. In the wider Himalayan Buddhist world, this garment or its equivalent is worn only for ceremonies such as confession and ordination, and only by fully ordained monks (*gelong*). Practices surrounding vestments in Bhutan differ slightly from other regions – in Bhutan few monks have received full ordination, although they are respectfully addressed as *gelong*.

The second important garment for Bhutanese monks is a maroon patchwork shawl or shoulder cloth for everyday wear *(zen)*.[7] This style of garment is said by Bhutanese to be what the Buddha was wearing when he was enlightened at Bodh Gaya. Its length should equal twenty-one spans of the wearer's hand, measured from the thumb to the tip of the third finger. The cloth may be made of wild silk, wool, or cotton.[8] In colloquial speech, the monk's shawl *(zen)* is often called a *kabné* ('covering'), the term used for a layman's ceremonial shoulder cloth. Like the latter, the monk's shawl is arranged in folds on the left shoulder and its color reveals the wearer's rank. A garment dyed maroon with lac (*jakham,* 'lac covering') is for ordinary monks. Orange is for the most senior monks of the Drukpa Kagyü hierarchy, the four *lopön* ('masters') – master of religious teachings, master of grammar, master of chanting and liturgy, and master of philosophy. These four, along with four other senior monks,[9] also wear a special dark brown woolen shawl *(therzen)* on top of their orange shawl. The king and the chief abbot wear yellow shoulder cloths.

The third essential monastic garment, also made of pieced-together cloth, is a tubular, maroon lower garment (colloquially, *shamtha*), worn folded into a long skirt.[10] Always put on over the head, rather than by stepping into it, the lower garment extends from the chest to the ankles. It is arranged with a fold in the back and one or more pleated folds on the right and left in front, which vary according to the monk's level of learning. These folds are likened by Bhutanese to the two flat pieces of wood that bind a sacred text. Bhutanese also say that, in theory, this garment should not be washed because it contains many blessings *(jinlab)*. A tailored underskirt (*meyö,* 'lower covering') of pleated white cotton is worn inside the wrapped maroon garment.

Depending on their rank, Bhutanese Drukpa Kagyü monks wear one or two tailored upper garments: a heavy vest of maroon cloth *(tötsi)* with a high collar and ornamental fabric at the shoulders, and an inner vest of cotton (colloquially, *tögo*) for senior monks.[11] The upper garments and underskirt are put on and secured at the waist with a yellow cloth cummerbund (*phoching,* 'stomach tie'). Then the lower garment is wrapped, arranged, and belted with a thin, plain, card-woven belt of red cotton or wool (*kuching,* 'body tie'). The upper edge of the lower garment is folded down over the belt and hides it. Some monks assisting in ceremonies wear belts decorated with intermittent supplementary-weft patterns like those more often seen on women's belts.[12]

The style and fabrics of a monk's vest(s) vary according to his rank and means. Usually, the garments have panels of silk at the shoulders and stiff cloth piping or edging at the armholes. Under the arms, a piece of felt or wool cut in a saw-toothed shape (*chabsham,* 'something that waves or dances') may be attached [fig. 6.4]. The piping is said by some

Bhutanese to represent a monk's vows, and the five saw-teeth, the volumes of major teachings that a monk must master. In recent decades, a number of Bhutanese monks wore blue shoulder trim on their jackets, but in 1988 the chief abbot, Je Khenpo Kunley Gyaltshen, ordered that they wear the more orthodox red color – an indication of the conservatism that governs monastic dress and other textiles for religious use.

Boots *(lham)* can be worn by any monk, but in practice only the most senior in the Bhutanese hierarchy wear them, and only on formal occasions. Similar to the traditional footwear of laymen, the boots have a thick leather sole with upturned toes and uppers made of heavy silk or thick woolen cloth ornamented with appliqué. Yellow, orange, or red uppers distinguish the rank of the wearer. The uppers are held in place below the knee by thin woven straps. Ordinary monks used to go barefoot, but nowadays they wear rubber thongs or Western-style shoes.

Bhutanese monks' garments traditionally were made of cotton cloth *(ré)* and woolen cloth *(nambu)*, with some silk used in the apparel of high-ranking monks. Although women did dye and weave maroon panels for monks' clothing, woolen fabrics imported from Tibet *(shema, therma)*, and wild silk cloth from Assam *(bura, for shawls)*, were preferred. The red or yellow belts worn by monks, as well as their boot ties, are woven by women on card looms. When a young boy enters a monastery, his parents provide him with two sets of clothes, replacing them as needed over time.

In contrast to lay dress, only minor changes have occurred in monks' attire. Nowadays, polyester and synthetic-blend fabrics from India are common for stitched garments – but the style and color of the garments have not changed. The most apparent innovations are in accessories, such as Western footwear, socks, and Seiko digital watches, that monks sometimes receive as gifts. Monks may also wear knitted sweaters and down jackets in cold weather; these are always maroon, in keeping with ecclesiastic guidelines.

There are fewer nuns than monks in Bhutan, but they, too, have a special dress. Women who have taken vows wear a purple or maroon dress in the Tibetan style *(bhokku, bögo)*. This full-length sleeveless garment overlaps in front and is belted with a plain, narrow red or yellow belt like that of a monk. A rectangular piece of maroon cotton *(jabté)* is wrapped around the lower body to protect the dress. Under her dress, a nun may wear a red blouse *(wonju)* or sweater, and over it a maroon jacket *(tögo)*. The fabrics of her outfit are usually cotton and wool, and sometimes polyester; Bhutanese say silks represent the sort of finery that nuns should take care to avoid. Nuns formerly went barefoot, but now wear thongs or plain, Western-style shoes without heels.

Dance Costumes

Religious festivals are held at different times of the year in almost every dzong of the country. Very important regional events, they last for several days and feature a series of dances. Dances reenacting episodes from Himalayan Buddhist history, and portraying important deities and their heavenly retinues, are performed by monks who undergo rigorous physical, mental, and spiritual training. Monk dancers wear masks and elaborate costumes that were inspired by Tibetan sacred dance traditions [figs. 6.5, 6.6]. Similar costumes are seen wherever these dances are staged, from Bhutan to Ladakh to Tibetan refugee communities in South India, because the dances themselves are similar throughout the Himalayan Buddhist world.[13] Other dances, derived from a uniquely Bhutanese heritage, vary from locality to locality and usually are performed by laymen. Lay dancers often wear what Bhutanese say is an archaic local dress or other costumes that existed before the Shabdrung.

Bhutan's two major Buddhist schools, the Drukpa Kagyü and the Nyingma, have similar dance traditions and costumes because each has incorporated the other's dances into its own festivals. Only a few dances remain specific to one or the other school. The main differences are in the choreography, music, and identity of the dancers. In central and eastern Bhutan where the Nyingma tradition is prevalent, in rare cases all the dances may be performed by monks. If there are no monks, they may be performed by the married laymen who have taken some religious vows (*gomchen*) and are a characteristic feature of the Nyingma tradition in Bhutan.

Dance costumes *(cham go)* are made primarily of Chinese silk brocades, which used to come from Tibet but nowadays are imported from Hong Kong. Characterized by a Western spectator in the eighteenth century as "extremely rich and showy ... [and] of the brightest coloured satin," the patterns and appearances of the costumes are governed by tradition, and have probably changed little over the years (Davis 1830, in Aris 1982, 59).[14] In 1774, monks wore "many-coloured satin cloaks ... [and] masquerade dresses, with visors like the beaks of birds, horses' heads, and other grotesque figures," much as they do today

Fig. 6.5
A monk-dancer performs the Black Hat dance (shanag cham), *which represents tantrists with supernatural powers; they drive out evil spirits and purify the surroundings with their footsteps. The dance also tells the story of the assassination in 842 of the anti-Buddhist Tibetan king, Langdarma, by a monk, Pelkyi Dorje, who had hidden his bow and arrows in the voluminous sleeves of his garment.* (Guy van Strydonck)

(Markham [1879] 1971, in Collister 1987, 17). Sometimes the same costumes are used in several dances. Dance robes are sewn by the monks responsible for tailoring, and new ones are made whenever a patron will pay for them, usually every twenty or thirty years. The costumes are stored in large wooden boxes in a special room and taken out only on festival days. The monks rehearse in their ordinary clothes, dancing barefoot.

One common type of costume, seen, for example, in the famous Black Hat dance, is an ankle-length tunic with long, kimono-like sleeves [fig. 6.5]. The full skirt is gathered at each hip in a series of pleats kept erect by a piece of wood secured to a padded belt worn under the dress. A long white cotton petticoat and vest are worn under the robe. Over this robe, depending on the dance, a dancer may wear a cotton apron painted with a terrifying deity's face and a short brocade or appliqué cape with fringed edges. Dancers often wear "cloud collars" made of floral brocade, an accessory whose form is seen also in traditional Chinese dress, in Tibetan dance costumes, and on the tops of Central Asian tents. Dancers wear a distinctive hat or mask, with a protective skullcap of thick cotton cloth. In the Drukpa Kagyü tradition, monk dancers generally wear boots decorated with appliqué.

Other costumes have knee-length skirts with an unusual construction, or trousers. The Lords of the Cremation Grounds, for example, wear a white cotton skirt with trousers or leggings underneath [fig. 6.6]. The skirt consists of a string to which long, narrow loops of cotton cloth are attached; these panels overlap when the dancer is at rest and swirl dramatically when he is in motion. This costume also includes a white cotton shirt, a short white cape, white footwear that separates the toes, and white gloves. Knee-length trousers are worn by the Ging, celestial beings who live in the paradise of Padma-sambhava, the saint

FIG. 6.6
This dance depicts the Lords of the Cremation Grounds, deities who protect regions symbolically situated on the periphery of the cosmic homes of the gods. The dancers' costumes, made of white cotton, yellow silk cloth, and brocade, evoke a world where life and death meet. (Guy van Strydonck)

who brought Buddhism to Bhutan in the eighth century. The garments are made of cotton cloth, printed like leopard skin. The Ging also wear front and back aprons sewn in the shape of a tiger skin. They dance bare-chested, their only upper garment being a brocade cloud collar.

Other dances feature 'heroes' *(pawo)* dressed in costumes that blend elements of archaic lay dress with aspects of dress now associated with village oracles of the same name. These dancers, when they represent attendants of Padmasambhava, are dressed in skirts constructed from loops of yellow patterned silk *(mentsi)* and waist-length blue silk jackets. Two panels of green-and-red brocade crisscross their chests, meeting in a diamond-shaped cloth emblem that recalls the amulets worn by ancient warriors. The *pawo* carry small drums and wear a diadem with five pointed panels *(rignga)*, a headdress worn by Bhutanese oracles that resembles crowns worn by shamans in Nepal and throughout Asia (Aris 1980b, 42), as well as the crowns worn by Buddhist priests for certain tantric rituals.

One unusual jacket for a festival performer is in the collection of the Museum of Ethnography at Neuchatel (Montmollin 1982, 119). Worn by a clown *(atsara)* who amuses onlookers, it is cut like jackets women wear *(tögo)*, with deep dolman sleeves and a shawl collar. However, it is neither woven nor made of brocade; it is stitched together of appliqué panels stylistically similar to ritual textiles and archaic women's tunics *(shingkha)*. The jacket shows a wheel of law on the back, flanked by the grinning visages of four "guardians." Bands of scrolling foliage, meander patterns, and flaming gems constitute the sleeves and front, almost as if the jacket had indeed been assembled from a *thrikheb*. The jacket is attributed to Bumthang.

Accoutrements of the Elite

Men skilled at embroidery and appliqué produce other items of apparel for Bhutanese of rank. These include sword accessories, hats, and the decorated boots worn by men and women of the court earlier in this century. While boots and sword accessories continue to be essential to a man's dress on formal occasions, the hats are very seldom used today.

Men of *dasho* rank or higher must wear a *pata losé* hanging from their sword belt on the left hip. While it may be woven, the decorative textile is often constructed of one or more pieces of brocade, silk, or cotton fabric about 30 cm long and arranged like neckties lying on top of each other. Sometimes the top cloth is embroidered with lucky symbols or flowers. In the past, this accessory was looped around the end of a man's sword and tucked in at the back of his belt, to hold up the sword while he walked or rode a horse. On meeting a superior, as etiquette required, the man released the sword, with one tug.

Although the queens of Bhutan do not wear crowns, photographs of the 1930s show women of the royal family wearing silk, pillbox-style hats *(peshasham)* [figs. 6.7, 6.8]. The front of the hat is often embroidered with a cluster of three flaming gems representing the Buddha, his teachings, and the community of the faithful. Colorful lotus blossoms or a pair of rampant, golden-scaled dragons may be depicted on the sides of the hat. Bhutanese relate

these hats to those worn in Tibet, where headgear was associated closely with social rank, and attribute their appearance in Bhutan to the royal family's contacts with Lhasa in the early twentieth century.[15] The custom of wearing this kind of hat was discontinued by the third queen, Queen (Mother) Ashi Kesang.

Like the queens, the kings of Bhutan have worn elaborate and unusual hats in lieu of a crown. The first king was photographed in different hats *(usha)*, several of which are now on display at the National Museum in Paro. They are round, usually with a stiff, upturned brim made of silk and brocade streamers hanging down the back. The brim is characteristically embroidered with a pair of dragons flanking a cluster of three flaming gems. In photographs seen today in government offices, hotels, shops, and other public places, the first and second kings both are wearing a hat associated with the office of Tongsa Pönlop (governor), a now honorary position customarily held by the crown prince. The hat is topped with a sculpted raven's head, recalling how Shabdrung Ngawang Namgyel was guided to Bhutan from Tibet by a raven. The bird's presence on the hat signifies the king's link to this spiritual ancestor and affirms his legitimacy. The "raven crown" continues to be a powerful symbol of the monarchy and was worn by the present king at his coronation.

Senior lay and religious officials wore hats associated with rank as well. Lay hats were mostly closefitting and stitched from silk or velvet. One style seen in old photographs has a trefoil panel at the front of its upturned brim; this panel is adorned with a prominent auspicious emblem, perhaps a double thunderbolt, or the cluster of flaming gems, also worn by royalty. The hats are topped with a silver or brass finial. Senior monks and lamas always wore headgear stitched of woolen cloth and silk, much as they do today. The most distinctive examples are the stiff, flared maroon hats worn by Drukpa Kagyü hierarchs [fig. 1.6].

Among well-to-do Bhutanese, hats made of silk damask and brocade are occasionally worn by a bride and groom [fig. 6.8]. They are worn on the counsel of a lama, who also selects the most felicitous date for the marriage ceremony, specifies the proper rituals to perform, and identifies auspicious colors for the couple's garments. Like the queens' hats, wedding hats are said to have been adapted from traditions among the aristocracy of south central Tibet. The hat of a groom is shaped somewhat similarly to that worn by heroes in sacred

FIG. 6.8

Embroidered silk hats were worn by Bhutanese queens and princesses earlier this century [fig. 6.7]. This example (foreground) has a whirling emblem surrounded by lotus petals on the top and two dragons clutching wish-fulfilling gems on its upturned brim. Three flaming jewels issuing from a lotus, at the front of the hat, represent the Buddha, his teachings, and the community of the faithful.

Brides and grooms may wear hats on the advice of a lama. The shapes and colors of the bridal hats shown here – red for the bride and green for the groom – were selected by consulting the horoscopes of the couple. The hats were stitched by male tailors in the service of the bride's and groom's households. (see Catalog)

FIGS. 6.9-10

Men's robes and women's jackets made from sumptuous Chinese silks have been favored among the elite at least since the early twentieth century. The jacket (above) was made from a robe worn by King Jigme Dorji Wangchuck in the early 1950s; his daughter, Her Royal Highness Ashi Choeki, later had the garment stitched into a jacket for her use. Today, such jackets are treasured heirlooms, packed in trunks most of the year and worn by the young women of a family for special occasions (see right). (fig. 6.10, Anthony Aris 1983) (see Catalog)

153

dances and may derive its auspicious quality in part from this association.[16] Related hats, made of wool with small areas of embroidery, were once worn by villagers in the Pelé La and Bumthang regions.[17]

Religious Scrolls and Banners

Thangka are religious scrolls found, made, and used in the greater Himalayan Buddhist area, from Ladakh to Bhutan and Mongolia to Nepal. The images are painted, embroidered, or appliquéd, and some combine embroidery and appliqué [figs. 6.11, 6.12].[18] Mounted in a frame of silk brocade, backed with cloth, and attached to a wooden dowel at either end,

Fig. 6.11

This image of Tsepamé, the Buddha of long life, with his consort illustrates the genre of religious scrolls (thangka) made by monks and trained laymen in Bhutan. Tsepamé is seated on a lotus pedestal and surrounded by a rainbow, a phenomenon often associated with the sudden appearance of deities. The plinth on which the lotus pedestal rests is carved and painted in typical Bhutanese fashion with two phoenixes, symbols of long life. The small figure at bottom center is possibly the sixteenth-century lama, Pema Karpo ('white lotus'), wearing the distinctive hat of a Drukpa hierarch.

The image is surrounded by narrow bands of yellow and red silk, called the thangka's 'rainbow,' and a main border of blue Chinese silk. The square panel at the bottom is called the 'door' of the thangka, a reminder of the images' role in Buddhist practices that involve contemplation of and spiritual entry into a thangka. *The image itself is constructed of cut and pieced Chinese silk damasks and brocades, heavily embroidered with silk threads and couched with gold cord. (see Catalog)*

scrolls are hung on walls in temples and private chapels, and are easily rolled up for transport or when not in use. These hangings are longer than they are wide and range in size from roughly 30 cm long to over 10 m long. Bhutan has a well-developed tradition of making embroidered and appliqué scrolls. *Thangka* are commissioned by donors, and the images' artistic value depends on which artist and materials a donor can afford. Commissioning a *thangka* is a virtuous action that earns merit, removes all sorts of obstacles from one's life, or brings a better rebirth to a deceased relative.

In Bhutan, *thangka* are made by monks or pious laymen who come from families of artists. Because of the nature of a *thangka*, it is considered better if the layman has a "proper mind attitude," that is, some religious inclination. Some painters are ex-monks or married lay priests *(gomchen)* of the Nyingma school. Most have received religious initiations that enable them to paint deities. However, with the development of the tourist trade, many *thangka* are now painted without any religious commitment.

The making of a *thangka* is a long process, involving different skills at different stages, from preparing the cloth support to sewing the image to its brocade frame. Often several people participate in making the scroll, with a master supervising the work. Most *thangka* are painted on a base cloth of fine, plainweave Indian cotton (in rare cases, silk). This is stretched on a wooden frame, stiffened with a coat of specially prepared glue on either side, and allowed to dry. A coat of glue and chalk is applied to the canvas and smoothed, to render the ground even and easy to work on. The subject, whose dimensions are dictated by written iconographic rules, is sketched in charcoal or graphite pencil. Alternatively, the painter may use a ready-made pattern, such as a woodblock or a stencil, to outline the image. Then organic colors or acrylic pigments are applied. A master painter will often leave parts of the image for his assistants to fill in.

More rarely, a *thangka* is made by embroidery or appliqué. In these cases, a pattern will be sketched or stenciled onto a silk or cotton ground cloth. The image is assembled first into several sections. Paper patterns guide how pieces of plain silk and patterned brocade are cut and joined, or embroidered, to compose primary and secondary deities and pattern elements. Once the component sections are ready, they are stitched one by one to the background cloth until the *thangka* is complete.

The *thangka* is then mounted in a frame of brocade panels, which may have been salvaged from an earlier textile. Between the image and the main brocade frame, which is traditionally blue, narrow panels of red and yellow brocade generally appear; they are called the *thangka*'s 'rainbow' *(ja)*, a phenomenon often associated with the sudden appearance of deities. A contrasting panel of brocade, called the 'door of the *thangka*' *(thang go)*, may be sewn onto the main border below the image. Usually, the *thangka* is backed with different, plain cloth. Finally, the scroll is secured to wooden rods with brass or silver knobs at each end. A piece of lightweight silk or cotton cloth, often yellow silk printed with a red-and-green floral pattern *(mentsi)*, is sewn to the upper rod as a cover for the entire image. This cover conceals the image if the deity represented is not meant to be seen by casual viewers, and it protects the *thangka*'s surface from damage when the scroll is rolled up for transport or storage.

Bhutan is known for very large appliqué *thangka*, which are unfurled over the entire façade of a religious building at festival times [fig. 1.4].[19] These *thangka* – sometimes five stories tall – are called *thongdröl*, meaning that the mere sight of the image liberates a viewer. A knowledgeable Bhutanese told this story about how the first large appliqué *thangka* in Bhutan, now stored in the dzong at Thimphu, was made about 300 years ago:

An important lama, the reincarnation of Shabdrung Ngawang Namgyel's son, had a dream one night in which Pelden Lhamo [the goddess who is Bhutan's protective deity] urged him to make a *thangka* of this kind. The next morning, he began cutting silk into pieces, but he was confused because he had no pattern for such a large image. That night he had a second dream that a bee would help him. The following morning, the bee appeared and buzzed over the silk cloth, showing him the shape of the pieces to cut, and this is how *thongdröl* came to be made in Bhutan.[20]

There are now about twenty monumental *thangka* in Bhutan, at most of the major dzongs and other important temples. Because of the size of the image and the financial outlay involved, commissioning a *thongdröl* brings considerable merit to the donor. This merit is increased by the fact that the image is not just for the donor but will benefit all the people who see it at festivals. Except for a few hours on one day of an annual festival, *thongdröl* are kept rolled and carefully wrapped in a storeroom of the dzong. In the 1980s, several *thongdröl* were commissioned by the royal family and private individuals; these can take up to a year to complete and exhibit a level of intricacy and workmanship that did not exist previously.

A religious scroll, be it a *thongdröl* or a smaller image for a monastery or private shrine, is not complete and has no religious value without a consecration. Sacred syllables are written on the back of the *thangka* in a ceremony that brings life and power to the textile image. It then becomes a hallowed object of worship.

Ceremonial Textiles and Shrine Furnishings

Many textiles are required for furnishing audience halls and shrines in dzongs, monasteries, temples, and private chapels. The ceremony – and brilliant textiles – of the court of Bhutan have been described by visitors since the seventeenth century in terms that hardly differ over time. Many of the textiles that add color to these accounts were imported Chinese silk robes; others were banners on poles, streamers on trumpets, ceremonial umbrellas, and cloth accessories for animals. In 1774, the first British emissary observed how the Druk Desi (temporal ruler) traveled: he was preceded by "twelve led horses, ... a hundred and twenty men dressed in red and blue, ... thirty archers, thirty horses laden with cloth, forty men on horseback ... and six musicians." Attendants waved fly whisks and twirled a white silk umbrella with colored fringes over his head (Markham [1876] 1971, cited in Collister 1987, 15). Twentieth-century visitors remarked on similar splendor and richly caparisoned animals at occasions like the wedding of the third king (Todd 1952). Animal trappings included embroidered and appliqué saddlecloths, bridles decorated with ribbons, and pile textiles imported from Tibet. Triangular face ornaments for horses and pile saddle carpets were popular among the well-to-do and are still seen in Bhutan, but the trappings of silk and appliqué are now used only on special occasions.

The sumptuous interiors at the Bhutanese court were described by the diplomat John Claude White, who presented the insignia of a Knight Commander of the Indian Empire to Ugyen Wangchuck at a ceremony in Punakha Dzong in 1905:

The centre or nave ... was hung with a canopy of beautifully embroidered Chinese silk. Between the pillars were suspended *chenzi* [silk brocade banners] and *gyentsen* [*gyetshen*, cylindrical silk] hangings of brilliantly coloured silks ... and [nearby] a fine specimen of *kuthang*, or needlework picture, a form of embroidery in which the Bhutanese excel. ... On the opposite side of the nave, ... was a low dais with a magnificent cushion of the richest

FIG. 6.12

This thangka *of Shakya Gyaltshen (1813-75) is assembled from pieces of imported Chinese silk tabby, damask, and brocade, cut and stitched together to form the ground and the figure. Details are embroidered with multi-colored silk floss in satin, chain, and seed knot stitches, and the outlines are couched in gold-wrapped thread.*

A Bhutanese inscription on a paper tag attached to this thangka *identifies Shakya Gyaltshen as the 35th and 38th head abbot (je khenpo) of Bhutan, who ruled from 1865 to 1869 and again in 1875. He is depicted in the robes of an abbot, seated on a throne, with his legs wrapped in his outer garment. His red hat identifies him with the Drukpa school of Mahayana Buddhism, the dominant school in Bhutan. Along the top of his throne is draped a white silk* khada *('presentation scarf'), while lotus blossoms spring from behind. The* thangka's *cover, made of flowered yellow silk (mentsi), is gathered at the top of the image. This* thangka *is thought to have been a diplomatic gift given to Lt. Col. J.L.R. Weir in Bhutan in the 1930s. (see Catalog)*

Fig. 6.13

"Floating banners of brocade and gyaltshen [hangings], and ... precious religious picture-scrolls embroidered in silk" decorated the audience hall at Punakha Dzong on the occasion of Sir Ugyen Wangchuck's coronation as Bhutan's first druk gyalpo in 1907. This photograph shows rows of cylindrical silk hangings (gyetshen) at the left and right and a long silk patchwork banner (chenzi) on the far side of the room. A ceremonial multipurpose cloth (chagsi pang-kheb) is visible on the table around which some men have gathered. Piles of cloth and other gifts are in the foreground. The ecclesiastic officials at left are garbed in the robes of senior Drukpa monks and miter-like silk hats. Several of the lay officials are wearing striped supplementary-warp-patterned (aikapur) robes, and all are swathed in their shoulder cloths. (John Claude White 1907, Courtesy National Geographic Society)

salmon-coloured brocade, on which Sir Ugyen Wangchuck sat, dressed in a handsome robe of dark blue Chinese silk, embroidered in gold with the Chinese character 'Fu' (White [1909] 1984, 140-41).

At Sir Ugyen Wangchuck's coronation as Bhutan's first king two years later, the audience hall at Punakha was "gaily decorated with floating banners of brocade and *gyaltshen*, and with precious religious picture-scrolls embroidered in silk" (White [1909] 1984, 224) [fig. 6.13]. In the past, similar textiles adorned the shrine rooms and living quarters of senior religious and lay officials within the dzongs. Most of these furnishings are assembled as patchwork from cut pieces of cloth – traditionally silk and nowadays often silk-like acrylic, rayon, and polyester. Others are composed of silk, cotton, or woolen broadcloth appliqué.

Almost every Bhutanese home has a private chapel or shrine room on the second or uppermost floor. As in monasteries and temples, three kinds of hangings, collectively called *chephur gyetshen*, are suspended from the ceiling [fig. 6.14]. Their sizes vary according to the size and height of the room. The first (*phen, baden*) has a cloud shape at the top and four narrow, ribbon-like panels of silk hanging below it. The second (*gyetshen*) is a cylindrical construction with a valance at the top, a plain center panel, and another valance at the lower edge. The third (*chephur*) is also a cylindrical textile, made up of narrow, overlapping, vertical panels of brocade. Typically, each type of hanging is mounted in a pair so that six hangings make a set. Other ceiling decorations are a rectangular canopy (*ladri*) made of patterned silk with a valance that hangs from its edges, and joined silk roundels that look like a string of colored pearls (*drawa draché*). A long banner of narrow brocade panels (*chenzi*, 'offering of silk to the gods') adorns the top of the walls of a shrine room. This type of hanging is idealized as made from garlands of gold, silver, and silk; some examples are latticework, composed of delicate brocade strips, silk ribbons, and gilt tassels that emulate this vision.

The shrine itself, constructed of wood, often covers most or all of one wall. The shrine has tiered altars where offerings are placed, niches where statues are displayed, and shelved compartments where religious texts, bound neatly in cloth and woven ties, are stored. Each

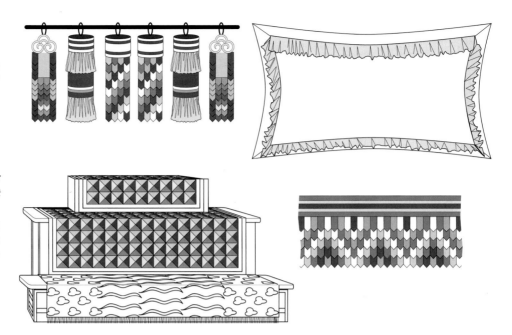

FIG. 6.14

Shrine Room Textile Furnishings. *The same textiles that decorate dzongs and temples adorn the shrine rooms of well-to-do homes. Three kinds of hangings (upper left) are suspended, in pairs, from the ceiling. From left to right they are: a* phen, *a* gyetshen, *two* chephur, *another* gyetshen, *and another* phen. *A canopy (*lathi, *upper right) is hung from the ceiling in front of the shrine, over the area where lamas and monks are seated when they conduct rituals for the family. Around the walls of the room, a long banner of brocade panels (*chenzi, *lower right) is installed.*

Bhutanese shrines are large wooden structures, intricately carved and painted, that include at least three altars (lower left). The lowest level, for food offerings, is draped with a tiger or leopard skin, or a textile patterned to resemble the animals' hides. The middle and upper levels, for water offerings, butter lamps, and incense, are covered with silk patchwork textiles. (After a drawing by Tenzing Namgay)

of the surfaces where offerings are placed is covered with a cloth (collectively, *chökheb*). The first and lowest altar of the shrine (*tshogthri*, 'multitude throne'), for food offerings, is supposed to be draped with a tiger or leopard skin; in practice this is more often a textile with patterns of tiger stripes or leopard spots and a fringe at its lower edge (*tshogkheb*, 'multitude covering'). The middle altar (*chöthri*, 'shrine throne'), where water offerings, butter lamps, and incense are placed, is covered with a multicolored patchwork textile that hangs over the altar's front edge (*tenkheb*, 'offering cover,' or *chökheb*). The top altar (*torthri*, '*torma* [butter offering] throne'), where ritual sculptures made of colored butter are arranged, is covered with a similar cloth, here called a *torkheb* ('*torma* cover'). All of these textiles can be draped over any raised place where ritual or other objects are kept.

The patterning of patchwork altar covers [figs. 6.15-6.16] is related to paintings that appear on monastery walls. Showing a checkerboard of colored squares, the paintings have complex significance. Bhutanese say that, as whole images, these are cosmograms or 'wheels of excellent existence' *(kunzang khorlo)*, in which the colors of the squares correspond to levels of spiritual and psychological awareness. The squares themselves may be inscribed with poetic anagrams and mystical syllables. The same checkerboard pattern is often painted onto a wooden shrine, and decorates the silk cloth on a table for an abbot's ritual instruments.

Special additional textiles are found in shrines dedicated to wrathful forms of Buddhism's protective deities (*gönkhang*, 'protector deity chapel'). These incorporate imagery suited to the deities – skulls that underscore the ephemeral nature of human existence, body parts that represent a loosening of sensual attachments to this world, and motifs showing a multitude of symbolic offerings to the gods (*gyentshok*). Rectangular and square appliqué panels of silk or woolen broadcloth may decorate an altar and the walls, and long banners are hung around the four walls of the room (Hill 1993; Rhie and Thurman 1991, 380, no. 158).

In shrine furnishings, there has probably been virtually no change in several centuries, except for the recent use of imitation silks. The interiors of temples and monasteries are often richly hung with decorative textiles, some new and some older, which are replaced as pious laypeople commission or donate them. If they are in good condition, fragments of older textiles will be reused in a new patchwork banner, so it is not unusual to see seventeenth- and eighteenth-century silks joined to panels of nineteenth-century brocade.

FIGS. 6.15-16
Patchwork silk altar covers (tenkheb) may cover one or more altars within a Bhutanese shrine. Examples like this one (fig. 6.16, below) are used on low tables in a shrineroom where ritual instruments are kept. Assembled from Chinese silks, tenkheb always show triangular pieces that are often fragments salvaged from old textiles. The unusual woven textile (fig. 6.15, left) emulates this patchwork and may have covered an altar or a seat, or wrapped a pair of cymbals for ritual use. In the secular world, patchwork is associated with long life. (see Catalog)

FIG. 6.17
This seat or saddle cover (gayok, at left) is assembled of Bhutan-woven, rather than imported, cloth and features an auspicious swastika (thenma yurung) surrounded by supplementary-weft patterning that imitates the patchwork in ritual textiles. The fringe incorporates the five primary colors that correspond to the elements [fig. 6.3], like a rainbow around the cloth. (see Catalog)

FIG. 6.18

Riding was a privilege reserved for men of rank and the nobility because Bhutan had few horses. Many of the textiles used on horseback are embroidered or appliquéd woolen broadcloth, emblazoned with long-life phoenixes and other propitious symbols [fig. 6.1]. Some horse trappings show checkerboard patterns like those on altar covers. The syce holding the horse's bridle has his shoulder cloth wrapped around his neck, and the lower part of his robe is protected by an apron from dust raised by the horse's hooves. The apron (damkhi) is striped, handspun cotton cloth from southwestern Bhutan. (Joan Mary Weir 1931, Courtesy Maybe Jehu)

Seat covers

Square and rectangular textiles loosely called 'throne covers' *(thrikheb)* are placed on cushions where high lamas sit in temples, as well as on cushions in audience halls, living quarters, and sitting rooms used by important people. They also serve to seat guests in lay homes on special occasions. In the past, a *thrikheb* was also carried by an attendant of the king to place on the floor when the monarch did prostrations while visiting temples. The same textiles arranged on a horse's back for the king, a nobleman, or a lama were called *gayok* ('saddle covering') when used in this fashion [figs. 6.17, 6.18]. Most of these textiles are made of broadcloth *(jachen)* or other woolen fabrics decorated with appliqué and embroidery and surrounded by a multicolored silk fringe. When for ecclesiastic use, *thrikheb* have a red or maroon ground. Seat covers typically show Buddhist symbols such as thunderbolts *(dorje)*, swastikas *(yurung)*, or whirling emblems *(norbu gongkhil)*, and they are sometimes intricately patterned with secondary motifs including phoenixes *(bja tshering)*, snow lions *(singye)*, flaming gems *(norbu)*, and ritual offerings *(gyentshok)*. More rarely, square seat covers resembling altar cloths are made of patchwork assembled from small triangles of broadcloth or brocade. Square seat covers are approximately 90 by 90 cm and rectangular covers roughly 90 by 170 cm.

Plainer versions of the same textiles, for less important occasions, have a name that is not honorific: *khaden*. These cushion covers are made of red, blue, yellow, and green broadcloth or local woolen fabric and lack silk fringes. They furnished elite homes and residences of the royal family, and were traditionally offered to visitors. Ordinary households often had a seat cover for distinguished callers as well. Square seat covers with auspicious symbols continue to be part of marriage ceremonies among the elite: the bride sits on a textile with a swastika, an emblem of eternity and long life, and the groom on one with a thunderbolt, a symbol of power and wisdom.

Rectangular appliqué textiles *(bokheb,* 'bedding cover,' or simply *kheb,* 'cover') likewise show thunderbolts and other Buddhist symbols fashioned from colorful broadcloth [fig. 6.20], and are typically fringed on their two narrow ends. Like more modest woven *denkheb*

FIG. 6.19

Square textiles that covered sitting cushions (thrikheb) *were taken along when traveling and spread on chairs or on the ground. This portrait shows the Paro Pönlop (governor) seated on a textile comparable to that in fig. 6.1, with floral corners and phoenixes in the field. A plainer but similar textile is on the grass in front of the governor. The governor and two other officials are wearing striped robes of supplementary-warp-patterned cloth from eastern Bhutan* (aikapur), *while the man at right is garbed in silk brocade. The various hats are associated with rank. (John Claude White c. 1907, Courtesy National Geographic Society)*

FIG. 6.20

Rectangular appliqué textiles (bokheb, kheb) *are constructed in the same way as square seat covers. This example shows a central double* dorje, *which has come to be a symbol of the royal government in the twentieth century; its presence could indicate that this textile was used at the court. The wild silk backing* (shabthrawo) *is similar to that for stitching brogpa women's dresses. (see Catalog)*

in ordinary homes, these covers were arranged on raised mattresses. They were also carried by attendants in court entourages and spread on the ground for officials to sit upon or as decoration. While a group was traveling, the bedding of the most senior officials would be rolled up in a textile of this kind.

While the silk textiles for altars and shrine rooms are made by men with techniques not used for lay textiles, ceremonial seat covers do not always have inherent ritual significance and may incorporate handloomed cloth of local manufacture rather than imported silk and woolen broadcloth. The center panel of some square examples is woven of cotton or wool patterned with woolen or wild silk supplementary wefts in the style of north central Bhutan (kushü) [fig. 6.17]. One rare woven panel has the appearance of silk patchwork [fig. 6.15].

FIG. 6.21 (opposite)

Phoenixes, snow lions, water deities, and winged guardian figures animate this superb appliqué seat cover. The central ring of lotus petals, which also forms pedestals for Buddhist images [cf. figs. 6.11, 6.12], symbolically elevates the person seated on the textile. All of these motifs are common to appliqué textiles used throughout the Buddhist Himalayas, making provenance difficult to determine. This exceptional example may be of Bhutanese manufacture, or a gift or commission of Tibetan origin. (see Catalog)

Small Bags

At one time, the Bhutanese used a variety of bags whose shapes reflected their different functions. While one still finds examples in use, several bag types are disappearing because plastic carrying sacks and Western-style purses and briefcases now serve the same purposes.

Kechung ('little neck'): This soft, round bag is about 20 cm in diameter, has a drawstring neck, and is carried by a leather strap or in the pouch of a garment [fig. 6.22]. A bag like this is made from scraps of wild silk and cotton cloth or of woolen broadcloth. It can carry coins, cowrie shells, betel nuts, dried chilies, and other sundries. *Kechung* are not common today.

Thrikhu: This cylindrical cloth bag is 20 cm or more in diameter and up to 60 cm long. It also has a drawstring neck and is usually pieced from circular strips of imported broadcloth; it may have a large central panel that is specially woven to become part of the bag or is salvaged from a robe *(go)* or dress *(kira)*. A distinctive feature of this bag is a wooden slat (or two) attached near the mouth to support the closing cord and leather carrying strap so that the filled container can be slung over a shoulder and carried easily. *Thrikhu* are used especially by lamas and monks to carry ritual objects for meditation or performing a ceremony.[21] These bags are no longer seen very often.

FIG. 6.22

Bhutanese men stitch bags from scraps of woven cloth and imported fabrics, tailoring the shapes of the containers to particular uses. The small drawstring bag (kechung; left) *is pieced from bits of wild silk cloth, perhaps left over from assembling garments. Ordinary people used pouches like this to carry coins, cowrie shells, betel nuts, and other sundries. The long cylindrical bag* (rear) *is a* thrikhu, *constructed of woven fabric from north central Bhutan with bright broadcloth at each end.* Thrikhu, *filled with personal effects or ritual objects, were slung over one shoulder by a leather strap. The pair of pouches in the foreground are an elite style, presented to their present owners by the third king in 1955. Their most unusual features are the carved silver rings that slide down to secure the mouths of the pouches and gilt ornaments in the shape of a lucky knot at the bottom of each pouch. All three of the bag types shown here are rarely seen today because Western-style purses and shopping bags are taking their place.* (see Catalog)

Chabshub ('water cover'): One of the attendants of the early kings and senior nobility carried a specially designed bag in which a drinking flask covered in cloth or leather, silver boxes of betel nuts and lime, and other sundries were easily accessible. This textile consists of a 20-cm-wide strap of broadcloth or silk, with pouches formed by strips of colorful silk, woolen, or cotton cloth joined to both ends of the strap. When the strap was slung over a shoulder, the pouches hung above waist level, one in front and one in back. The example illustrated [fig. 6.22, bottom], presented to its owner by the third king in 1955, has two small silver rings that slide downward to neatly secure the mouths of the pouches. This type of bag is also used by monks and resembles cloth containers kept in shrine rooms for storing sandalwood and other incense, in the form of sticks, leaves, or powder.[22]

Tsamkhu ('flour container'): This cylindrical drawstring bag, similar to a *thrikhu*, is still very much in use for transporting or storing flour, roasted grain, or rice. New examples found in use today generally incorporate a center panel of machine-made rather than handwoven cloth and usually have ends made from commercial woolen felt.

FIG. 6.23

Animal trappings include appliqué saddle pads of Bhutanese manufacture, saddle covers sewn from lengths of central Bhutanese yathra, *and pile saddle carpets woven in Tibet. Today, with the advent of motor roads, horses are less used for transport and the traditional saddle gear photographed here in Bumthang in 1971 is seldom seen. (Anthony Aris)*

Animal Trappings

Like some of the bags described above, many animal blankets and saddle pads are "second-generation" textiles fashioned out of cloth once used for another purpose. Stitched from old wild silk clothing or woolen blankets, they are backed and edged with blue or red cotton or broadcloth. Pile face ornaments for horses and mules (imported from Tibet and Kalimpong), and more unusual, locally made appliqué face decorations and appliqué or embroidered saddlecloths, were used by lay and religious elites.

Tents

Especially in the past, decorative cloth tents *(gur)* were used for temporary living quarters and for holding special outdoor events. Ceremonial tents housed officials and their entourages while on tour and were erected for court banquets, promotion festivities, and other ceremonies. Unlike the black yak hair tents woven by nomadic herders, these tents are square or rectangular and have a sharply peaked roof. They are made of white cotton fabric from India, trimmed with cotton or broadcloth appliqué on the roof and at intervals around the sides [fig. 6.24]. The appliqué shows architectural motifs such as window frames, and Buddhist symbols – a pair of deer (associated with the Buddha's first sermon at Sarnath), lucky knots, and wheels of law. A colorful valance, perhaps of yellow silk patterned with red flowers *(mentsi)*, flutters at the edges of the roof, along the top of the tent's cloth walls. Over such a tent, another panel of plain cloth was customarily erected as a dew shield.[23]

Ceremonial tents were once commissioned by regional governors *(pönlop)* for distribution to the dzongs under their respective jurisdictions and were made by monk communities housed in the dzongs. Similar tents, still used by well-to-do families for banquets celebrating

FIG. 6.24
Ceremonial tents create special environments for viewing archery contests and festivals, eating a banquet at a marriage or promotion celebration, and other celebratory occasions. They are made of imported Indian cotton, embellished by skilled laymen or monks with appliqué that adds architectural veracity: window silhouettes, roof details, and auspicious Buddhist symbols, which are also painted on houses. The tent here, photographed at the Paro Tsechu festival, shows a cluster of flaming gems on the narrow end and a wheel of law flanked by two rampant dragons on the broad side; lucky knots and wheels of law decorate the sides. Today, ceremonial tents are usually borrowed when needed; new ones are seldom made. (D.K.M. 1987)

weddings and promotions, and at archery tournaments, may be commissioned from skilled laymen or tailors who are former monks and specialize in appliqué work. Today tents are generally borrowed, and new ones are rarely made because of the expense involved and their infrequent use.

The most elaborate tents used by the court were made of cloth decorated with supplementary wefts in the style of north central Bhutan *(kushü)*. A 1904 photograph [fig. 5.58] shows one such tent with plain sides and a sloping roof of patterned cloth with appliqué added to the corners. An even more extraordinarily decorated tent, now privately owned, is constructed entirely of handloomed cotton cloth decorated with supplementary-weft wild silk and wool motifs, like an archaic tunic *(kushung)*. Broadcloth appliqué has been attached at the corners and seams. Measuring approximately 180 cm by 300 cm, it is in excellent condition. Bhutanese shown photographs of this tent said similar tents were kept in the royal stores in Bumthang and Wangdichöling for use by governors and other senior officials. In the mid-1950s, when a decision was made to move the capital to Thimphu, the tents were not transferred to the new capital, perhaps because government officials no longer require this kind of shelter when they are on tour.[24]

PART THREE

Weaving
in
Bhutan

Chapter Seven

The Weaving Regions of Bhutan

Three areas of Bhutan have strong, distinctive weaving traditions – eastern Bhutan, north central Bhutan, and central Bhutan. Western Bhutan has a much more modest, fragmented history of textile production. Except for north central Bhutan, each of these areas is a north-south corridor with a range of climatic zones from subtropical hills to alpine valleys and a corresponding variety of weaving. Areas of southern Bhutan that were settled by people of Nepalese ethnic origins are not presently known for weaving, although some women there, like their forebears in Nepal, may have worked at looms at one time.

Eastern Bhutan

The hills of eastern Bhutan [Map 2, page 170] are inhabited mainly by Shachops ('easterners'), the country's most numerous group. Shachops speak Tshangla, a language shared with Sherdukpens and some Mönpas in neighboring Arunachal Pradesh (India). The east, somewhat lower and drier than the rest of the country, is blessed with a temperate climate. Wild bananas, papaya trees, poinsettias, giant lilies, and orchids abound. Many people live in dwellings of bamboo matting on stilts, a reminder of the region's close proximity to Southeast Asia.

Eastern women are Bhutan's most celebrated weavers. Most learn the craft as very young girls, and if they bring income to their family by weaving they are freed from other household and farming tasks. Otherwise, they may weave during the winter (January-March), when the harvest is over and agricultural demands on their time are minimal. In this region, where madder and other wild dyeplants abound and lac and Bhutanese indigo flourish, dyeing skills are also highly developed. The northern part of the east is associated especially with wild silk cloth and the south with cotton fabrics.

On Bhutan's eastern border, the seminomadic herders of the high valleys of Merak and Sakteng are also weavers and have a unique dress style. They fashion hats, ropes, and bags out of yak hair and weave garments, floor mats, and blankets of yarn spun from their sheep wool. Some women spin wild silk cocoons into fiber, which they dye with lac and weave into tunic-style dresses (*shingkha*), women's jackets, and belts. During the winter months the herders make extended trips to lower parts of the region and even to Samdrup Jongkhar on Bhutan's southern border with India, bartering their yak products for wild silk cocoons, ready-made cloth, and other items they need. The Merak Sakteng people share the lifestyle, language, and dress of several groups across the border in India and preserve stories of how they migrated from Tibet in the seventh century.

For centuries, cloth was central to the internal economy of eastern Bhutan. Tax in some areas was paid in the form of lengths of plain and patterned cotton and wild silk cloth until the 1950s. The local nobility employed many weavers in their households. A brisk trade was carried on every fall when people from central Bhutan came to exchange their woolen cloth

FIG. 7.0 (page 167)
Working on the shady porch of her home in Duksam, north of Tashigang in eastern Bhutan, this woman is weaving flowers into the field of a red shoulder cloth (rachu). Her cummerbund is the wide style that older village women still favor. (D.K.M. 1987)

FIG. 7.1
Am Rinzi Pedon, born in 1907 in the Chumé Valley of Bumthang, worked as a weaver for Ashi Wangmo, daughter of Bhutan's second king. She is holding a raincloak (yathra charkab) with the same patterns she wove into woolen textiles for the princess's household in the 1930s and 1940s. This raincloak was one of the last things she made for her own use before she stopped weaving in the 1960s. (Begana, D.K.M. 1992)

Map 2 Bhutan's Weaving Regions

for lac, indigo, and wild silk textiles from the warmer valleys of the east.

Cloth is still an important product of the region, although not as many women weave. Wild silk fabric is particularly sought after, and sets of cloth panels for men's robes and women's dresses are sold in local market towns or taken to the capital.[1] Traditionally patterned cotton fabrics are also popular throughout the country, admired as being sturdy and attractive for curtains, cushion backing, and garment facings. The villages of Radi, Phongmé, Bartsham, and Yabrang continue to weave women's jackets, dresses, and belts, which they exchange with the Merak Sakteng herders for butter, meat, and cheese. Families of means, such as the local nobility at Chungkhar in Pemagatshel District, still employ weavers, although their work is mostly sold in Thimphu now rather than reserved for the household. And traditional barter with central Bhutan continues, albeit on a smaller scale.[2]

Looms, Fibers, and Dyes
Backstrap looms are a fixture outside many eastern Bhutanese homes, set up on porches, under bamboo mats, or in thatched sheds to protect weavers from the sun and rain. In Pemagatshel District, shelters on stilts are constructed in fields near the house so that girls and women can weave in the shade while watching the crops and livestock. Card looms and horizontal frame looms are also used.

Wild silk, cotton, and acrylic are the main fibers for weaving today. Most wild silk is imported from India through Samdrup Jongkhar. Shachops generally purchase yarn, while men from Merak Sakteng buy less costly cocoons, which they carry north for their wives to process. Some local cotton is prepared for weaving in Thongsa and Mikuri in Pemagatshel District, but most women weave with bright cotton and acrylic yarns from India.

Eastern Bhutan is known for lac and for native dyeplants that thrive in the mild climate. Lac is the preferred source for red and will be used even when synthetic dyes tint other yarns in the same cloth. Madder grows abundantly but is not considered as rich or fast a dye ("it goes after six washings"), so it is used mainly where lac is not produced. Bhutanese indigo *(Strobilanthes sp.)* is grown in kitchen gardens, and *Symplocos* leaves for yellow are either gathered on the ridges above villages or brought from Mongar District. Nowadays many villagers use tiny amounts of commercial acid as a mordant.

Types of Cloth and Patterning Techniques

Eastern Bhutan is renowned for plainweave fabrics, supplementary-weft-patterned fabrics, and supplementary-warp-patterned fabrics. The number of words in Tshangla to describe kinds of cloth and their patterns is evidence of a dynamic weaving tradition and very sophisticated popular awareness of cloth. Gift lists of the mid-1700s, such as those in Yönten Thayé, refer to 'eastern cloth' *(sharé)*, and Captain Welsh's report of 1794 lists several types of silk and cotton cloth from the east among the products of "Botan" known in India.

The areas of eastern Bhutan most associated with patterned and unpatterned plainweave fabrics are parts of Mongar and Pemagatshel districts.[3] They produced a multitude of cotton and wild silk fabrics tendered to the dzongs each year. Yönten Thayé mentions at least six types of relatively undecorated, white cloth *(karjyang, '*white and simple'), which were woven for the local authorities. Only some can be identified now, and examples of others are no longer easy to find, but might still be lying in the storeroom of a dzong or monastery.[4] One type of cotton fabric *(dungsam kamtham,* 'cloth from Dungsam'), often described by Bhutanese as "thick," is remembered particularly because it was once used for soldiers' clothing.

Plaid and striped fabric for garments and household use is still characteristic of these southern hills. The plaids resemble designs woven by the Burmese, the Khamptis and Singphos in Arunachal Pradesh, and the Assamese, underscoring the historical and cultural links between Bhutan and areas farther east. Two color combinations are popular: red-and-black (or -blue) plaid on a white field [fig. 7.2]; and yellow, white, and black on a rust-colored field *(sethra, '*predominantly gold pattern'). At one time, there were at least four versions of the red/black/white pattern whose names indicate how local they were. One of these, *decheling kamtham* (from Decheling in Samdrup Jongkhar District), was known throughout Bhutan and copied widely. *Kamtham thrawo* ('multicolored cloth') and *pangtsi,* an Assamese pattern copied in Bhutan, are more intricate plaids used to line cushions and clothing.

Shabthrawo ('eastern multicolored cloth') refers to two predominantly red, wild silk fabrics, one plaid and the other striped. The plaid had a reddish field crisscrossed with yellow and white lines, and may have been a version of what is now called *sethra.* Used in Bhutan and exported to Tibet, it was made into underskirts for lamas and women. Two versions of the rust-colored plaid called *sethra* are seen today: *sethra dokhana,* which has black in it, and *dalapgi sethra,* which does not. Among eastern Bhutanese, the term *shabthrawo* also applies to red-and-white-striped wild silk cloth from Pemagatshel and Mongar districts that was traded to the people of Merak Sakteng, who used it for women's garments.

Warp-striped cloth is another eastern hallmark occurring in many varieties, all of which have special names. The most popular type is a wild silk or cotton fabric simply called 'country cloth' *(yütham)* [fig. 5.41]. Very popular as rural dress, it was noted by a hill man exploring for the British in the 1860s (Survey of India 1915, 8[2]:49).[5] Today, Indian factory-

Fig. 7.2

The hills of southeastern Bhutan are renowned for patterned fabrics that were once woven from homegrown cotton, used in every household, and tendered to the local authorities as taxes-in-kind. Today, only a few villages in Pemagatshel District still cultivate cotton and weave fabrics such as these for household use and occasional sale. Native indigo, madder, and turmeric are natural dyes still in use, although commercial dye powders may be added to a dye bath to intensify the color of the yarns.

Most local fabrics from which clothing is made feature warp-striped or plaid patterns that Bhutanese say are old and indigenous. The two examples at the right are typical for women's dresses: thara *or* shardang thara *(white ground with colorful warp stripes) and* möntha*, which is understood to mean 'Bhutanese (*mön*) weaving' (warp-striped ground with supplementary-warp-pattern bands in red and blue). The two most popular fabrics for men's robes, at left, are* samkhongma *(white, blue, and red warp-striped plainweave) and a plaid called* pangtsi*, adopted from patterns in nearby Assam. (see Catalog)*

made versions of this pattern are worn more often than the handwoven cloth. *Shardang thara* ('striped woman's dress') is a local pattern showing multicolored warp stripes on a white field, while *samkhongma* has narrow red-and-blue warp stripes on a white field. *Möndré* ('Mön [understood as 'Bhutanese'] dress') is a similar pattern that Bhutanese say has a an early origin. Today, mainly older people in rural areas wear these fabrics [fig. 7.2].

In the past fifty years, rows of small supplementary-weft patterns have appeared in some striped plainweave cloth used for women's dresses, an innovation loosely described as 'new design' *(pesar)* [fig. 7.3]. In eastern Bhutan, people describe these fabrics as having 'designs in blank space' *(tongpang rigpa)*. In western Bhutan, dresses made from this cloth are often known as *dromchu chema* ('having little boxes') in allusion to the localized patterns. Pattern wefts are usually worked in pairs and are discontinuous, being interworked with the ground weave only where the motif appears on the face of the cloth. The patterns are single-faced, visible only on the finished side of the weaving.

Many other textiles that originated in the east, such as traditional women's belts *(kera)*, are decorated with supplementary wefts that create two-faced patterning. Here, the supplementary wefts float on one surface of the plainweave ground when not floating on the other and create a negative pattern on one side of the cloth. Four to eight very fine, unplied supplementary-weft yarns usually function as a single patterning unit. Pattern wefts may be worked across the entire fabric from one edge to the other (continuous) or used in discrete areas (discontinuous). Both continuous and discontinuous supplementary wefts decorate multipurpose textiles *(pangkheb)* used for tax payments, rough toweling, doorway curtains, cushion linings, and bundle carriers. The most elaborate of these cloths, the ceremonial *chaksi pangkheb*,

Fig. 7.3

Since the 1940s, rows of small supplementary-weft designs have appeared on warp-striped women's dresses. Whatever fabric they decorate, their presence gives a cloth the secondary designation pesar, *'new design.' Typical motifs include (top to bottom): an eight-pointed star that Bhutanese call a 'butterfly' (*phenphenma*) or sometimes a 'water mill' (*chüta shokpa*); a stylized version of the Chinese character for long life; a lotus flower (*pema*); and another type of flower. Similar designs have decorated the garments of the elite since at least the turn of the century. (see Catalog)*

FIGS. 7.4-5

*Supplementary-warp-patterned
fabrics* (aikapur) *are the most
popular, prestigious textiles made in
the northern region of eastern Bhutan.
The girls at right were photographed
in Radi, a village famous for producing this cloth. Characterized by
alternating bands of plainweave*
(pang) *and supplementary-warp
patterning* (hor), *aikapur is woven in
five color combinations. The four types
shown above are (left to right):*
mensé mathra, *gold patterning on a
red ground;* lungserma, *green and
red patterning on a yellow ground;*
jadrima, *yellow and white patterning
on a red ground; and* dromchu
chema, *red, green, yellow, and white*

*patterning. Colorful warp striping in
any of these textiles gives it the
descriptor 'arranged with a rainbow'*
(jadrima). *The fifth type of aikapur,
called* möntha, *is shown in figs. 7.2
and 7.6.*

*The warp-pattern bands in these
fabrics are measured by crosshatches
on the horizontal bars in the pattern
bands. These crosshatches are known
as 'legs'* (kang), *making a fabric 'five-
legged,' 'nine-legged,' and so on [see
fig. 3.3]. Although the textile on the
far right does not have 'legs,'
Bhutanese can still tell how many it
ought to have by the width of its
pattern bands. (fig. 7.5, Anthony Aris
1983) (see Catalog)*

has a center panel patterned from one end to the other with bands of continuous supplementary wefts.[6]

Eastern Bhutan is especially famous for supplementary-warp-patterned fabrics collectively known as *aikapur*. Woven of cotton, wild silk, or cultivated silk, they are so admired that eastern weavers who knew this technique were retained in the noble households of central, and later western, Bhutan. These cloths are probably the ones mentioned in a British report of 1794: "Nainta, ... Goom, Sing, an embroidered cloth, [and] Daroka, a silk of a mixture of green, red and yellow colours" (Welsh 1794, in Mackenzie [1884] 1989, 387). To an untrained eye, the cloths do appear to be embroidered – and to an untrained ear, gathering information secondhand from Assamese merchants, the cloth names recorded could have been rough approximations of unfamiliar Bhutanese terms.[7]

Aikapur features alternating bands of plainweave *(pang)* and supplementary-warp patterning *(hor)* on a plainweave ground.[8] Five color schemes, several with Bhutanese names indicating that they are considered very old and indigenous, are distinguished [figs. 7.4-7.6]:

> *mensé mathra* ('*mentsi*-like red pattern' or 'Mön [understood as 'Bhutanese'] yellow and red pattern'):[9] yellow pattern bands on a red field [fig. 7.7];
> *lungserma* ('yellow, valley[-woven] cloth'): green and red pattern bands on a yellow ground;
> *jadrima* ('cloth arranged with a rainbow'): yellow and white pattern bands between colorful warp striping;
> *möntha* ('Mön [understood as 'Bhutanese'] weaving'): blue or black and red pattern bands between colorful warp striping; and
> *dromchu chema* ('with little boxes'): red, green, yellow, and white pattern bands.[10]

Multicolored warp stripes in any version of these cloths inspire the apt secondary designation 'having a rainbow' (*jadrichem*, or *jadrima* for short). In some weavings, pattern bands alternate with bands of single-faced supplementary-weft patterning showing 'tree

FIG. 7.6

These two panels show eastern Bhutanese supplementary-warp patterns (aikapur) woven of commercial cotton yarn from India. On the left is möntha, *which is worn only by women and has red-and-black warp-pattern bands, alternating with warp striping in which black and white are characteristically prominent. Another version of the same pattern is shown in* fig. 7.2. *The pattern of the cloth on the right is what eastern Bhutanese say was the original* dromchu chema *('[design] having little boxes'). Today the "box" motifs, no longer fashionable, are rarely seen. The term* dromchu chema, *particularly in western Bhutan, is often applied instead to the pattern seen at the far right in* fig. 7.4, *or to cloth decorated with tiny supplementary-weft designs, like that in* fig. 7.3. *The fringe on the panel at right is not plied or trimmed because the panel has not been stitched into a dress. Note the rows of weft twining that finish women's dress panels near the fringe.* (see Catalog)

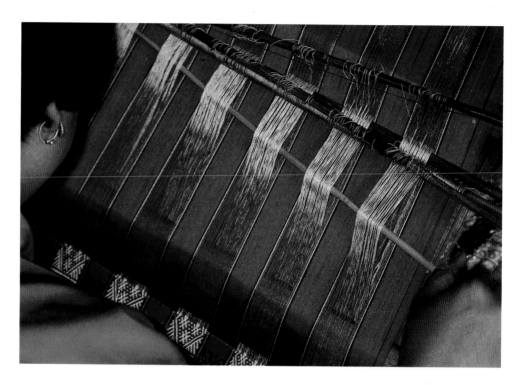

FIG. 7.7
Sonam Pema, who weaves for the queens of Bhutan, is at work on a panel of aikapur mensé mathra, *a specialty of her native Tashigang District. She is inserting a stick to raise a shed created by the pattern-heddle rod just above where she is working. The heddle rod, one of about nine needed to make the motif, is tied to a set of warp yarns in the pattern sequence. Sonam Pema is making a space through which she will pass the shuttle carrying the weft yarn. The textile she is weaving combines patterns created by supplementary warps, as illustrated in this picture, with patterns made with supplementary wefts [see fig. 7.8]. (S.S.B. 1994)*

leaf' *(shinglo)* motifs [fig. 3.3]. Bhutanese examine the delicate branches and leaves of these trees when assessing the quality of a fabric. *Shinglo* that are crisply executed and have innovative or especially delicate details are associated with garments made for the nobility and well-to-do.

Aikapur is a special Bhutanese cloth because its patterns reflect gradations associated with social status. Qualities of the cloth are differentiated by the width of the supplementary-warp-pattern bands. Vertically, in the warp direction, these bands have a standard format [fig. 3.3]: a primary motif; followed by a solid horizontal bar, a crosshatched bar, and another solid bar; a primary motif; and so on. While primary motifs may repeat or vary within a given pattern band, the intervening bars are identical and there are always an odd number of crosshatches – three, five, seven, or nine – all auspicious to Buddhists. Bhutanese describe an *aikapur* according to how many crosshatches (*kang,* 'legs') its pattern has and regard highly examples with nine or more 'legs' because they have more intricate patterns. Cloth with nine 'legs' is said to have been reserved for the nobility and the kings, but one often sees cloth with eleven or thirteen 'legs.' Even when 'legs' are not present, Bhutanese can identify an *aikapur* cloth by the width of its pattern bands.

Prized by Bhutanese for many generations, *aikapur* has been a cloth of distinction, saved for special occasions. In fact, in the market at Samdrup Jongkhar, mothballs are called *aikapur,* a term that Bhutanese say refers to how mothballs, like the cloth, are put away in chests. The patterns are worn by both men and women with one exception. *Möntha* ('Mön [understood as 'Bhutanese'] weaving') [figs. 7.2, 7.6] is so closely associated with women that men do not wear it under ordinary circumstances. The contexts in which men do wear it reinforce the notion that the cloth is quintessentially female and that women are somehow peripheral to Bhutan's Buddhist culture. *Möntha,* whose name alludes to the 'unenlightened' or 'non-Buddhist' (an early connotation of *mön*), was often worn by men playing the parts of women in folk dances and at archery contests, where female servants, usually weavers, or men in *möntha* cloth wrapped like a *pakhi,* once danced and teased the opposing teams. Here, Bhutanese say that men took the role of a shabby, but loyal servant-joker in traditional dramas *(phento)*. This figure has a complex background and origin. He is somewhat laughable and rather on the margins of mainstream Buddhist culture. The fact that these jokers and women dress in 'unenlightened cloth' suggests that the fabric on some level symbolizes limited integration in the current social order.[11]

Some of the distinctive garments of the Merak Sakteng people – men's upper garments and short pants and women's wraps for the upper and lower body – are woven by their women and made of sheep's wool. Women's tunic-style dresses, jackets, and belts, however, are made of wild silk cloth and often obtained from nearby villagers who weave them specially for bartering to the herders. The jacket pattern is always the same, showing rows of horses, elephants, and peacocks that are reminiscent of patterns in distant Southeast Asia [fig. 2.2]. Geometric patterning on the belts, showing auspicious swastikas and flowers, is similar to that on jackets.

North Central Bhutan (Lhuntshi District)

Lhuntshi District lies high in the hills near Bhutan's northern border. The northern part of this district (Kurtö) is renowned for its weaving and as the original home of the royal family, whose forebears migrated to central Bhutan, taking their weavers with them. The culture and special language of Kurtö's famous weaving villages link these communities both to Bumthang (central Bhutan) and to regions east of Bhutan that have important weaving traditions and preserve tunics as a dress style for women. The language (Dzalakha or, locally, Khomakha), which is different from that spoken nearby (Kurtötkha), resembles both the major language of central Bhutan (Bumthangkha) and that of Tawang in Arunachal Pradesh (Driem 1992, 11-17). Linguistic studies may eventually shed light on the origins of these now very distinct peoples and the textile-related practices they share.

Everyone in the region – and some Bhutanese outside the area – can name at least one or two of the villages that were celebrated for their weaving.[12] They are all located in the northern sector of the district (Kurtö). The Wangchuck family, who lived at Dungkhar, and other Kurtö nobility are said to have retained weavers for generations, many of them from Khoma and Yomining.[13] The products of local looms served as tax payments, as in eastern Bhutan. For example, the village of Khoma paid in butter, rice, pork, and beef, and in three kinds of cloth. These fabrics included *pangkheb* (multipurpose cloths), *chikpa tharé* (a kind of woman's dress), and *phechung* (bags). Houses with more than 5 acres of land were assessed three *pangkheb* annually.

Unfortunately, although the legacy of local weaving is strong enough to maintain its reputation in Bhutan, much of the cloth now being manufactured is undistinguished. Even in the village of Gompakap – where Bhutanese enjoy telling visitors that men do all the "women's work," including cooking, and the women just weave all day long – the lengths of cloth being woven for the Thimphu market in 1993 were of mediocre quality at best.[14] This appears to be a result of weavers' perceptions of their market and their limited financial resources, which make acrylic and medium-quality cotton yarns most affordable. Also, some of the best weavers have moved to Thimphu to weave for clients. The village has no old cloth left to be seen, evidently because of the market for Bhutanese textiles, which has led middlemen to scour the hills for items that can be sold in Kathmandu.

Looms, Fibers, and Dyes

Lhuntshi District has always imported the materials for its most famous textiles. Cotton was available from villages to the south and east (Chali and Chaskar in Mongar District) or from regions farther south. Wild silk cocoons came all the way from Samdrup Jongkhar on the Indian border, a ten-day walk to the south, where local people obtained them in exchange for rough bags made of nettle and pig's whiskers used for brushes. Lac was acquired from eastern Bhutan and mordants from Tibet.

The most significant local weaving materials were bast fibers (generically called *zowa* or *ki*, 'nettle'), which Bhutanese say were once the only ones used. Three villages still have a reputation for weaving with nettle, and others are said to have been well known in earlier times.[15] Of dyeplants, madder was found in nearby forests in such abundance that basketloads were carried north into Tibet. Bhutanese indigo was cultivated in household gardens and *Symplocos* was known as a source of yellow. Now very little dyeing is done because people import yarns from India and use commercial dyes if they must color them. Men from Chaskar and Yadi villages to the south still come to a few homes in the village of Khoma every November to barter their oil seed and lac for dried chilies.

FIG. 7.8

The elaborate technique of supplementary-weft patterning developed in Kurtö in north central Bhutan now epitomizes skill among weavers throughout the country. Known as kushü, *it involves two types of patterning, both utilizing short pattern yarns that are interworked only in particular areas of the cloth. The weaver here is inserting two pattern wefts, worked as one unit, so that they create blocks of color and appear to lie flat on the surface of the cloth* (sapma). *To both sides of where she is working are diamond-shaped motifs. Here, pattern wefts are wrapped around warps on a diagonal and interworked with each other, so that the design is raised above the surface of the cloth* (thrima) *[fig. 7.11]. The weaver is thirty-year-old Chösung Lhamo, a native of Radi, Tashigang District, who has been weaving for the queens in Thimphu for nine years. (D.K.M. 1994)*

Types of Cloth and Patterning Techniques

Kurtö (northern Lhuntshi District) is famed for cloth decorated with *kushü*, a regional style of discontinuous supplementary-weft patterning on a white field. Older Bhutanese recall that the area was also known in the 1930s for plaid cloth (*mathra*, 'predominantly red pattern'), sometimes woven with stripes *(khacha)* at the edges. Nowadays, this plaid is associated more closely with Bumthang (central Bhutan).

The most celebrated of Kurtö's supplementary-weft-patterned weavings is the woman's dress called *kushüthara* ('brocaded dress'), decorated in the *kushü* technique also seen on bags and other textiles [fig. 7.8]. Some patterning *(sapma)* is composed with supplementary wefts that appear to lie on the finished face of the cloth; when not floating, they are laid in with wefts of the ground weave. More intricate motifs are created by a group of four supplementary wefts that are interworked with warp elements and each other by twining and wrapping (*thrima*, 'to wind, coil around'). *Thrima* patterns appear to ride on the surface of the cloth, and some look very much like embroidery. For example, the four supplementary wefts are sometimes handled as two complementary pairs, which crisscross one another, like shoelaces achieving what resembles a vertical "cross-stitch." Alternatively, the supplementary-weft pairs may be wrapped around ground warps to form what looks like a horizontal "chain stitch." Because Bhutanese fabrics are warp-faced, a skilled weaver can insert *sapma* and *thrima* pattern wefts so that neither is visible on the back of the cloth.

The designs for *kushü* patterning are so varied that they are impossible to classify. Several dozen basic patterns are modified and interpreted, or combined together, at a weaver's pleasure [fig. 7.10]. Bhutanese looking at the cloth give the patterns graphic names. The evocative descriptors – 'pigeon's eye' *(parewa mik)*, 'monkey's nail' *(prai tsimba)*, 'rooster's comb' *(bjapé zewa)*, 'cooking pot lip' *(therpai chi)*, 'fly's wing' *(brang shokpa)*, and many others – reflect a rich, complex imagery. A few of these names are consistent, but most vary according to where the observer comes from, his or her gender and knowledge of weaving, and purely subjective interpretation. Patterning that looks like patchwork *(tenkheb, phup)* is believed to bring long life. Swastikas *(yurung)* and a lattice pattern that Bhutanese call a 'lucky knot' *(dramé, peyab)* are both auspicious Buddhist emblems. According to some older women, these three motifs – patchwork, swastikas, and lucky knots – were supposed to appear on women's dresses, and indeed they commonly form the end borders of many older examples [fig. 5.7]. Natives of Kurtö also say that animal designs, which are no longer in fashion, were associated primarily with the villages of Gompakap and Minjé.[16]

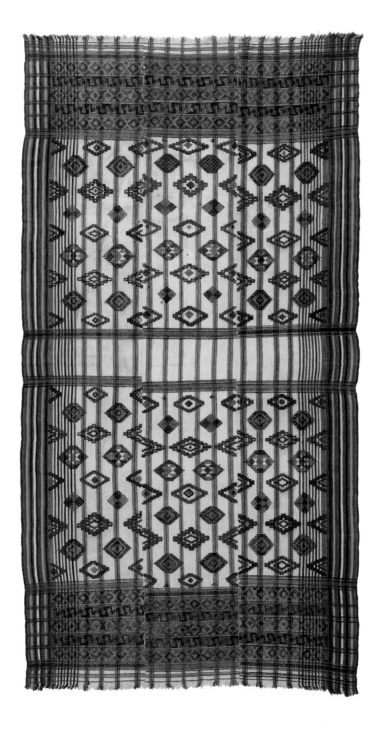

Fig. 7.9

As the kushüthara *style of woman's dress was popularized at the turn of the century, it was adopted and copied by ordinary women. Interpreted on looms outside the palace weaving workshops, motifs were enlarged and simplified, becoming ever bolder. To save time, sometimes an undecorated area was left in the center of the textile, which is not visible when the dress is worn.*

The ground of the dress here is mostly undyed cotton, but the colored warp stripes at the edges of the textile are wild silk, which becomes soft and flexible with wear, causing a slight unevenness evident in the photograph. The richly colored yarns are tinted with native indigo, madder, and, probably, turmeric. Women from Bumthang say the dress's style, colors, and materials point to its having been made in Kheng, in what is now Shemgang District. The elite of Bumthang traditionally viewed this heavily forested, lower-altitude region as being 'at the edges of civilization' (matpala), *and use this term to describe weaving – like this dress – that is not up to the "Bumthang standard." (see Catalog)*

FIG. 7.10
The variety of motifs in kushü *patterning defies classification. Bhutanese call them by different names, according to what they personally see in a design. Among the few standard characteristics of the motifs are edge treatments, illustrated in the first three rows shown here. The top row features triangular elements around each motif that are called 'rooster's combs.' The second row of motifs is edged with straight lines known as 'monkey's nails.' The third row shows trapezoids that resemble 'fly's wings.' The bottom row shows motifs known as* (left to right) *a 'vase'* (bumpa), *a 'cooking pot lip'* (therpai chi), *an amulet or charm box* (gau), *and a crossed thunderbolt or double* dorje (dorje jadam).

FIG. 7.11
This detail of a kushüthara *dress shows the extraordinarily intricate – and varied – patterning created with* thrima. *Motifs measure about 4 to 8 cm from top to bottom, and a dress such as this one could well take a year to weave. Worked in silk on a cotton ground, the motifs include many variations on basic pattern elements that are selectively illustrated in* fig. 7.10. (see Catalog)

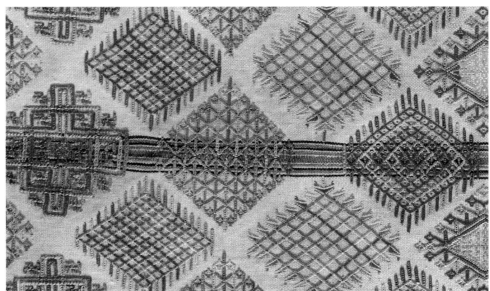

179

FIG. 7.12

Sheep's wool is the primary weaving fiber in the colder valleys of central Bhutan, where weavers produce heavy twill fabrics made into blankets, raincloaks, shawls, and winter garments. Although backstrap looms were once widespread, now almost all weaving is done on horizontal frame looms, a technology imported from Tibet in the 1930s. The color combination and style of weft stripes in the rolled loom length indicate that it was woven in the Sephu area, west of Tongsa Dzong. This panel would be cut and stitched into a blanket or cloak. The finished textile underneath it has a pattern called tarichem *('[design] having tiger stripes'), used for women's dresses* [cf. fig. 5.16] (see Catalog)

Central Bhutan

The four valleys of Bumthang District – Chumé, Chökhor, Tang, and Ura – figure in some of the earliest historical tales and records of Bhutan. The area's major language, Bumthangkha ('language of Bumthang'), is related to languages spoken in Lhuntshi District to the northeast, the forested hills of Shemgang District to the south, and Arunachal Pradesh (India). Bumthang's ancient nobility, some of whose lineages still exist, enjoyed trade and cultural links with Tibet, to which they were nominally subject before the seventeenth-century Drukpa conquest. Other local families are counted among the religious aristocracy (*chöjé*), whose members have in more recent centuries included important Buddhist teachers. Some Bumthang families had branches in Kurtö (northern Lhuntshi District) and some intermarried with Kurtö families who maintained homes in Bumthang (for example, the royal family). The Wangchuck family's migration from Kurtö to Bumthang around 1850 helped bring about the nationalization of what were previously local weaving traditions.

The four valleys of central Bhutan (Bumthang) are acclaimed for weaving with sheep wool, and all paid tax in cloth from local looms. Households in Ura, for example, tendered the following three items: one plain white woolen cloth (*nambu karthi*, a thin cloth for making prayer flags and tearing into thin strips used as butter lamp wicks); one woolen cloth patterned with traditional designs (*yathra*, 'pattern from the upper regions'); and one length of red plaid woolen cloth *(mathra)*. Yarns in these fabrics were colored with the cheapest available dyes – madder rather than lac for red and pine cones rather than indigo for blue.[17]

The Bumthang area is also significant because it was here that workshop weaving flowered from the mid-1800s until around 1960. Noble households are still remembered well for this activity, although it disappeared after hereditary service obligations were abolished in 1957.[18] The Kurtö *ashi* (princesses) who were born or married into the royal family brought their servants, including weavers, to Bumthang. Women of local noble families were also honored to weave for the princesses. In the mid-1940s, the staff at one palace there included seven full-time dyers and forty weavers, as well as twenty people who did nothing but spin and wind yarn. In a courtyard at another residence, Lamé Gompa, there was a large mortar stone for preparing dyes, which were ground with a wooden pestle turned by a water wheel.

Skilled weavers in these households [fig. 7.1] were free from the pressures of the marketplace and wove some of the most exquisite surviving *kushüthara*, as well as other fine cloth. Their work epitomizes *hingtham* ('heart weaving') as opposed to *tshongtham* ('weaving for sale').

Women who grew up in Bumthang recall that loads of silk and cotton yarn were delivered to the compounds, along with baskets full of local raw wool for spinning. They remember how the princesses' weavers employed spindles that rested in a little bowl, or even spinning wheels, while villagers used drop spindles that enabled them to spin while going about other tasks. Weavers sang songs to pass the time, and the mood is characterized even now as always happy. From time to time, the women were called upon to dance at archery competitions, which was a part of their obligation to the family. There were special names for the women who spun yarn and wound it into balls *(belabemi)* and for dyers *(tshochabmi)*. The good weavers stayed busy weaving clothing that the family kept for its own use. The most skilled of these women are still remembered by name.[19] Those with lesser skills produced the pieces of cloth that had to be prepared to give as gifts to peers and inferiors.

Villages to the west in Bumthang and neighboring Tongsa District are also known for weaving with wool, although there were no workshops like those at the palaces in the four Bumthang valleys. People from Horjé, Rukubji, and Sephu still barter their woven products for textiles and dyes from other parts of Bhutan, which are being carried through by traders.

South of the Bumthang valleys, the densely forested hills of Shemgang District – most of which can be penetrated only on foot – have weaving traditions. In the past, wild silk and cotton were cultivated. Natural coloring agents of all kinds are plentiful in the forests. Only *Symplocos* does not flourish at this lower altitude, so turmeric was used instead for yellows. Most cotton and wild silk cloth produced in Shemgang resembles that from neighboring Mongar and Pemagatshel districts in eastern Bhutan. Residents also wove with bast fibers; people in Kheng Tali, above Dakpai, for example, are said to still have nettle-cloth garments, although these have not been worn for many years. The local nobility had close contacts with

FIG. 7.13

Plaid woolen fabrics whose predominant color is red (mathra) *are a trademark of Bumthang in central Bhutan. Narrow panels from a horizontal frame loom are stitched into both men's robes and women's dresses. The patterns are suitable for many occasions. The rolled loom lengths here were a gift to their owners in 1978, while the similar, finished textile at left is a woman's dress woven of Bumthang wool, colored with vegetable dyes, in 1985-86. Since the late 1950s, small supplementary-weft patterns have been added to plaid fabrics, an innovation known as 'new design'* (pesar). *The* mathra pesar *example here, woven of machine-spun Indian woolen yarn in Thimphu in the mid-1980s, is patterned with 'thunderbolt' (double* dorje) *motifs in silk. (see Catalog)*

FIG. 7.14

Colorful woolen cloth from central Bhutan is sought after throughout the country for stitching into mattress covers, jackets, blankets, raincloaks, and car-seat covers. The most traditional yathra *patterning combines weft stripes with rows of standard motifs, arranged at a weaver's pleasure. In the center of each loom length, there is supposed to be a horizontal panel composed of little triangles that form diamond shapes. Called* tenkheb *('offering cover') because it resembles the patchwork seen in silk altar cloths, this motif should also be centrally positioned in a finished textile stitched from* yathra.

The loom length on the left, woven from imported Australian wool, shows (top to bottom): *'water and mountains in the patchwork style'* (churi tenkheb), *'coins'* (tranka), *'sun rays'* (zerpa), *'little white thorn flowers'* (se'u chungku), *'stars and thunderbolts'* (karma dorje), *'big white thorn flowers'* (se'u chunma), *'stars like in a lap cover'* (karma pangkheb), *and 'scissors'* (gimtsi). *The loom length on the right, woven from Bumthang sheep's wool, shows* (top to bottom): *'diamonds in the patchwork style'* (khorlo tenkheb), *a variety of lotus blossom* (pema tongden), *'butterflies'* (phen-phenma), *two rows of diamonds* (khorlo), *patchwork* (tenkheb), *a variation on the lotus flower, and lucky knots* (peyab). (see Catalog)

Bumthang and employed weavers. Some made brocaded women's dresses in the *kushüthara* style [fig. 7.9], but these never had the prestige of examples made in Bumthang or Kurtö.[20] Today most silk and cotton yarns come from India, and a mix of natural and synthetic dyes are used.

The Mangdé River valley in Tongsa District is likewise known for cloth production. At royal residences and winter homes of the nobility south of Tongsa Dzong, weavers were kept busy, although not on the same scale as at the palaces in Bumthang. More notably, a number of villages on the west bank of the river between Nabji Korphu and Kela also have weaving traditions. They are particularly known for nettle cloth, which was made, among other things, into wrapped garments *(kurel pagi)* worn by women that cross over the chest and fasten at the shoulders, like the *pakhi* formerly worn by men in this area.[21] All the village names contain the element *mön*, associated with indigenous non-Buddhist people.

Looms, Fibers, and Dyes

Although the backstrap loom was once universal in the Bumthang region, almost all woolen cloth is now made on a horizontal frame loom introduced from Tibet in the 1930s.[22] Local sheep are sheared twice or three times a year.[23] Additional wool, instead of coming from Tibet as it used to, came in recent years from Australia and was distributed by the National Women's Association of Bhutan. Today flocks of hybrid sheep are being raised to provide better fleece for weaving. Acrylic and woolen yarns, manufactured in Ludhiana and the Chandigarh area, are brought from India.

Many of the natural dyes used in the Bumthang valleys come from temperate areas to the south such as Shemgang and Mongar districts. Madder, Bhutanese indigo, *Symplocos* leaves, turmeric, and various mordants are still acquired when central Bhutanese take their flocks south to graze or when southern traders come north. Villagers from the Ura Valley travel east to bring back lac and indigo, which they in turn market in the other three valleys of central Bhutan. Villages closer to Tongsa, like Rukubji, are visited each year by traders from Tashigang District in eastern Bhutan. In remote areas of central Bhutan, there are still women who have never bought or used commercial dyes.

Types of Cloth and Patterning Techniques

The wool-weaving areas of central Bhutan produce striped plainweaves, fine plaid twills, and heavier, supplementary-weft-patterned twills. The occasional plainweaves are woven on backstrap looms. Twills were also formerly woven on backstrap looms equipped with three heddle rods. These weaves now predominate, perhaps because the shafts that are integral to the horizontal frame loom, which is ubiquitous in this region, make twills very easy to produce. Until workshop weaving declined in the late 1950s, fabrics that originated in the east were also woven here by native easterners retained especially to produce them.

Indigenous to Bumthang and parts of Tongsa District are woolens made of natural brown, black, and white yarns and yarns tinted dark blue or shades of red. Characteristic plaid, checkered, and striped loom lengths, for example, from the Sephu area around Rukubji, are used mainly for stitching raincloaks and blankets. The simplest cloths are somewhat rough black woolens (*pchana*, 'black woolen cloth') for winter dresses and robes. Similar fabric, dyed a rich orange-red with madder, is stitched into blankets that monks use as shawls (*pchana map*, 'red black woolen cloth') [fig. 2.11]. A coarser variety of black woolen textile covers loads on horses during the rain. Other fabrics show black-and-white, black-and-red, or red-and-white checks or stripes; the most colorful are *sephu charkab* ('Sephu raincloaks'), which are striped in the weft direction with broad bands of white, orange, green, and blue [fig. 7.12]. Four to six panels make up the finished textile, under which a baby can be carried very easily. The products of this area immediately bring to mind the goods so often cited as products of Bhutan in British Indian accounts: "coarse red blankets and striped woolen cloth in half yard widths" (Bogle, in Collister 1987, 20).

Most central Bhutanese woolen fabrics for garments feature wide or narrow stripes. The village of Horjé, for example, is associated with women's dresses 'striped like a tiger' (*tarichem*) [fig. 7.12].[24] *Hothra* ('Mongolian pattern') [fig. 2.8], very popular earlier in this century, is decorated with narrow, multicolored weft stripes. Both it and a variant pattern showing weft stripes alternating with horizontal rows of crosses on a plain ground (*jalo*) were manufactured in Tibet and obtained through trade before the introduction of horizontal looms enabled Bhutanese to produce their own versions of the Tibetan patterns [fig. 2.10].[25]

Plaid patterns are also specialties of central Bhutan. The best known are based on one of two designs: varicolored plaid on a maroon field (*mathra*, 'red pattern') [fig. 7.13]; or yellow, white, and black plaid on an orange field (*sethra*, 'gold pattern') [fig. 5.41]. The latter was originally from eastern Bhutan, where it was woven of wild silk on backstrap looms. The first woolen versions are said to have appeared in the early 1950s and are very popular now.[26] The maroon plaid is an indigenous design whose name is still synonymous with central Bhutan (*bumthang mathra*). At some point this pattern was copied by Tibetan weavers and introduced back into Bhutan as a trade textile (*tsangthra*) produced in narrow rolls on a horizontal frame loom.[27] An important recent innovation in the plaid fabrics are supplementary-weft designs [fig. 7.13], introduced during the reign of the third king (1952-72). Their presence gives a fabric the secondary designation *pesar* ('new design'). Lengths of woolen plaid cloth are sold in rolls ready to be cut, stitched, and lined.

Another cloth equally characteristic of Bumthang is the decorative woolen called *yathra* ('pattern from the upper regions'). Earlier, it seems to have been plainweave or twill made on a backstrap loom, but now it is almost always twill produced on a frame loom. Uncut lengths of the cloth measure about 65 cm by 300 cm or more and show several patterns. The traditional palette of naturally dyed yarns is rich and warm: rainbow hues of pink, plum, and maroon, a handful of blues and greens, with accents in white and gold. Today in the Chumé Valley, two roadside shops opened in 1991-92 feature examples in brilliant orange, lime green, turquoise blue – the tones in which Indian acrylic yarns are available.

There are many variations of *yathra*, all with single-faced supplementary-weft patterning, either on a plain ground or on a weft-striped ground. Pattern wefts are paired and quite thick; they are tied down with warp yarns, laid into the shed of the ground weft, and interworked diagonally on what will be the finished face of the textile in such a way that they appear to ride on the surface of the twill. The bold designs, arranged in horizontal or diagonal rows, include familiar motifs: diamonds, stars, 'coins,' lucky knots, 'scissors,' 'long-life vases,' and floral motifs [fig. 7.14]. Traditionally, cloth with a dark brown ground is reputed to come from the Chumé Valley, while *yathra* with predominantly white and rust grounds comes from the Ura Valley farther east. Both types are now made in the Chökhor Valley around Jakar Dzong and to a lesser extent in the Tang Valley. Names of designs vary slightly, especially in the Ura dialect.

There have been noticeable changes in *yathra* "fashion" over time. During the second king's reign (1926-52), Bhutanese remember the appearance of cloth that departed from the conventional pattern format described above.[28] The first major innovation occurred in wool lengths that were cut in half and stitched together to form a cushion or floor covering (*denkheb*). These began to be woven to resemble pile rugs from Tibet, with traditional design elements enclosed in a lattice in the field and framed all around by a 'Chinese wall' meander (*janachari*) [fig. 5.55]. Today lengths of wool are decorated with designs like those on fancy women's dresses (*kushüthara*). New pattern combinations appear regularly, and some become known as the design of a particular woman or weaver.

Yathra was traditionally used for cushion covers or blankets (two panels) and for cloaks (three panels). Since the 1950s, it has also been made into jackets that are very popular with Bhutanese women and foreigners who find them in the bazaars of Thimphu, Darjeeling, Kalimpong, and Kathmandu. In the late 1980s, well-to-do Bhutanese began ordering *yathra* cloth in sizes and design formats to fit Western-style couches and car seats. The entire interior of a vehicle is sometimes handsomely appointed in this gaily patterned fabric.

Western Bhutan

Today there are weavers in Thimphu and other areas west of the Pelé La, the high pass that divides western Bhutan from the very different cultures and traditions farther east, but Bhutanese often volunteer that the west lacks native weaving traditions. Admittedly, the weaving may not compare with the sophisticated practices elsewhere, but oral traditions, a few records, and textiles themselves indicate that the inhabitants of the west did produce cloth. The first possible clue about weaving appears in a sixteenth-century text that describes how a famous Bhutanese saint, Phajo Drukgom Shigpo, first encountered the girl who was to become his wife. Though a religious text cannot be interpreted as historical fact, it relates how, in the thirteenth century, Phajo caught sight of Sonam Pedon sitting and weaving with a group of girls on an island in the Wang River that flows south of Thimphu.

The next clue is an unambiguous statement by the first British visitor to Bhutan, who only traveled in western Bhutan. In 1774, George Bogle commented specifically on how families bartered their produce for wool from Tibet – which was spun, dyed, and woven at home. The villagers also obtained coarse cotton and broadcloth, dyes, and spices from India, most of which they sent on to Tibet, but some of which were used locally (Bogle, in Collister 1987, 17-18). As late as 1911, another observer noted that at Pasakha (Buxa Duar), near the present-day border town of Phuntsholing, large quantities of wool from Bhutan, Tibet, and Ladakh entered India (Gruning 1911, 11:147). It would not be surprising if some western Bhutanese households still processed and wove as well as traded in this wool at that time.

Today weaving is an integral part of daily life in a handful of villages in western Bhutan that were settled by people from east of the Pelé La. For example, a few communities in Punakha and Wangdi Phodrang districts weave with wool, wild silk, and occasionally cotton. Their residents speak a language (Henkha) related to that of Bumthang and presumably came from beyond the Pelé La long ago.[29] Three textiles known throughout Bhutan today include the name of one of these villages – Adhang, in Wangdi Phodrang: a particular pattern of woman's ceremonial shoulder cloth (*adha rachu*) [fig. 5.15] that originated as a local design; a clothing fabric (*adha mathra*) [fig. 5.41] styled "the dress of the Wangchuck king" in a folk song; and a ceremonial shoulder cloth for men whose association with the town is unclear (*adha khamar*, a textile with a white center panel flanked by red panels) [fig. 5.37].

Other textile names allude to weaving traditions that no longer exist.[30] For example, the Uma area in Wangdi Phodrang District gave its name to belts that were quite plain except for patterning near each end (compare the 1855 belt in fig. 1.5). The locality is said to have been settled by people from south central Bhutan (Kheng), who would have brought cloth production skills with them. More puzzling is a cloth called *dalapgi sethra*, a kind of yellow plaid that has no black in it. Bhutanese say that it "came from" the village of Nub Dalap, near Phuntsholing, and that other distinctive cloth was also made there.[31] Pasakha (Buxa Duar) was once the source of "nice women's ceremonial shoulder cloths," and the Dagana region west of there produced cotton cloth (Nado 1987, 24).

Older Bhutanese acknowledge that weaving does exist in the west and was once more widespread there. They note that nomads in Ha and Laya Lingshi, on Bhutan's western and northwestern borders, fashion clothing and other utilitarian textiles from yak, sheep, and goat wool. They also mention that "poor families" living at lower altitudes wove cloth from nettle fiber and made it into garments. Bast-fiber cloth, for example, is closely associated with Upper Karchi in Punakha District and with Wang Sisina south of Thimphu. Nettle was also the most common weaving fiber among the Lhops ('southerners'), a group living in several villages in Samtse District. Perhaps because western Bhutan had easy access to cloth from other areas, native production of cloth never supported more than the most basic needs.

Bhutanese weaving is the sum of many local traditions, some of which have moved with their weavers beyond their origins and some of which have found markets far away from the locality of their manufacture. Today in Bhutan this composite of local traditions has become valued as a national artistic and cultural asset.

Chapter Eight

Fibers, Dyes, and Looms

I may be wearing a dress made of nettle cloth, and have no silver brooches,
But I have two husbands!
You have a dress made of *adha mathra* [colorfully striped cloth], and jewelry –
But you have no husband!

> – *The end of a folk story about a poor woman from Shengana in Punakha*
> *District and a rich woman from Wang Sisina near Thimphu*

This provocative remark reflects the universal view in Bhutan that nettle is a very humble fiber. However, people from all parts of the country honor it as the original fiber used by local weavers long before native cotton or wild silk, for which Bhutan is now much better known, was popular. Contemporary weavers seldom work with nettle, choosing instead a wide assortment of other handspun or machine-spun fibers, both indigenous and imported. Natural and commercial dyestuffs are utilized in every possible scenario: separately, in adjacent yarns, and one overdyeing the other. In contrast, the processing of local fibers and the technology of weaving have changed much less than present possibilities would allow.

Fibers

Nettle

What Bhutanese call 'nettle' is today judged too coarse for most uses. People use the term *zocha* ('nettle thing') for fibers obtained from several plants. One of them is indeed a common variety of nettle grass (*Girardinia palmata*) (Nakao and Nishioka 1984, 132). Another is extracted from the stalk of *Cannabis sativa* (hemp), which grows wild in much of Bhutan, and a third comes from a tree bark. The plant stalks are soaked, sometimes boiled, and then shredded for twisting into yarn with the aid of a drop spindle. Throughout the country and nearby regions of India and Nepal, local bast fibers are processed similarly for weaving.[1] In Bhutan, 'nettle' is also used by archers for stringing traditional wooden bows.

Past and current use of bast fibers is associated with regions and villages in Bhutan where weaving is thought to be a particularly ancient skill [fig. 8.2].[2] Use of the fibers was once widespread, because bast-fiber cloth (*yüra, yüré,* 'country cloth') was the chief material for clothing until people learned to work with other fibers or, later, were able to obtain machine-spun Indian cotton yarn. Bast-fiber clothing had become rare by the 1940s, but it is remembered by older Bhutanese and was worn in parts of southern Bhutan until the mid-1960s.[3] Women's nettle-cloth dresses, which were fastened with thorns or sharpened bamboo slivers, disappeared before men stopped wearing nettle-cloth robes. Today, some

FIG. 8.1

Bhutanese women are skilled in coloring their weaving yarns with local plants and minerals, commercial dyes from India, and mixtures of the two. Skeins of yarn to wind into balls for weaving, a basket of yarns ready for use at the loom, and a circular cake of waxy lac residue were photographed in the home of Am Rinchen Zangmo, a master weaver and dyer, in Chumé Nanggar, Bumthang. (D.K.M. 1986)

people are reluctant to admit that the fabric was ever worn because it is considered such humble apparel.

Rough and sturdy, bast-fiber carrying cloths, sacks, and bags are sought after throughout Bhutan. This cloth is now gaining value, in eastern Bhutan because it is labor intensive to produce, and in western Bhutan because it is hard to replace.

Silk

Silk is the most prestigious fiber in Bhutan. Silk yarns, which are essential for creating very intricate patterns, are the most expensive to obtain. Among a family's cherished possessions is often a densely patterned robe or dress presented to a forebear by the first or second king or queen. These garments are sometimes patched, their silk patterns frayed, and the luster gone from their silver and gold yarns, but they are treasured heirlooms.

Although Bhutanese may call all silk *bura* ('insect cotton'), they distinguish several types of yarn: wild silk *(bura)*; cultivated, reeled silk *(seshu)*; Khaling silk (varieties of silk imported from Assam); and parachute silk *(namdru küp)*. The significant characteristics of silk yarn are whether it is produced by the domesticated, mulberry silk moth *(Bombyx mori)*, or by a wild or semidomesticated, nonmulberry silk moth; and whether it is reeled or spun.[4] Bhutan is most famous regionally for cloth made of, or patterned with, spun wild silk *(bura)*. This fiber was used much more than reeled silk until around 1970. Since then, a wider range of reeled silk yarns has become available, and more Bhutanese can afford to use them.

Wild silks are produced by a variety of moths that belong mainly to the *Saturnid* family (Giant Silkworm Moths). Common cultivated silk is reeled as a long fiber from the cocoons of domesticated *Bombyx mori* moths fed on mulberry leaves. Most wild silk is thicker than cultivated silk and is off-white in color, because *Saturnid* moth larvae feed on the leaves of trees and shrubs rich in tannin, which colors the silk the larvae extrude. Another important feature of wild silk is that it is rarely reeled. Cocoons gathered in the forest are often found after the larvae have already metamorphosed into moths and eaten through their cocoons, severing the silk filament in many places. Wild silk fibers are, therefore, shorter than the silk from domesticated moths. The broken cocoon is pulled apart and the fibers are spun, like cotton or wool. Some moths used for wild silk production have over the centuries become semidomesticated, in that people provide them with food and places to spin cocoons, which, as in the wild, are collected once the moths have emerged.

Several genera of *Saturnid* moths are native to southern Bhutan and adjacent hill areas of India. Assam has been noted for its "tree silk" for centuries; wild silk cloth was a staple of the region's commerce with "Bhutan, Towang, and the tribes inhabiting the lower Himalayan hills" (*Provincial Gazetteer* [1906] 1983, 65). Of the three best-known local *Saturnid* silks, Bhutanese have always preferred the one called *endi*, a coarse, beige fiber produced by *Samia ricini* [fig. 8.3].[5] This moth (a.k.a. *Attacus ricini*), whose larvae feed on the castor oil tree *(chamaling shing; Ricinus communis)*, is not a true species but a semidomesticated form cultivated on a large scale in Assam and Bhutan. The wild *Samia* in Assam and Bhutan is *S. canningii*, not *S. cynthia*, and seldom if ever used for silk these days.[6]

This account describes wild silk rearing in Goshing village in Bhutan's Shemgang District:

> Moths are kept in a special, closed-off room of the house where they can fly a little or rest on clean white cloth spread with "white" and "red" grass that we bring from the forest … in a short time they lay tiny white eggs. The eggs are rolled gently into small balls and

FIG. 8.2
Villages south of Tongsa are among those known for weaving with nettle fiber. This man's carrying cloth is typical of the utilitarian textiles made from nettle and other bast fibers. (Anthony Aris 1983)

wrapped in cloth for five days, when the tiny caterpillars are born. We put them onto flat baskets and cover them with a cloth. They are fed tender shoots of the castor oil tree and then bigger and bigger leaves. As they grow, we place branches of *shakoi shing* [a tree] in the room and put the caterpillars onto them. They climb up by themselves and eat the leaves. Then they begin making cocoons, which takes about three days. The branches with cocoons are cut off, and when they are ready, we tap the branches with a stick to make the moths come out. We release the males, which are smaller, and keep the females and some intact cocoons for the next breeding cycle.[7]

Whether collected from the forest or cultivated in this fashion, the cocoons are steeped in a solution of hot water, which has been drained through fermented rice, to soften and de-gum the cocoons. While still moist, the fiber is drawn out of each cocoon by hand. As the thread is wound onto a spindle, fiber ends are joined by pressing them together and lumps are smoothed between thumb and forefinger.

Although they may take precautions "to make the moths come out" before cocoons are simmered, Bhutanese acknowledge that in silk rearing they risk violating the Buddhist tenet of not killing living beings, even accidentally. Therefore, many cocoons and most yarn used in Bhutan, at least today, are from Assam. Bhutanese can safely weave and dye wild silk as long as they are one or more steps removed from the gathering or heating of cocoons. The herders of Merak Sakteng and other eastern Bhutanese travel to the Indian border to obtain cocoons, but many people prefer to purchase plain and colored wild silk yarns from India.

Much more wild silk was cultivated in southern and eastern Bhutan at one time. Bhutanese say that this practice has been declining for at least two generations. Late-nineteenth-century trade records note that thousands of pieces of *endi* (wild silk) cloth were exported from Assam at annual fairs in towns near the Bhutan border, but there is no mention of cocoons or yarn, implying that Bhutan had a domestic supply. Nonetheless, noble households in central Bhutan did import silk yarn, and small quantities of both cocoons and yarn probably also changed hands through petty trade along the border.

Today only a handful of relatively isolated villages in southern and eastern Bhutan rear wild silk moths.[8] The small quantities of fiber manufactured are produced mainly by families who cannot afford imported yard goods, yarns, or cocoons. Heightened sensitivity about violating Buddhist beliefs and increased prosperity have led more Bhutanese to purchase ready-spun and -dyed yarn. Indeed, a government-sponsored silk production unit in eastern Bhutan closed down several years ago because of public sentiment against the taking of life that might be involved in the enterprise.

Cultivated silk, for which the Orient is so famous, is produced by domesticated silk-worms (mostly *Bombyx mori*) that feed on mulberry leaves and extrude a fine liquid protein coated with sericin. When exposed to air, this becomes the fiber we know as silk. The larvae, which cannot survive in the wild, are carefully protected and fed handpicked leaves. After molting several times, the worm spins a cocoon, inside of which it metamorphoses into a moth over several weeks. If not prevented, it will then eat through the cocoon, breaking the silk fiber. In order to reel long, unbroken, smooth fibers, mature cocoons are simmered, killing the moths inside. Waste fibers from breakage are also spun, yielding a coarser, less desirable yarn often termed "raw silk" in the West.

Cultivated, reeled silk *(seshu)* has always been the most expensive yarn. In the past, Bhutan obtained its yarn from India and China, both famous for their mulberry silk industries. The small quantities of Chinese silk were purchased at festivals and trade fairs in

Fig. 8.3

Wild silks used in Bhutan and neighboring Assam are obtained from several varieties of Saturnid *moths (Giant Silkworm Moths). The moth shown here is today known as* Samia ricini, *a semidomesticated form that produces the type of wild silk* (endi) *favored in Bhutan. (Reproduced from Wardle 1881, pl. 8,* Attacus ricini; *Courtesy Lotus Stack)*

Tibet. Reportedly, reeled silk was little used until the early decades of this century, when it was popularized among the aristocracy by Ashi Pema Dechen, junior queen of the second king, and began to replace wild silk as the fiber of choice. Bhutanese now import most of their reeled silk from India, Japan, and Hong Kong, but are quick to point out the superior quality of "old silk" from India and China.

Small amounts of *Bombyx* silk are produced in a few villages in southern Bhutan that rear the larvae on native mulberry leaves *(shagongma shing)*. Although some efforts have been made to develop this modest activity into an industry, families are reluctant to become involved because of the stigma attached to taking the life of the silk moths.[9]

Two other types of silk are distinguished by Bhutanese. Khaling silk refers to Assamese yarns imported by the National Handloom Development Project in Khaling (Tashigang District). Most of them are spun from the waste fibers of mulberry-fed *Bombyx mori* silkworms.[10] This cultivated, spun silk is not as fine as cultivated, reeled silk, but is somewhat rough and slubby. Parachute silk *(namdru küp,* 'sky-ship [airplane] yarn') was introduced to Bhutan from India during the Second World War. Old women remember that the royal grandmother, Ashi Phuntsok Chöden, senior queen of the second king, was the first person to have the fiber, which came in the form of a heavy rope. The braided outer layer was unraveled for use as weft, and the straight strands of the rope's inner core were used for warps and pattern wefts. This fiber was thicker and cheaper than silk yarn from India and was dyed locally. Some say it is not of the same quality as other silk because it shows wear and does not hold color well.[11]

Cotton

In temperate areas of Bhutan, cotton is the fiber for ordinary garments and other utilitarian textiles. In 1838, Capt. R.B. Pemberton noted the manufacture of coarse cotton cloth and the custom of wearing cotton during the summer (Pemberton, in Collister 1987, 67, 65). Until the middle of this century, the majority of the cotton used in Bhutan was grown, spun, and woven locally [fig. 8.4]. Native cotton is known as *kabé*.

Cotton was once cultivated throughout the warm, southern hills, especially in Shemgang, Mongar, Pemagatshel, and Samdrup Jongkhar districts. In 1774, the annual yield was estimated at 40,000 maunds (1,490 metric tons) (Markham 1876, 55). In some areas, a portion of the crop was turned over to the state in return for salt from Tibet. The cotton was then redistributed to villagers to spin and weave into cloth, much of which was again given to the state as a form of tax. Cotton cultivation has greatly diminished over the past thirty-five years with the decline of tenant farming, the monetization of taxes, and the increased availability of commercial Indian yarns. Access to machine-spun yarn now makes local cultivation so uneconomical that it continues only in a few places for household use.[12]

Another fiber that the Bhutanese call cotton comes from a small tree. The Tibetan woman who is said to have introduced weaving in Tashigang centuries ago taught people first how to weave simple designs in wool and then how to make yarn from a "cotton tree" *(chemashing; Gossypium?)* native to the area. Fiber from this tree is still occasionally used for weaving in eastern Bhutan.[13]

Wool

In high-altitude areas, herding is a mainstay of the economy and wool *(bé)* is the chief weaving fiber. According to tradition, Ashi Jyazum (Wencheng), the Chinese bride of the seventh-century Tibetan king Songtsen Gampo, introduced sheep to Bhutan. As the story

Fig. 8.4

The village of Thongsa, Pemagatshel District, is one of the few places where cotton is still cultivated and processed for household weaving. A hand-operated cotton gin to remove seeds from the bolls is in the foreground. (Singay Namgay 1983)

goes, her parents had flocks of sheep of all colors of the rainbow. She was so angry at being sent so far away from home that she decided to steal some of the sheep, and off she went. When her mother discovered the sheep were gone, she said, "How could my daughter turn on her parents this way?" and spat in the direction the girl had gone. Her spittle turned into a river that ran across her daughter's path. As the girl led the flock across the bridge, it collapsed and the sheep fell into the river. She called out to them, "*Kar nap, sho, sho!* (Black and white, come, come!)," and those sheep scrambled after her, but the colored sheep were lost. This is why, say the Bhutanese, they have only black and white sheep.[14]

In colder areas, local fleece was spun and made into the cloth needed by each household, as well as handed over in raw form to authorities, who redistributed it to villagers for processing into cloth due to the state as tax.[15] Red and blue woolen cloth of domestic manufacture *(tshönam ngomar)* also figures in lists of gifts dating from the mid-1700s.[16] Panels of this cloth were surely stitched into the "blankets" mentioned so often in British records as an article of Bhutanese men's dress and the most important export to India. Although Bhutan also imported woolen cloth from Tibet and broadcloth from British India, local wool was the major source of clothing and utilitarian textiles in regions such as north central Bhutan.

Sheep wool still provides the primary fiber for villagers in Bumthang District (central Bhutan) and for seminomadic herders in western Bhutan (Laya Lingshi) and eastern Bhutan (Merak Sakteng). Flocks are sheared twice a year: in April-May before they are taken to their summer grazing areas and in September-October. Until the late 1950s, raw Tibetan wool, and occasionally woolen yarn, were imported sporadically. In the 1970s and 1980s, modest quantities of raw merino wool were imported from Australia. In recent years, Australian breeding stock has helped establish hybrid flocks whose fleece is popularly known as 'the trade minister's wool' *(tengye lyönpogi bé)*, because the stock was introduced when His Royal Highness Namgyal Wangchuck, the king's uncle, was minister of trade. In 1992-93, Australian experts and funds were helping to see if wool-washing and -carding machines would aid in processing the hybrid wool.

Yak wool and hair are also woven by herders in northern and eastern Bhutan and by villagers in central Bhutan. The soft inner wool from the chest and underbelly of yaks is suitable for making clothing and blankets. More commonly, the yak's outer coat, which is hair-like and highly water repellent, is woven into coarse raincloaks, blankets, tents, bags, and rope and fashioned into hats. Yak tails are used in Bhutan and exported as fly whisks.

Imports: Commercial Yarns and Synthetic Fibers
Small quantities of Tibetan woolen yarn, Indian cotton yarn, and silk yarns from India and China have been known in Bhutan for centuries. The first machine-spun cotton yarns probably reached Bhutan around 1870, but they were imported in very small quantities. Not until forty years later did cotton yarn figure as one of the chief exports to Bhutan from Assam, entering mainly through the market town of Samdrup Jongkhar in the southeast.[17] This yarn was known as *lata*, a name that Bhutanese explain reflected cultural perceptions of the time. Eastern Bhutanese, who were the predominant clients of Indian merchants along the border, spoke only their own languages and had to rely on sign language to communicate, pointing to what they wanted. The Indian merchants, not known for their patience, would cry out in exasperation, *"Lata!"* – meaning simpleton, but which the Bhutanese came to think was the name of the yarn. The term spread to Tibet via the Bhutanese, who still use the word for Indian cotton yarn.[18]

The new fibers penetrated Bhutan unevenly. Bhutan's trade with India was always relatively modest, and until the 1960s most Bhutanese traders must have bartered only what they could transport back to their home or village. Those who represented noble households might have purchased goods in some quantity, but few others would have been affluent enough or even interested in purchasing novel fibers. Many traders would have come from nonweaving areas, such as western Bhutan, and presumably found ready-made cloth of more use and value.

Imported goods, therefore, did not necessarily compare well or even compete significantly with indigenous products for some years. Even for the well-to-do, there were no dramatic economic advantages to machine-spun yarn; labor for the noble workshops was plentiful, as were supplies of indigenous wool and cotton and Assamese wild silk. It was apparently between 1955 and 1965, when serfs were released from their traditional obligations and began weaving on their own and when the road to Bhutan's capital was completed, that more significant quantities of inexpensive commercial yarn were brought in—and found eager consumers.

Bhutanese weavers today have access to fibers from around the world and buy the best they can afford. Popular varieties of Indian yarn include: cotton *(lata, tukuli)*; mercerized cotton *(Japan tukuli)*; and blended cotton and polyester *(terikot;* or *küpsap,* 'new yarn'). Silk-like acrylic yarn *(silik)* is an inexpensive alternative to reeled silk yarns *(seshu)* from India, Hong Kong, and Japan. Affluent Bhutanese prefer silver and gold threads from Japan to similar threads from Banaras (India) because the former remain shiny and last longer. Machine-spun woolen yarn *(them)* and acrylic yarn *(jachen)* from India have been popular since the 1960s for patterns on women's cotton dresses and new-style belts. Indian yarns are also an inexpensive alternative to local wool in central Bhutan, and while they have been available to some weavers for decades, between 1988 and 1992 they revolutionized the color palette of patterned cloth *(yathra)* woven there.

Fiber Preparation

Bhutanese fibers are almost always spun with a drop spindle *(phang)* [fig. 8.5].[19] Only locally grown cotton is traditionally spun first with the aid of a spinning frame, then twisted again, using a drop spindle to produce a tighter yarn. Spinning is usually women's work, although men in the herding communities of Laya Lingshi and Merak Sakteng spin yarn from sheep, yak, and goat wool. Bhutanese women also employ drop spindles to ply yarn and to tighten the twist of woolen, acrylic, and silk yarns from India. From the spindle, or the spinning frame, yarn is transferred to a rotating winding wheel [fig. 8.6] or hand-held skein winder. It is then wound off into balls or skeins for weaving in natural colors or for dyeing.

Fig. 8.5
Bhutanese women spin fibers and ply yarn – or, as here, tighten the twist of a yarn – with the aid of locally made drop spindles whose designs vary from village to village. The blue cloth wrapped about the woman's kira *protects her dress while she goes about her work. (Ellen Kaplowitz)*

Fig. 8.6
After yarn is spun, it is transferred from the spindle to a rotating winding wheel, and then lifted off, as a skein, for dyeing. Dyed skeins of yarn are transferred back to the same winding wheel (at right) to be wound into balls or onto a bobbin for weaving. Here, the yarn is being drawn off onto a slender, metal bobbin with the aid of the hand-operated spinning frame (at left). The bobbin will be inserted into a boat-shaped wooden shuttle for use on a horizontal frame loom. (Tongsa, D.K.M. 1992)

192

Dyes

Coloring yarns for weaving is a particularly delicate step in cloth production. Recipes are passed down from mother to daughter and are not usually shared with outsiders. Good colors are valued so much among the Bhutanese that strong taboos guide the dyeing process. Strangers should not witness it, lest they take away the color, and pregnant women should not dye yarns (lest the yarns' color be "stolen" by the baby). During the first half of this century, dyeing in the noble households of central Bhutan was done by specialists. These women prepared dyestuffs on a large outdoor grinding stone turned by several people, and then they colored silk and cotton yarns by steeping them in huge pots. In the 1930s and 1940s, most of the dyeing at these workshops still was done with indigenous materials.[20]

Bhutanese formerly used a standard selection of dyeplants found throughout Bhutan as well as local variants. Many of these dyestuffs grow in other Himalayan regions, and specific procedures for extracting color closely resemble recipes popular in Ladakh, Nepal, Sikkim, and southern Tibet. Although commercial dye powders were known in Bhutan before 1900 and have been very popular since the 1950s, they coexist with vegetable dyes.

Red

Stick lac *(jatsho)* is a resinous secretion deposited on tree branches by the parasitic *Laccifer lacca* insect [fig. 8.7]. The larvae draw their nutrients from the sap of the trees and secrete a viscous fluid that covers their bodies and encrusts the twigs. This encrustation is scraped off for processing as a red dye. Probably the most ancient of animal dyes, lac has been used in India since the beginning of recorded history (Ferris 1979, 355).

The warm eastern valleys of Bhutan, like adjacent Tawang and Assam (India), were noted for lac production. A small number of villages still register, for tax purposes, the trees on which insects are reared.[21] During the winter, twigs crusted with the insects are hung on a host tree *(khangaling shing; Zizyphus sp.)* that grows along rivers and streams. There the next generation of lac insects begins. When the weather warms in May or June, branches bearing the insect colonies are cut and placed on summer host trees that flourish on hillsides between 1,200 and 1,500 m.[22] In October, as soon as the mature insects begin emerging from the encrustations, the dyestuff is harvested by scraping hard nodules (stick lac) off the branches. Some seed colonies are cut and draped over branches of the winter host tree to propagate another brood of insects.

For centuries, lac was valued primarily as a dye, but its residue was also useful as sealing wax. Supplies from eastern Bhutan and adjacent Tawang (India) were sold in Assam to the south and thence reexported to north central India and Tibet. A very precious commodity in regions as far off as Ladakh, lac was a trade staple until the early 1870s,[23] when synthetic dyes began reaching India from Europe. Export taxes on lac initially were repealed to help keep the local product competitive, but over the next decade the imports to Bengal of alizarin and aniline dyes grew exponentially. Commerce in lac fell by more than ninety percent between 1883 and 1885 and was of no significance after that (Watt [1889] 1972, 2:409).

Although the Indian demand for Bhutanese lac ended, synthetic dyes made their way north relatively slowly, so lac cultivation for Tibetan and Bhutanese markets continued. In the 1890s, production in the Tashigang Valley was evident but not systematic (White [1909] 1984, 190), just as it is today. Although the border with Tibet was closed in 1959, Bhutan's own market for the dye still creates steady traffic to the east during harvesting season. In fact, demand outstrips supply, keeping prices high and on the rise. Families who cannot or do not wish to work the production trees they own sometimes give seed *(li,* from the *khangaling shing)* to tenant cultivators, who then utilize the trees. The tree rent in 1992 was seven *pathi* (measures) of stick lac per tree.

Bhutanese say that although native host trees abound, production remains desultory for the same reason that wild silk cultivation is not greater: many Bhutanese are happy to use lac, but feel it is sinful to produce because some insects are unavoidably killed during harvesting. Villagers often believe the red dye is actually the insects' blood. The dire consequences of being involved in lac production and use are graphically described in a Bhutanese text:

This large lake surrounded by mountains of fire is the lake in which sinners are cooking. ... Those who are thrown into the lake tied up with a hot iron chain have killed many of the larvae that produce red dye while they were on earth. The punishment for this act is to be cooked in an intense heat. Those who are hit on the head with a black axe are enduring the punishment for having traded the red dye. Those whose mouth is filled with a lot of blood are incurring the punishment for having dyed yarns by cooking them in the red color. Those who are crushed under a big stone are suffering the punishment for having worn many garments dyed with this red color. The people who have done all these things related to the red dye will not be delivered from this lake for three *kalpa* [cycles of existence] *(Delog sangye chözom namthar* [c. 1800?] 1980, 82, quoted in Pommaret 1989, 49).

Extracting color from stick lac is a slow process. One recipe, collected from Nanggar village in the Chumé Valley of Bumthang District,[24] calls for placing the lac in hot but not boiling water and grinding it into small pieces with some yeast and roasted wheat or barley grains. The pot is covered so the mixture ferments and a white cream rises to the surface; the mixture is stirred on five consecutive mornings. The liquid is then strained through a sieve, and the residue hardens into a wax used for sealing documents. Finally, the yarns are steeped for up to a week in the covered pot. If wool is being dyed, yarns are soaked first in a solution of hardwood ash *(thekhu),* and the dye-to-fiber ratio is two to one. If wild silk is being dyed, the ratio is from five to one to nine to one. Silk yarns are first boiled in an alum solution, then dried and wrapped in a thin cotton cloth so that they do not become tangled with chunks of the lac when immersed in the dye bath. As the red color emerges, the dye bath is boiled and ingredients are added to produce darker shades. Hues from pink to rich, deep red result, with true maroon and plum tints achieved by plunging yarns briefly into a solution of indigo.

Lac produces a superior color, but it is five times as costly as Bhutan's other indigenous red dye – madder. This climbing creeper, called *tsö* or *tsut (Rubia manjitha* and *R. wallichiana),* grows wild in the middle hills between 1,200 and 2,700 m (Nakao and Nishioka 1984, 134; Sonam Tshering 1990, 16). In western Bhutan, the vine flowers in August and is harvested soon afterward, when the seeds turn black. In the east, its orange blossoms line the roads in October, and the plant is picked in late November. Typically, the stems are coiled like a rope and air dried, or dried over a fire, and then chopped into small pieces that can be stored.

Like lac, madder was a staple of commerce between Bhutan and its neighbors. A Jesuit visitor in the mid-1700s noticed a brisk trade at Phari, in Tibet near Bhutan's northwest border, in "certain red twigs which give a most excellent red dye, especially to woolen cloth" (Desideri 1932, 140-41). In 1870, one of the so-called *pandit* explorers, sent surreptitiously by the British into the then little-known Himalayan regions, noted:

> a scandent plant, called *chud* ... found growing wild in these parts, entwining round the trunks of trees, and ... a most important article of trade. The people gather it in the jungle, cut it up into small pieces and carry it away into Tibet, where a rich red dye is extracted from it, when dry. This dye is in great demand throughout Tibet (Rinzin Namgyl, in Survey of India 1915, 2:373).

From other parts of Bhutan, basketloads of madder were carried north to the fair in Tsona Dzong (Tibet) and south to the Assam plains.[25] In eastern Bhutan, local taxes were paid in basket-loads of madder *(tsö do)*.

Madder is readily available in Bhutan and still popular for dyeing wool, cotton, and silks. Much simpler than using lac, the process involves boiling about a handful of madder twigs per pound of fiber, removing them, and then steeping the yarns. Varying the dye-to-fiber ratio and steeping time produces different shades of orangish- or brownish-red. Alumaceous earths are sometimes used as mordants, or the yarn may be soaked first in a solution of *Symplocos* leaves.[26]

Yellow

The leaves of at least four varieties of *Symplocos* trees contain a yellow pigment.[27] The shrubs are generally found on slopes above 1,000 m, so Bhutanese pick the branches when they ascend ridges to cut bamboo and firewood. Around Radi in eastern Bhutan, autumn is the best time to bring down leaves, which can be used fresh or dried. Recipes from central Bhutan involve placing well-washed woolen yarn in a boiling pot of the leaves and leaving it there until the desired shade of yellow is obtained. After the wool is rinsed and dried for a day, it may be steeped in a second dye bath of turmeric and coarsely ground buckwheat grains *(jobche)* which heightens its color. If the second bath contains madder, a rich rust or orange will be the result.[28]

In Mongar, Tashigang, and Pemagatshel districts, native turmeric *(yongka; Curcuma sp.)* is another source of yellow. Used for coloring and spicing food in India and Nepal, this rhizome produces a fine, bright yellow. Alumaceous earth may be added to the dye bath, which does not need boiling. Because turmeric yellow is somewhat fugitive, many Bhutanese women mix turmeric with another dyestuff that strengthens the color.

Blue

Bhutan's main blue dye comes from broad-leafed shrubs that contain indigotin and are collectively called indigo *(ram; Strobilanthes flaccidifolius* and *S. sp.)* (Sonam Tshering 1990, 13).[29] The plants are cultivated in kitchen gardens because they are so useful as coloring agents. Picked in the fall, the leaves must be used fresh or immediately prepared for storage [fig. 8.8]. In Mongar District, they are packed tightly in a tin or other container lined with banana leaves, and sprinkled with yeast. Alternatively, they can be covered with cow dung. In about twenty days, after the leaves are fermented and rotted, they are taken out and mixed with water dripped through hardwood ashes *(thekhu)*. One can either dye with this compound or mold it into balls or cakes, which are dried and stored for future use.

Bhutanese indigo is not the same indigo that is cultivated in India (Hindi: *nil; Indigofera tinctoria*). Indian indigo, which was grown first in Bombay and Gujarat, and from 1795 onward in Bengal, was much sought after in Tibet, and, as middlemen, the Bhutanese held

FIG. 8.8
The indigotin-rich leaves of several species of Strobilanthes *are the main source of blue dye. The plants are cultivated in many parts of Bhutan for their dyeing properties. (Thinleygang, D.K.M. 1986)*

local monopolies on the transit of the dye through their country. It was not used in Bhutan because reliable local substitutes were so abundant.

As in other Himalayan areas, Bhutanese indigo dyeing is a long, laborious process that can easily go wrong. It should be done by one person, in a quiet place, unobserved. The dried cake must be ground into powder, mixed with water, and fermented in an alkaline solution of hardwood ashes. The mixture is then kept warm but not boiled, and after about a week the yarn is immersed. The first dye lot is a light blue, with two to four successive steepings yielding deeper shades. Yeast and *chang* (local rice beer or other fermented grain beverage) are added during the dyeing to maintain the proper level of fermentation.[30]

Other Colors and Mordants

Compound colors are achieved by overdyeing. For example, greens result when yarns tinted blue with indigo are dyed in a second solution of one of the *Symplocos* leaves. Because "good" greens are hard to obtain, Bhutanese invariably consider these tones when judging the overall quality of a woven cloth.

Numerous other local plants are exploited to supplement the weaver's palette. Walnut (*tagoshing; Juglans regia*) bark and husks, and the sour fruit of a tree called *chorgenshing* (*Phyllanthus emblica L.*), are sources of black and brown dyes, especially in Bumthang and Mongar districts. Another source of black is a mud mixed with a poisonous root (*chukchumé* in Bumthang) that causes swelling to the face and hands. Leaves called *photorshing* yield a yellow dye in eastern Bhutan (Sonam Tshering 1990, 17-18). In western Bhutan, red is obtained from the purple-skinned berries of thorn bushes (*kipetsang*). Light blue and purple are obtained from pine cones (*dungshing*) gathered in areas of central Bhutan over 3,000 m. Easier to use than indigo, this dye is said to have been used chiefly for yarns required for making tax cloth.[31]

Mordants are substances that fix a dye on a yarn by combining with the dye to form an insoluble compound. Traditional mordants include the *Symplocos* leaves, alumaceous earths, and sour fruits. The earths and a mineral known as 'stone indigo' (*doram*) are found in small deposits along roads and riversides. Sour fruits native to temperate regions of central and eastern Bhutan serve as mordants, as does pomegranate skin in western Bhutan. In eastern Bhutan, crabapples are used as a mordant – and numerous other fruits with the suffix -*churpo* ('sour') are known elsewhere.[32]

The National Handloom Development Project in Khaling has experimented with various other natural dyestuffs and imported mordants. The Dyeing Unit there has developed recipes for dyeing with rhododendron leaves (yellow); marigolds (yellow); *Artemisia sp.* (*khempa*; green); and several other flowers and leaves.[33]

Imported Dyes

Introduced in Europe in 1856, commercial dyes (*tshosar,* 'new color') were widely available in India by 1880. They quickly reached the border markets of West Bengal and Assam and were rapidly introduced into Sikkim and Tibet. By 1885, synthetic dyes had seriously affected the regional trade in most natural dyes, whose use declined even more dramatically in the following decade. While the dyes could have reached Bhutan, too, by the turn of the century, Bhutanese believe this was not the case. Older people remember their grandparents bringing back some pink dye powder from festivals in Tibet, but this was a rarity. Moreover, textile gifts presented to Sir Charles Bell in 1910, which would have represented a fine grade of recently made, local cloth, show only vegetable colors [figs. 3.5, 5.5].[34]

Fig. 8.9
Bhutanese regard natural dyes as superior to commercial dyes, but they like the brightness achieved with synthetic powders. Today, many women add a pinch of these dyes from Armenian Street in Calcutta to a natural dye bath to heighten the hues attained with traditional dyestuffs. Alternatively, women will dip commercial yarns into a dye bath of native indigo or lac to enhance their tint. (Radi Dukpiling, D.K.M. 1992)

Synthetic dyes, as opposed to commercial yarns that were already dyed, appear to have been introduced into noble households by the 1920s, if not before. They gained popularity among the well-to-do very quickly. Textiles from this time onward show increasingly numerous and gay colors. In the late 1940s, traders were bringing powder dyes north to towns as far from the Indian border as Tashigang. During those years, the easily available dyes became fashionable among ordinary people. Many women who were young girls at this time say that, while their mothers routinely continued to use natural dyes alongside synthetic colors, they themselves never learned to use natural dyes because of the growing popularity of commercial dyes (and imported, colored yarns).[35]

As late as the mid-1980s, vegetable dyes were still in wide use in Bhutan's towns and countryside. But in the past decade, dyeing practices, even in rural and relatively remote areas, have changed radically. Women say vegetable dyes require too much work or are too expensive compared with dyes from Calcutta, or that dyes are no longer needed because handloomed cloth is being replaced by the new factory-made cloth from India. As a result, fewer women are dyeing yarn at all and, of those, fewer are using vegetable dyes.

Practices in Bhutan today exhibit a tension between custom and convenience. Many people say they still prefer vegetable colors to commercial tints, and certainly they esteem natural-dye colors more highly. Thus, well-to-do families continue to use indigenous dyestuffs as a matter of principle, as do some villagers who have easy access to them. Very often the color of a commercial yarn will be enhanced by steeping it in a natural dye bath. At the same time, women like the brightness obtained with synthetic dyes and commonly add a dollop of Indian dye powder [fig. 8.9] to a natural dye bath to enhance *its* result. In recent years, the Bhutanese also have come to realize that Westerners favor vegetable dyes. Especially in areas frequented by tourists, one will quickly be assured that the woolen cloth for sale is colored with natural dyes – despite the vivid oranges and hot pinks. While many bright yarns may be dipped into natural dye baths, purely vegetable-dyed fibers are rarely seen in textiles for the public market.

Looms

Three types of looms *(thagshing)* are used in Bhutan, but one is predominant: the backstrap loom. Horizontal frame looms were introduced from Tibet in the first half of this century. Card looms, a form of backtension loom that perhaps also entered Bhutan from Tibet, have long been used for making a select group of narrow textiles.[36]

Backstrap Looms
Most weaving in Bhutan is done on two types of backstrap loom *(pangthag,* 'body or lap loom') [fig. 1.10].[37] One type, the most common, has two warp beams that require a wooden frame, so these looms are usually set up against the wall of a porch, in a special weaving shed, or indoors near a window or doorway. On this loom, the warp slants upward, away from the weaver, and around the upper warp beam. In contrast, the second type of loom has a single warp beam, which is usually positioned so the warp rides parallel to the ground in front of

the weaver. These looms, which can be moved easily, are used by seminomadic herders. Bhutanese weavers employ a length of bamboo as the shuttle case and a wooden sword to beat in the weft.

The warp is prepared for the loom by winding it around upright wooden posts. One method of warp winding utilizes two vertical posts about 150 cm apart, fixed in a board laid on the ground. A thin, joining rod connects the posts near their top ends. Depending on the pattern of the cloth to be woven, two to five thin wooden or bamboo rods are propped against the joining rod. One of them, around which warp yarns are looped, will become the cross, helping to keep warp yarns in order during weaving. Another one will become the shed rod for the ground weave; and, if needed, others will serve as shed rods for pattern warps. Ground warps are tied with loops of thread to a heddle rod, and supplementary (pattern) warps to pattern heddle rods, as the warp is prepared. The warp is most often wound in a circular direction as a continuous length, with different-colored warp yarns tied end to end. When a panel of this cloth is removed from the loom, it is tubular and must be cut across a narrow section of unwoven warps in order to create a flat rectangle.

The warp may also be wound in another manner, using a third fixed post (*sogshing*, 'life wood'), which becomes the closing rod when the warp is transferred to a loom. In this case, the winding direction is reversed every time the warp loops around the closing rod; alternatively, the direction may be reversed at other regular intervals. When a panel of this type of cloth is completed, the closing rod is pulled out, releasing the warp-end loops. The fabric is a flat panel that does not require cutting. The name of the closing rod, *sogshing*, is also the term for the pole of a prayer flag and for the wooden molds for making butter offerings. This shows the critical, parallel importance of these three "life-giving" items.

When the warp is moved to a loom, the two fixed (end) winding posts are replaced by the upper and lower warp beams, inserted into holes in the vertical frame beams. The breast beam, typically a length of bamboo split in half lengthwise so that it grips the cloth, is tied to the weaver's backstrap with leather or nylon cords. The backstrap is a piece of animal hide, a woven bamboo panel, or a length of canvas with wooden dowels at each end. By leaning backward, the weaver maintains warp tension as she weaves. As the weaving proceeds, she moves the entire warp by loosening the two halves of the breast beam to release the cloth, and sliding the unwoven warp downward toward her.

Backstrap looms with a single warp beam are used in herding communities in northwest Bhutan (Laya Lingshi). The warp beam is positioned 1 to 3 m in front of the weaver, roughly level with the breast beam at the sitting weaver's waist. The warp beam may be braced in a frame or with stones or heavy sacks of salt. The advantage of this loom is that it can easily be rolled up and moved with partially woven cloth on it. During the winter, when most weaving takes place, herders carry their looms as they move their flocks or make trading trips, and set them up wherever they camp. Weavers in Phobjikha, a high valley near the Pelé La, use a similar loom, whose warp of 3 m or more is sometimes supported by a low crossbeam, propped on two sticks, midway down its length.

Fabric woven on backstrap looms is limited in width to roughly 65 cm. Garments and other textiles are fashioned by stitching together two or more lengths of cloth. A woman's dress *(kira)*, for example, if made of silk or cotton, consists of three panels joined in the warp direction and oriented horizontally in the finished dress. If made of wool on a backstrap loom, the dress will contain six panels oriented vertically.

Most fabric woven on a Bhutanese backstrap loom is warp-faced plainweave. A fabric may be embellished with supplementary warps, supplementary wefts, or both. Examples of supplementary-warp-patterned textiles are the *aikapur* from eastern Bhutan [figs. 7.4, 7.7]. The pattern warps float on one face of the cloth when not floating on the other, creating a negative pattern on the back of the textile.

Supplementary-weft patterning may be created by yarns that extend from one selvedge to the other (continuous wefts), or by shorter yarns that are interworked with ground wefts and ground warps in a limited area (discontinuous wefts). Women's traditional cummerbunds *(kera)* and the center panels of multipurpose textiles *(chagsi pangkheb)* usually show continuous supplementary wefts, moving back and forth across the entire width of the fabric [figs. 5.11, 5.45-5.48]. The pattern yarns float on one side of the cloth when not floating on the other. The most uniquely Bhutanese examples of discontinuous supplementary-weft patterning are textiles decorated with the technique called *kushü*, which originated in north central Bhutan [figs. 7.8, 7.9]. *Kushü* pattern yarns are laid in with the ground weft so that they are visible only on the front surface of the cloth.

FIG. 8.10

Two women are needed to prepare the warp for a horizontal frame loom. The woman in the foreground is threading warp yarns through the hedddles that will control the ground weave. Her companion is looping the yarn around a stick that will become the warp beam when the yarn is transferred to the loom. (D.K.M. 1986).

Horizontal Frame Loom

The horizontal frame loom *(thrithag)* does not use a circular warp, and it is worked with treadles [figs. 8.11, 8.12]. The warp is wound around narrow rods laid parallel to the ground. At one end of the warp, as the winding proceeds, yarns are tied to or inserted through the heddles that will control the ground weave [fig. 8.10]. Four shafts are customary. Supplementary (pattern) warps are not used on this type of loom. The warp is then transferred to the loom, and the shafts are suspended by cords from the pulley frame. The ground weft is wound on a long, bamboo bobbin with forked ends (for example, for weaving *yathra*) or on a very short bobbin that is inserted into a boat-shaped, wooden shuttle (for example, for weaving *mathra*).

For the ease of the weaver's arm motions, which vary depending on the patterning techniques used, the width of cloth made on this loom is between 20 and 65 cm. Panels of fabric from the loom are cut and sewn into finished textiles. For example, a woman's woolen dress may have between ten and fourteen narrow panels made on the frame loom, which are oriented vertically when the dress is worn. Blankets and raincloaks consist of two or three panels cut from the same loom length and joined in the warp direction.

The horizontal frame loom is mainly used for weaving with woolen and acrylic yarns. Typically, the cloth produced is a twill weave *(bjichu mito, 'little bird's eye')*. The most common weave, seen in textiles such as narrow *mathra* panels for stitching into garments and wider panels of *yathra* cloth, is a plain 2/2 twill. Older examples show staggered 2/2 diamond, staggered 2/2 vertical herringbone, and other twills. Very often, as in *mathra pesar* and *yathra*, the twill ground cloth is patterned with discontinuous supplementary wefts.

This loom was introduced to central Bhutan from Tibet sometime around 1930. In north central Bhutan, the story is well known:

Around 1920, a young man named Sonam Dondhrup [c. 1895-1975] from Kurtö Yomining [a town in northern Lhuntshi District] went off to Tongsa Dzong, then the home of the royal family, to seek his fortune in the king's service. There were many people from

Lhuntshi at the court because the royal family had originally come from Dungkhar in the northern part of Lhuntshi. In Tongsa, Sonam Dondhrup discovered he was interested in weaving and in his free time, he learned to work at a backstrap loom from some of the weavers there. He became a good weaver.

Ashi Wangmo, the young daughter of the first king, also lived at Tongsa. She is fondly remembered in Bhutan not so much for weaving, but for her religious devotion – she became a nun. She noticed Sonam Dondhrup's curiosity about looms and his skill in weaving, and one day asked him to stay with her as an attendant, saying she had over 100 women weaving for her, but not one man. Moreover, she knew that a different kind of weaving was done in Tibet, using a different loom. She asked Sonam Dondhrup to go to Tibet to learn that weaving and then train Bhutanese how to do it. He did go, and spent nine months there, but no one would teach him. Then Ashi Wangmo sent two sets of gift cloth (*zong*) to him to give the Tibetans and after that they taught him. He came back, made a horizontal frame loom, and taught her how to weave on it. The two of them trained many of the women at the court in Tongsa. Later Ashi Wangmo went back to her home in Lhuntshi and taught women there how to weave on the horizontal frame loom.[38]

The loom was popularized in western Bhutan in the late 1940s by Thimphu Zimpön (chamberlain) Rinchen Dorji, who brought two Tibetan families from Phari to weave in Thimphu because he admired their work. They brought their wooden looms with them and soon the looms were being copied locally.[39] Today the horizontal frame loom is seen mainly in Thimphu, central Bhutan, and Merak Sakteng.

FIG. 8.11

Horizontal frame looms, operated with foot treadles, were introduced to central Bhutan from Tibet in the 1930s and to the Thimphu area the following decade. This young woman in Thimphu is weaving a panel of the woolen twill called mathra, *of which her dress is made. She is about to insert the weft yarn, which is wound around a bobbin in a boat-shaped shuttle. Her loom has four shafts, which is typical for weaving twill cloth, and the basket secured to the loom frame holds weaving yarns and tools. (Anthony Aris 1983)*

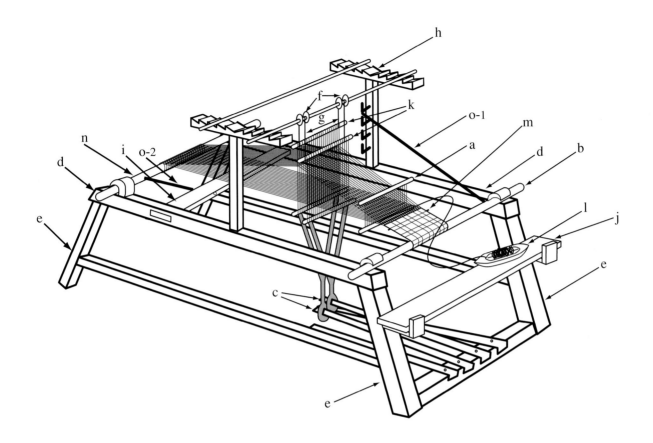

Fɪɢ. 8.12

The Horizontal Frame Loom.

Dzongkha (Dz)/Bumthangkha (Bu)/Kurtö-tkha (Ku)/Tshangla (Tsh): *thrithag* (khri 'thag)

(a) Beater/reed

Dz/Ku: *tham, thama* (thagm, thag ma), Bu: *thama, thamagi khwa*, Tsh: *nas* ('comb')

(b) Cloth beam

Dz: *drim* (sgril ma), *dongdrim*, Bu: *namdri, namdrim*, Ku: *do ngé, drishing*, Tsh: *drishing*

(c) Foot treadles

Dz: *kangthrab* (rkang 'khrab), Bu/Ku: *kangthra*, Tsh: *bitingshing*

(d) Frame beam

Dz: *thagshing* ('thags shing), Bu: *thrithag kera*, Ku: *thrithag seng*, Tsh: *thangshing*

(e) Frame foot

Dz: *thagshing kam* ('thags shing rkang ma), Bu/Ku: *thrithag tawa*, Tsh: *thagshing bi*

(f) Pulley

Dz/Bu/Ku/Tsh: *khorlo* ('khor lo)

(g) Pulley cords

Dz: *né thagpa* (gnas thag pa), Bu: *na thagpa*, Ku: *nat thagpa, nat prengpa*, Tsh: *nyé do*

(h) Pulley frame

Dz: *thrithaggi nam* (khri 'thag gyi rnam), Bu: *khorlogi shing*, Ku/Tsh: *changzer*

(i) Rear crossbeam

Dz: *bushing* (sbug shing), Bu/Ku: *barshing*, 'mid-beam', Tsh: *chudang*, 'belt'

(j) Seat

Dz: *enta* (a'n ta), Bu/Ku/Tsh: *pang*

(k) Shafts

Dz/Ku/Tsh: *néshing* (gnas shing), Bu: *nat tseng, nashing*

(l) Shuttle

Dz: *wachu* (wa chung), Bu: *drimpu*, Ku: *pundung*, Tsh: *phunduptsham, phunpalang*

(m) Temple

[This slender stick is hardly visible because it is always inserted underneath the web.]

Dz/Bu: *tser* (tser, btsir), Ku: *tser, nitma*, Tsh: *lizi, lizu, tser*

(n) Warp beam

Dz: *judrim* (rgyu sgril ma), *juchi, juthi*, Bu: *jhapagi drim, ama kening*, Ku/Tsh: *drishing*

(o) Warp tension system

(o-1) front element

Dz/Bu: *drim kotha* (sgril ma ko thag), Ku: *thrithaʼi la*, Tsh: *per*, 'iron, metal'

(o-2) rear element

Dz/Bu: *japagi drimgi kotha*, Ku: *kotha*, Tsh: *per*

Card Loom

The Bhutanese card loom utilizes a continuous, circular warp mounted on the same frame as a backstrap loom *(pangthag)* and similarly held taut by a weaver's body position [fig. 8.13]. The Bhutanese call the loom a 'paper loom' *(shogu thagshing)* because the cards were once made of sheets of sturdy local paper or animal hide. Today they are often made from X-ray film or cardboard. The warp units are made of four yarns, each passing through a different hole in the four corners of a card. Two cards with eight warps make up a set. The cards are rotated by quarter turns to open and close each shed, and the weft is beaten down with a wooden sword. For a new-style woman's belt, about sixty cards are used.

Bhutanese use this type of loom to produce very narrow textiles such as men's belts. The ground is usually a countered four-strand, warp-twined fabric, with twining that is inverted at intervals throughout the textile. Triple wefts are common. When a woman's belt is card-woven, it is decorated with various techniques of supplementary-weft patterning. Wool, acrylic, and cotton are used for the ground weave of textiles made on this loom.

Card weaving flourished in Burma, India, and Tibet (Schuette 1956, 9-11) and may have been introduced to Bhutan from Tibet.[40] The strongest evidence for this hypothesis is the range of textiles traditionally made on this loom. They are all similar to textiles made in Tibet and are used in contexts that were introduced from Tibet: for male dress (men's belts and garters for securing boots) and

religious purposes (ties for binding religious texts [*petha* or *singtha*] and, sometimes, straps to hold reliquaries worn on the chest). Before Bhutan was unified as a Buddhist nation in the mid-1600s, men's customary dress was different, so belts and boot ties of this type were probably unknown. Charm boxes were secured with narrow strips of cotton fabric, as they sometimes still are. Since the 1960s, narrow women's belts have also been made by card weaving. The adaptation of women's belts to this loom, formerly reserved for men's apparel and religious items, seems something of a paradox. Perhaps it was only possible because of the social and cultural changes that have led to the relaxation of other textile and dress traditions since the 1950s.

Fig. 8.13

This weaver in Kabesa, near Thimphu, maintains the tension of the warp on her card loom by leaning slightly back against her backstrap. The warp yarns are threaded through holes in the pack of yellow cards, which are small cardboard squares cut from government file folders rather than traditional pigskin. The loom's wooden frame, the wooden sword for beating in the weft, and the breast beam positioned in the weaver's lap are features seen on other Bhutanese backtension looms (pangthag). Card looms are employed for weaving narrow textiles such as men's belts, garters for securing boots, straps for tying up religious texts, and, in the past thirty-five years, women's belts. (D.K.M. 1992)

The twentieth century has seen rapid changes in the materials used by Bhutanese weavers. The imported fibers and commercial dyes available even in remote villages have increased exponentially and been readily incorporated in textile production. In embracing new materials, Bhutanese have not abandoned their traditional fibers and indigenous dyestuffs, but use them side by side or in combination with commercial yarns and dyes. In contrast to this change in materials, weaving technology has changed relatively little. Local fibers are still spun by hand, and imported yarns are often respun or plied on a drop spindle. The backstrap and card looms—and, for the past sixty years, the Tibetan horizontal frame loom—have not been displaced by mechanized looms or other "improved" technology. They continue as the exclusive means of cloth production, providing weavers with technical options that are flexible enough to create an ever-evolving array of textiles.

Notes

Chapter One

1. See in particular Pallis 1960, 141-59.

2. Indo-Tibetan Buddhism does, however, commemorate a male weaver among the eighty-four *siddhas*. He was Tantipa of Sandhonagara, who was from India, where men do weave. See Abhayadatta 1979, 65-68.

3. See Driem 1994 (forthcoming) and also his unpublished 1991 ms. Here and below I rely heavily on these two sources for details of linguistic affiliation and population figures, as they represent a considerable advance on my own findings published in Aris 1979, xiv-xviii.

4. All groups use Tibetan script either in its formal "headed" style known as *uchen* (dbu can) or in the local Bhutanese cursive hand known as *gyuyig* (rgyug yig). My renderings of Dzongkha and Tibetan words as they are pronounced are given in italics. Their proper orthography is given in Roman after their first occurrence. Where the orthography is not known or is the same as the phonemic rendering, it is omitted.

5. Unspun cotton or local cotton yarn is not termed *ré* but rather *kabé* (ka bal); the classical Tibetan *singbé* (srin bal, literally 'insect wool') is also used in writing.

6. Notice that the single syllable "ras," pronounced *ré* both in Tibetan and Dzongkha, becomes *ra* in the second element of most Dzongkha compounds but remains *ré* in the equivalent Tibetan compounds.

7. See Aten Dogyetshang 1993, 87-90. See also that volume, p. 122, n. 29, for the editor's comment that an extensive 'eulogy of silk' (dar bshad) was composed by the seventh incarnate lama and 'minor abbot' (mkhan chung) of *Dragyab Dongkong* (brag g.yab gdong kong), Thubten Deleg Gyamtsho (1898-1972), with the title "Dar bshad 'bel gtam pad dkar phreng ba." I do not know if this work has been published.

8. See Tendzin Dorje n.d. [1986?] ms., 38-44. This fascinating work on the marriage customs of eastern Bhutan awaits study.

9. See Petech 1990, 103-11, which builds on and supersedes my own findings in Aris 1979, 120-23. See also Aris 1980a, 10-11.

10. This is also the conclusion of Driem 1991 ms., 20-22.

11. *Pha drukgom shikpai namthar* n.d [c. 1580?]. In 1993 this work was being serialized in the Dzongkha edition of *Kuensel,* Bhutan's national newspaper. On this saint see Aris 1979, 168-74.

12. "tha ra" = "'thags ra." The text is obviously corrupt here. Perhaps "tha ra" could be "'thags ras" ('woven cloth') instead of "'thags ra" ('weaving yard').

13. "thag skyed" = "thags sgye"? My emendation is a tentative one based on the identification by my Bhutanese informants of "sgye sne" in Ashi Nangsa's song (see n. 36 below) as a backstrap, usually known to the Bhutanese as a "sked 'thag" (literally 'waist-strap').

14. "stag mo" = "thags mo"? Again my emendation is uncertain, based on a possible reconstruction of the Tibetan from the Dzongkha "thagm." Certainly "stag mo" ('tigress') cannot be correct.

15. I first drew attention to these paintings in Aris 1979, 176-77, and 178 (pl. 15). My suggestion there that they might date from the time of the temple's enlargement by Kunga Sengge (1314-47) must be revised in the light of the radiocarbon date now obtained (see next note).

16. See Aris 1989a on the radiocarbon dating of Chang Gangkha wall paintings.

17. A similar phrase is found in the code of the *pazap* militia (referred to in this chapter), translated in Aris 1976, 622, 628.

18. The lady in question was Tshokye Dorje (1680-98), the only grandchild of Shabdrung Ngawang Namgyel.

19. For example, see the *Kathrim* [Bhutan's Legal Code of 1729], quoted in Aris 1986, 160-61. See also Yönten Thayé [n.d.] 1970, fols. 4or, 69r, 73v, 75v, 93v.

20. The source frequently combines the standard Tibetan decimal counting system with Bhutan's unique vigesimal system, the only text where I have found both systems used in parallel.

21. Other local terms in this source which await elucidation are "khra khra" and "ta tsha." Several Tibetan terms also fail to turn up in any dictionary.

22. "arti dkyil dkar gyi rgyab bkab." Chandra Das [1902] 1985 defines "ar ti" or "ar ti kha dmar" as 'cloth of raw silk imported from Assam, having three stripes lengthwise.' The item is still used by yogins of the older Tibetan schools.

23. On the gifts of cloth exchanged between Bhutan and Assam on the occasion of the first "official" embassy sent from Bhutan, see also Phukan 1981, 225-33.

24. Here are some examples of these compounds: mdzod chen, mdzod rnying, mdzod thung, mdzod btags, mdzod sgag, gos mdzod, bar mdzod, phyi mdzod, nang mdzod.

25. I have depended here on the spellings and definitions used in the *Bögya tsigdzö chenmo* 1985.

26. For example, "sman bar" ('middling'), "sman rnying" ('old'), "sman kha rnying kha" (?).

27. See the account of Tibet by the missionary Domenico da Fano, in Petech 1952-56, 3:13-15, "The handkerchiefs of silk which come from China and which are used in Tibet as

money are called Manse or Mancia." (I owe this reference and its translation to my friend Nicholas Rhodes.) The Bhutanese Legal Code of 1729 forbids the acceptance of even a "square of 'sman [rtse]'" by a judge when trying cases; see Aris 1986, 152-53.

28. *Ashi nangsai namthar* [n.d.] 1984; the song translated below is on pp. 143-46. An English translation of the song has already appeared in Allione 1984, 110-12. My version aims at greater technical and conceptual accuracy. A Tibetan edition of the same work in my collection has the title "Rigs bzang gi mkha' 'gro ma snang sa 'od 'bum gyi rnam thar," published in 1977 and 1984 by the Tibetan Cultural Printing Press (Dharamsala).

29. Our knowledge of the *delog* cult in Bhutan today derives entirely from the detailed research of Françoise Pommaret (1989).

30. "thags chas," lit. 'loom things' (Dzongkha: *thagcha*, 'thags cha), parts of the loom.

31. "rkang khung," lit. 'foot hole' (Dz: *kangthé*, rkang theg), ground frame beam.

32. "gdan chung," lit. 'little mat' (also Dzongkha), ground mat on which a weaver sits.

33. "phur ba," lit. 'peg' or 'ritual dagger' (Dz: *thagshing*, 'thags shing), frame beam.

34. "thags mgo," lit. 'loom head' (also Dzongkha), front portion of the loom.

35. "thags shing," lit. 'loom stick' (Dz: *jushing*, rgyu shing; also *théshing*, the shing), warp beam.

36. "sgye sne," lit. 'bag-hem' (?) (Dz: *kethag*, sked 'thag), backstrap.

37. "tshigs pa" (Dz: *tshig*, tshig), breast beam.

38. "snal ma" (Dz: skudp; also *ju*, rgyu), warp.

39. The "abiding nature of the universal basis" is the primordial emptiness of reality.

40. "'thag pa'," lit. 'rope' (also Dzongkha), cord for fastening the backstrap to the breast beam.

41. The Ten Virtues consist in the renunciation of the Ten Non-Virtues and the practice of their opposites: murder, theft, sexual misconduct, falsehood, slander, irresponsible chatter, verbal abuse, covetousness, vindictiveness, and holding wrong views. The translations and lists of the enumerated terms which appear in this poem are taken from Gyurme Dorje and Kapstein 1991.

42. "srog smug," lit. 'life-?' (Dz: *thaggi sog*, 'thags gyi srog, lit. 'loom's life'; or *sogshing*, srog shing, lit. 'life wood'), closing rod.

43. The 'female consort' is the yogin's tantric partner.

44. "yar gnas," lit. 'upper place' (Dz: *néshing*, gnas shing), heddle rod for ground warp.

45. The Three Upper Realms are those inhabited by the gods, the antigods, and the humans.

46. "mar gnas," lit. 'lower place' (Dz: *néshing* [see n. 44]), heddle rod for ground warp.

47. The Three Evil Destinies are those occupied by the denizens of hell, the tormented spirits, and the animals.

48. "'u lu" (Dz: *'u lu*; or *udung*, 'u dung), shed rod.

49. "bkad" (Dz: *pün*, spun), weft.

50. "Giving and taking" refers to the meditative technique attributed to Atisa whereby one's own merit and happiness are "given" to all sentient beings and their demerit and suffering are "taken" by the meditator as a means of cultivating the mind of enlightenment.

51. "bsang smyug" (Dz: *pündung*, spun dung), shuttle case.

52. The Two Obscurations are those of conflicting emotions and those concerning the knowable.

53. "sil le" (also Dzongkha), bobbin.

54. The Two Provisions are those of merit and of pristine cognition.

55. "btsir (rgyab?)" (Dz: *tser*, btsir), temple (a stick that holds the woven fabric taut from edge to edge).

56. "snam bu" (Dz: *bé*, bal; or *nambu*, snam bu), woolen cloth.

57. The Eight Worldly Concerns are those of profit, loss, pleasure, pain, fame, defamation, praise, and blame.

58. *Tak-tak* represents the sound of the sword (Dz: thagm), a stick used for beating in the weft.

59. The number is an allusion to the 84,000 teachings which the Buddha is said to have propounded to counter the same number of mental afflictions.

Chapter Two

1. Most of Bhutan's twenty-one languages belong to the Tibeto-Burman branch of the Sino-Tibetan family. Other speakers of Tibeto-Burman languages include the Kachins and Chins of Burma and the Akhas, Lahus, and Karens of Burma and Thailand. Closer relationships exist between the languages of central Bhutan and northern Arunachal Pradesh (India) and between the Tshangla spoken in eastern Bhutan and the language of Pemakö in southeast Tibet (Aris 1979, xiv-xviii, 122).

The eastern Bhutanese, the Akas of Arunachal Pradesh, the Shans of Burma, and the Tibetans share origin legends derived from the mythology of the Ch'iang people of western China; also, origin myths of the Bhutanese and the Thulung Rais of eastern Nepal are closely linked to Tibetan myths recorded before the tenth century (Aris 1979, 125-38; Milne [1910] 1970, 18).

2. The lands outside Bhutan that were once part of this north-south corridor have been partitioned in the twentieth century between China (the northern, Tibetan area) and India (Kameng District in Arunachal Pradesh).

3. The people of Merak and Sakteng are known to other Bhutanese as *bjop*, a term also sometimes applied to the Dakpas, Bhutanese herders who live between Tashigang and Merak Sakteng and dress similarly to the Merak Sakteng people.

4. The Tibetan exile is said to have been Prince Tsangma, son of King Tridé Songtsen. His story is related in an important Bhutanese text, the *Gyelrig* (Ngawang 1728, fol. 10v-14r, quoted in Aris 1986, 27-29).

5. For example, in the fifteenth century, the famous central Bhutanese lama Pemalingpa traveled in Tawang; his younger brother established temples there and married a local girl (Aris 1989b, 111-12). Another link was established in the early seventeenth century when a half-brother of Shabdrung Ngawang Namgyel, the founder of Bhutan, settled in Tawang (Imaeda 1987, 195).

6. See, for example, Aris 1979, 119-23; and Pommaret 1994.

7. Both groups were probably living in the region before the seventh century AD and speak Tshangla (Aris 1979, 122; Imaeda and Pommaret 1990, 119). On the Mönpas, see Dhar 1984, 295-306.

8. The border was created when Tawang was annexed under the Tibetan governor of Tsona Dzong in 1680, in response to the eastward advance of the Bhutanese military, consolidating the new state established by Shabdrung Ngawang Namgyel.

9. They are woven less in Merak Sakteng than in lower-lying villages (such as Radi and Phongmé) just to the west.

10. The Sherdukpens believe that they came

from Tibet and also have historical links with Bhutan (Sharma 1961, 5-9; Fürer-Haimendorf 1982, 172-75). For a drawing of a Sherdukpen loom, see Sharma 1961, 22.

11. In 1668, the Lepcha chief of Sikkim asked the Tibetans to help him repulse a Bhutanese army, and periodic military engagements between Bhutan and Sikkim occurred for the next two centuries. From 1678 until 1865, Bhutan controlled the Kalimpong area, which it ceded to the British only after the Anglo-Bhutan War. The Bhutanese still maintain strong links with the town. In 1904, Sir Charles Bell estimated that in southwestern Bhutan there were 700-800 "Bhutanese," 300-400 Lepchas, and 14,000 Nepalese (Bell Collection 1904, 1-3).

12. The "coarse silk" robe was made from "the cocoon of a large caterpillar that is found wild at the foot of the hills, and is also cultivated" (Hooker 1855, 1:123). The coat covered with crosses is recognizable as tie-dyed fabric imported from Tibet.

13. For example, Sir Charles Bell received a gift from the Paro Pönlop (governor) in 1915 that was annotated as a "Lepcha *chadar* [man's shawl]" (Bell Collection 1915a). Some Lepchas lived within Bhutan's borders, so it is certainly possible that the textile was a Lepcha shawl woven in Bhutan; however, Bhutanese and Lepcha fabrics are so alike that, even were the cloth woven by other Bhutanese, its patterns could well have been seen as "Lepcha" by a secretary in Darjeeling or Kalimpong. Similar striped cloth is still machine-woven in India for sale in the Kalimpong region. Known throughout the Himalayas as "Kalimpong cloth," it is widely used in Nepal and India to make inexpensive, decorative items for tourists.

14. Chinese visitors described the seventh-century kingdom of Kamarupa (Assam) as including what is now Bhutan. On this early Assamese history, see Gait [1905] 1967, 1-36, and Lahiri 1991, 134.

15. For example, *gapé pore* refers to twelve designs that Padams and Minyongs, Adi groups living in Siang District, weave in women's skirts (Elwin 1959a, 35). In 1794, the Nagas were noted for producing, among other textiles, "*narakapore*, an embroidered silk" (Welsh 1794, reproduced in Mackenzie [1884] 1989, 387).

16. For example, a scroll of patterned, woven cloth (*vrindabaniya kapor*), a talisman cloth worn by Ahom warriors (*kavach kapor*), and a "protective garment of bridegroom and bride" (*ana kata kapor*) (Das 1985, 228, 231).

17. At least a dozen major ethnic groups and many subgroups were once known for their weaving: the Mönpas, Sherdukpens, and Buguns (Khowas) in Kameng District; the Apa Tanis and Daflas (Nishis) in Subansiri District; the two dozen Adi (Abor) tribes and Gallongs of Siang District; the Khamptis and Mishmis of Lohit District; and the Singphos, Tangsas, and Wanchos of Tirap District. Major sources are: Baruah 1960; Bhattacharjee 1983; Dutta 1990; Elwin 1959a and b; Fürer-Haimendorf 1982; Hodson [1911] 1989; Jacobs 1990; Kumar 1979a and b; Mackenzie [1884] 1989; Marak 1986; Saha 1987; and Srivastava [1962] 1988.

18. Wild silk was utilized only by two groups immediately adjacent to Bhutan and by communities of Burmese origin far to the east; the others were important consumers of Assamese wild silk cloth obtained through trade.

19. Madder also was widely used and traded north to Tibet (Butler 1847, in Elwin 1959b, 328). More parallels in dyeing practices and beliefs probably exist, but no studies have carefully documented weaving in this region of northeast India.

20. Although *plaid* was an Anglo-Indian term for any shawl, the Khamptis and Singphos are noted specifically for their plaid-patterned textiles.

21. In the mid-nineteenth century, the Akas' dress was "a kind of toga of rough Assamese silk or of Bhutia blanket cloth" (Hesselmeyer 1867, in Elwin 1959b, 445; Macgregor 1884, in Elwin 1959b, 450). For sketches of that garment and another one worn by Dafla men, see Butler 1847, in Elwin 1959b, pls. 9, 10. In Chowdhury 1990, pls. 4 and 6 illustrate Miji and Dafla men wearing similar wrapped garments today.

22. The wives of chiefs also carried "egg-shaped silver cases obtained from Bhutan," which must have been similar to the amulets that Bhutanese wear (Macgregor 1884, in Elwin 1959b, 450) [cf. fig. 5.14, lower right].

23. The Akas are thought to have migrated to Arunachal Pradesh from Burma around AD 1300 (Hesselmeyer 1867, in Elwin 1959b, 438-39).

24. A belt was called *kerak* or *nenak* by the Boris, Adis, and Tanis (Kumar 1979a, 49-50) and *serak* or *cherak* by the Pailibos (Kumar 1979b, 33, 36). This may be due to linguistic affinities or a loan word that has spread through the region.

25. Dunsmore 1993 is a good overview of Nepalese weaving.

26. Bhutanese do not consider the place of religious textiles' manufacture to be very important. For example, a magnificent temple banner on display at the National Museum in Paro (1994) was recently purchased in Nepal. Although it was probably made in Tibet, the hanging is one that might have adorned an important temple in Bhutan and is therefore considered appropriate for the museum's collection.

27. Although weaving continues in Tibet, the Chinese occupation has altered the craft so fundamentally that the past tense here refers to practices before 1951. Activities related to cloth production were the domain of women – nomads and villagers alike – who spun and dyed yarn and wove cloth for their own use. As in Bhutan, weaving was often a form of service owed to the local nobility. Vertical frame looms were used for weaving pile carpets. See Myers 1984 and Yuthok 1990, 120, 163-64, 198.

28. Tibetan connections with China were well established by the Tang dynasty (618-907), and the country's early relations with India, Central Asia, and Iran are also well known (Leeper 1984, 21-25).

29. On *therma*, see Rockhill [1891] 1975, 282. *Shema* was "very soft wool ... collected off the necks of the sheep," woven into cloth so fine that a length about 25 cm wide could be drawn through a ring (Taring 1986, 120).

30. Information provided by Ian Baker, Himalayan scholar who visited Pemakö and Kongpo in 1993; personal communication, December 1993. One group that may constitute a link between the regions are the so-called Drukpas (discussed in Nair 1985), who migrated about 200 years ago from eastern Bhutan to their present home in northeast India, just south of Pemakö. Drukpa women wear a tunic (p. 75) that also seems to resemble the Bhutanese *shingkha*. See also Chapter Five, n. 11.

31. In the seventeenth century, "Bhutan merchants" were bartering goods at Balkh in northern Afghanistan (Gait [1905] 1967, 274), a tantalizing reference that unfortunately, at that time, could have refered to *any* ethnic

Tibetan from the southern Himalayas.

32. Liebenthal 1956, 9-11, gives accounts by Hsuan Tsang and by I-tsing, written between AD 685 and 689. Both Chinese noted that the eastern border of Kamarupa (Assam) was the frontier of southwestern China, a region inhabited by the "Southern Man" and Laos. In the nineteenth century, Assamese traders traveled to Yunnan, and sold small quantities of Chinese goods at the Assam border town of Sadiya (Basu 1970, 190).

33. The value of this trade in 1809 was Indian rupees (Rs.) 200,000, fully half the amount of trade between Assam and the more accessible neighboring state of Bengal (Mackenzie [1884] 1989, 15).

34. The Tremo La and Pemé La were the most important passes for the Tibet-western Bhutan-India trade.

35. The Bhutanese earlier had allowed two Kashmiri trading families who fled Nepal and settled in Lhasa to transport selected goods through Bhutan, but this enterprise does not appear to have been very profitable.

36. *Moleskin* was a thick cotton cloth coated with varnish to make it look like dark green or black leather.

37. The passes are called the Duars, related to the word *door* – an indication of their age-old importance as channels of intercourse between the hills and the plains. Bhutanese texts sometimes use the word *lago* (las sgo, 'work-door'), connoting a border market at the foot of one of these passes (Aris 1979, 108-14). Most of the Duars were Bhutanese territory or under Bhutanese jurisdiction until 1865.

38. "[This official] had some lands, and paid nothing to the king except presents. All the messengers and traders of Bhutan, all servants of the Deva Raja [temporal ruler of Bhutan], must go first to Siliambari. [The official] ... levied no duties, but received presents in order to prevent his throwing impediments in the way of business, and no one was allowed to purchase at Siliambari without employing him as a broker" (Basu 1970, 192).

39. The *gya drungpa*, mentioned in the *Kathrim* [Bhutan's Legal Code of 1729], fol. 107r, quoted in Aris 1986, 141 and 168, n. 51.

40. The site at Hajo is said to have been "discovered" by a ruler of eastern Bhutan and his

lama in the late sixteenth century (Ngawang 1728, fol. 50r, quoted in Aris 1979, 71).

41. Fairs specifically for the "Bhutan Bhutias" were held at Kuriapara Duar, "Kerkeria ... and at Daimara, north of Udalguri (Mackenzie [1884] 1989, 15). Fairs also were held at Darrang, Subankhata, Udalguri, and Ghagrapara in Darrang (*Provincial Gazetteer* [1906] 1983, 65). The Udalguri fair was the most important, held for three to four weeks every February-March.

42. These traders are also called Manangis, after their native valley of Manang in north central Nepal. They traveled by train from Calcutta to the Assamese towns of Dhubri, Gauhati, Nowgong, Dimapur, and Tinsukia between January and March each year (Van Springen 1992, 131-34).

43. Use of Bhutanese cloth in Ladakh may date to the first half of the seventeenth century, when a very close relationship existed between Ladakh and Bhutan. By the 1670s, Bhutan had been granted several monasteries and associated estates in Ladakh, properties that were looked after by Bhutanese monastic officials and delegates for more than 200 years.

44. From 1765 onward, Bhutan posted a representative (*gya pchila*) and some troops at Cooch Bihar, which was also minting Bhutan's coins at the time. As early as the twelfth century, political and economic ties between Bhutan and this area were close and strong.

45. Rights to revenue from the inhabitants of the plains below the Duars were periodically disputed, and from time to time punitive expeditions resulted when dethroned kings, bandits, and mercenaries took refuge in the jungles on either side of the Duars. These tensions led to outright war in 1864-65, after which Bhutan ceded its right to the last of the Duars land revenue in exchange for annual payments from the British.

46. Information given by the late Lam Nado, Bhutanese historian and scholar, and by Dasho Shingkar Lam, Secretary (*gyal drung*) to the third king and former Speaker of the National Assembly. The Tibetans themselves did not use this cloth, which like other woolen twills came from from Dachi, Nang, and Chedeshö in Lhobrak across the border from central Bhutan (Nado 1987, 24).

47. Bhutan also exchanged official gifts each year with Chinese representatives in Lhasa, who typically sent Bhutan flowered scarves

and silk (Collister 1987, 43).

48. Although Bhutanese say they mostly used *endi* silk, White may indeed have seen more costly *tussar* silk being woven at what was the most influential – and soon to be royal – household in the country. He may also have mistaken *endi* for *tussar*, which was better known in India.

49. When the Duars were under Bhutanese jurisdiction in the eighteenth and nineteenth centuries, the Kacharis paid taxes to the Bhutanese government in grain and this cloth (Endle [1910?] 1990, 21-22). On other Kachari cloth specially made for the Bhutia market, see note 54 below.

50. In 1815, Kishan Kant Bose noted that the annual caravans to Rangpur in Bengal brought back, among other goods, "woolen cloth, *pattus* [Indian cotton cloth], indigo, ... and coarse cotton cloths, of which they use part in Bootan and send the rest to Lhassa" (Bose 1815, in *Political Missions* [1865] 1972, 350). In 1911, at Pasakha (Buxa Duar), British cloth was still a major item of exchange (Gruning 1911, 11:147).

51. Its name referred to the figure of a sheep (*lu*) that appeared on the red wax seal (an import tax stamp?) on each bale.

52. This was *haathi nambar*, 'elephant brand,' so called because of the elephant on the wax stamp that sealed a bundle of this cloth.

53. For example, on blankets as a part of soldiers' dress in 1774, see Turner [1800] 1971, 118. A century later, blankets selling for 3 rupees each were the second most numerous item brought by Bhutanese to the Udalguri trade fair – and the import into Assam with the highest total value (Rs. 15,174) (Hunter [1879] n.d., 1:143). As late as the 1940s, woolen blankets from Bhutan were sought after by the Apa Tanis in Subansiri District of Arunachal Pradesh (India) – not for use in their original form, but so they could be unraveled and the yarns dyed and woven into ceremonial woolen cloth (Fürer-Haimendorf 1980, 64).

54. The *kharu* and *dunko lepa* cloths were made by Kachari villagers specially for sale to the Bhutanese (Hunter [1879] n.d., 1:144).

55. The "Central Asian" wool most likely did come from distant points because the British Indian market was diverting supplies from western Tibet at this time.

56. For example, in 1905 the chief imports to Lhakhang Dzong, just north of central Bhu-

tan, were white rice, madder, and stick lac (White [1909] 1984, 201).

57. Information given by Chungkar Dasho, Pemagatshel, November 1992. Indigo was the sole Indian product that transited Bhutan without a local market. This was because Bhutanese indigo was an excellent dye itself, although not produced in export quantities like the Indian variety.

58. Recent scholarship on the textiles of the widely dispersed Tai groups of mainland Southeast Asia, for example, helps document traditions to which Bhutanese cloth can be linked. Major sources for this section are: Cheesman 1988; Fraser-Lu 1989; Gittinger and Lefferts 1992; Lewis and Lewis 1984; and Prangwatthanakun and Cheesman 1987.

59. Chiefly the Kachins, Chins, Akhas, Lahus, Lisus, and Karens. In contrast, Tai peoples speak languages belonging to the Tai branch of the Tai-Kadai linguistic family. Designs in textiles of Southeast Asian groups that speak Miao-Yao languages exhibit similarities with Bhutanese textile designs as well (for example, Boudot 1994, 65, fig. 19).

60. The exceptions are the Akhas, who do not use backtension looms, and the Lahus, who also use foot-treadle looms.

61. Am Kunzang (of Shingkar, Bumthang), Thimphu, 1990; and Ashi Chhemey Wangmo Norbu (of Kheng Buli and Bumthang), Thimphu, 1990. Tai-Lao techniques that the Bhutanese know are: discontinuous extraweft patterning (Thai: *chok*), continuous extra-weft patterning (*khit*, or *phaa khit*), extra-warp patterning (*muk*), and twill weaves (*yok dok*).

62. Other Phu Tai blankets show familiar diamond patterning and hooked ornaments (Gittinger and Lefferts 1992, fig. 5.36). On the Tai Nueas, for example, see Prangwatthanakun and Cheesman 1988, 38.

63. The Tai textiles whose motifs and/or formats most resemble Bhutanese examples are: shoulder cloths (Thai: *phaa biang*), head cloths (*phaa mon*), certain blankets (*phaa hom*), temple banners (*tung*), and the various textiles known as *phaa chet*. Like the Bhutanese *chagsi pangkheb*, the literal translation of *phaa chet* indicates the textile's use as a 'towel.' Also like the Bhutanese *chagsi pangkheb*, some *phaa chet* are ceremonial textiles worn as shoulder cloths or offered to temples (Prangwatthanakun and Cheesman 1988,

77-79).

64. Among the Tai (Lao) Nueas, this pattern is reportedly associated with tantric Buddhism, which, in combination with animist beliefs, is practiced solely by this group (Cheesman 1982, 123).

65. Head cloths, door curtains, pillows, and towels made by the Phu Tais utilize similar diamonds and horizontal pattern bands in a smaller format (Gittinger and Lefferts 1992, figs. 2.23, 2.24).

66. Cut and sewn tunics have been worn in the region for centuries, although little is known about their past and current use. For example, in the first century AD, the Ngai-Laos, who lived in Sichuan Province (China) and are related to the Ahoms of Assam, paid a per capita tax of two tunics similar to those Karen women now wear (Milne [1910] 1970, 7). In 1826, Kamaon Mishmi women in Arunachal Pradesh (India) wore a knee-length dress with "merely a slit in it to let the head through," apparently a tunic that has since disappeared (Wilcox 1832, in Elwin 1959b, 304). The Karen and Chin tunics collected in 1898 are both in the collection of the Museum of International Folk Art in Santa Fe, New Mexico.

Chapter Three

1. Bhutan has had elements of a monetary economy alongside its important barter economy for several hundred years. Since the mid-1950s, the government has issued new currency and otherwise stimulated the country's transition to a cash economy, but barter is still very common in rural areas.

2. This ceremony takes place at the convenience of a family, generally during the winter when agricultural tasks have been completed and monks are free to come to the house and conduct the ritual. Over one or more days, the deities of most importance to the family are worshipped before an altar decorated with offerings of butter lamps, butter sculptures, incense, and fruits. During the course of the prayers, cloth from the *yanggam* and the household is piled before the altar.

3. White scarves are articles of social intercourse throughout the Buddhist Himalayas. Tibetans often present them to someone who is going away, but this is not done in Bhutan. Today, most silk *khada* used in Bhu-

tan are manufactured in Surat (India); inexpensive cotton gauze *khada* come form Manipur (India).

4. The position of Druk Desi lapsed when the monarchy was established in 1907.

5. The bride and groom do not exchange cloth gifts routinely, although the groom might present his bride with a new set of clothes, and dresses are generally part of her dowry.

6. The *pangkheb* is annotated in the margin of the English typescript of the letter as a "box cover?" and the *tagre* as a "Lepcha *chadar* [man's shawl]." Because it was an official gift, the latter may in fact have been a Bhutanese textile that resembled Lepcha weaving.

7. The *khati* is annotated in the margin of the letter's English typescript as a "comforter."

8. Orchard Street in New York is a favorite place to find plaid woolen cloth for women's dresses, and Hong Kong and Bangkok are sources of silks for making women's blouses and jackets.

9. In fact, yearly obligations of this kind existed as early as the thirteenth century, when the local rulers of western Bhutan complained of having to supply higher authorities with huge quantities of rice, butter, cotton, and iron, as well as undertake three periods of corvée (Aris 1979, 169).

10. Delegations came from Paro, communities in central Bhutan, and pastoral regions in northern Bhutan, all of which were under the Shabdrung's control. Missions also came from the clan leaders of eastern Bhutan, which was not yet administered by the Drukpas, and from Phari in Tibet, Cooch Bihar, Hajo in Assam, and other adjoining Indian lands.

11. In Pemagatshel District of southeastern Bhutan, for example, households were assessed one panel of cloth per 3 *langdo* (officially equivalent to 1 acre) of land. From the seventeenth century, cloth belonged to the category of 'fresh tax' (*lönkhé*), which also included meat, butter, salt, wood, and cereals, as opposed to 'dry tax' (*kamkhé*), which was levied in cash.

12. Bhutanese scholars give "spen" as another spelling of the element *pön* (dpon), and say that it has been preferred since the 1950s because the older spelling with its feudal connotations is now inappropriate. Information given by Dasho Shingkar Lam, Secretary to the third king and former Speaker

of the National Assembly.

13. Yönten Thayé (n.d.) is a rich source of references. *Pönthag* ('official's weaving') also occurs as a term for the white and colored wild silk cloths woven for taxes. Tibetans knew *pentog*, a variety of *pöntshe*, as 'a kind of country chintz with figures of tamarisk, imported ... from Assam or Bhutan' (Chandra Das [1902] 1985, 800).

14. Sets of three panels of cotton "tax dresses" sometimes had a center panel with a white ground and side panels with a blue ground [fig. 5.6]. Belts given to women laborers were known as *khem*, and were worth a small coin. Information given by the late Lam Nado, Bhutanese historian and scholar, and Pönlop-Dep Töchu of Thinleygang.

15. For example, in 1880, Pema Thallong Bhutia of Bhutan was assessed Rs. 20, four brass pots, and four pieces of cloth for stealing a horse from across the border in Tawang (India) (Mackenzie [1884] 1989, 19).

16. Information given by Dr. Yoshiro Imaeda, February 1987, citing his copy of the blockprint, fol. 13r. Lam Nado; the Venerable Mynak Tulku Rimpoche, Director, National Museum; and Dr. Imaeda helped locate and interpret other references from Yönten Thayé (n.d.) as well.

17. Information given by Dasho Shingkar Lam, Lam Nado, and others.

18. Most of the fabrics listed in this source are not familiar to Bhutanese today, although scholars can sometimes infer what they looked like from a descriptive name. For example, *ashom göchen* (Assamese brocade), *kashikai ré* (Indian [Banaras?] cotton), and *athang khamar* (a striped red-and-white ceremonial textile from Adhang in Wangdi Phodrang District) were given to the incarnations of the Shabdrung and his son, Jampel Dorje.

19. Information also given by Dr. Yoshiro Imaeda, citing Yönten Thayé, fol. 32.

20. The insights of Dr. Marc Dujardins on the cultural significance of house construction and the roles of men and women in the process are gratefully acknowledged (October 1993, personal communications).

21. An early documented example of this practice occurred when the famous saint Pemalingpa visited what is now Arunachal Pradesh (India) in 1504. Many of the gifts he received there were textiles, one of them a length of red-and-white-striped silk (*khamar*

thrasum, dkar dmar khra gsum) (Aris 1979, 104). This was probably a ceremonial cloth for covering the legs and feet.

Chapter Four

1. For much of the information here, I am especially indebted to: Am Yeshe Chöden and her sister Am Kunzang (of Bumthang and now Thimphu); Am Tshering Dem and her sister Am Ugen Doma (Thimphu); Am Sonam Yödön (Dechenchöling); Ashi Kesang (Dorjibi); Am Karma (Jakar); Am Rinchen Zam (Nanggar); Ugen Tshomo (Tang); Künchen Norbu (Ura); Khoma Ashi Phuntsok Wangmo (Kurtö); Ai Chuni (Kurtö Gompakap); Am Zangmo and Pema Chöden (Radi Dukpiling); the Wamrong Lam and his daughter, Choeki Ongmo (Wamrong and Khaling); Ugen Wangda (Thongsa); and Norbu Zangmo and Sengge Chezam (Pemagatshel).

2. The Pelé La is a high pass in the Black Mountains between Wangdi Phodrang and Tongsa. Bhutanese view it as the gateway to eastern Bhutan and associate the lands beyond it with traditions that are different from, as well as more indigenous and older than, those in the west.

3. Information given by Ashi Kesang, Dorjibi, 5 May 1987; and others. Chöden Lhamo is said to have been an early queen in Tashigang, and may be connected with Ama Jomo, the Tibetan noblewoman who led the original settlers of Merak Sakteng south (Sonam Wangmo 1990, 141-43); or with Ache Lhamo, a goddess honored in well-known annual dances in the region.

4. Story told by Ai Chuni, Gompakap, 21 October 1992.

5. Stories told by Am Yeshe Chöden and Am Kunzang, 18 November 1992. The Sherdukpen people of Tawang (Arunachal Pradesh, India) have a similar legend, which says the princess came from Assam and passed through Tsona Dzong (Tibet) near the Bhutan border. The details of the legend (Sharma 1961, 5-6) relate it to the Bhutanese story of Khyikharathö.

6. Agricultural activities also reflect women's association with fertility. For example, in 1907, J.C. White observed a ceremony of blessing the rice fields in Tongsa where women defending an irrigated upper field were attacked by the men from an unwatered

lower one. When, as on this occasion, the women managed to drive the men off, he was told, the victory forecast "fertility of the soil and increase among the flocks" ([1909] 1984, 160).

7. Wikan 1990, 38-39, discusses Bhutanese concepts of birth pollution and beliefs about the spiritual vulnerability of a delivering woman.

8. Many Bhutanese – especially men and women native to eastern and central Bhutan, but also people living in Thimphu – acknowledge that they were taught not to walk on or step across a loom warp. Some say this taboo relates to the universal habits of not stepping over or permitting the soles of one's shoes to face another person, which would dishonor the "divine" within that person (or the gods that older Bhutanese believe live on every hair of the body). Others say that parts of the loom were made from a special, high-altitude bamboo that was hard to get, so the wood itself was considered sacred.

9. Famous saints, especially Padmasambhava, who introduced Buddhism to Tibet and Bhutan in the eighth century, appear in these contexts as apocryphal figures whose presence gives a story greater weight.

10. Story told by Choeki Ongmo, Khaling, 31 October 1992.

11. For example, when the first king planned the formal education of an initial group of Bhutanese in 1921, he sent one boy to India for training in weaving (Collister 1987, 175). Who he was and what he did on his return are unknown. Also, Ashi Pem Dem, who manages the weaving workshop in Tamshing (Bumthang), learned to dye yarns from an uncle who worked for the royal grandmother, and a male weaver who worked for Ashi Wangmo is credited with introducing the Tibetan horizontal frame loom (see Chapter Eight).

12. Generally, the more privileged one's rank in the hierarchy of reincarnation, the less work one does. Men's superiority is expressed even more explicitly in several gender-allocated tasks. For example, only women are supposed to handle manure, which is used as fertilizer. Because contact with dung, it is said, degrades a man's 'mind,' women also build and tamp down earthen (mixed with dung) walls during house construction. In practice both men and women are exoner-

ated from the consequences of crossing gender boundaries if no more appropriate person is there to do the task. On women, see Wikan 1990.

13. Many of these hardships – pregnancy, birth, infant care, and child raising – flow directly from the body in which a woman finds herself "trapped" during this lifetime. Dzongkha, however, does not reflect the same lower-class nature of women as the common Tibetan word for 'woman,' *kyimen* (skye dman), which literally means 'of lower birth.' On Buddhism and women, see Havnevik n.d. [1991?], 144-81.

14. Sir Charles Bell's report of 1910, 15-16, mentions the prominence of eastern Bhutanese officials in western Bhutan at the turn of the century. The more recent resettlement of eastern Bhutanese in the west during the construction of the Chukha hydroelectric plant in the 1980s created a true community of weavers in this region, but *natives* of western Bhutan have rarely taken up weaving.

15. Studies around 1990 reported eighty to ninety percent of Bhutanese women contributing to household income by weaving, which is probably a high estimate. Countrywide, eighty percent may know how to weave, but weaving as a cottage industry is still concentrated in central and eastern Bhutan, and in Thimphu.

16. Translation from Khengkha: Pema (Goshing); Dasho Sithey, Director, National Academy of Performing Arts; and Sangay Wangchuk, Undersecretary in the Council for Ecclesiastical Affairs and Acting Director, National Library.

17. *Tsangmo* ('songs of Tsang [south central Tibet]') were popularized by the Sixth Dalai Lama (1683-1706). Each four-line verse, which may be sung in Tibetan, Dzongkha, or another Bhutanese language, metaphorically addresses subjects from ribald humor, to love, to religious devotion. *Alo* are songs from Kurtö and eastern Bhutan.

Chapter Five

1. Wild silk is used sparingly for the ground weave of *kushüthara*, which like most Bhutanese weavings are warp-faced textiles. Wild silk is never used for the white ground warps, but frequently appears in some of the colored warps that form the stripes at the

upper and lower edges of the dress.

2. This is not the first time Bhutanese patterns have been produced externally for the Bhutanese market. Copies of indigenous patterns, machine-woven in Amritsar (India), were marketed by the Kalimpong merchant known as Khadebu in the late 1960s. Including colorful striped plainweaves, plaids (*mathra*), and supplementary-warp-patterned cloth (*aikapur*), these fabrics were made into clothing in Bhutan and stitched into vests and bags that are still popular tourist items in Darjeeling and Kathmandu. The fabrics' use was banned in Bhutan in the early 1970s. Information: Binod Agarwal, Phuntsholing, and others. Since the early 1990s, a flourishing industry in Nepal has been producing imitation woolen *yathra* for the export market as well.

3. *Thok* ('varicolored') is a word that also describes the colors of the fields. The convention of using two colors every fourth band is no longer strictly followed.

4. This cloth came in bales bearing the image of an elephant, so the fabric was known to Bhutanese as *hathi nambar* ('elephant brand'). The same cloth was used to line men's robes. Information given by Pönlop-Dep Töchu of Thinleygang.

5. Bhutanese point out that the necklace should be called *dongtha* ('front thread'). The term *jabtha* derives from the days when women wore needle-like pins to secure their dresses; a necklace that helped balance these pins was draped on the wearer's back, hence the name. Longer necklaces of semiprecious stones were worn in the normal fashion on a woman's chest.

6. The headbands, known locally as *nyelempa* or *welempa*, are identical to ornaments still worn by the Miji and Aka people [fig. 2.6] of Arunachal Pradesh (Chowdhury 1990, figs. 4, 5; Nair 1985, 36). The young girl in Chowdhury (fig. 5) is also wearing large silver wire earrings that resemble the old-fashioned Bhutanese ornaments.

7. Phajo Drukgom Shikpo's wife, Ashi Sonam Pedon, is said to have proved her power to him by thus creating the spring at Phajoding above Thimphu. Although forgotten by many, the traditional name of the spring is *Thin Chu* ('pin spring'). Information given by Tshering Dolkar, Thimphu, and others. Similar dress fasteners were part of Lepcha dress in the mid-1800s (see Chapter Two).

8. White tennis shoes are seen, for example, in photograph 115b, vol. 4, Williamson Collection. Other photographs of the period appear in Williamson 1987.

9. Tunics in Bhutan are difficult to date because they have been relegated to ceremonial use for at least eighty to 100 years. They are, therefore, stored in boxes most of the year, and their condition is sometimes quite good. Based on local information, most examples probably date to the nineteenth century.

10. The same tunic is occasionally worn by older women in Tashiyangtse District.

11. People of Kurtö also associate *shingkha* tunics with the Shingkhar Lauri region on Bhutan's eastern border, south of Merak Sakteng. Whether tunics exist there is not known. A "long garment of dark red" is worn by Aka women farther east (Nair 1985, 36), and tunics resembling *shingkha* are found among the so-called Drukpas who migrated to northern Arunachal Pradesh from eastern Bhutan several centuries ago (Nair 1985, 74-75).

12. The villages are in Kurtö (Lhuntshi District), Bumthang District, Tashiyangtse District, and Mongar District. The figures are called *gatpo-gatmo/ganmo* ('old man, old woman'). In Takila Gompa (Kurtö), for example, the male figure wears a robe made of nettle and the woman a white tunic with designs on it. In the shrine room at a private residence in Tangsibji (Bumthang District), the female figure wears a *shingkha*.

13. Villages where *pcha* ceremonies are known to occur are: Jang, Ne, Tshamang, Taya, Tsawang, Khaujung, Yomining, Gangzor, and Tsangmo. The temples of Takila Gompa, Shungkhar Kesibi Lhakhang, and Rawabi Gompa also are associated with these festivals. The Bhutanese rituals are discussed by Pommaret 1994 (forthcoming), and similar ceremonies in Tawang (Arunachal Pradesh) are noted by Fürer-Haimendorf 1980, 170, and Nanda 1982, 112.

14. This summary is based on accounts given by Dorji Wangchuk, patriarch of a leading Tangmachu family who own a *shingkha*, his wife, the former headman (*gup*) of Tangmachu, and two other villagers (February 1987 and October 1992). Information was also provided by Khoma Ashi Phuntsok Wangmo and Kesang Chöden of Jasibi (February 1987), and by B. Wangdi of Mongar

and Ugyen Wangdi of Thimphu. See Myers 1988.

15. Information given by Künchen Norbu, Ura, 23 October 1992.

16. Sonam Wangmo 1990, 152-53, gives further details on Brokpa dress, and Sharma 1961, 16-21, illustrates the similar apparel and jewelry of Sherdukpens in adjacent Arunachal Pradesh (India). See also Chapter Two.

17. Translation compiled with the assistance of Sangay Wangchuk, Undersecretary in the Council of Ecclesiastic Affairs and Acting Director, National Library; Thinley Wangchuck, Ministry of Trade and Industry; Michael Aris; and others. The current version of this folk song reflects a change in fashion, substituting *bumthang mathra* (maroon plaid) for the *adha mathra* cloth that was popular previously. According to Dasho Sithey, Director, National Academy of Performing Arts, the song relates to the old custom of court soldiers in Punakha teasing poorly dressed citizens by saying, "Oh, what a nice robe you have!" In response, the man being taunted sang these verses to himself.

18. Explanation of this change given by Colonel Dhendup, Dechenchöling, 8 October 1992.

19. Some Bhutanese relate the "opening" of the shoulder cloth to long-ago etiquette that required a man to show a superior that he had no weapon concealed in the folds of the bulky textile.

20. Much of the information on shoulder cloths and men's garments in this and the following paragraphs was given by Dasho Shingkar Lam, Secretary to the third king and former Speaker of the National Assembly; the late Lam Nado, then Dzongkha Advisor in the Department of Education; Lopön Pemala, former Director, National Library; the late Lyönpo Sangye Penjor; Dasho Lam Sanga; and other Bhutanese scholars.

21. For example, similar shoulder cloths are donned by Tibetan laymen who have taken the first monastic vows. In Nepal, Buddhist lamas who are permitted to marry use a red-and-white shoulder cloth, as do Tamang lamas. Ladakhi men and women wear red-and-white *kabné*, imported from Bhutan, across their shoulders in folk dances and on other occasions.

22. Information given by the late Lam Nado, citing Yönten Thayé. A similar red-and-white textile is clearly seen in a Samuel Davis drawing of eighteenth-century soldiers (Aris 1982, pl. 27).

23. According to Dasho Sithey, the garment identified the dancers with an archetypal folk character – the intelligent buffoon (*phento*) – whose roots are secular and who appears in the Acho Phento dance. Male dancers were the attendants of the nobleman who organized the archery, or from households that owed service to the nobleman's family. Sometimes the dancers were women, in which case they were weavers serving the noble household. The custom of men dancing stopped when hereditary service and many minor administrative ranks were abolished during the third king's time (1950s). Today the dancers are always women. Their participation may be organized by a contest sponsor, but it is entirely voluntary.

24. For a Darjeeling photograph, see Watson 1868, pl. 43, showing "Three Bhutia Chiefs."

25. "*Lebi adha mathra, wangchuk pönpoi namza* (The beautiful *adha mathra* is the dress of the Wangchuck king)." Like the striped woman's shoulder cloth (*adha rachu*) that it somewhat resembles, this pattern originated in Adhang in Wangdi Phodrang District.

26. The quote and details of layered dress come from Pönlop-Dep Töchu. The quilted garments were described by H. E. Ugyen Tshering, Bhutan's Permanent Representative to the United Nations.

27. Details on Merak Sakteng clothing are also given in Sonam Wangmo 1990, 152-53. The Dakpas, a group of Bhutanese yak herders who live between Tashigang and Merak Sakteng, wear similar clothing, except that trousers are substituted for the leather leggings and *kanggo*. See Chapter Two on related apparel worn by Mönpa men in adjacent Tawang (India).

28. Doorway curtains (*goré*) are found throughout the Buddhist Himalayas. Made of many fabrics, the curtains are edged with bands of narrow blue or red cotton cloth; similar bands of cloth may be stitched down the center of the textile in the warp direction and across the middle in the weft direction as well. Usually the curtain is backed with a lining before a cotton valance is added as trim at the top end.

29. Information given by Am Yeshe Chöden. *Pangkheb* are also required for rituals conducted by a female diviner (*jum*) to forecast a family's future. The diviner draws a swastika on the ground with rice or flour and places the folded textile on top of this emblem. She then sits on the cloth and goes into a trance. At the end of the ceremony, the cloth is lifted to see whether the swastika has remained intact, in which case all will be well. If it has turned or been smudged, rituals should be performed to avert possible adversities. Information given by Yum Thuji Zam, Punakha, February 1994.

30. Much of this information and that on bags (*phechung*) was provided or confirmed by Dasho Shingkar Lam and by Dasho Tseten Dorje, Master of Protocol (*dasho dronyer*) for the late king and present king. Dasho Tseten Dorje is currently contributing to a book in Dzongkha on *driglam namzha*, under the auspices of the Special Commission for Cultural Affairs.

31. Information given by Dasho Shingkar Lam and by Am Rinzi Pedon, who wove for Ashi Wangmo in the 1930s.

Chapter Six

1. Translation compiled with the particular help of Dasho Shingkar Lam, Secretary to the third king and former Speaker of the National Assembly; Sangay Wangchuk, Undersecretary in the Council of Ecclesiastic Affairs and Acting Director, National Library; and the Venerable Mynak Tulku Rimpoche, Director, National Museum.

2. The lists of property that are maintained in dzongs and temples in Bhutan are a rich source for future study. If they could be examined, they would enable identification of extant textiles from different places of manufacture as standards for a better understanding of stylistic characteristics and variations.

3. Explained by Lopön Pemala, former Director, National Library, 10 November 1992.

4. Dr. Marc Dujardins provided very helpful information on the role of cloth in some of these rituals; October 1993, personal communications.

5. Information in this section was provided by Lopön Pemala; the late Lam Nado, Bhutanese historian and scholar; Dasho Lam Sanga; Sangay Wangchuk; and Gelong Konchog Tenzin (Matthieu Richard).

6. Used alone, the term *chögo* can apply to the patchwork cloth called *namjar* or to monks'

clothing in general.

7. In classical tradition, the second essential garment is not the shawl but the *chögo lagö* (Tibetan), which resembles the *namjar* but has fewer patchwork panels. For ceremonies, the *lagö* is worn on top of the shawl and, on special occasions, the *namjar* is worn on top of the *lagö*; the shawl *(zen)* is worn every day to protect the *lagö* and the other two sacred garments from perspiration and body dirt. Bhutanese monks do not wear a *lagö*.

8. If made of wild silk, the garment is called *bura kabzen* ('wild silk shawl'); if made of wool, it is a *therzen* ('woolen shawl'); and if cotton, it is a *rézen* ('cotton shawl'). Monks should have one *zen* of maroon wool and another of wild silk or cotton, as well as a white woolen shawl for use at night *(shachukab, pchemkar)*.

9. The other four senior monks are the master of discipline, the master of arts, the master of the choir, and the Shabdrung's chamberlain.

10. This corresponds to the *chögo thangö* of Tibetan tradition, which in colloquial Dzongkha is called *shamtha leuma*. The garment in theory is compulsory for fully ordained monks.

11. The inner upper garment is the classical *töthung* and the outer vest is the *tönga*.

12. Information given by Dasho Shingkar Lam. These unusual belts are said not to have any particular significance, except that they are associated with rituals in which the monks who wear them make water offerings *(chablup)*.

13. For background on the dances, see Aris 1980b.

14. Davis's vivid description, written in 1783 and quoted in Aris 1982, 57-60, touches on a number of dances still seen today at the Thimphu Dromchö and Tsechu each September. The *Druk chamyig [Manual of Bhutanese Sacred Dance]*, written by Dasho Nagphel, the lay master of dances, in 1967, does not discuss how or when costumes were standardized in Bhutan. The costumes worn by lay and monk dancers both deserve further detailed study.

15. Information given by Dasho Shingkar Lam and by Karma Ura, Planning Commission, March 1993.

16. Information given by Karma Ura, March 1993.

17. Information given by Dasho Shingkar Lam.

18. On ritual art and its meanings, see Pal 1983, 35-47; on *thangka*, including appliqué and embroidered images, see Béguin 1991, 385-89; and on *thangka* painting, the best and most exhaustive source is Jackson and Jackson 1984.

19. See, for example, Huntington 1986 and Stratton 1986.

20. Story related by Dasho Lam Sanga, November 1992.

21. Information given by Thinley Dorji, New York, March 1994.

22. Information given by Thinley Dorji, March 1994.

23. This dew shield was known as a *gur jayap*; information given by Dasho Shingkar Lam.

24. Information given by Dasho Shingkar Lam, who remembers seeing the tents at the court forty years ago.

Chapter Seven

1. The price of a set of supplementary-warp-patterned wild silk panels for making into a man's robe was calculated in Radi village (Tashigang District), in October 1992, as follows (Ngultrim [Nu.] 30 = US $1). The raw materials were: 2 1/2 kg of wild silk thread at Nu. 240 per kg in Samdrup Jongkhar (Nu. 600); synthetic dyes (Nu. 100); and 7 *pathi* (measures) of lac from Yadi at Nu. 25 per measure (Nu. 175): total Nu. 875. It took approximately five weeks to dye and wind the thread, prepare the warp, and weave the cloth. The robe panels sold locally for about Nu. 3,500. An enterprising woman might hire another woman to weave the cloth. The rate paid to her for weaving a large panel of supplementary-warp-patterned cloth was Nu. 120; for a small panel *(zurtsi)*, Nu. 60; and for a large panel of warp-striped plainweave, Nu. 70.

2. In October 1992, one measure of lac was worth five measures of homemade liquor *(ara)*; one-third measure of pork, beef, or butter; half a measure of rice; or Nu. 17 in cash. Transported to Bumthang (central Bhutan), the measure of dye would sell for Nu. 30. In Tongsa, farther west, one measure of lac was worth ten measures of any unmilled grain.

3. These areas, and most of what is now adjacent Shemgang District (central Bhutan), form a region traditionally known as *kheng*, or *khengri namsum* ('three types [of people]

of Kheng'), which refers to the indigenous inhabitants of this densely forested section of the hills.

4. These tax cloths were collectively known as *kamtham* ('dry [-tax] weave,' that is, 'cloth'), and sometimes as *pönthag* ('official's weaving,' which referred to white and colored cloth). Specific types were: *kamtham karpo*, a plain white cotton; *gandru*, a set of two panels of white cotton with a little pattern, for making doorway curtains; *pönchu*, a thin, loosely woven white cotton; *pöndab*, a white cotton with green stripes, for lamp wicks; and *pöntshe*, a plain white cloth or one with red stripes at the edges. See Glossary.

5. This pattern comes in two variations: *yütham jadrima* ('country cloth arranged with a rainbow') has five primary colors; *yütham marchang* ('country cloth, only red') is predominantly red, green, and blue. Dungsam Pemagatshel was famous for these patterns.

6. Traditional women's belts *(kera)* and multipurpose textiles *(pangkheb)* also show some selvedge-to-selvedge patterning that is double-faced. This patterning appears at the fringed ends and at intervals between two-faced patterning.

7. "Daroka," from its description, appears to be *lungserma*; "nainta" might have been *menta (möntha)*; "sing" perhaps *mensi (mensé mathra)*; and "goom" possibly *domchum (dromchu chema)*.

8. For eastern Bhutanese, the salient feature of *aikapur* is the presence of supplementary-warp patterns, and any cloth so decorated may be called *aikapur* or *kapur* (e.g., *kapur phatsa*, 'supplementary-warp-patterned bag'). In western Bhutan, *aikapur* normally refers only to the pattern eastern Bhutanese would call *aikapur jadrima*, yellow and white supplementary-warp-pattern bands alternating with colorfully striped plainweave.

9. Bhutanese offer three etymologies for the name of this pattern. The spelling "mon ser mar khra" associates the cloth with an indigenous, non-Buddhist *(mön)* past and names the sole colors of the fabric (yellow and red). The spelling "sman rtse mar khra," in contrast, alludes to a Chinese silk *(mentsi)* that is yellow, red, and green – and has a more prestigious cultural association. A final explanation is that the pattern originated among the Mechi people residing on the Indian side of Bhutan's southern border and was originally called *mechi mathra*.

10. *Dromchu chema* refers to different supplementary-warp-patterned fabrics in different parts of Bhutan. In Thimphu, it commonly means a fabric with red, green, yellow, and white pattern bands; it can also describe fabric patterned with units of three very narrow warp-pattern bands. In eastern Bhutan, where supplementary-warp-patterned fabric originates, the fabric with red, green, yellow, and white pattern bands is generally considered a version of *aikapur jadrima*. Eastern Bhutanese tend to use *dromchu chema* for another pattern that *does* resemble little boxes but that has gone out of vogue in this century [fig. 7.6, right].

11. Information on *phento* was given by Dasho Sithey, Director, National Academy of Performing Arts. Furthermore, men garbed in *möntha* often wear the cloth crossed over their chests in the style of a *pakhi* (the wrapped garment once worn by men of some indigenous groups). Lopön Pemala, former Director, National Library, believes *möntha* was the earliest dress of Bhutan and that the technology and designs for weaving it came from the east (November 1992).

12. The most frequently mentioned are Khoma and Gompakap (Gompa Karpo), but also Taya, Pangkhar, Tsango, Tangmachu, Nyelamdung, Minjé, and Yomining.

13. Ai Chuni, born around 1902 and a resident of Gompakap, said that when some of the Wangchucks still lived at Dungkhar around the turn of the century, their weavers were from Khoma and Yomining. The family took many of these women with them when they moved to Bumthang, and later to Tongsa. The Wangchucks' collateral descendants at Dungkhar and Né are said still to employ weavers from Khoma (interviews in Lhuntshi and Gompakap, October 1992).

14. The women of every household weave, producing up to six supplementary-weft-patterned women's dresses (*kushüthara*) per year. Buyers come in April-June and pay Nu. 3,000 (US $100) for good-quality dresses decorated with cotton designs, Nu. 1,000 for those with designs in acrylic yarn, and Nu. 450 to Nu. 600 for the lowest-quality weavings.

15. The villages best known for presently working with bast fibers are Ngalakhachu, Takila Gompa, and Né.

16. For a variety of *kushü* patterns, see Barker 1986 and Myers 1989. See also Barker 1985.

17. Information given by Künchen Norbu, Ura, November 1992. Taxes were paid to authorities at Tongsa Dzong, formerly the administrative center for all regions of Bhutan farther east. Tongsa Dzong in turn handed the goods over to Punakha Dzong, Bhutan's capital from the seventeenth to the mid-twentieth centuries.

18. One such workshop was at Lamé Gompa, the home of Ashi Pedon and Ashi Yangzom, daughters of the first king by his first wife, Ashi Rinchen of Tamshing. Others were: Wangdichöling, home of Ashi Chöden, the younger sister of the first king (see photographs in White 1914); Thinley Rabten, home of Ashi Wangmo, the daughter of the first king by his second wife, Ashi Lemo of Kurtö Timnyong; and Tang Ugyenchöling, home of the descendants of Dorje Lingpa. At Tang, many of the villagers also wove for the local *dasho* (lord) until 1957, "when the weavers who came from Kurtö went home." A few Bumthang noblewomen have maintained their strong interest in weaving. At Tamshing, for example, Ashi Pem Dem manages a weaving workshop with a teacher from the Chumé Valley. Another prominent family has a group of weavers working privately at Dorjibi.

19. For example, Tham Kabum was a leading weaver for the late Queen (Dowager) Ashi Pema Dechen at Wangdichöling, and Tham Döma was a leading weaver for Queen (Dowager) Ashi Phuntsok Chöden. Information given by Ashi Pem Dem.

20. The people of Bumthang traditionally viewed south central Bhutan as *matpala* – "at the edges of civilization" – and accordingly did not admire its weaving. Older women use this word to describe *kushüthara* whose patterns and intricacy are not up to the "Bumthang standard."

21. Information given by Karma Ura, Planning Commission, February 1994.

22. *Tarichem* (striped women's dresses) and *yathra* (supplementary-weft-patterned twill cloth) are sometimes still woven on a backstrap loom. At Ugyenchöling in Tang, however, only one out of twenty-four weavers uses a backstrap loom today.

23. In Tongsa Tsangkhar, for example, the best wool is obtained in June-July when the flocks return from the mountains. Fleece from the January shearing is shorter and used for weft yarns. The third shearing is in April.

24. According to Lopön Pemala and the late Lam Nado, Bhutanese historian and scholar, this village, whose name means 'lineage of Mongols,' was settled by remnants of the army under Lajang Khan that invaded Bumthang in 1714. Both scholars also speculated about whether textile patterns, such as *hothra* ('Mongolian pattern'), may have been introduced by these immigrants.

25. *Hothra* and *jalo* came from Lhobrak, just north of central Bhutan (Nado 1987, 24). *Kham metok* ('design from Kham [Tibet]') was another woolen, once popular for making into men's robes, that is no longer seen; information given by Dasho Shingkar Lam, Secretary to the third king and former Speaker of the National Assembly.

26. Dasho Shingkar Lam remembers being "amazed!" when he saw woolen *sethra* for the first time between 1952 and 1954.

27. This cloth was called *tsangthra* ("pattern from Tsang" [Tibet]) to distinguish it from its prototype woven in Bhutan on a backstrap loom (*mathra*). Later, *tsangthra* came to mean any *mathra* cloth woven on a frame loom, even in Bhutan. Today, because only frame looms are used for weaving this fabric, the term has almost disappeared in favor of *mathra*. There are four major varieties of *mathra* whose names correspond to the sequencing of warp colors: *khempa*, *dorshongba*, *khrachikpa*, and *churichem*.

28. Information given by Dasho Shingkar Lam and other natives of Bumthang.

29. Henkha is spoken in villages on both the eastern and western slopes of the Black Mountains (Driem 1992, 14-15). The villages especially known for weaving are Phobjikha, Adhang, and Nyala, all west of the Pelé La, and those in the Sephu region, east of the pass.

30. Information in this paragraph was given by Am Yeshe Chöden and Am Kunzang and by the late Lam Nado.

31. For example, plaid cotton (*pangtsi*) and a supplementary-warp-patterned fabric (*mensé mathra*) whose local style had very wide pattern bands and "different" designs. The village name is sometimes given as Nub Dalakha.

Chapter Eight

1. For nettle use among northeast Indian groups, for example, see Dalton 1872, in Elwin 1959b, 337, and Bhattacharjee 1983, 50, on the Mishmis; and Sharma 1961, 22-23, on the Sherdukpens.

2. For example, the villages of Ngalakhachu and Takila Gompa (Tangmachu) in Lhuntshi District; the villages of Kabesa and Shengana in Punakha District; the Kheng region in Shemgang District; the Mönpa villages of southern Tongsa District; and villages in Samtse District that are home to the Lhop (Doya) people.

3. For example, in the Kheng region of Shemgang District and Dorokha region of Samtse District. Information from the late Lam Nado, Bhutanese historian and scholar; see also Nado 1987, 24. Dasho Shingkar Lam, Secretary to the third king and former Speaker of the National Assembly, recalls seeing people in nettle-cloth garments in Bumthang and Mongar districts as a young man (1930s and 1940s).

4. Although the literature to date has called Bhutan's most ubiquitous fiber "raw silk," this term more accurately refers to silk as it comes from a cocoon, no matter what type of silkworm moth produces it. At this point, the silk is coated with a sticky gum that keeps the fiber strong and elastic, but that is later totally or partially removed, usually by simmering the cocoons, to faciliate spinning and weaving. Major sources for this section on silks are: Butler 1888; *Encyclopaedia Britannica* 1911; Feltwell 1990; Ferguson 1971-72; Kolander 1985; Peigler 1993; and Wardle 1881.

5. I am grateful to Douglas C. Ferguson, Research Entomologist, Systematic Entomology Laboratory, U.S. Department of Agriculture, c/o National Museum of Natural History, and to Dr. Richard S. Peigler, Curator of Entomology, Denver Museum of Natural History, for identification of *Samia ricini* as the species found in Bhutan.

   The other two principal types of silk in the region are *tussar* and *muga*. *Tussar*, the finest and costliest, is a silvery fiber produced by *Antheraea mylitta*. This form feeds on several host trees, the best known to Bhutanese being *Ziziphus jujuba* and *Z. zizipha* (Dzongkha: *khangaling shing*). *Muga* is produced by *Antheraea assamensis*, which feeds on a half-dozen trees that tint it shades from gold to brown (Peigler 1993, 152-55). Somewhat coarser than *tussar*, *muga* is also more durable. *Endi* is coarser still, and was the type least valued in Assam, although favored in Bhutan. On Assamese wild silk moths and silk production, see *Provincial Gazetteer* [1906] 1983, 61, and Hunter [1879] n.d., 1:138-41.

6. Peigler, 18 January 1994, letter to author.

7. Dolma, a young woman from Goshing, 20 November 1992, interview.

8. The villages still known to cultivate wild silk include Goshing, Pangbang, Ngangla, Pangkhar, and Bjokha.

9. Samples of "100 percent Bhutan-made mulberry silk" were formerly on display at the silk production center in Phomshing, near Tashigang.

10. The project also imports a little spun wild silk (*muga*).

11. In 1993, one sample of unraveled rope that had never been woven into cloth dissolved in a solution test just as silk would. If the rope came from Allied parachutes or supplies, it would most probably have been nylon (then called vylon), because the Allies had no large, steady source of reeled (monofilament) silk. Although the Japanese had a thriving silk industry, Japanese materials would not have been on the market in India. The rope, therefore, was very likely of Indian manufacture and, indeed, made of reeled silk. Tests performed and information given by Camie Campbell and Mary Ballard, Conservational Analytical Laboratory, Smithsonian Institution; confirmed by Dr. Norman Endichter.

12. In Pemagatshel District, the villages of Thongsa and Mikuri are still known for growing cotton. In Thongsa, two households maintain modest fields by the riverside, planting the cotton in different places each year so that it grows better. Men sow the cotton in March-April and pluck it in August-September. Women dry, seed, card, and spin the fiber. They sell some of the cloth they weave in Pemagatshel, but make most of it for their own use.

13. Two other sources of cotton-like fiber are *Bombax malabericum* (Dz. *pem getsar*), a tree found in southern Bhutan from which batting for pillows and quilts is obtained, and a tree that grows in Samdrup Jongkhar whose flowers resemble cotton bolls. Information given by Lyönpo C. Dorji.

14. The moral of the story, heard in October 1992 from Ai Chuni, a ninety-year-old native of Gompakap (Kurtö), is to obey your parents and not incur their wrath.

15. One early reference to wool is found in Bhutanese laws promulgated in the mid-1600s, instructing government officers not to force wool on tenants so that they would have to weave it (Department of Education 1992, 11).

16. The late Lam Nado, and the Venerable Mynak Tulku Rimpoche, Director, National Museum, located these references, chiefly in Yönten Thayé n.d.

17. For example, in 1875, "20 bundles of cotton thread" were among the items purchased by Bhutia traders in Kerkeria (Bhutan) at the annual trade fair (Hunter [1879] n.d., 1:144). Machine-spun cotton, the "European cotton twist and yarn" of contemporary records, made its breakthrough into Assam between 1883 and 1885, and supplies increased steadily thereafter. See, for example, Government of Assam 1881-82, Appendix iv; Government of Bengal 1884-85, 32ff and Appendix E, lxxxvi.

18. This story was heard from several Bhutanese who are not resident in eastern Bhutan. For Tibetan use of the term, see Laufer 1918, 5.

19. See Mickle 1984 on spindles in Bumthang. The Textile Booklist 1984a and b include a series of short essays, like Mickle's, on aspects of Bhutanese weaving.

20. Information in this section was provided or confirmed by Ashi Kesang, Dorjibi, August 1986; Am Yeshe Chöden, Thimphu, November 1992; and Ashi Pem Dem, Tamshing, January 1994.

21. Lac is cultivated around the villages of Gomkora, Phongmé, Yerba, Yabrang, and Udzarong in Tashigang District; Drametsé, Chaskar, Ngatsang, and Yadi in Mongar District; and Yurung and Chebar in Pemagatshel District (Sonam Tshering 1990, 14). In 1984, Chaskar, Ngatsang, and Drametsé together had 100 acres of registered *jatsho shing* lac trees.

22. Several trees are suitable summer hosts: *lilumshing* (*Engelhardtia spicata* Juglandaceae); *sershing* (*Albizzia* sp. Leguminosae); *chambak-tang* (*Kydia calycina* Malvaceae); and *tshoshing* (*Butea monosperma*); see Nakao and Nishioka 1984, 137, and Sonam Tshering 1990, 14.

23. In the early 1870s, more than 4 metric tons of

lac sometimes were sold by the Bhutias at a single fair (Hunter [1879] n.d., 1: 143; Government of Assam 1881-82, Appendix ii).

24. The recipe was given by Am Rinchen Zam, Nanggar, March 1987.

25. A vast amount of the madder in British trade statistics came from Bhutan proper rather than Tawang. For example, in 1875, some 11,500 bundles of twigs, worth just Indian rupees (Rs.) 79, were sold by Bhutias (people from Tawang and Bhutan) at two trade fairs in Assam, but at the Doimara fair within Bhutanese territory, the amount of madder that changed hands was 14 metric tons, worth Rs. 1,875 (Hunter [1879] n.d., 1:143-45).

26. Recipes given by Am Rinchen Zam, Nanggar, and Ashi Kesang, Dorjibi, August 1986.

27. Bhutanese call these trees *zim, shungkhé,* and *pangtsi* (the berries of the latter are pressed for oil). In Radi (Tashigang) and Kheng (Shemgang), an apparently related leaf called *shingshaba* is used as well. Depending on the region, the species are *Symplocos racemosa, S. ramosissima, S. paniculata,* and *S. glomerata* (Sonam Tshering 1990, 14-15).

28. Recipes were given by Am Rinchen Zam, Nanggar, and Ashi Kesang, Dorjibi, August 1986.

29. On "Assam indigo" *(Strobilanthes cusia)* in Bhutan, see Nakao and Nishioka 1984, 138-39.

30. A typical recipe from central Bhutan goes as follows: The leaves are cut like grass, cleaned, dried, and then stamped on so that they crumble into "tiny ashes." They are placed in a bamboo container with a little hot water; when the substance turns dark red, hardwood ash *(thekhu)* is added. The mixture is kneaded well and placed in a warm location, sometimes near a stove, and covered to ferment. When it becomes the consistency of mud or butter (one to three weeks), it is strained and more hot water and hardwood ash are added before placing it in a warm spot for another week. A creamy residue *(sha)* appears on its surface. Wool immersed one evening is left overnight and then dried in the sun to see if the color is ready. The mixture is kept warm for another few days and then the wool is steeped again, turning a darker color. The third steeping produces a fine blue if the dye has been properly prepared; otherwise, one or two more steepings are needed. *Chang* (local rice beer) may be mixed in while the yarn soaks for up to one week. Recipes give by Am Yangchen, Jakar; and Ashi Kesang and Lemo, Dorjibi, August 1986.

31. Information on local dyes provided by Am Sonam Yangzom, Ngang Lhakhang, August 1986; Tshering Thondup and other villagers of Shingkar, September 1986; Sangay Dolma, Thongsa Pemagatshel, March 1987 and October 1992; Künchen Norbu, Ura, November 1992; and others. The yellow root and bark of *kipetsang* bushes are also used as an eye medicine, according to Pönlop-Dep Töchu of Thinleygang.

32. The mineral substances are collectively called 'sour stones' *(dochur).* Three samples analyzed at the Conservation Analytical Laboratory, Smithsonian Institution, were mixtures of magnesium aluminum sulphate hydrate and potassium aluminum hydrate sulphate (Camie Campbell and Mary Ballard, February 1993, communication to author). *Dochur* is also said to refer to natural salt (Sonam Tshering 1990, 19-20). The sour fruits are from three principal trees: *khomang (Choenomeles lagenaria* and *C. wilsonii); robtang (Rhus simialata Murr.);* and *chorgenshing (Phyllanthus emblica L.);* see Sonam Tshering 1990, 16, 18-19.

33. See also Choeki Ongmo 1991 and Choeki Ongmo and Purna Prasad 1991.

34. Observations by visitors to Bhutan at the time confirm that ordinary people dressed in sober colors. This may have been due in part to sumptuary laws regulating dress (Bell Collection 1904, 6). Descriptions of the court, on the other hand, are vivid – filled with mentions of bright Chinese silks, gay wall hangings and banners, and colorful dress, which were all made of imported rather than local fabric.

35. Various factors fostered this wholesale, if relatively late, national adoption of synthetic dyes. Wider use of bright colors must have been possible partly because by then the well-to-do had established them as a fashion. Their use must likewise have been encouraged by the abolition of hereditary service and relaxation of some conventions about dress, even though today one must still be careful not to "outdress" a social superior.

36. In the past few years, Tibetan vertical frame looms also have been introduced to support a modest industry of weaving Tibetan-style pile carpets in Phuntsholing.

37. Rita Bolland, well known for her studies of Southeast Asian looms, is preparing a monograph on a Bhutanese backstrap loom in the collection of the Royal Tropical Institute (Tropenmuseum) in Amsterdam that will be an important contribution to the field.

38. This account was compiled from information given by one of Sonam Dondrup's granddaughters; Ai Chuni of Gompakap; Dorji Wangchuk of Tangmachu; and Am Sitharmo of Khoma.

39. This story was related by two of the Zimpön's daughters, Am Ugen Doma and Am Tshering Dem. The Zimpön also designed an experimental loom at which two weavers could work opposite one another.

40. In Tibet, the card loom is called *kothag,* 'leather loom,' because the cards were typically made of animal hide. On similar looms in Darjeeling that use a pseudo-continuous warp and closing rod, see Collingwood 1982, 37 and fig. 10.

Glossary of Selected Terms

Most of the non-English terms used in the text are from three of Bhutan's twenty-one languages: Dzongkha (Dz), 'the language of the dzong,' which is the cultivated form of the native language of western Bhutan and is Bhutan's national language; Bumthangkha (Bu), the major language of Bumthang District (central Bhutan), variations and dialects of which are spoken in surrounding regions from Tongsa to Lhuntshi District; and Tshangla (Tsh), commonly called Shachobikha, the principal language of eastern Bhutan.

Compiling a glossary of weaving and textile terms is a challenge because of Bhutan's linguistic diversity. People may use Dzongkha or Bumthangkha in conversation but draw on specialized words from their own dialect or language as needed. Some formerly regional or local terms relating to weaving and cloth are now also used by native Dzongkha speakers. Pronunciation of a word (especially when borrowed from another Bhutanese or non-Bhutanese language) often varies from speaker to speaker, and the meaning of a term in eastern, central, and western Bhutan may be slightly or markedly different.

Wherever possible, the region or language of apparent origin is indicated: Bumthang (Bu), eastern Bhutan (Tsh), Lhuntshi District (Kurtötkha [Ku] and Dzalakha [Dzal]), and Merak Sakteng (MS), Mön villages in southern Tongsa (Mönkha), particular districts, as well as Tibetan (Tib), Lepcha, Anglo-Indian English, Hindi, and Chinese. Words used by Nepalese-speaking southern Bhutanese are indicated as Lhotsakha (Lho), 'southern border language.'

Ascertaining spellings and etymology is also complicated because most Bhutanese languages lack written forms. Written Dzongkha, which has existed since the 1960s, is still undergoing development. Dzongkha is written in Tibetan script and, like Tibetan, contains many silent letters that make the written and spoken forms of a word very different. The "official" system of rendering Dzongkha words in Roman transcription employs many diacritical marks to achieve linguistic accuracy; it is not yet widely known or used in Bhutan, and it is also somewhat daunting for a general reader. Many Bhutanese are guided instead by the weekly newspaper *Kuensel*, which employs Roman transcriptions that have become conventional because of wide use rather than linguistic accuracy. Complexity arises also in personal names; a name that is spelled only one way in Dzongkha may be Romanized several different ways according to individual preference.

Contents of the Glossary

Bhutanese and other non-English terms relating to textiles are represented in simplified phonetic forms in the Glossary in bold italics. The *é* indicates a sound like the vowels in the English word *aid*, and is commonly represented as *ey* or *ay* in Roman Dzongkha. The umlaut over *o* or *u* conveys frontal, rounded vowel sounds similar to those in the German words *göttlich* and *tür*, and are sometimes written as *oe* and *ue*. With apologies to Bhutanese and other scholars who have labored to bring precision to the use of Dzongkha, the transcriptions here avoid diacritical marks that would improve their accuracy but be strange to a wide audience.

Consistency in the phonetic renderings of similar and identical written forms is elusive for several reasons. Spoken Dzongkha tends to contract the longer written forms that sometimes, but not always, preserve Tibetan orthography; their pronunciation in Dzongkha may also differ slightly from that in spoken Tibetan. Scholarly opinions about Dzongkha spellings, and therefore correct pronunciations, sometimes also diverge, particularly around terms, like so many of those included here, that are not related to the realms of religion and state. The same English sound often corresponds to several written Dzongkha elements, and the same Dzongkha element may have a slightly different quality at the middle or end of a word. At the request of Bhutanese authorities, and again with general readers in mind, this work adheres to conventional spellings of placenames and forms of address, whose spellings are anything but linguistically consistent.

Scholars and linguists will want to consult the entries in parentheses immediately after the phonetic forms for transliterations based on Western scholarly traditions. Where Bhutanese scholars prefer different spellings of the same word, alternative transliterations are provided. Alternatives occur especially when terms are derived from Tibetan, in which case their spellings are sometimes simplified to correspond more accurately to Dzongkha pronunciation. Terms related to religious textiles are more likely to retain Tibetan spelling and pronunciation. Alternative spellings also occur in historical literature (approximate dates of the texts are indicated when known). No spellings or transliterations are given for words from other languages of Bhutan, although Bhutanese may write them phonetically in *uchen* (printed script). The *Guide to Official Dzongkha Romanization* and the first chapters of *The Grammar of Dzongkha* (Driem 1991, 1992) are good sources to consult for more extensive discussion of transliteration and Roman transcription, as well as pronunciation.

See figs. 1.10 (page 44) and 8.12 (page 201) for keys naming the parts of the backstrap and horizontal frame looms.

In spite of its shortcomings, this Glossary can nonetheless be a basis for further study and correction. The individuals who assisted in the research certainly prevented many errors from appearing, and those that do appear are entirely my own. (D.K.M.)

adha khamar (a thang kha dmar) A man's red-and-white ceremonial shoulder cloth, a style that originated in Adhang in Wangdi Phodrang District (c. 1760).

adha mathra (a thang dmar khra) A warp-striped plainweave fabric that originated in Adhang (showing blue, green, red, yellow, and sometimes black stripes).

adha rachu (a thang rags chung) A woman's warp-striped ceremonial shoulder cloth, a style that originated in Adhang.

adholishi (a dho li shi, a rdo li shi) Indian silk used for making dance costumes in Bhutan (c. 1760).

ai (A'i) (1) Grandmother. (2) Polite term for an old woman.

aikapur (a'i ka pur, a'i ka spur) (1) Tsh: any supplementary-warp-patterned fabric. (2) Dz: a supplementary-warp-patterned fabric with pattern bands in yellow and white (Tsh: *aikapur jadrima*).

am (Am) (1) Honorific term for the wife of a high-ranking man. (2) Polite form of address for any adult woman.

ashi (a zhe) (1) Princess. (2) Honorific term for a high-status woman. An *ashi khada* (shortened to *ashida*) is a superior quality of silk presentation scarf.

baden (ba dan) See *phen*.

barbjang (bar byang) The center panel of a woman's dress.

bé (bal) Wool, woolen yarn. Tsh/MS: *mé, mi*.

békhu (bal khur) Basket for keeping wool or other yarns in readiness for weaving or beside the loom. Bu: *békhur, tsangter*. Ku: *kurma*. Tsh: *shöskom, kudpa shoma*.

belabemi (bal la' 'bad mi) Women who spun yarn and wound it into balls at weaving workshops in noble households.

bharati (bha ra ha ti, bha ras ha sti) From *bharat*, Hindi term for 'India'. White, Indian cotton used for lining walls prior to painting them (c. 1760). Cf. the modern term *bharé*, 'Indian cotton.'

bhokku [Lepcha] A Tibetan-style woman's dress, worn especially by Bhutanese nuns. Also called *bögo* (bod gos), 'Tibetan dress.'

bidar [Merak Sakteng] Boots; see *lham*.

bja tshering (bya tshe ring) 'Long-life bird.' Phoenix; a symbol of long life seen in textiles.

bjajé (bya rjes) 'Bird's footprint.' A trident-like motif stitched into a Bhutanese Drukpa Kagyü monk's patchwork shawl (*chögo namjar*).

bjang (byang) A panel of cloth from a loom. Bu:

jangtha.

bjichu mito (byi'u chung mig to) 'Little bird's eye.' Twill weave, such as that characteristic of cloth woven on a horizontal frame loom. Sometimes called *churi*, 'river, mountains,' because of its zigzag elements.

bokheb (sbog khebs) 'Bedding cover.' An appliqué textile edged by fringe, used for sitting on and for wrapping up bedding, and on which bedding is laid out. See *denkheb*.

brokpa ('brog pa) (1) Dz: seminomadic herder. Also *bjop* ('byogp). (2) MS: The name the people of Merak Sakteng in eastern Bhutan call themselves.

bubjang (bubs byang) A set of three panels of cloth for a woman's dress. See *barbjang* and *thama bjang*.

bündri (bun bsgril, sbog 'gril) 'Round, collected.' A wrapping cloth, often decorated with *kushü* patterning. Ku/Dzal: *kushü bogdri*.

bura, buré ('bu ras) 'Insect [bug] cotton' (1) Wild silk cloth. (2) Silk yarn, especially wild silk. Tsh: *bakha kutpa, baha*.

buramap ('bu ras dmar po) 'Red wild silk.' Maroon ceremonial shoulder cloth worn by men with the title of *dasho*. Bu: *bura shindi*. Ku/Dzal: *bura yabma leu*. Tsh: *bura tsalo*.

chabsham (chab gsham, rkyab 'cham) 'Something that waves or dances.' The ornamentation at the lower edge of the armholes of a monk's vest.

chabshub (chab shubs) 'Cover for a water bottle.' Cloth containers used by the lay elite and monks.

chagsi pangkheb (phyag gsil spang khebs) 'Hand wash lap cover' (honorific). An intricately decorated multipurpose textile used by the well-to-do and in ceremonial settings.

chamgo ('cham bgo, 'cham gos), 'Dance garments.' Costumes worn in religious dance.

chang (chang) Homemade alcohol or local beer made from fermented grain and used in dyeing.

changjé (phyag mjal) Gift (often of cloth) from an inferior to a superior.

charkab (char bkab) 'Rain covering.' (1) Any textile used as protection (for a person or animal) against the rain. (2) A cloak made of three panels of woolen cloth from central Bhutan. *Pchana charkab* have red-and-black or white-and-black checks; *sephu charkab* are striped; and *yathra charkab* have various designs.

chashumi (phyag zhu mi) An attendant of a high official who traditionally carries a woven

bag or ceremonial textile.

chemashing [Tshangla] A tree (*Gossypium?*) from which "cotton" is obtained for weaving in eastern Bhutan.

chenzi, chenzi darchung (spyan gzigs dar chung) 'Offering of silk to the gods.' A special banner for decorating the upper walls of a shrine room.

chephur (phye phur) A textile made of narrow, overlapping panels of brocade, two of which should hang in a shrine room. Also heard as *chedphur*.

chephur gyetshen (phye phur rgyal mtshan) The set of six textiles (two each of three types: *chephur, gyetshen, phen*) required for a shrine room or temple.

chögo, chögö (chos bgo, chos gos) 'Religious garments.' (1) Monks' clothing. (2) The patchwork shawl worn by monks (*chögo namjar*). Honorific: *kuchö* (sku chos).

chögo lago (chos gos bla bgo, chos gos bla gos) 'Religious garments, lamas' garments.' (1) Dz: Monks' clothing. (2) Tib: A shawl that is one of the three essential garments of a monk; not used by Bhutanese Drukpa Kagyü monks.

chögo namjar (chos gos rnam byar) A patchwork shawl, made of orange cotton cloth, that is one of the three essential garments worn by a monk.

chögo namsum (chos gos rnam gsum) 'Three religious garments.' The three most essential sacred garments (*chögo namjar; chögo lago; shamtha*) of a Mahayana Buddhist monk.

chöjé (chos rje) 'Lords of religion.' Local noble families throughout Bhutan whose lineages include important Buddhist teachers.

chökheb (mchod khebs) 'Offering covering.' (1) Textiles for covering the various altars of a shrine. (2) A textile for covering the particular altar (*chöthri*) on which water offerings and butter lamps are placed.

cholo [Lhotsakha] Tight-fitting, short-sleeved blouse worn with a sari. A *chaubundi cholo* has long sleeves and ties at the shoulder and waist.

chom (chogm) Gift (often of cloth) between equals.

chorgenshing [Tshangla] A tree (*Phyllanthus emblica L.*) whose leaves are used for black dye in eastern Bhutan and whose sour fruits serve as a mordant. Also called *chorgéshaba, chorginsé*. Lho: *amla, churu*.

chözhé (chos gzhas) 'Dharma song.' Dances, mostly religious, performed at festivals.

chuba [Bumthangkha] (1) Tibetan-style man's

robe (Tib: *phyu pa*). (2) MS: A man's long-sleeved woolen upper garment. Also called *goidung* (Merak) and *tshoskam chuba* (Sakteng).

chukchumé [Bumthangkha] A poisonous root used as a black dye.

dakpa (dwag pa) Seminomadic herders of eastern Bhutan, similar to *brokpa*. Also called *dap*.

damki ('dam dkris) 'Mud cover.' A lower garment like an apron, usually of striped cotton cloth, traditionally worn by attendants walking near a high-status person on horseback to protect them from dust raised by the horse's hooves.

dar (dar) Dz/Tib: (1) Silk, silk yarn (*dar küp*). Also *jadar* (rgya dar, 'Chinese [or Indian] silk'). (2) Flag. (3) To flourish, prosper, spread.

darpa (dar spar) 'Printed flag.' A narrow textile with woodblock-printed prayers on it; prayer flag (cf. Tib: *darpoché, darchang*). White flags are properly *darpa*, while sets of five, colored flags are *darcho*. Once the flag is erected, the pole and banner together are called *darshing* ('flag wood').

dasho (drag shos) 'Excellent one.' A Bhutanese title awarded by the king that carries with it the right to wear a red shoulder cloth; hence, a "red scarf officer."

deb raja [Anglo-Indian] See *druk desi*.

decheling kamtham (bde chen gling skam 'thag ma) 'Cloth from Decheling.' (1) A white cotton fabric with a red-and-blue or -black plaid pattern, formerly made in southeastern Bhutan, for making door curtains and cushion linings; also a tax cloth. (2) Contemporary fabric, sometimes machine-woven, with the same pattern. See *kamtham*.

denkheb (gdan khebs) 'Seat or mattress cover.' (1) Any textile to cover a sitting cushion. (2) A cushion cover made from two panels of patterned woolen cloth from central Bhutan, edged with broadcloth or felt. See *bokheb*.

dharma raja [Anglo-Indian] See *shabdrung*.

dö (mdos) Outdoor household shrine, made from a wooden wand having crosspieces wound with thread (especially in eastern Bhutan).

dobchu (dob chung) Bracelet. *Baso dob* is an ivory bracelet.

dochur (rdo skyur) 'Sour stone.' Alumaceous earths used as mordants. Also called *brakchur*.

dokcha (rdog cha) Skein (of yarn). Bu/Ku: *dokpa*. Tsh: *kudpa sharang*.

dokshing (rdog shing) Skein winder. Bu: *kinthang*. Ku: *dokshing*. Tsh: *jhinang*.

domtha (dorm thag) Semifitted trousers of wild

silk or cotton traditionally worn under a man's robe.

dongkheb (gdong khebs) 'Front cover.' A striped woolen apron worn by women in central Bhutan. Bu: *thüden*. Tib: *pangden*.

dongtha (gdong thag) 'Front cord.' A necklace.

doram (rdo ram) 'Stone indigo.' An alumaceous earth used as a mordant.

dorje (rdo rje) Thunderbolt; a depiction of a sacred thunderbolt. Crossed or double thunderbolt: *dorje jadam*.

dos pani [Hindi?] A type of bleached or grayish-white Indian cotton (*markin*) formerly imported for lining men's robes.

doya [Lhotsakha] See *lhop*.

dozum (sgro bzum) A sharp, pointed dagger traditionally carried by Bhutanese men. Similar knives with different-shaped blades are *baché* (sba chem), *chethem* (phyel tham), and *redi* (ral gri).

dramé (dra meg) A lattice pattern composed of eternal or lucky knots, one of the eight auspicious symbols of Buddhism. See *peyab*.

dramnyen chözhé (sgra snyan chos gzhas) 'Stringed instrument dharma song.' A Bhutanese dance performed at festivals.

drawa draché (drwa wa drwa phyed) A textile for a shrine room, resembling a string of pearls made from colored cloth.

driglam namzha (sgrig lam rnam gzhag) (1) Code of monastic and court discipline. (2) Traditional Bhutanese etiquette governing dress and behavior.

dromchu chema, dromchem (sgrom chung can ma) 'With little boxes.' (1) Tsh: A fabric with supplementary-warp-pattern bands containing designs that resemble little boxes. Very often the cloth shows sets of three narrow pattern bands, side by side, worked in two alternating colors. (2) Dz: A supplementary-warp-patterned fabric with alternating pattern bands of red, green, yellow, and white. (3) Dz: A plainweave, warp-striped fabric with supplementary-weft patterning.

druk ('brug) Dz/Tib: Dragon; thunder dragon.

druk desi ('brug sde srid) Temporal ruler of Bhutan, a position that lapsed when the monarchy was established in 1907.

druk gyalpo ('brug rgyal po) King of Bhutan.

drukpa ('brug pa) (1) A Bhutanese. (2) The particular school of Kagyü Buddhism practiced in Bhutan and its followers.

drukyul ('brug yul) 'Thunder dragon country.' The Dzongkha name for Bhutan.

dungsam kamtham (gdung bsam skam 'thag ma

) 'Cloth from Dungsam.' A cotton fabric formerly made in southeastern Bhutan. See *kamtham*.

dungshing (gdung shing) Pine trees, whose cones give a light blue or purple dye (central Bhutan).

dzögo (mdzod gos) Dz/Tib: 'treasury clothes'; general term for Chinese silk. Chinese: *kuduan* ('treasury satin'?).

dzong (rdzong) Fortress-monasteries, where civil and religious authorities have been housed jointly since the seventeenth century.

dzöpön (mdzod dpon) 'Treasury [store] master.' The keeper of the storerooms where tax cloth and other goods were kept in a *dzong*.

endi, eri [Anglo-Indian] A variety of wild silk from Assam and Bhutan, produced predominantly by *Samia ricini* (a.k.a. *Attacus ricini*), which feeds on the castor bean tree (*Ricinus communis*; Dz: *chamaling shing*).

gandru (gang gru [?]) A set of two pieces of white cotton with a little pattern, used for doorway hangings and lamas' raincloaks, and exported to Tibet. Formerly 'worth thirty coins.'

gau (ga'u) Charm box or amulet, typically of silver and traditionally worn by men and women.

gayok (sga g.yogs) 'Saddle covering.' (1) An appliqué or woven textile, with or without fringe, to cover a saddle. (2) Any textile to cover a saddle. A *gayok tenma* (sga g.yogs brtan ma) has a swastika in the center. See *thrikheb*.

gelong (dge slong) (1) A fully ordained monk. (2) Honorific term for any monk.

go (bgo, gos) 'Garment, coat.' (1) A man's robe. Bu: *chuba* (q.v.). (2) Clothing, especially men's clothing. Tsh: *khamung*.

göchen (gos chen) 'Great garment.' (1) Chinese silk cloth, including damask and brocade. (2) Any silk fabric.

gomchen (sgom chen) A lay priest, sometimes married, in the Bhutanese Nyingma Buddhist tradition.

gönkhang (mgon khang) 'Protector deity chapel.'

goré (sgo ras) 'Door cloth.' A doorway covering made of any one of various textiles.

goshab (gong shab) Cloth facing at the collar of a man's robe.

goshub [Tib: gos shubs] Tunic worn by women of Kongpo and Pemakö (southeastern Tibet), similar to archaic Bhutanese tunics (*shingkha*).

gotsum, gotsuma (mgo btshum) 'Over the head.' (1) A sleeveless shift worn as a woman's petticoat or undergarment. (2) Bu: An archaic tunic made of cotton or bast-fiber cloth. See *kushung*.

gur (gur) Tent, referring to all varieties from the plainest shelter to a ceremonial tent decorated with appliqué.

gur jayab (gur rgya yab) A rain and dew shield formed by two slanting panels of cloth erected like a roof several feet over a tent.

gyentshok (rgyan tshogs) Offerings to the gods, often depicted on textiles, especially those that decorate protector deities' chapels.

gyetshen (rgyal mtshan) 'Banner of victory,' one of the eight auspicious symbols of Buddhism. This tubular textile should decorate a shrine room (as a pair).

hathi nambar [Hindi] 'Elephant brand.' A coarse Indian cotton fabric formerly imported for stitching into women's petticoats and lining men's robes.

hingtham (hing 'thag ma) `Heart weaving.' Tib: snying 'thag ma. The finest textiles, woven for family use or by a skilled weaver in a noble household and known for their intricate patterning. See *tshongtham*.

hor [Tshangla] Bands of supplementary-warp patterning in a fabric.

hothra (hor khra) 'Mongolian pattern.' A striped woolen fabric, originally from Tibet, used for men's robes and women's dresses. Also called *hothra janchu*. Bu: *hothra atsa*. Tsh: *shardang thara*.

hothra jalo (hor khra rgya lo, hor khra 'ja' log) 'Mongolian pattern with a rainbow.' A woolen fabric, originally from Tibet and patterned with weft stripes and tie-dyed or stamped crosses (Tib: *thigthra, thigma*). Sometimes simply called *jalo*.

ja ('ja') 'Rainbow.' (1) Multicolored warp or weft stripes in a textile. (2) Facing on the inside upper and lower edges of a woman's wrapped dress. (3) Facing at the cuffs and hem of a man's robe. (4) Narrow red and yellow silk borders forming the border of a *thangka* image.

jab (rgyab) 'Back.' The supplementary-weft patterning at either fringed end of a *kushüthara*. Also called *ja, jabgang, japang*. Bu: *zhipi*. Ku/Dzal: *janthap*. Tsh: *manglem*.

jabkab (rgyab bkab) 'Back cover.' A man's wrap or shoulder cloth (1700s).

jabté (rgyab stan) 'Back cover.' A cloth wrapped around a woman's lower body to keep a dress clean.

jabtha (rgyab thag) 'Back cord.' (1) A necklace worn at the back of the neck to help balance the pins that formerly fastened a woman's dress. (2) A necklace (worn in front) that joins contemporary dress fasteners.

jachen, jaching (rgya phying) (1) Broadcloth made in England and formerly imported from British India for making appliqué textiles, for edging and backing textiles, and for making boots. (2) Wool-like acrylic yarn, which now comes from India.

jadrima ('ja' sgrig ma) 'Cloth arranged with a rainbow.' Also *jadrichem*. (1) A fabric with yellow-and-white supplementary-warp-pattern bands between colorful warp striping. (2) A secondary designation for any textile with bands of colorful warp striping.

janachari (rgya nag lchags ri) 'Chinese wall.' A meander or key pattern [e.g., fig. 2.3].

jandha An aesthetic quality associated with women's dresses. A dress that "has *jandha*" has designs whose colors contrast agreeably with the field color and make a strong visual impression.

jangsham (ljang gsham) 'Green background.' A woman's dress with a green field.

jatsho (rgya tshos) 'Chinese or Indian color.' Lac, a dyestuff produced by the *Laccifer lacca* insect. Tsh: *tshos* ('color').

je khenpo, je khembo (rje mkhan po) Bhutan's supreme religious leader (chief abbot).

jinlab (byin brlabs) Blessings, said to be "contained," for example, in monk's lower garments and men's belts.

jobche (byo phye) 'Buckwheat flower.' Coarsely ground grains added to dyebaths of *Symplocos* leaves to heighten the resulting yellow color.

ju (rgyu) Warp. Bu: *aamaa, tha aam*. Ku: *tha, rotman*. Tsh: *renang, ju*.

kabé (ka bal) (1) Cotton, cotton yarn (handspun). Also called *singbé* (Tib: srin bal). (2) Cotton cloth made from handspun yarn. Ku/Dzal: *kampé*. Tsh: *mongan, mo-an, kaba*.

kabné (bkab ni) 'Covering [with ceremonial connotations].' A man's, or woman's, ceremonial shoulder cloth. *Alu banegi kabné* is a double-width cloth that women use to carry babies on their backs. Bu: *botok*. Ku/Dzal: *yabma*. Tsh: *sari*.

kabné map (bkab ni dmarp) 'Red covering.' See *buramap*.

kamar thrasum (dkar dmar khra gsum) Red-and-white striped wild silk textile (c. 1504). See *khamar*.

kamtham (skam 'thag ma) 'Dry [-tax] weave,' meaning cloth. Varieties of relatively undecorated, plainweave cotton cloth that were once important forms of tax payment in southeastern Bhutan.

kamtham karpo (skam 'thag ma dkar po) 'White cloth.' Plain white cotton cloth formerly made in southeastern Bhutan.

kamtham thrawo (skam 'thag ma khra bo) 'Multicolored pattern cloth.' Plaid cloth formerly made in eastern Bhutan.

kanggo [Merak Sakteng] Short pants, with an apron-like flap in front and back, woven of thick white wool and worn by men.

kapur [Tshangla] Supplementary-warp patterning; for example, a *kapur phatsa* is a bag (*phatsa*) so decorated. Bengali: 'cloth.' Assamese: certain kinds of cloth.

karjyang (dkar skyang) 'White and simple.' (1) Plainweave cloth. (2) Varieties of plainweave cotton formerly made in southeastern Bhutan and used as taxes-in-kind.

kashika ré (ka shi ka ras) 'Indian [Banaras?] cotton.' Varieties of fine muslin and other cloth formerly imported to Bhutan. Cf. *kasha*, 'Indian cotton,' and *kachi*, (1) coarse white Indian cotton for making prayer flags; (2) fine cotton from Banaras.

kechung (skyal chung, rkyal chung) 'Little neck.' A round, patchwork bag with a drawstring neck.

kera (sked rags) 'Waist cloth.' A man's or woman's belt. *Matrami keré*, 'belt worth one coin.' *Lungsem kera*: a belt with a yellow ground. Ku/Dzal: *kichin, atshing*. MS: *kichin, kera*. Tsh: *chudang*.

khab thinkhab (khab 'thin khab) A style of dress fastener resembling a long, straight pin with a round brooch at one end and a ring at the other.

khada (kha dar) Presentation scarf of cotton, silk, or synthetic fiber, imported from India and China (via Tibet). Tib: *khata* (kha btags).

khaden (kha gdan) (1) A floor mat or rug for sitting on. (2) A seat cover decorated with appliqué. Tib: *khaden* (kha stan, kha gdan).

khaja (kha 'ja') Stripes, such as the warp stripes at the upper and lower edges of a woman's dress. Bu: *chikhor*. See *thama bjang*.

khamar (kha dmar) 'Red mouth'; sometimes dkar dmar ('red and white'). (1) Ceremonial shoulder cloth with a white center panel flanked by red panels, worn by village headmen and some lay priests (*gomchen*). Sometimes *adha khamar* (q.v.) and *khamar kabné*; formerly also *tangka sari* (c. 1760). Bu: *botok*. Ku/Dzal: *khamar yabma*. Tsh: *khamar sari*. *Tshoré khamar* (tshos ras kha dmar, 'dyed cloth, red mouth') was a textile to cover the feet and knees (c. 1760).

khangaling shing [Tshangla] *Zizyphus sp.*, trees on which lac insects are reared and on which the wild silkworm moths that produce *tussar* silk are fed. Sometimes *jatsho shing*, 'lac tree.'

khé zong (khral zong) 'Tax cloth.' Also heard as *thré zong.* Tsh: *zong sari.*

kheng (khengs) A heavily forested region of south central Bhutan that now lies within Shemgang District. Also *khengri namsum* (khengs rigs rnam gsum), 'the three types [of people] of Kheng.'

khomang, khomachurpo (kho mang skyur po) Sour fruits of *Choenomoles lagenaria* and *C. wilsonii* used as mordants. See *chorgenshing* and *robtang.*

khoptang rigpa [Tshangla] 'Designs to throw away.' Supplementary-weft patterning on a warp-striped plainweave ground. Also called *tongkhang rigpa*, 'designs in empty space.' See *dromchu chema.*

khorlo ('khor lo) (1) Spinning wheel; also called *khorli.* Bu: *chyaphang.* Ku: *sondaling.* Tsh: *sondaring.* (2) A diamond pattern that dominates many textiles and individual pattern bands.

ki, kui [Kurtötkha] Nettle or other bast fiber; see *yüra* and *zocha.*

kichin [Merak Sakteng] Belt. Also called *kera* (Dzongkha).

kipetsang (skir pa'i rtshang) A thorn bush whose berries yield a red dye (western Bhutan).

kira (dkyis ras) 'Wrapping cloth.' A wrapped woman's dress. Tsh: *thara.*

kobtin [Merak Sakteng] Felted yak hair sitting cushion worn suspended from the back of the belt.

koma (rko ma, ko ma) Woman's dress fastener.

kuching (sku bching) 'Body tie' (honorific). A red, woven belt worn by monks.

kunzang khorlo (kun bzang 'khor lo) 'Wheel of excellent existence.' A checkerboard design with mystic significance painted on monastery walls. See *tenkheb.*

küp (skud pa) Yarn, thread. Bu: *nema* (cf. Tib: snal ma), *rotman.* Ku/Dzal: *pun, tütpang.* Tsh: *kudpa, tütpang.*

küp drigo (skud pa'i sgril sgod) Ball of yarn. Bu: *tü.* Ku: *tü-i, pong.* Tsh: *kudpa lomnang.*

küpsap (skud pa gsar pa) 'New yarn'. Tericotton, a recently available synthetic-blend yarn. Also called *jaküp*, 'Indian yarn.'

kushü, küshü, kushu (ku shud, skud shud) Loosely, 'brocade'; a technique and style of

patterning with supplementary wefts that originated in Kurtö (north central Bhutan). See *sapma* and *thrima.*

kushü bogdri [Kurtötkha/Dzalakha] A wrapping cloth decorated with *kushü* patterning.

kushung [Kurtötkha/Dzalakha] A tunic made of cotton or nettle. Also called *shingkha, kishung, kibu, kigu,* and *kigo* ('nettle garment'). Bu: *gotsum*, 'over the head'; *atsa; kushü atsa*, 'brocaded dress or petticoat'; *ganmo atsa*, 'old woman's dress.' Pemagatshel: *kujung, kuji, kushung; gongdong (jaimo) khamung*, 'spirits' clothing.' Mongar: *paga, nang go.* Radi: *ngang go.*

kushüthara (skud shud thag ras, ku shud 'thag ras) 'Brocaded dress.' A wrapped woman's dress with a patterned, white ground, originally from Kurtö in north central Bhutan.

ladri (bla bre) A rectangular canopy for a shrine room; when used over a lama's head. Also called *babtré*, 'what is spread above,' and *namyöl*, 'curtain of heaven' (Bell 1905).

lama, lam (bla ma) (1) Buddhist monk of a senior rank. (2) Polite term for monks who perform ceremonies.

lata (la kra) Dz/Tib: Shiny, machine-spun cotton yarn imported from India.

lham (lham) (1) Boots with leather soles and woolen uppers. *Tsholham* (tshogs lham) are ceremonial boots worn during formal meetings. (2) Shoes in general. MS: *bidar.*

lhamju (lham rgyu) Boot ties (garters). The honorific *lhamching* (lham bcing) is also heard.

lhemdru (lhan drub) Appliqué work.

lhop (lho pa) 'Southerner.' Indigenous communities in southwestern Bhutan that call themselves *lhokpu* and are also known by their Lhotsakha name, *doya.*

lochag (lo phyag, lo chags) Annual goodwill missions that carried gifts to Tibet.

lopön (slob dpon) 'Teacher.' Title for senior lamas and lay teachers.

lungserma, lungsem (lung ser ma) (1) Originally Tsh: 'yellow valley [cloth]'? A supplementary-warp-patterned fabric with red and green pattern bands on a yellow ground. (2) A woman's belt with a yellow field (*lungsem kera*).

lyönpo (blon po) Minister (of the government).

mabjang (ma byang) A set of three matching panels of cloth for a man's robe. If needed, a fourth, smaller panel is called *zurtsi.*

mapsham (dmar po gsham) 'Red background.' A woman's dress with a red field.

markin [Hindi] Varieties of Indian cotton fabric

formerly imported for lining commoners' robes.

mathra (dmar khra) 'Predominantly red pattern.' A twill woolen plaid fabric, predominantly maroon or red, that is closely associated with central Bhutan (*bumthang mathra*). There are four varieties of *mathra* whose names correspond to the sequencing of warp colors: *khempa, dorshongba, khrachikpa,* and *churichem.*

mensé mathra (sman rtse dmar khra) 'Mentsi-like yellow-and-red pattern.' A fabric with yellow supplementary-warp-pattern bands on a red ground. An alternative spelling (mon ser dmar khra) suggests an early indigenous origin.

mentsi, mensé (sman rtse) From Chinese *mianzi.* A yellow silk fabric with red-and-green floral patterning, of Chinese manufacture and imported via Tibet. Now also produced in India.

metok (me tog) 'Flower.' Design, pattern on cloth. Tsh: *rigpa.*

meyö (smad g.yogs) 'Lower covering.' (1) A tailored underskirt worn by monks. (2) Full overskirts worn with *go* by some laymen who perform regional dances at festivals.

mön, mon (mon) An early Tibetan name for regions to the south of Tibet that were (in contrast to Tibet) not Buddhist. Bhutanese scholars often use Bhutan's traditional names, such as the 'southern Mön land of medicinal herbs' (*lhomon menjong*, lho mon sman jong). Eastern Bhutan was once part of a region still known to scholars as *mönyul*, 'the land of Mön.'

möndré [Tshangla] 'Mön [understood as Bhutanese] dress.' A white, red, and black or blue cloth from eastern Bhutan, thought to be early and indigenous.

mönpa (mon pa) 'Person or people of Mön.' (1) An early Tibetan term for peoples living south of Tibet. (2) Today a name referring to several completely unrelated ethnic groups in the Himalayas, including communities in Arunachal Pradesh (India) as well as southern Bhutan.

möntha (mon 'thag) 'Mön [understood as Bhutanese] cloth.' A supplementary-warp-patterned fabric with prominent use of blue- or black-and-red pattern bands between colorful warp striping, and not ordinarily worn by men.

muga, munga [Anglo-Indian] A variety of wild silk from Assam, produced by *Antheraea assamaea*, which feeds on several native trees that tint the silk it extrudes shades from white to brown.

nambu (snam bu)Dz/Tib: Woolen cloth, especially fine woolens made in Tibet. *Nambu karthi* (snam bu dkar khrigs) was thin, plain white woolen cloth made in central Bhutan as a tax payment.

namdru küp (snam gru skud pa) 'Sky-ship [airplane] yarn.' A silk fiber imported as rope from India between the late 1930s and late 1940s and unraveled for weaving.

napsham (gnag po gsham) 'Black background.' A woman's dress with a black field.

nashab (nang shabs) Lining of a man's robe.

ngosham, onsham (sngo gsham) 'Blue background.' A woman's dress with a blue field. Also applied to a dress in which the center panel has a white field and the flanking panels have blue fields.

norbu (nor bu) Gem. A pearl or flaming gem, often seen in ritual art and in textiles in sets of three, representing the Buddha, his teachings, and the community of the faithful.

pakhi [Lepcha, Toktop] (1) Man's wrapped garment that crosses over the chest, formerly worn by various groups from eastern Nepal to Arunachal Pradesh. Lhokpu: *pokwi*; Sherdukpen (Arunachal Pradesh): *sapé*. (2) Cf. Mönkha: *pagi*, a similar woman's garment traditionally worn in Mönpa communities in southern Tongsa District.

paktsa [Merak Sakteng] A man's sleeveless vest made of deerskin or other hide.

pang [Tshangla] Bands of plainweave in the ground of a fabric.

pangkheb (spang khebs)'Lap cover.' A multi-purpose textile made in different varieties and qualities. *Chhuré pangkheb*: a raincloak used by lamas.

pangthag, pangtha (spang 'thag) Body-tension (backstrap) looms, excluding card looms. Tsh: *dangshing*. See fig. 1.10.

pangtsi (spang rtsing) A red-and-black plaid cloth whose pattern is said by Bhutanese to have come from Assam. Bhutanese like the similarity of this term to *pangtse*, which describes the patterns of fields and meadows.

pangtsi (spangs rtsi) *Symplocos paniculata*, whose leaves are used as a yellow dye. See *zim*.

pata (dpa' rtags) Sword.

pata losé (dpa' rtags blo tsel) An accessory textile worn hanging from the belt with a sword.

pazap (dpa' rtsal pa) Ceremonial militia.

pchana (chel nag) 'Black woolen cloth.' Several types of thick fabric from central Bhutan that are not necessarily black. For example, *pchana map* ('red black wool') is a shawl used by monks.

pentok [Tib: spen mdog] 'A kind of country chintz with figures of tamarisk, imported . . . from Assam or Bhutan' (Chandra Das 1905). A variety of *pöntshe*.

pesar (dpe gsar) 'New design.' (1) A fabric with small supplementary-weft designs on a striped plainweave ground. (2) Any unfamiliar, innovative fabric pattern.

peshasham (pad zhwa zhwam) 'Lotus hat.' (1) Embroidered hats with floral designs worn by the queens of Bhutan until the 1950s. (2) Less ornate hats formerly worn by village women in central Bhutan (*amtsogi peshasham*, 'women's lotus hats').

petha (dpe 'thag) A narrow, woven tie to bind a religious book within its wooden covers; also called *singtha* (sing 'thag).

peyab (dpa' g.yab) Eternal or lucky knot, one of the eight auspicious symbols of Buddhism that often appears in textiles. Tib: dpal gyi be'u. See *dramé*.

phang (phang) Drop spindle. Bu: *yokpa*. Ku: *yoga*. Tsh: *yokpa, yokpu*.

phariya [Lhotsakha] A woman's lower garment, consisting of a generous length of fabric wrapped around the lower body and arranged with pleats in front.

phechung (phad chung) 'Small bag,' often decorated with *kushü* patterning. Bu: *phetsé*. Ku/Dzal: *kushü phechung, phatsa*. Tsh: *phatsé, kapur phatsa* (with supplementary-warp patterning), *shepé phatsa* (with warp stripes).

phen (phan) A cloud-shaped textile with four ribbons hanging from it, considered to represent one type of 'banner of victory' (*gyetshen*). Two *phen* should hang in a shrine room or temple. Called *baden* when they are not part of a set.

phoching (pho bcing) 'Stomach wrap.' A yellow cummerbund worn by monks.

pishup [Merak Sakteng] Men's leather leggings.

pönchu (dpon chung, spen chung) 'Little piece for the official.' Thin, white cotton cloth ('worth five coins'), formerly made for tax payments.

pöndab (dpon 'dab, spen 'dab) 'Official's leaf.' White cotton cloth with green stripes, formerly tendered to the dzong and used for making lamp wicks.

pönlop (dpon slob) Governor of a district or region.

pönthag (dpon thag, spen thag) 'Official's weaving [cloth woven by the command of the chief local official].' White or colored wild silk or cotton cloth formerly woven as taxes-in-kind. Also *pönthag tshoré* (dpon thag tshos ras), 'dyed tax cloth'; and *pönthag buré* (dpon thag 'bu ras), 'wild silk tax cloth' (c. 1760).

pöntshe (dpon tshad [1700s], spen mtshed), 'Official's measure.' White cotton cloth worth twenty coins, formerly used for lining blankets, covering walls, making lamp wicks, and paying the lowest laborers at a dzong (*logo pöntshe*, 'annual clothes, official's measure').

pün (spun) Weft. Ku/Tsh: *phun*.

rachu, rechu (rags chung) 'Small cloth or sash.' A woman's ceremonial shoulder cloth; also called *kabné*. Cf. Tib: ske rags chung ma. Bu: *botok*. Ku/Dzal: *yabma, rechu*. Tsh: *sari*.

ram (ram, rams) (1) Indigo, or other blue dye. (2) Shrubs native to Bhutan (*Strobilanthes flaccidifolius* and *S. sp.*) whose leaves contain indigotin and are used as a blue dye. Tib: rams. Bu: *tsanja*. Ku/Dzal: *tsanja, ja*. Tsh: *yangshaba*. Kheng: *rujag*.

ré (ras) (1) Cotton cloth. (2) Cloth (in compound terms).

rep, repa (ral pa) Fringe. Bu: *ma*. Ku/Dzal: *romba, repa*. Tsh: *prema*.

reth [Kurtötkha/Dzalakha] See *thra*.

risoktsa [Tshangla] 'Water rubbing.' A corn cob used to moisten the warp on a loom and to apply sizing (corn porridge).

robtang [Tshangla] *Rhus simialata Murr.*, a tree whose sour fruits are used as a mordant. See *chorgenshing* and *khomang*.

rumnang [Tshangla] An archaic braided silver headband worn in eastern and north central Bhutan. Ku/Dzal: *nyelempa, welempa, moipi*.

samkhongma [Tshangla] A plainweave fabric with narrow red-and-blue warp stripes on a white field. Similar to *möndré*.

sapma [Kurtötkha] A technique of *kushü* patterning in which pattern wefts are interworked with warps so that they lie on the surface of the ground weave.

sengge (seng ge) 'Lion.' A snow lion seen in appliqué textiles; the national emblem of Tibet.

seshu (ser shu) 'Gold yarn.' Cultivated, reeled silk yarn.

sethra (ser khra) 'Predominantly gold pattern.' Plaid cloth woven of wild silk or wool, in which orange or rust predominates. *Sethra dokhana* has black in it; *dalapgi sethra* does not.

shabdrung (zhabs drung) From Tib: *shab* (zhabs), honorific for 'foot,' and connoting respect. (1) The title of the religious leader and statesman Ngawang Namgyel, who unified Bhutan in the early seventeenth century. (2) The short name for the most important of Shabdrung Ngawang Namgyel's three reincarnations, who was the religious ruler of Bhutan (Anglo-Indian: *dharma raja*) until the death of the last officially recognized incumbent in 1931.

shabthrawo (shar khra bo) 'Eastern multicolored pattern.' A red (or pink), yellow, and white plaid fabric formerly made in Bhutan for domestic use and export to Tibet. See *sethra*.

shachop (shar phyogs pa) 'Easterner.' General term for the inhabitants of eastern Bhutan, whose language, Tshangla, is often called *shachobikha*, 'language of the east.'

shagongma shing [Tshangla] Mulberry, a shrub whose leaves are the food for *Bombyx* silkworms.

sham (zham) (1) Hat, including that worn by a bride or groom. (2) MS *shamu*: Felted yak hair hat worn by men and women. Also called *mukhuling*.

shamtha, shamtha leuma (bsham thabs le'u ma) One of three essential garments for a monk, the tubular lower garment. Tib: *chögö thangö* (chos gos thang gos). Honorific: *kusham* (sku bsham).

shardang thara [Tshangla] 'Striped woman's dress.' (1) A dress with multicolored warp stripes. (2) Any striped dress.

sharé (shar ras) 'Eastern cloth' (c. 1760).

shema [Tibetan] A very fine woolen cloth made in Tibet.

shingkha [Bumthangkha, Kurtötkha, Tshangla] (1) A sleeveless shift or tunic ('petticoat'). (2) An archaic, patterned tunic made of cotton or nettle (*delemé shingkha*, 'olden time dress'). (3) An archaic tunic made of wool (Bu: *kandomé atsa*, 'angel's dress'), called *ngaushingkha* if the fabric is blue and *leushingkha* if the fabric is red. Also called *pcha go, pcha atsa* (*pcha* referring to the ritual in which the garment is now worn). Pemagatshel: *shungkha, nongnongma*. (4) MS: A red-and-white warp-striped wild silk tunic worn by women in Merak Sakteng, in Tashiyangtse District, and in nearby Arunachal Pradesh. Also called *dongalhema* (Sakteng).

shinglo (shing lo) 'Leaf of a tree.' (1) A tree-of-life design executed in supplementary-weft yarns [e.g., fig. 3.3]. (2) Secondary designation for a textile with these motifs, as, for example, *aikapur shinglo*.

shogu thagshing (shog bu 'thag shing) 'Paper loom.' Card loom, whose cards were formerly made of sturdy local paper. Tib: *kothag*, 'leather loom' (because tablets were formerly made of leather [*kowa*]). Tsh: *shigu thagshing*.

shubda (shub da) Wheel for winding yarn off spindle or into balls or skeins. Also called *küpshubnye*. Bu: *shubda, shidang*. Ku: *shidang*. Tsh: *yumnang*.

shungkhé (zhung khe) *Symplocos racemosa*, whose leaves are used as a yellow dye and a mordant in Bhutan and nearby regions of Sikkim, Nepal, and Tibet. Cf. Tib: shu mkhan. See *pangtsi* and *zim*.

silik [English, Hindi] Imported, synthetic yarns, such as silk-like acrylic.

sintha lu nambar (sin thag lug nam bar) 'Sheep brand [?].' A heavy Indian cotton fabric formerly imported for making men's robes.

sogshing (srog shing) 'Life wood.' (1) The pole for a prayer flag. (2) The wooden mold used for making offerings of butter or dough. (3) Dz/Tib: The closing rod of a backstrap or vertical frame loom.

söra (gsol ras) 'Cloth [honorific?].' Gift (often of cloth) from a superior to an inferior.

sunkü (srung skud) Protective neck cord presented by a lama.

tagoshing (star go shing) Walnut tree (*Juglans regia*), whose fruit husks and bark are used in dyeing black and brown. Tsh: *khéshing*.

tahung (ta hung) Dz/Tib: A Chinese red silk cloth. From Chinese *dahung*.

tarichem (stag ris can ma) 'With tiger stripes.' A woolen fabric with broad bands of maroon, blue, brown, and black made in central Bhutan. Cf. Tib: stag ras, 'a chintz with stripes resembling those of a tiger' (Chandra Das 1905).

tenga kema ([Merak Sakteng] A panel of woolen cloth worn by women around the hips; also called *mé kema* or *meyö* (q.v.).

tenkheb (rten khebs) 'Cover for religious offerings.' (1) A patchwork textile usually patterned with a checkerboard design and placed upon the middle and upper altars of a shrine (*chöthri* and *torthri*). (2) A checkerboard design in any textile. In *kushüthara*, the design is called *phup* [e.g., fig. 3.7]. See *kunzang khorlo*.

thag (thag) Warp. Bu: *thag*. Ku: *tha, kan*. Tsh: *renang*.

thag ('thags) (1) Cloth or fabric. Bu: *thathab*, *nambu* (wool). Ku: *tha*. Tsh: *nam chhuma*. (2) Rope or cord (thag, thag pa).

thagcha, thagché ('thags cha, 'thag cha) 'Loom things.' Parts of a loom and other tools for weaving. Tsh: *khamung namé chala*.

thagshing ('thags shing) Loom.

thagthami ('thags 'thag mi) Weaver. Also shortened to *tham*.

tham, thama ('thag ma, thagm) Sword, a stick to beat the weft on a body-tension (backstrap) loom.

thama bjang (mtha' ma byang) The upper and lower panels of a woman's dress, which usually have warp stripes at one edge, *thama* refering to 'the end, outermost side, border, or hem of a dress.' Also called *ja* ('rainbow'; Bu), *khaja* ('stripes') or *khabjang* (especially Ku), and *shabjang* (Tsh). See *bubjang* and *barbjang*.

thanggo (thang sgo) 'Door of the *thangka*.' A square inset of contrasting cloth in the cloth mount of a *thangka*, at bottom center.

thangka (thang ka) A religious image on a scroll that may be painted, embroidered, appliquéd, or a combination of embroidery and appliqué. Also called by the honorific terms *göku* ('silk body, image') and *kuthang*.

thara, tharé, thari ('thag ras) 'Woven cotton.' (1) Dz: A wrapped woman's dress made of plainweave cotton patterned with stripes. (2) Tsh: Any wrapped woman's dress (the equivalent of the Dzongkha word *kira*). See *shardang thara*. (3) any woven cloth (c. 1760). *Chikpa tharé* (a variation of *mathra*) was a kind of woman's dress made in north central Bhutan for tax payments.

thebthem (kreb krem) Simple footgear made from pieces of leather tied to the feet with thongs.

thekhu (thal khu) Water dripped through hardwood ashes and used in dyeing. Ku/Dzal: *bja, bla, kwe*. Tsh: *khari, thulu*.

them (ther ma) (1) A fine woolen cloth made in Tibet. Tib: *therma*. (2) Fine, machine-spun woolen yarn, which now comes from Kalimpong and Amritsar in India.

themba [Merak Sakteng] Maroon woolen woman's shawl. Also *hlemba*.

thigthra (thig khra) See *hothra jalo*.

thinkhab ('thin khab) 'Holding needle.' The long, sharp pins with which Bhutanese women used to fasten their dresses. Tsh: *turpang*.

thongdröl (mthong sgrol) 'Liberation at sight.' A monumental appliqué *thangka*, displayed outdoors at annual religious festivals.

thra (khra) A very fine warp stripe in the ground cloth that a weaver uses to help position discontinuous supplementary-weft patterns in the textile. Bu: *khra*. Ku/Dzal: *reth*. Tsh: *rit*. Kheng: *ri*.

thrikheb (khri kheb) 'Throne cover.' A textile made of appliqué or patchwork and used to cover the seat of an important person.

thrikhu (khrid khug) A cylindrical bag with a drawstring neck, made of panels of Bhutanese and imported cloth, with an external wooden slat attached to help support it when slung over a shoulder.

thrima ('khyil ma) 'To wind, coil around.' A technique of *kushü* patterning in which pattern wefts are interworked with each other and warp yarns so the designs they form appear to be raised above the surface of the ground, sometimes resembling a chain stitch or cross-stitch. Tsh: *taksing* ('starting place') *thrima* (or *khodang*) is patterning at the lower edge of a *kushung*.

thrithag [Tib: khri 'thag] Horizontal frame loom, introduced from Tibet. See fig. 8.12.

thruk [Tibetan] Thick Tibetan woolen cloth imported and used for men's robes. Tib: *purug* (spu phrug), *pulo*.

tögo (stod bgo, stog gos) 'Upper garment.' (1) A woman's jacket. (2) A man's shirt worn under the robe. (3) Colloquial: An inner cotton vest worn by monks; also called *meshab* or *ngöshab*. (4) Any upper garment or jacket. Bu/Tsh: *töthung, tethung*. See *töthung*.

tora (lto ras) 'Food [cooked rice] cloth.' A small square cloth carried by Bhutanese for use as a plate.

torkheb (gtor khebs) '*Torma* [butter offering] covering.' A textile that covers the altar on which butter offerings are placed (*torthri*).

töthung (stod thung) (1) MS: jacket worn by women. If the jacket is red and patterned with animals, it is also called *zukthya töthung* or *nornang töthung*. (2) Tib: the inner cotton vest worn by monks. See *tögo*.

tötsi (stod rtsi) A sleeveless vest of maroon woolen cloth worn by monks. Tib: *tönga* (stod dga). See also *tögo*.

tranka (kran ka) 'Coin.' A round design that appears in textiles [e.g., fig. 3.3]. A motif resembling a Chinese coin is a *hortang* ('Mongolian coin'); and an elongated Chinese character for 'long life' is a *tranka tshering* ('long-life coin').

tsamkhu (rtsam khug) 'Flour container.' A cylindrical bag with a drawstring neck, made of panels of Bhutanese and imported fabric joined together.

tsangthra (gtsang khra) 'Pattern from Tsang [Tibet].' (1) Formerly: A red plaid (*mathra*) cloth made on a horizontal frame loom in Tibet for export to Bhutan. (2) Now: Any fabric woven from *them (therma)*, fine yarn from Tibet or now from Kalimpong.

tshemdru (tshem drub) Sewing, stitchery.

tshempön (tshem dpon) 'Sewing chief.' Master tailor. A *tshempa* is an ordinary tailor and a *tshemdru thumi* is one skilled in embroidering ritual textiles.

tshö (tshos) Madder (*Rubia manjitha* and *R. wallichiana*). Bu/Ku: *tsöt, tsut*. Tsh: *lanyi, lanyinang*.

tshochabmi (tshos rkyab mi) Women who dyed yarns at weaving workshops in noble households. Also *tshokhemi*.

tshokheb (tshogs khebs) 'Covering for a multitude [of offerings].' A textile to cover the low altar at the front of a shrine (*tshogthri*).

tshongtham (tshong 'thag ma) 'Commercial weaving.' Cloth woven for other than one's own use and not for the nobility; contrasted with 'heart weaving' (*hingtham*).

tshosar (tshos gsar) 'New color.' Commercial, synthetic dyes.

tsi sokpa [Tshangla] Corn porridge, used as sizing for wild silk warp yarns.

tsugtru (btsugs phrug) Dz/Tib: A woolen blanket with long, shaggy pile, once from Tibet but now also made in Bhutan by Tibetans and Bhutanese.

tukuli [Hindi] Machine-spun cotton yarn from India. *Japan tukuli* is mercerized yarn from India. Pemagatshel: *tangting*.

tussar, tussah [Hindi] The costliest variety of wild silk from Assam, produced by *Antherea mylitta*, which feeds on *Ziziphus sp.* (Tsh: *khangaling shing*).

usha, usham (dbu zhwa) Honorific term for the embroidered hats worn in lieu of a crown by the kings of Bhutan. See also *peshasham*.

walakthang [Sakteng] An ornamental string of silver coins worn suspended from a woman's belt. Merak: *bhari thagpa hiki*.

wonju ('og 'jug, 'on rju) A woman's blouse. Tib: *wangchuk*. Also called *gyenja* (Tib: khyen 'jar, kheng 'jar).

yanggam (g.yang sgam) 'Box of prosperity' in which tokens of household wealth, including textiles, are kept.

yathra (ya khra) 'Pattern from the upper regions.' A woolen cloth with supplementary-weft-patterning from Bumthang in central Bhutan.

yerbo [Merak] A decorative bunch of cowrie shells worn suspended from a woman's belt. Sakteng: *dronba*.

yongka (yongs ka) Turmeric (*Curcuma sp.*), a yellow dye. Tsh: *jung*. Lho: *haldi*.

yüra, yüré (yul ras) 'Country cloth.' Cloth made from nettle or other bast fiber. Sometimes *yöphé*. See *ki* and *zocha*.

yurung, yungdrung (g.yung drung) Swastika; an auspicious Buddhist symbol connoting continuity or eternity.

yütham (yul 'thag ma) 'Country [-woven], soft-textured [cloth].' A wild silk or cotton cloth with multicolored warp stripes. *Yütham jadrima* has five primary colors, while *yütham marchang* is predominantly red, green, and blue.

zen (gzan) Monk's maroon shawl or shoulder cloth; also known as *kabné* or *jakam* (when dyed with lac, *jatsho*). The garment can be made from wool (*therzen*), wild silk (*bura kabzen*), or cotton (*rezen*).

zhé (gzhas) 'Song.' Traditional secular dances, reenacting stories from various parts of Bhutan and performed by laymen at annual festivals.

zi (gzi) A highly prized black agate with white patterning used in jewelry. A *zitha* is a necklace featuring one or more of these stones.

zim (zim) Species of *Symplocos* trees whose leaves are used as a yellow dye and a mordant. Also called *zimshing, domzim, serzim*. Tsh: *shingshaba*. Lho: *kharane*. Very similar to and often confused with *shungkhé*.

zocha (zwa cha) 'Nettle thing.' (1) Nettle (*Girardinia palmata*) or other bast fiber, such as that from *Cannabis sativa*. (2) Cloth made from nettle or other bast fiber. Ku/Dzal: *ki, kui, kuli, kuela paku, zowa*. Tsh: *bjazu, zangru*. Mönkha: *kurel*. See *yüra*.

zong (zong) Woven cloth; goods. Also *zongcha*, 'woven things.'

zongshé (zong shes) 'Absence cloth.' A fine formerly paid in cloth when one was not able to perform the annual labor required of each household by the state.

223

Catalog of Exhibition Objects

Regional attributions are based on pattern, style, and fibers. Because the documented history of Bhutanese textiles is minimal, and no fiber or dye analyses have as yet been carried out, most dates are approximate.

Measurements reflect first the warp and then the weft dimension, or other dimensions as noted. Fringe is plied unless otherwise indicated.

Bhutanese weavers combine different yarns and dyes freely, so many textiles exhibit tremendous variety in their fibers and colors. Pending fiber and dye analyses, the material identifications are visual. When warps are made of two or more materials, the predominant fiber is mentioned first. Wefts are usually of the predominant warp fiber and are not specifically mentioned. Fibers are typically dyed before weaving (the exception is Assamese wild silk cloth, which may be dyed, with lac for example, to make a man's or monk's shoulder cloth). Imported cotton is generally from India, while silk yarns come from China, India, Hong Kong, or Japan.

Discontinuous supplementary-weft-patterning techniques include what Emery 1980 classifies as single-faced and two-faced patterning, while continuous supplementary wefts form double-faced and two-faced patterning.

*An asterisk preceding an entry indicates an object is illustrated but not exhibited.

Introduction

Fig. I.1
Woman's dress (kira; kushüthara)
Central Bhutan, early twentieth century. 256 cm (including 1.5-cm fringe at each end) x 152 cm. Lent by Lisina and Frank Hoch. Warp-faced plainweave ground, with warps of undyed cotton and colored wild silk; several kinds of silk used for discontinuous supplementary-weft patterning and for continuous supplementary-weft patterning at the fringed ends; one row of weft twining at each end. Natural and synthetic dyes. Machine stitched.
Presented by King Jigme Dorji Wangchuck and Queen (Mother) Ashi Kesang in 1955. The dress was probably made in a palace workshop in Bumthang.

Fig. I.5
Woman's belt (kera) (detail)
Bhutan, before 1855. 139.5 cm (including 28-cm fringe at each end) x 21.5 cm. Lent by the Board of Trustees of the Victoria and Albert Museum (05575 [IS]). Handspun cotton, plainweave ground (possibly mixed with nettle or wool); continuous supplementary-weft patterning in wool yarns dyed blue with native indigo and red with lac.
Presented to Sir Charles Bell by the king of Bhutan in 1910.

Chapter One

Fig. 1.3
Raincloak (charkab)
Bumthang, mid-twentieth century. 107 x 109 cm. Lent by Barbara Adams. Wool; twill ground with discontinuous supplementary-weft patterning. Natural and synthetic dyes. Handstitched. Remnants of red cotton cloth facing at upper and lower edges.

Chapter Two

Fig. 2.2
Panel for a woman's jacket (töthung) (detail)
Merak Sakteng, eastern Bhutan, c. 1980. 235 x 57 cm (including 3.4-cm fringe at lower edge). Phillips Collection, Peabody Essex Museum (E70019). Wild silk warp-faced plainweave ground (yarns dyed with lac); commercial Indian cotton used in continuous and discontinuous supplementary-weft patterning.

Fig. 2.7
Woman's dress (kira; thara) (detail)
Southeastern Bhutan, 1930s. 264 cm (including 18-cm unfinished fringe at each end) x 128.5 cm. Lent by Mr. Lobsang Lhalungpa and Ms. Gisela Minke. Handspun (undyed) Bhutanese cotton and machine-spun (colored) Indian cotton; warp-faced plainweave ground with one row of weft twining at each end. Handstitched.
Presented to Mr. Lhalungpa's father, Kungo Chozur Gyaltshen Tharchin of Lhalung Zimkhang, Lhasa (Tibet), by Dasho Gyurme Dorji, brother of the second king of Bhutan, in the 1930s.

Fig. 2.8
***Panel from a woman's apron** (dongkheb)
Central Bhutan or Tibet, third quarter of the twentieth century. 81.5 x 67 cm. Phillips Collection, Peabody Essex Museum (E73337). Wool; twill. Natural and synthetic dyes. Handstitched.

Multipurpose covering (yangtsep charkab)
Tashiyangtse District, third quarter of the twentieth century. 320 cm (including 11-cm fringe at each end) x 125.5 cm. Phillips Collection, Peabody Essex Museum (E77738). Wool; warp-faced plainweave ground with three rows of weft twining at each fringed end.

***Multipurpose textile** (charaki charkab)
Dhur, Bumthang, c. 1980. Diana K. Myers. Yak hair, plainweave; stitched with yak hair thread; tufts of yak tail.

Fig. 2.11
***Madder twigs** (E200205)
***Lac dye** (E200202)

*Bhutanese paper made from the *Daphne* shrub. Phillips Collection, Peabody Essex Museum

Container used as a measure
Shemgang District, mid-twentieth century. H: 11 cm; circ: 56 cm. Phillips Collection, Peabody Essex Museum (E200254). Bamboo and wood.

Basket with lid
South central Bhutan, twentieth century. H: 13.5 cm; circ: 75.5 cm. Phillips Collection, Peabody Essex Museum (E74544). Bamboo.

Water container covered with basketry
Bhutan, twentieth century. H: 33.5 cm; circ: 31 cm. Phillips Collection, Peabody Essex Museum (E70699). Wood; bamboo; metal trim; leather strap.

Brick of tea with lucky knot imprint
Tibet, twentieth century. 9.5 x 12 x 2 cm. Phillips Collection, Peabody Essex Museum (E75274).

Yak tail
Northern Bhutan, 1993
L: 71 cm. Phillips Collection, Peabody Essex Museum (E200443). Hair; wooden handle.

Lengths of wild silk (*endi*) cloth
Assam (India), twentieth century; received as gifts in Bhutan, 1978-90. Lisina and Frank Hoch.

Monk's wrap or blanket
Sephu, Tongsa District, 1993. 119 x 235 cm. Lent by Diana K. Myers. Wool; twill ground, dyed with madder. Small diamond-shaped cotton cloth appliqué. Handstitched.

Fig. 2.12
Panel for a skirt (detail)
Kachin people, Burma, early twentieth century. 22 x 164 cm. Lent by the Textile Museum (1986.10.2), Gift of Elva Hendershot. Cotton weft-faced plainweave ground. End panels with continuous supplementary-weft patterning and center field with discontinuous supplementary-weft patterning in wool.

Fig. 2.14
Blanket (detail)
Phu Tai people, Kalasin Province, Thailand, mid-1930s (?). Patricia C. Naenna, Chiang Mai (Photograph by Mattiebelle Gittinger). Silk and cotton ground warps, silk supplementary warp, cotton weft; supplementary-warp patterning.

Fig. 2.15
Woman's dress (*kira, mensé mathra*) (detail of first entry in fig. 7.14)

Fig. 2.16
Head scarf (detail)
Northeastern Laos, twentieth century. 195 cm (including 11-cm fringe at each end) x 48-51 cm. Lent by Diana K. Myers. Silk; plainweave ground with continuous supplementary-weft patterning.

Fig. 2.17
Shoulder cloth (*phaa biang*) (detail)
Sam Neua people, northern Laos, c. 1870. 185 x 42 cm. Lent by the Museum of International Folk Art (1987.372-2). Silk; warp ikat and supplementary-weft patterning; braided and knotted fringe.

Fig. 2.18
Tunic (detail)
Chin [Sandowan] people, Burma, collected c. 1890. 105 x 98 cm. Lent by the Museum of International Folk Art (FA 77.43.12). Cotton with continuous and discontinuous supplementary-weft patterning.

Fig. 2.19
Sash (detail)
Laos, early twentieth century. 139 x 50 cm. Lent by the Museum for Textiles (T86.336). Handspun cotton plainweave ground with silk supplementary-weft patterning.

Fig. 2.20
Multipurpose ceremonial cloth (*chagsi pangkheb*) (detail)
Central or eastern Bhutan, early twentieth century. 322 cm (including 16-cm fringe) x 86.5 cm. Lent by Barbara Adams . Warps of red (lac-dyed) wild silk, and undyed white, black, and blue (indigo-dyed) handspun cotton. Warp-faced plainweave ground; wild silk and cotton discontinuous and continuous supplementary-weft and supplementary-warp patterning. One row of weft twining at each end. Natural dyes. Handstitched.

EXHIBITED BUT NOT ILLUSTRATED:

Woman's dress (*shingkha*)
Sakteng, c. 1990. 126 cm (including 1.5-cm fringe at lower edge) x 79 cm. Phillips Collection, Peabody Essex Museum (E200219). Wild silk plainweave; yarns natural white or dyed with lac and indigo. One row of weft twining at lower edge in commercial wool yarn. Handstitched.

Woman's belt (*kichin, kera*)
Sakteng, c. 1990. 260 cm (including 29-cm fringe at each end) x 32 cm. Phillips Collection, Peabody Essex Museum (E200221). Wild silk plainweave; yarns dyed with lac. One row of weft twining at each end in commercial cotton yarn.

Woman's jacket (*töthung*)
Sakteng, c. 1990. 63 cm (including 3-cm fringe at lower edge) x 143 cm (armspan). Phillips Collection, Peabody Essex Museum (E200220). Wild silk plainweave; yarns dyed with lac. Imported cotton used for continuous supplementary-weft patterning, imported acrylic for discontinuous supplementary-weft patterning. Green wool twill piping (synthetic dye).

Woman's hip blanket (*tenga kema*).
Sakteng, c. 1980s. 71 x 62 cm. Phillips Collection, Peabody Essex Museum (E200222). Wool twill with hem handstitched in wool yarn.

Woman's shawl (*themba*)
Sakteng, c. 1980s. 64 x 59 cm. Phillips Collection, Peabody Essex Museum (E200223). Wool twill; lac dye. Imported wool and acrylic ornaments. Leather straps attached with imported cotton yarn.

Woman's boots (*bidar*)
Merak, c. 1993. H: 31 cm; w: 9.5 cm. Phillips Collection, Peabody Essex Museum (E200437 A-B) Woolen twill; embroidery in wool yarn; leather soles.

Woman's hat (*shamu, mukhuling*)
Sakteng, c. 1990. H: 8 cm; diam: 21 cm. Phillips Collection, Peabody Essex Museum (E200218). Felted yak hair.

Woman's sitting cushion (*kobtin*)
Merak, c. 1993. Diam: 24.5 cm; tie: 53 cm long. Phillips Collection, Peabody Essex Museum (E200441). Felted yak hair embroidered with pink and white yarns.
Part of a set of clothing commissioned in 1992 from the household of Chukpo San Tsewang, a leading citizen of Merak who served as headman of the village in the early 1970s. Probably made by one of his two wives, Tsering Chhonzom or Phurpa, who are sisters.

Hip ornament with needle case (*yerbo*)
Sakteng, 1980s. L: 47 cm. Phillips Collection, Peabody Essex Museum (E200224). Needle case: horn. Leather tassels; cowrie shells.

Chain of coins for hanging pocketknife (*walakthang*)
Sakteng, 1980s. L: 53 cm. Phillips Collection, Peabody Essex Museum (E200225).

Man's upper garment (*chuba*)
Sakteng, c. 1980s. 88 cm (collar to hem) x 150 cm (armspan). Phillips Collection, Peabody Essex Museum (E200210). Wool twill; lac dye. Green (synthetic dye) wool twill piping. Local repairs. Handstitched in wool yarn.

Man's belt (*kichin, kera*)
Sakteng, c. 1980s. 320 x 10 cm. Phillips Collection, Peabody Essex Museum (E200211). Twined yak hair.

Man's short pants (*kanggo*)
Sakteng, c. 1990. 61 x 66 cm. Phillips Collection, Peabody Essex Museum (E200212). Wool; twill, handstitched. Three rows of decorative stitching in commercial cotton thread. Leather ties.

Man's leggings (*pishub*)
Sakteng, c. 1990. L: 65 cm; w: 22 cm. Phillips

Collection, Peabody Essex Museum (E200213). Leather.

Man's vest (*paktsa*)
Merak, c. 1993. 76 x 85 cm. Phillips Collection, Peabody Essex Museum (E200433). Mountain goat skin.
Part of a set of clothing commissioned in 1992 from the household of Chukpo San Tsewang.

Man's boots (*bidar*)
Merak, c. 1993. H; 34 cm; l: 24 cm; w: 11 cm. Phillips Collection, Peabody Essex Museum (E200217 A-B).
Part of a set of clothing commissioned in 1992 from the household of Chukpo San Tsewang.

Man's hat (*shamu, mukhuling*)
Merak, c. 1993. Diam: 21 cm. Phillips Collection, Peabody Essex Museum (E200438). Felted yak hair.
Part of a set of clothing commissioned in 1992 from the household of Chukpo San Tsewang.

Woman's dress (*kira; hothra jalo*)
Bhutan, first half of the twentieth century. 142 x 252 cm. Phillips Collection, Peabody Essex Museum (E77737). Tibetan wool twill with tie-dyed crosses; natural and synthetic dyes. Pink cotton cloth facing. Handstitched.

Blanket (*charkab*)
North central Bhutan, c. 1970s. 146 x 91 cm. Phillips Collection, Peabody Essex Museum (E72825). Yak hair; warp-faced plainweave with yak tail tufts at corners; handstitched with yak hair thread.

Skirt
Tai Neua people, Laos, mid- to late nineteenth century. 132 x 63 cm. Lent by the Museum for Textiles (T86.334). Plainweave ground of handspun silk warps and cotton wefts; silk supplementary-weft patterning; weft ikat.

Banner (*tung*)
Shan people, Burma, c. 1890. 122 x 49 cm, plus fringe. Lent by the Museum of International Folk Art (FA.77.43.28). Cotton ground with supplementary-weft patterning.

Chapter Three

Fig. 3.1
***Striped cloth panel** (*samkhongma* pattern)
Pemagatshel District, c. 1985. 294 x 54 cm. Phillips Collection, Peabody Essex Museum (E200264). Handspun cotton, warp-faced plainweave; natural dyes.

***Striped cloth panel** (*adha mathra* pattern)
Kheng Nangla, Shemgang District, c. 1980. 266 x 55.5 cm. Phillips Collection, Peabody Essex Museum (E200260). Wild silk, plainweave; natu-

ral dyes.

***Two loom lengths of cloth** (type of *mathra* pattern)
Jakar, Bumthang District, 1985. A: 10.56 m x 25 cm; B: 10.70 m x 25 cm. Phillips Collection, Peabody Essex Museum (E200266 A, B). Wool; twill, natural dyes.
Commissioned by Am Thinley, wife of the then-deputy governor.

Four cloth panels (*mensé mathra*), for a man's robe (detail shown in fig. 3.3)
Thimphu, c. 1989. Panels A-C: 300 (including 1-to-6-cm fringe at each end) x 48-50 cm; Panel D: 219 x 25.5 cm. Phillips Collection, Peabody Essex Museum (E200380 A-D). Cultivated silk (from Hong Kong); warp-faced plainweave ground with supplementary-warp and discontinuous supplementary-weft patterning. Synthetic dyes. Commissioned by Am Rinji Om Dorje for her husband.

***Panel of yellow silk** (*mentsi*)
India, contemporary. Lisina and Frank Hoch. Imported silk plainweave fabric; stamped with patterns. Synthetic dyes.

***Presentation scarf** (*khada*)
Probably Surat (India), contemporary. 319 x 62 cm. Phillips Collection, Peabody Essex Museum (E200409 E). Imported silk fabric, with prayers, lucky knots, and wheels of law woven into the ground.

Fig. 3.3
Panel of cloth (*mensé mathra*), **for a man's robe** (detail of fig. 3.1)
Phillips Collection, Peabody Essex Museum (E200380)

Fig. 3.5
Multipurpose ceremonial textile (*chagsi pangkheb*)
Central Bhutan, c. 1900. 264 x 98 cm. Lent by the Board of Trustees of the Victoria and Albert Museum (IM 20-1933). Cotton warp-faced plainweave ground; continuous and discontinuous supplementary-weft patterning in wild silk dyed with lac and native indigo, and supplementary-warp patterning in cotton dyed with native indigo.
Presented to Sir Charles Bell by the king of Bhutan in 1910.

Fig. 3.6
Two panels of cloth for making a *pangkheb*
Bhutan, 1950s
Panel A: 284 cm (including 22-cm unplied fringe at each end) x 52.5 cm. Panel B: 299 cm (including 20-cm unplied fringe at one end and 24-cm at the other) x 51 cm. Lent by Diana K. Myers. Panel A: handspun cotton, warp-faced plainweave ground with discontinuous supplementary-weft patterning and supplementary-warp patterning;

one row of weft twining at each end. Panel B: handspun cotton, warp-faced plainweave ground with discontinuous and continuous supplementary-weft patterning. Undyed ground; pattern yarns tinted with synthetic dyes.

Fig. 3.7
Woman's dress (*kira; ngosham*)
Bhutan, c. 1974. 242 x 132.5 cm (including 2-cm fringe at each end); warp length differs in the three panels (235 cm, 236 cm, and 242 cm). Lent by Mr. Lobsang Lhalungpa and Ms. Gisela Minke. Several kinds of imported cotton; warp-faced plainweave ground with discontinuous and continuous supplementary-weft patterning; one row of weft twining at each end. Machine stitched.

Chapter Four

Fig. 4.2
Woman's dress (*kira; ngosham*)
Bumthang, 1920s. 260 cm (including 3-cm fringe at each end) x 145 cm. Lent by Her Royal Highness Ashi Choeki Wangchuck. Blue cotton and imported, colored silk warps; warp-faced plainweave ground with several kinds of silk and metallic yarns used for supplementary-weft patterning (*sapma* and *thrima*). One row of weft twining at each end. Natural and synthetic dyes. Machine stitched.

Fig. 4.3
***Woman's dress** (*kira*)
Khaling, c. 1985-86. Patrizia Franceschinis. Wild silk; warp-faced plainweave ground with supplementary-warp patterning.

Woman's dress (*kira*)
Khaling, 1992. 228 cm (including 1.5-cm fringe at each end) x 150.5 cm. Lent by Her Majesty Queen Ashi Sangay Choden Wangchuck. Warp-faced plainweave ground of imported cotton yarn; discontinuous supplementary-weft patterning in imported wild silk.

***Woman's dress** (*kira*)
Khaling, 1985. Patrizia Franceschinis. Wild silk; warp-faced plainweave ground with discontinuous supplementary-weft patterning.

Fig. 4.4
***Woman's dress** (*kira*)
1993. 292 x 224 cm. Phillips Collection, Peabody Essex Museum (E200435). Indian machine-woven cotton fabric.

***Woman's dress** (*kira; möntha*)
Thimphu, 1993. Diana K. Myers. Indian cotton (*lata*); warp-faced plainweave with supplementary-warp patterning.

EXHIBITED BUT NOT ILLUSTRATED:

Woman's dress (kira; aikapur jadrima)
Bhutan, before 1960. 264 x 141.5 cm (including 2.5-cm fringe at each end). Lent by Mr. Lobsang Lhalungpa and Ms. Gisela Minke. Several kinds of imported commercially-dyed cotton; warp-faced plainweave ground with supplementary-warp patterning; three rows of cotton weft twining at each end. Machine stitched.

Woman's dress (kira)
Khaling, c. 1989. 242 cm (including 1-cm fringe) x 160 cm. Lent by Patrizia Franceschinis. Imported cotton yarns; warp-faced plainweave ground with supplementary-warp patterning. One row of weft twining at each end. Synthetic dyes.

Man's robe (go), aikapur pattern with five 'legs'
Khaling, c. 1987. 150 cm (collar to hem) x 203.5 cm (armspan). Lent by His Excellency Ugyen Tshering. Imported cotton yarns; warp-faced plainweave ground with supplementary-warp patterning. Faced with green cotton fabric.

Chapter Five

Fig. 5.5
Woman's dress (kira; kushüthara)
Central Bhutan, c. 1910. 277 x 141 cm. Lent by the Board of Trustees of the Victoria and Albert Museum (IM 19-1933). Cotton warp-faced plainweave ground with wild silk supplementary-weft patterning in yarns dyed with native indigo and lac.
Presented to Sir Charles Bell by the king of Bhutan in 1910.

Fig. 5.6
Set of three panels for a woman's dress (kira)
Southeastern Bhutan, before 1960. Panel A: 304 cm (including 14-cm unplied fringe at each end) x 56.5 cm; Panel B: 304 cm (including 16-cm unplied fringe at each end) x 56.5 cm; Panel C: 300 cm (including 15-cm unplied fringe at each end) x 57 cm. Phillips Collection, Peabody Essex Museum (E200267 A-C). Handspun cotton; warp-faced plainweave ground with supplementary-warp patterning and continuous and discontinuous supplementary-weft patterning. Natural dyes.

Fig. 5.7
Woman's dress (kira)
South central Bhutan, early twentieth century. 254 cm (including 7-cm fringe at each end) x 142 cm. Lent by Barbara Adams. Warp yarns of undyed and indigo-dyed handspun cotton, and of wild silk in other colors. Warp-faced plainweave ground; continuous and discontinuous supplementary-weft patterning in blue cotton and colored wild silk. One row of weft twining at each end. Natural dyes. Handstitched.

Fig. 5.8
Woman's dress (kira)
Bhutan, mid-twentieth century
238 cm (including 2.5-cm fringe at each end) x 134.5 cm. Lent by Barbara Adams. Most warps of imported cotton, with some imported silk yarns. Warp-faced plainweave ground with discontinuous supplementary-weft patterning in several kinds of imported silk and metallic yarns. One row of weft twining at each end. Synthetic dyes. Machine stitched.

Fig. 5.9
Woman's dress (kira)
Bumthang, 1960s. 262 cm (including 2-cm fringe at each end) x 152 cm. Phillips Collection, Peabody Essex Museum (E200387). Imported cotton, warp-faced plainweave ground; imported silk and metallic yarns used for discontinuous supplementary-weft patterning (sapma). Three rows of cotton weft twining at each end. Machine stitched.
Designed by and woven for Am Damchu.

Woman's dress (kira)
Thimphu, 1980s. 243 cm (including 1.5-cm fringe at each end) x 161.5 cm. Lent by Jane A. Phillips. Imported cotton, warp-faced plainweave ground; imported silk and metallic yarns used for discontinuous supplementary-weft patterning (sapma and thrima). One row of silk weft twining at each end.

Fig. 5.10
Woman's dress (kira; mapsham)
Thimphu, 1983. 225 cm (including 1.5-cm fringe at each end) x 154 cm. Lent by Her Majesty Queen Ashi Sangay Choden Wangchuck. Cultivated silk (from Hong Kong); warp-faced plainweave ground with discontinuous supplementary-weft patterning. One row of weft twining at each end. Machine stitched.

Fig. 5.11
Woman's belt (kera)
Bhutan, early twentieth century. 254 cm (including fringe at each end) x 42 cm. Lent by the Asian Art Museum of San Francisco (1991.22), Gift of Betty Alberts. Cotton warp-faced plainweave ground; wild silk supplementary-weft patterning. Native indigo and lac dyes.

Fig. 5.12
Woman's belt (kera)
Drakten (Kurtö), Lhuntshi District, 1950s. 226 cm (including 44-cm fringe at one end) x 41 cm. Lent by Diana K. Myers. Cotton warp-faced plainweave ground, with wild silk discontinuous and continuous supplementary-weft patterning. Native indigo and lac; synthetic yellow and green dyes. One end cut.

Woman's belt (kera)
Bhutan, mid-twentieth century. 180.5 cm (including 30.5-cm fringe at one end) x 21.5 cm.

Phillips Collection, Peabody Essex Museum (E70187). Imported cotton, warp-faced plainweave ground; continuous and discontinuous supplementary-weft patterning in several kinds of wild silk, imported cotton, and cultivated silk yarns. Lac, and synthetic dyes. One end cut.

Woman's belt (lungsem kera)
Thimphu, 1984. 186 cm (including 13-cm unplied, knotted fringe at each end) x 21 cm. Lent by Diana K. Myers. Indian cotton, warp-faced plainweave ground; discontinuous and continuous supplementary-weft patterning in acrylic yarns from India.

Woman's belt (kera)
Thimphu, late 1980s. 274 cm (including 32-cm fringe at each end) x 6 cm. Phillips Collection, Peabody Essex Museum (E200402). Imported wool; imported silk used for kushü-style discontinuous supplementary-weft patterning and one row of weft twining at each end.

Woman's belt (kera)
Thimphu, early 1990s. 264 cm (including 31-cm fringe at each end) x 8 cm. Phillips Collection, Peabody Essex Museum (E200404). Imported wool; imported silk discontinuous supplementary-weft patterning (sapma and thrima) and one row of continuous supplementary-weft patterning at each end.

Fig. 5.14
Dress fasteners shaped like pins (thinkhab), joined by two thick necklaces
Bhutan, nineteenth century. Pins: 31.5 cm long; rings: 8.5 cm diam; necklaces: 68 cm long. Phillips Collection, Peabody Essex Museum (E73243). Silver alloy.

*****Dress fasteners** shaped like pins (thinkhab)
Bhutan, c. 1930s. Lisina and Frank Hoch. Silver with gilt; turquoise.
Presented by Dasho Karma Galey in 1988.

Dress fasteners shaped like pins with rings at one end and brooches at the other (khab thinkhab)
Eastern Bhutan, 1930s. Pins: 21 cm long; rings: 6.5 cm diam. Lent by Diana K. Myers. Silver; turquoise.

Pair of brooches (koma) joined with a chain of diamond-shaped floral ornaments
Bhutan, c. 1930. Lisina and Frank Hoch. Silver with gilt.
Presented by Am Yeshe of Rongthongwoong (Tashigang District), who wore this jewelry from the 1930s to 1950s.

Pair of brooches (koma)
Bhutan, early to mid-twentieth century. Diam: 8 cm. Phillips Collection, Peabody Essex Museum (E72563). Silver compound; turquoise.

Necklace (*jabtha*) made of nine British Indian coins
Pemagatshel, mid-twentieth century. L: 51 cm. Phillips Collection, Peabody Essex Museum (E200261). Silver. Coins dated 1941-44. Obverse faces read *George VI King Emperor* and show king's profile; reverse faces read *One rupee India*, with the date. Safety pin attached to one of the rings joining the coins was used as a toothpick.

*Pair of brooches (*koma*) joined with a chain and lucky knot ornament
Bhutan, before 1955. Lisina and Frank Hoch. Silver; turquoise. Presented by King Jigme Dorji Wangchuck and Queen (Mother) Ashi Kesang in 1955.

Pair of brooches (*koma*) joined with a chain of thunderbolts (*dorje*)
Thimphu, 1990-92. Brooches: 5.5 cm diam; necklace: 49 cm long. Phillips Collection, Peabody Essex Museum (E200393). Silver with gilt; turquoise.

*Pair of brooches shaped like thunderbolts (*dorje koma*)
Bhutan, mid-twentieth century. L: 4.5 cm; w: 2 cm. Phillips Collection, Peabody Essex Museum (E69791). Silver with gilt; turquoise.

Pair of dress fasteners, new style
Dechenchöling, 1993. L: 21 cm; w: 6.5 cm. Anonymous lender. Silver with gilt.

*Amulet
Bhutan, early twentieth century. Lisina and Frank Hoch. Silver with new gold leaf; turquoise. Presented by Queen (Dowager) Ashi Phuntsok Chöden in 1970.

*Earrings (*sinchu*)
Thimphu, 1992. Diam: 2 cm and 2.2 cm. Phillips Collection, Peabody Essex Museum (E200396 A and B). Silver with gilt; turquoise.

Pair of bracelets (*dobchu*)
Merak, early twentieth century. Diam: 8 cm; h: 3 cm. Phillips Collection, Peabody Essex Museum 1994 accession. Silver compound made of melted Chinese coins (*dayang*); coral, turquoise.

*Bracelet
Bhutan, twentieth century. Lisina and Frank Hoch. Silver with gilt; turquoise. Presented by Queen (Mother) Ashi Kesang in 1955.

*Pair of bracelets
Bhutan, early twentieth century. Circ: 17 cm; diam: 6.5 cm; w: 1.5 cm. Phillips Collection, Peabody Essex Museum (E200395 A and B). Silver compound with turquoise.

*Bracelet
Dechenchöling, mid-twentieth century. Lisina

and Frank Hoch. Silver with gold. Presented by Queen Mother Ashi Kesang in 1992.

*Bracelet
Bhutan, before 1955. Lisina and Frank Hoch. Silver with gold. Presented by Queen (Mother) Ashi Kesang in 1955.

*Bracelet
Bhutan, before 1965. Lisina and Frank Hoch. Gold (gilt silver?) with turquoise. Presented by King Jigme Dorji Wangchuck in 1965.

*Bracelet
Bhutan, twentieth century. Lisina and Frank Hoch. Ivory with gold; turquoise. Presented by Her Majesty Queen Ashi Tshering Pem Wangchuck in 1992.

Fig. 5.15
Woman's shoulder cloth (*adha rachu*)
Bhutan, mid-twentieth century. 304 cm (including 26-cm fringe at each end) x 40 cm. Phillips Collection, Peabody Essex Museum (E69833). Wild silk warp-faced plainweave ground; wild silk discontinuous and continuous supplementary-weft patterning; one row of weft twining at each end. Natural dyes (pink possibly synthetic).

*Woman's shoulder cloth (*rachu*)
Pemagatshel District, 1970s. Anonymous. Cotton; plainweave ground with discontinuous supplementary-weft patterning in field and continuous supplementary-weft patterning at fringed ends.

*Woman's shoulder cloth (*rachu*)
Thimphu, 1980s. 260 cm (including 25-cm fringe at each end) x 23 cm. Phillips Collection, Peabody Essex Museum (E200398). Cultivated silk (from Hong Kong); warp-faced plainweave ground with discontinuous and continuous supplementary-weft patterning.

*Woman's shoulder cloth (*rachu*)
Thimphu, 1980s. 261 cm (including 24-cm fringe at each end) x 30 cm. Phillips Collection, Peabody Essex Museum (E200400). Imported cotton, warp-faced plain-weave ground; cotton discontinuous supplementary-weft patterning in field and imported silk discontinuous and continuous supplementary-weft patterning at ends. One row of silk weft twining at each end.

Woman's shoulder cloth (*rachu*)
Thimphu, 1980s. 274 cm (including 27-cm fringe at each end) x 24 cm. Phillips Collection, Peabody Essex Museum (E200399). Imported cotton, warp-faced plain-weave ground; imported cotton, imported silk, metallic, and acrylic yarns for discontinuous supplementary-weft patterning. One row of silk weft twining at each end.

Fig. 5.17, 5.18 (and cover)
Tunic (*kushung*)
Lhuntshi District, nineteenth century. 137 cm (shoulder to lower edge, including 15-cm fringe) x 87.5 cm. Phillips Collection, Peabody Essex Museum (E69560), Given in memory of Stephen Phillips. Handspun cotton, warp-faced plain-weave ground. Wild silk discontinuous supplementary-weft patterning (*sapma* and *thrima*); wild silk, wool, and bast-fiber continuous supplementary-weft patterning in border at lower edge. Pattern wefts dyed with lac, madder, indigo, and *Symplocos* (?). Neck finishing: local blue cotton and red wool plainweave fabrics; embroidery in wild silk yarns. Ribbons: several kinds of imported silk cloth and brocade; local cotton cloth.

Fig. 5.19
Tunic (*kushung*)
Lhuntshi District, nineteenth century. 125 cm (shoulder to lower edge, including 24-cm fringe) x 86 cm. Phillips Collection, Peabody Essex Museum (E74578). Handspun cotton, warp-faced plainweave ground. Wild silk discontinuous supplementary-weft patterning; cotton, wool, and bast-fiber continuous supplementary-weft patterning in border at lower edge. Natural dyes. Neck finishing: local wool plainweave cloth; some imported wool broadcloth (?). Ribbons: local wild silk cloth, dyed with indigo and lac; imported silk and cotton cloth.

Figs. 5.20, 5.21
Tunic (*kushung*)
Lhuntshi District, nineteenth century. 138 cm (shoulder to lower edge, including 19-cm fringe) x 91 cm. Lent by Barbara Adams. Handspun cotton, warp-faced plainweave ground. Wild silk discontinuous supplementary-weft patterning; and wild silk, wool, and bast-fiber continuous supplementary-weft patterning in border at lower edge. Natural dyes. Neck finishing: local wool plainweave cloth; imported silk cloth; embroidery in wild silk yarns.

Fig. 5.22 (upper left)
Woman's dress (*kira; shardang thara, tharé*)
Pemagatshel District, mid-twentieth century. 262 cm (including 17-cm fringe at each end) x 140 cm. Phillips Collection, Peabody Essex Museum (E200234). Handspun cotton; warp-faced plainweave ground, with discontinuous and continuous supplementary-weft patterning at fringed ends. Probably natural dyes. Machine stitched.

Fig. 5.23 (upper right)
Woman's dress (*kira; kushüthara*)
South central Bhutan, early twentieth century. 278 cm (including 11-cm fringe at each end) x 135 cm. Lent by Barbara Adams. Handspun cotton, warp-faced plainweave ground; blue (indigo-dyed) cotton and red (lac-dyed) wild silk used in discontinuous supplementary-weft

patterning throughout, and in continuous supplementary-weft patterning at fringed ends. One row of weft twining at each end. Handstitched.

Fig. 5.24 (lower left)
Woman's dress (kira; kushüthara)
Central Bhutan, early twentieth century. 274.5 cm (including 4-cm fringe at each end) x 137.5 cm. Phillips Collection, Peabody Essex Museum (E73212), Given in memory of Augustus P. Loring. Warps of undyed and indigo-dyed handspun cotton, and dyed wild silk (blue and other colors). Warp-faced plainweave ground, with wild silk discontinuous supplementary-weft patterning and continuous supplementary-weft patterning at fringed ends. One row of weft twining at each end. Natural dyes.

Fig. 5.25 (lower right)
Woman's dress (kira; kushüthara)
Central Bhutan, early twentieth century. 259 cm (including 1.5-cm fringe at each end) x 145 cm. Lent by Barbara Adams. Warps of white (undyed) cotton and imported (colored) silk. Warp-faced plainweave ground, with imported silk discontinuous supplementary-weft patterning and continuous supplementary-weft patterning. One row of weft twining at each end. Synthetic dyes. Machine stitched.

Fig. 5.26
Woman's dress (kira) (detail)
Central Bhutan, mid-twentieth century. 254 cm (including 2-cm fringe at each end) x 152 cm. Lent by Barbara Adams. Imported cotton; warp-faced plainweave ground, with discontinuous supplementary-weft patterning and continuous supplementary-weft patterning at fringed ends. One row of weft twining at each end. Machine stitched.

Fig. 5.27
Tunic (ngaushingkha)
North central Bhutan, nineteenth century. L: 120 cm; w: 78 cm. Phillips Collection, Peabody Essex Museum (E77734). Wool twill ground dyed with indigo. Appliqué: imported wool broadcloth, local wool twill cloth, striped Tibetan twill fabric. Outlining and embroidery in twisted wool; silk yarns. Ribbons: local and imported silk and cotton fabrics.

Fig. 5.28
Tunic (leushingkha)
North central Bhutan, nineteenth century. L: 117.5 cm; w: 67.5 cm (top) to 87.5 cm (bottom). Lent by Barbara Adams. Wool twill ground dyed with lac. Appliqué: local wool twill and plainweave fabrics. Outlining in twisted wool or cotton, and silk yarns. Ribbons: local and imported silk and cotton fabrics.

Fig. 5.33
*Man's robe (go), mensé mathra pattern with five 'legs'

Thimphu, 1980s. 143 cm (shoulder to hem) x 194 cm (armspan). Phillips Collection, Peabody Essex Museum (E200377). Cultivated silk (from Hong Kong); warp-faced plainweave ground with supplementary-warp patterning. Lining: blue Indian cotton fabric and neck panel of black Chinese silk brocade. Facing: brown Chinese silk. Ties: mensé mathra.

*Man's robe (go; pangtsi)
Thimphu, 1980s. 143 cm (shoulder to hem) x 183 cm (armspan). Phillips Collection, Peabody Essex Museum (E200378). Wild silk plainweave cloth from Assam. Lining: blue Indian cotton fabric and neck panel of cotton fabric in sethra pattern. No separate facing fabric.

Man's robe (go), lungserma pattern with eleven 'legs'
Thimphu, 1980s. 151 cm (shoulder to hem) x 186.5 cm (armspan). Phillips Collection, Peabody Essex Museum (E200379). Wild silk; warp-faced plainweave ground with supplementary-warp patterning. Natural and synthetic dyes. Lining: blue Indian cotton cloth and neck panels of wild silk pangtsi cloth from Assam. Facing: red Chinese silk. Ties: Chinese brocade.

Fig. 5.34
Boy's robe (go), mensé mathra pattern with seven 'legs'
Thimphu, 1988. 103 cm (collar to hem) x 98 cm (armspan). Lent by Her Majesty Queen Ashi Sangay Choden Wangchuck. Cultivated silk (from Hong Kong); warp-faced plainweave ground with supplementary-warp and discontinuous supplementary-weft patterning. Lining: blue Indian cotton cloth. Facing and ties: red-and-gold silk brocade from Hong Kong.
Woven for His Royal Highness Dasho Khamsum Singye Wangchuck.

Boy's shirt (tögo)
Thimphu, 1988. 48 cm (collar to hem) x 128 cm (armspan). Lent by Her Majesty Queen Ashi Sangay Choden Wangchuck. Cotton fabric from India.
Made for His Royal Highness Dasho Khamsum Singye Wangchuck.

Boy's belt (kera)
Thimphu, 1988. 244 cm (including 25-cm fringe at each end) x 3.5 cm. Lent by Her Majesty Queen Ashi Sangay Choden Wangchuck. Wool.
Woven for His Royal Highness Dasho Khamsum Singye Wangchuck.

Boy's boots (lham)
Thimphu, 1988. H: 28 cm; l: 17 cm. Lent by Her Majesty Queen Ashi Sangay Choden Wangchuck. Several kinds of silk and silk brocade cloth; cotton and silk-like acrylic cord; leather trim; rubber and leather soles. Lining: orange plainweave wild silk cloth.
Made for His Royal Highness Dasho Khamsum

Singye Wangchuck.

Boy's boot ties (lhamching)
Thimphu, 1988 . 87.5 cm (including 6-cm fringe at each end) x 2.5 cm. Lent by Her Majesty Queen Ashi Sangay Choden Wangchuck. Cotton warp-faced plainweave ground with embroidery in silk and metallic yarns. Three rows of silk weft twining at each end.
Made for His Royal Highness Dasho Khamsum Singye Wangchuck.

Fig. 5.36
Sword (pata), of the type called kongdi maja ('Kong peacock')
Kham, eastern Tibet, nineteenth century. Sword: 77 x 5 cm; scabbard: 65.5 x 5 cm. Lent by Mrs. Ugen Norzom Namgyel. Sword: iron blade, silver with gilt grip. Scabbard: wood, leather, silver with gilt. Inscription on blade reads "sma bya" (maja). Paper tag reads: "rkong gri sma bya" (kongdi maja).
At the turn of the century, this sword belonged to Jakar Dzongpön Chimi Dorji, the grandfather of the lender's husband.

Wooden bowl decorated with silver (dza phop nyöshichem)
Bhutan, early twentieth century. H: 4.5 cm; circ: 5 cm; diam: 10 cm (lip) and 5 cm (base). Lent by Mrs. Ugen Norzom Namgyel. Wood; silver; lacquer (on bottom).
The bowl was given to the lender's husband by his father, the late Lyönpo Sangye Penjor.

Rectangular box for betel nuts and leaves (chakhar)
Bhutan, late nineteenth or early twentieth century. L: 13 cm; w: 8 cm. Phillips Collection, Peabody Essex Museum (E70789). Silver.

Round box for lime (drimi)
Bhutan, late nineteenth or early twentieth century. H: 4 cm; diam: 6.5 cm . Anonymous lender. Silver.

Sword belt
Tibet, late nineteenth or early twentieth century. L: 102 cm. Phillips Collection, Peabody Essex Museum (E71441). Leather; silver compound (plates); iron (studs and rings).

Fig. 5.37
Man's shoulder cloth (khamar kabné)
Bhutan, twentieth century. 216 cm (including 34-cm fringe at each end) x 90 cm. Phillips Collection, Peabody Essex Museum (E70021). Wild silk warp-faced plainweave ground, with wild silk and cotton weft twining at fringed ends. Natural and synthetic dyes. Handstitched.

Fig. 5.41
*Small panel of cloth (sethra pattern)
Woven by Dorje Chözom, Radi, Tashigang Dis-

trict, 1992. 213 x 27 cm. Phillips Collection, Peabody Essex Museum (E200449). Wild silk plainweave. Synthetic and natural dyes.

Small panel of cloth, left over from making a man's robe (*adha mathra* pattern)
Woven by Dorje Chözom, Radi, Tashigang District, 1992. 131 x 19 cm. Phillips Collection, Peabody Essex Museum (E200451). Wild silk plainweave. Synthetic and natural dyes.

Small loom length (*zurtsi*) for making a man's robe (*yütham* pattern)
Woven by Dorje Chözom, Radi, Tashigang District, 1992. 188.5 x 27 cm. Phillips Collection, Peabody Essex Museum (E200452). Wild silk plainweave. Synthetic and natural dyes.

Small loom length (*zurtsi*) for making a man's robe (*pangtsi* pattern)
Woven by Dorje Chözom, Radi, Tashigang District, 1992. 173 x 21.5 cm. Phillips Collection, Peabody Essex Museum (E200454). Wild silk plainweave. Synthetic and natural dyes.

Fig. 5.44
Multipurpose cloth (*pangkheb*)
Central Bhutan, c. 1910. 249 x 46 cm. Lent by the Board of Trustees of the Victoria and Albert Museum (IM 22-1933). Handspun cotton; warp-faced plainweave ground, with discontinuous supplementary-weft patterning in yarns dyed with native indigo and madder.
Presented to Sir Charles Bell by the king of Bhutan in 1910.

Fig. 5.45
Ceremonial multipurpose cloth (*chagsi pangkheb*)
Eastern Bhutan, late nineteenth or early twentieth century. 300 cm (including 21-cm fringe at each end) x 85 cm. Lent by Barbara Adams. Wild silk warp-faced plainweave ground; wild silk continuous and discontinuous supplementary-weft patterning and supplementary-warp patterning. One row of weft twining at ends. Natural dyes. Handstitched.

Fig. 5.46
Ceremonial multipurpose cloth (*chagsi pangkheb*)
Eastern Bhutan, mid-twentieth century. 287 cm (including 17-cm fringe at each end) x 75.5 cm. Lent by Diana K. Myers. Handspun, naturally dyed and imported (orange) cotton, warp-faced plainweave ground; wild silk continuous and discontinuous supplementary-weft patterning, and cotton and wild silk supplementary-warp patterning. Handstitched.

Fig. 5.47
Ceremonial multipurpose cloth (*chagsi pangkheb*)
Central Bhutan, early twentieth century. 284 cm (including 15-cm fringe at each end) x 88 cm.

Phillips Collection, Peabody Essex Museum (E78068). Warps of lac-dyed wild silk and indigo-dyed cotton. Warp-faced plainweave ground with wild silk (and white parachute silk?) continuous and discontinuous supplementary-weft patterning; wild silk supplementary-warp patterning. One row of weft twining at each end. Natural dyes. Handstitched.

Fig. 5.48
Ceremonial multipurpose cloth (*chagsi pangkheb*)
Southeastern Bhutan, early twentieth century. 254 cm (including 19-cm fringe at each end) x 103 cm. Phillips Collection, Peabody Essex Museum (E74570). Handspun cotton, warp-faced plainweave ground. Lac-dyed wild silk and indigo-dyed cotton used in continuous and discontinuous supplementary-weft patterning. Blue cotton also used for supplementary-warp patterning. Weft twining at each end. Handstitched.

Fig. 5.49
Multipurpose cloth (*pangkheb*)
Eastern Bhutan, twentieth century. 280 cm (including 25-cm fringe at each end) x 85 cm. Phillips Collection, Peabody Essex Museum (E74566). Handspun cotton, warp-faced plainweave ground. Lac-dyed wild silk and indigo-dyed cotton used in continuous and discontinuous supplementary-weft patterning, in supplementary-warp patterning, and in colored wefts. Handstitched

Fig. 5.52
Bag (*phechung*)
Central Bhutan, twentieth century. 54.5 x 51.5 cm. Phillips Collection, Peabody Essex Museum (E74599). Warp-faced plainweave ground of bast fiber, with wool and wild silk discontinuous and continuous supplementary-weft patterning. Natural and synthetic dyes. Handstitched. Local repairs in cotton twill and plainweave fabrics. Recently added: red felt corner trim, machine-stitched seams, and woven cotton strap from India.

Fig. 5.53
Wrapping cloth (*kushü bündri*)
Central Bhutan, twentieth century. 133 x 152.5 cm. Lent by the Minneapolis Institute of Arts (82.102.40), Gift of Bud Grossman. Warp-faced plainweave ground with handspun (undyed) cotton warps and wefts, and intermittent blue cotton and red wild silk warps; wild silk discontinuous supplementary-weft patterning. Native indigo and lac dyes.

Fig. 5.54
Raincloak (*charkab*)
Ura Valley (?), Bumthang, mid-twentieth century. 119.5 x 136 cm. Lent by the Minneapolis Institute of Arts (82.102.32), Gift of Bud Grossman. Wool plainweave with discontinu-

ous supplementary-weft patterning.

Fig. 5.55
Seat cover or blanket (*denkheb*)
Bumthang, twentieth century. 146 x 91 cm. Phillips Collection, Peabody Essex Museum (E74562). Wool; twill ground with discontinuous supplementary-weft patterning. Natural and synthetic dyes. Machine stitched. Pink Indian cotton plainweave fabric edging.

Fig. 5.57
Raincloak (*charkab*)
Bumthang, early to mid-twentieth century. 122 x 127 cm. Lent by Diana K. Myers. Wool; twill ground with discontinuous supplementary-weft patterning. Natural dyes.

EXHIBITED BUT NOT ILLUSTRATED:

Woman's dress (*kira; thara, tharé*)
Thimphu, early 1980s. 237.5 x 134 cm. Lent by the Asian Art Museum of San Francisco (1990.60), Gift of an anonymous friend of the museum. Imported cotton, warp-faced plainweave.

Woman's dress (*kira; kushüthara*)
Central Bhutan, early twentieth century. 260 cm (including 6-cm fringe at each end) x 144 cm. Phillips Collection, Peabody Essex Museum (E72828). Handspun cotton, warp-faced plainweave ground; wild silk discontinuous and continuous supplementary-weft patterning (*sapma* and *thrima*). One row of weft twining at each end. Most, if not all, natural dyes. Handstitched.

Woman's belt (*kera*)
Woven by Sangay Dolma, Thongsa, Pemagatshel District, 1992. 223 cm (including 20-cm fringe at one end and 38-cm fringe at the other) x 12.5 cm. Phillips Collection, Peabody Essex Museum (E200232). Handspun cotton plainweave ground with continuous supplementary-weft patterning. Yarns are unbleached or tinted with natural dyes (indigo and madder).

Woman's ceremonial shoulder cloth (*rachu*)
Bhutan, c. 1950. 266 cm (including 18-cm fringe at one end and 23-cm fringe at the other) x 11 cm. Lent by Her Majesty Queen Ashi Sangay Choden Wangchuck. Imported silk, warp-faced plainweave ground; several kinds of silk used for continuous and discontinuous supplementary-weft patterning.
This *rachu* was worn by Her Majesty's maternal grandmother, Am Ugen Dem, in the 1950s. The textile is half its original size, being one of two shoulder cloths made from the earlier garment for use by two granddaughters.

Woman's shoulder cloth (*rachu*)
Bhutan or Kalimpong (India), c. 1955-60. 168 cm (including unfinished fringe) x 18.5 cm. Lent by the Henry Art Gallery, University of Washing-

ton, Elizabeth Bayley Willis Collection (64.9-111), Gift of Virginia and Prentice Bloedel. Indian cotton yarns. Warp-faced plainweave ground, with continuous and discontinuous supplementary-weft patterning; weft twining at fringed ends.

Tunic (kushung)
Lhuntshi District, nineteenth century. 138 cm (shoulder to lower edge, including 21-cm fringe) x 90.5 cm. Lent by Barbara Adams. Handspun cotton, warp-faced plainweave ground. Wild silk discontinuous supplementary-weft patterning throughout (sapma and thrima); and wild silk, wool, and bast-fiber continuous supplementary-weft patterning in border at lower edge. Natural dyes. Neck finishing: local cotton twill fabric dyed with indigo; red wool plainweave fabric. Embroidery and stitching in imported silk yarns. Ribbons: local wild silk and imported silk fabrics.

Man's robe (go)
Bhutan, early twentieth century. 150 cm (collar to hem) x 218 cm (armspan). Lent by Mrs. Chhemey Wangmo Norbu. Chinese brocade. Lining: blue cotton twill cloth. Facing and ties: wild silk pangtsi fabric.
This robe belonged to the owner's father-in-law, Chapcha Penlöp Dasho Nakchung, who received it as a gift from the second king (i.e., before 1952), who had worn it himself.

Man's robe (go), pangtsi pattern
Thimphu, mid-twentieth century. 141.5 cm (collar to hem) x 140 cm (armspan). Lent by Mrs. Ugen Norzom Namgyel. Wild silk plainweave. Lining: sheepskin. Hand- and machine stitched.
This robe belonged to the late Gelong Nyerchen-Dep of Thimphu, Tshering Dorji (1902-84), who wore it in the last years of his life.

Blessing cords (sungkü)
Bhutan, contemporary. A: 65 cm long; B: 60 cm long; C: 68 cm long. Phillips Collection, Peabody Essex Museum (E200420) A (red), B (blue), C (yellow). Silk-like acrylic yarn from India.

Dagger (A), **sheath** (B), **and card-woven belt** (C)
Kheng Gojing, Shemgang District, 1980s. A: 42 cm long x 4 cm wide; B: 30.5 long x 5.5 cm wide; C: 130 x 2.3 cm. Phillips Collection, Peabody Essex Museum (E200238 A [dagger], B [sheath], C [belt]). A: iron blade, wooden handle. B: wood, bamboo. C: imported wool, with patterning in imported acrylic and cotton.

Panel for making a multipurpose cloth
(pangkheb) and used as tax payment
Mikuri, Pemagatshel District, mid-twentieth century. 240 cm (including 30-cm fringe at one end) x 47 cm. Phillips Collection, Peabody Essex Museum (E200258). Handspun cotton, warp-faced plainweave ground; cotton discontinuous supplementary-weft patterning and supplemen-

tary-warp patterning. One end cut. Synthetic (red and black) and natural (indigo blue) dyes.

Panel for making a multipurpose cloth
(pangkheb) and used as tax payment
From the household of Pema Chöden, Phongmé, Tashigang District, mid-twentieth century. 242 cm (including 28-cm unplied fringe at each end) x 29 cm. Phillips Collection, Peabody Essex Museum (E200259). Handspun cotton (from chemashing [Gossypium?]), warp-faced plainweave ground; cotton discontinuous supplementary-weft and supplementary-warp patterning. Synthetic and natural dyes.

Bag (phechung)
Central Bhutan, twentieth century. 63 x 56.5 cm. Phillips Collection, Peabody Essex Museum (E77733). Warps of undyed bast fiber and colored wool; warp-faced plainweave ground with wool and wild silk yarns used in discontinuous and continuous supplementary-weft patterning (sapma). Natural and synthetic dyes. Handstitched.

Carrying cloth (bündri)
Central Bhutan, mid-twentieth century. 107 x 120 cm. Phillips Collection, Peabody Essex Museum (E74567). Unbleached handspun cotton, warp-faced plainweave ground; wool discontinuous and continuous supplementary-weft patterning (sapma). Natural dyes. Handstitched. Braided cotton tie at each corner. Local repairs on reverse: corners reinforced with plainweave cotton and wild silk yütham fabric.

Carrying cloth (bündri)
Lhuntshi District, mid-twentieth century. 66 x 67 cm. Lent by Diana K. Myers. Unbleached, handspun cotton, warp-faced plainweave ground; wild silk discontinuous supplementary-weft patterning (sapma and thrima). Natural dyes. Cotton cloth tie at one corner; two other ties missing.

Ceremonial textile (chagsi pangkheb)
Indian region adjacent to eastern Bhutan (?), twentieth century (?). 354 x 106 cm. Phillips Collection, Peabody Essex Museum (E70016). Handspun cotton plainweave. Discontinuous supplementary-weft patterning in wild silk (dyed with lac and perhaps also with madder) and tan and indigo-dyed cotton. One row of weft braiding at fringe.
Although its structure and materials are characteristically Bhutanese, and its pattern format is typical of a chagsi pangkheb, this textile is composed of a single panel whose width exceeds the weft dimension that can be produced on contemporary Bhutanese looms. The geometric and animal motifs, and dyes, suggest the textile may have been made near eastern Bhutan in Assam.

Woman's dress (kira; aikapur jadrima) (detail)
Wangdichöling, Bumthang, c. 1950s. Diana K.

Myers. Cotton; warp-faced plainweave ground with supplementary-warp and discontinuous supplementary-weft patterning. One row of weft twining at each end.
This dress was woven for Her Royal Highness Ashi Choeki Wangchuck and given to its previous (Bhutanese) owner in 1982.

Chapter Six

Fig. 6.1
Throne (seat) cover (thrikheb)
Bhutan, c. 1900. 127 x 124 cm (including 16-cm fringe on each side). Phillips Collection, Peabody Essex Museum (E70014), Given in memory of Stephen Phillips. Cut and assembled imported wool broadcloth; embroidery in silk yarns; outlining and couching in tightly twisted wool. Wild silk fringe (natural and synthetic dyes). Edging: Bhutanese wild silk cloth (sethra). Handstitched. Backing (recent): cotton twill fabric, machine stitched.

Fig. 6.8
Queen's or princess's hat (peshasham)
Bhutan, 1900-40. H: 10.5 cm; circ: 60.5 cm; diam: 19.5 cm. Phillips Collection, Peabody Essex Museum (E73220.A). Cut and assembled imported silk damask; embroidery in several kinds of silk and gold and silver thread. Lining: imported red silk fabric. Handstitched.

Bride's hat
Thimphu, 1992. H: 10.5 cm; circ: 60.5 cm; diam: 22.5 cm. Lent by Mrs. Chöden Namgyal and Mr. Kinley D. Dorji. Cut and assembled imported silk brocade. Lining: imported red silk fabric. Handstitched.

Groom's hat
Thimphu, 1992. H: 13 cm; circ: 59 cm; diam: 16 cm. Lent by Mrs. Chöden Namgyal and Mr. Kinley D. Dorji. Cut and assembled imported silk brocade. Lining: imported white cotton cloth. Hand- and machine stitched.

Fig. 6.9
Woman's jacket (tögo)
Central Bhutan, 1950s. 59 cm (collar to hem) x 175.5 cm (armspan). Lent by Her Royal Highness Ashi Choeki Wangchuck. Chinese brocade. Collar facing: wild silk cloth (pangtsi pattern; dyed with native indigo and madder). Lower edge: red Chinese brocade.
This jacket was made from a robe that belonged to King Jigme Dorji Wangchuck, who wore the robe during New Year's celebrations in Bumthang in the early 1950s. The robe was later given to his daughter, Her Royal Highness Ashi Choeki, who had the jacket made.

Fig. 6.11
Religious scroll image (thangka) depicting Tsepamé

Bhutan, late nineteenth or early twentieth century. Image: 46.5 cm long x 36 cm wide. Scroll: 100 cm long x 65 cm wide. Phillips Collection, Peabody Essex Museum (E72571). Cut and assembled Chinese silk fabrics (tabby, damask); embroidery in imported silk and metallic yarns. Brocade panel at bottom shows the Chinese character *shou*, signifying long life. Backing: two varieties of wild silk cloth (one dyed with lac); imported (northeast Indian?) supplementary-weft-patterned cotton cloth. Hand- and machine stitched.

Fig. 6.12
Religious scroll image *(thangka)* depicting Shakya Gyaltshen (1813-75)
Bhutan, late nineteenth century. Image: 67 cm long x 51 cm wide. Scroll: 144 cm long x 87.5 cm wide. Lent by the Asian Art Museum of San Francisco (B62D34), Avery Brundage Collection. Cut and assembled Chinese silk fabrics (tabby, damask, brocade); embroidery in imported silk yarns. Wooden dowel; brass finials; paper tag with inscription.
This *thangka* was probably presented to Lt. Col. J.L.R. Weir in Bhutan in the 1930s.

Fig. 6.15
Altar or offering cover *(tenkheb)*
Central Bhutan, nineteenth or early twentieth century. 74 x 88 cm. Phillips Collection, Peabody Essex Museum (E67327). Handspun cotton, warp-faced plainweave ground; wool discontinuous supplementary-weft patterning *(sapma)*. Natural dyes. Edging: cotton plainweave fabric dyed with indigo. Handstitched.

Fig. 6.16
Altar or offering cover *(tenkheb)*
Thimphu, c. 1920-30. 49.5 cm square, plus 9-cm fringe at lower edge. Lent by Diana K. Myers. Cut and assembled fabrics including Chinese tabby, damask, and brocade and striped Indian silk. Fringe: silk. Backing: Indian cotton print fabric.

Fig. 6.17
Woven saddle cover *(gayok)*
North central Bhutan, early twentieth century. 89.5 x 84.5 cm (including 27.5-cm fringe on each side). Phillips Collection, Peabody Essex Museum (E76927). Handspun cotton, warp-faced plainweave ground; supplementary-weft patterning in wool yarns colored with natural dyes. Acrylic fringe (newly added). Backing: wild silk cloth dyed with lac.

Fig. 6.20
Seat cover *(thrikheb)*
Bhutan or Tibet, nineteenth century. 118 x 112 cm. Phillips Collection, Peabody Essex Museum (E70017), Given in memory of Augustus P. Loring. Cut and assembled imported woolen broadcloth; embroidery and outlining in tightly twisted silk and wool yarn.

Fig. 6.21
Rectangular seat cover *(denkheb, bokheb)*
Bhutan, early twentieth century. Approximately 170 cm (including 21.5-cm fringe at each end) x 64 cm. Phillips Collection, Peabody Essex Museum (E70013), Given in memory of Stephen Phillips. Cut and assembled imported wool broadcloth and cotton; embroidery and outlining in several kinds of tightly twisted silk and wool yarn. Wild silk fringe (brown has deteriorated or oxidized, so that only remnants visible), colored with natural and synthetic dyes. Backing: wild silk plainweave *(shabthrawo* pattern) cloth; yarns are unbleached or dyed with lac or indigo.

Cylindrical bag *(thrikhu)*
Central Bhutan, first half of the twentieth century. L: 81 cm; w: 31.5 cm; circ: 63.5 cm. Phillips Collection, Peabody Essex Museum (E77736). Undyed handspun cotton, warp-faced plainweave ground; wild silk discontinuous and continuous supplementary-weft patterning *(sapma* and *thrima)*. Natural dyes. Ends: imported wool broadcloth; several kinds of wild silk and cotton cloth; Chinese brocade. Cotton cord; leather strap; metal ring; bone slat at mouth. Handstitched.

Fig. 6.22
Round pouch *(kechung,* 'little neck')
Bhutan, before 1970. H: 22 cm; circ: 57 cm (open). Lent by Diana K. Myers. Wild silk cloth scraps (lac-dyed plainweave, *pangtsi, adha mathra, aikapur jadrima, mensé mathra)*; cotton plainweave and twill fabrics. Twisted cotton cord; metal rings; leather tassels and drawstring. Lining: cotton twill cloth. Handstitched.

Pair of joined pouches *(chabshub)*
Central Bhutan, c. 1955. L: 98 cm. Pouches: w: 16 cm; circ: 41 cm. Lent by Lisina and Frank Hoch. Cut and assembled imported silk tabby, silk brocade, and silk-like fabrics. Machine- and handstitched. Silver with gilt (rings and bottom ornaments); tassels of imported silk-like yarn. Presented by King Jigme Dorji Wangchuck and Queen (Mother) Ashi Kesang in 1955.

EXHIBITED BUT NOT ILLUSTRATED:

Woman's jacket *(tögo)*
Central Bhutan, 1930s. 64.5 cm (collar to hem) x 204 cm (armspan). Lent by Mrs. Chhemey Wangmo Norbu. Chinese brocade. Collar facing (new): patterned Indian cotton fabric. Lower edge: orange silk brocade.
Presented to the lender by her mother-in-law, Am Ngatshom, who wore it in the 1930s.

Woman's jacket *(tögo)*
Central Bhutan, 1930-1940s. 59 cm (collar to hem) x 164 cm (armspan). Lent by Mrs. Sonam Wangmo. Chinese brocade. Collar facing: silk cloth *(pangtsi* pattern). Lower edge: rainbow-hued patterned silk cloth.
Presented to the lender by Her Royal Highness Ashi Choeki Wangchuck in 1982.

Woman's jacket *(tögo)*
Central Bhutan, 1930s-1940s. 58 cm (collar to hem) x 174 cm (armspan). Lent by Mrs. Sonam Wangmo. Chinese brocade. Collar facing: cotton cloth *(sethra* pattern). Lower edge: rainbow-hued patterned cotton cloth.
This jacket was given to its owner by her former mother-in-law, Am Rinzi, in the 1970s. Am Rinzi, wife of the chief secretary to the third king, wore the jacket in the 1930s.

Five-part costume for Black Hat dance *(shanag chamgo)*
Lent by the Monk Body of Bhutan, Tashichö Dzong.
A. Robe *(chamgo)*, c. 1760. Chinese patterned silk (originally for a mandarin robe), lined with locally woven cotton fabric. Made by the Thimphu Nyerchen Shalé and presented to the Monk Body.
B. Cloud collar *(dorje gong)*, c. 1760. Imported, patterned silk, recently relined with cotton fabric.
C. Black hat *(shanag)*, c. 1660. Wood, leather, silver, peacock feathers, procupine quills.
D. Apron *(throshé)*, c. 1660. Painted cotton (?); recent cotton lining and ties.
E. Boots *(shab lham)*, contemporary. Silk, leather.

Set of six temple hangings *(chephur gyetshen)*
Main shrine, Punakha Dzong, c. 1940. Lent by the Monk Body of Bhutan, Tashichö Dzong. Imported Chinese and Indian silk fabrics; cotton backing.

Throne cover *(thrikheb)*
Central Bhutan, late nineteenth century. 148 x 145 cm. Lent by Mrs. Ugen Norzom Namgyel. Unbleached handspun cotton, warp-faced plainweave ground; discontinuous and continuous supplementary-weft patterning in wild silk colored with natural dyes (small area that appears to be patterned with imported silk in center). Three borders of plainweave cotton cloth, dyed tan and blue with natural dyes. Backing: coarser plainweave cotton fabric. Handstitched.
This textile came from the household of Kunzang Dorji, uncle of the lender's husband, in Bumthang Chumé Ngatsang.

Throne cover *(thrikheb)*
Bhutan or Tibet, c. 1900. 126 x 124 cm. Phillips Collection, Peabody Essex Museum (E74547). Cut and assembled imported wool broadcloth; white wool twill (Tibetan?). Outlining and embroidery in wool yarn, dyed with synthetic and natural dyes, and several kinds of silk yarns. Edging: imported wool broadcloth.

Saddle pad made of *yathra*
Bhutan or Tibet, twentieth century. 79 x 130 cm.

Lent by the Museum for Textiles (T88.0444). Wool; twill ground with discontinuous supplementary-weft patterning. Broadcloth edging and cotton twill backing.

Chapter Seven

Fig. 7.2
Man's robe *(go)*, *pangtsi* pattern (detail)
Woven by Sangay Dolma, Thongsa, Pemagatshel District, 1991. 141 cm (collar to hem) x 184 cm (armspan). Phillips Collection, Peabody Essex Museum (E200231). Handspun cotton plainweave; dyes are indigo and madder. Handstitched. Lining: neck panel of Assamese cotton cloth *(pangtsi* pattern). Facing: blue Indian cotton cloth. Sleeve cuffs: 13.5 cm of warp-faced plainweave cotton fabric *(aikapur dromchu chema* pattern). Tie: black cotton twill.

**Man's robe *(go)*, *samkhongma* or *möndré* pattern (detail)
Thongsa, Pemagatshel District, c. 1980.144 cm (collar to hem) x 161 cm (armspan). Phillips Collection, Peabody Essex Museum (E200230). Handspun cotton plainweave; dyes are indigo and madder. Handstitched. Lining: none. Facing: blue Indian cotton cloth. Ties: two kinds of Assamese cotton cloth *(pangtsi* pattern).

Woman's dress *(kira)*, *möntha* pattern (detail)
Thongsa, Pemagatshel District, c. 1978.234 cm (including 2-cm fringe at each end) x 125 cm. Lent by Diana K. Myers. Handspun cotton; native indigo and madder. Some Indian commercial cotton used for colored warp stripes. Handstitched.

One of three panels for a woman's dress, *shardang thara* pattern (detail)
Woven by Sangay Dolma, Thongsa, Pemagatshel District, 1993. A: 252 cm (including 2-cm fringe at each end) x 47 cm; B: 252 cm (including 2-cm fringe at each end) x 45.5 cm; C: 254 cm (including 2-cm fringe at each end) x 48.5 cm. Phillips Collection, Peabody Essex Museum (E200429 A-C). Handspun cotton plainweave, dyed with native indigo, madder, and turmeric. One row of weft twining at each end.
Fig. 7.3
Woman's dress *(kira)*, *pesar* patterning (detail)
Bhutan, third quarter of the twentieth century. 230.5 x 132 cm. Phillips Collection, Peabody Essex Museum (E72782). Imported cotton and silk warp-faced plainweave ground; imported silk and cotton discontinuous supplementary-weft patterning. Synthetic dyes. Machine- and handstitched. Ends hemmed.

Fig. 7.4
Woman's dress *(kira)*, *mensé mathra* pattern with nine 'legs' (detail)
Eastern Bhutan, mid-twentieth century. 267.5 cm (including 4-cm fringe at each end) x 137 cm.

Phillips Collection, Peabody Essex Museum (E200457). Wild silk warp-faced plainweave ground; supplementary-warp patterning and three rows of weft twining at each end. Natural and synthetic dyes. Handstitched.

Woman's dress *(kira)*, *lungserma* pattern with eleven 'legs' (detail)
Eastern Bhutan, mid-twentieth century.246 cm (including 2-cm fringe at each end) x 137 cm. Phillips Collection, Peabody Essex Museum (E69789). Wild silk warp-faced plainweave ground; supplementary-warp patterning and three rows of weft twining at each end. Natural and synthetic dyes. Handstitched.

Woman's dress *(kira)*, *jadrima* pattern with eleven 'legs' (detail)
Eastern Bhutan, mid-twentieth century. 256 cm (including 3-cm fringe at each end) x 132 cm. Phillips Collection, Peabody Essex Museum (E200456). Wild silk warp-faced plainweave ground; supplementary-warp patterning and three rows of weft twining at each end. Natural and synthetic dyes. Handstitched.

Woman's dress *(kira)*, *dromchu chema* pattern with no 'legs' (detail)
Eastern Bhutan, mid-twentieth century. 260 cm (including 4-cm fringe at each end) x 127 cm. Anonymous lender. Wild silk warp-faced plainweave ground; supplementary-warp patterning and three rows of wild silk weft twining at each end. Most, if not all, natural dyes. Handstitched.

Fig. 7.6
Woman's dress *(kira)*, *möntha* pattern (detail)
Bhutan or Kalimpong (India), c. 1955. 266 x 140 cm (including fringe). Lent by the Henry Art Gallery, University of Washington (64.9-128), Elizabeth Bayley Willis Collection, Gift of Virginia and Prentice Bloedel. Indian cotton yarn; plainweave ground with supplementary-warp patterning and weft twining at ends.

Panel for a woman's dress, *dromchu chema* pattern (detail)
Bhutan or Kalimpong (India), c. 1955. 267 x 44.5 cm (including unfinished fringe). Lent by the Henry Art Gallery, University of Washington (64.9-103, d2), Elizabeth Bayley Willis Collection, Gift of Virginia and Prentice Bloedel. Indian cotton yarn; plainweave ground with supplementary-warp patterning, and weft twining at ends.

Fig. 7.9
Woman's dress *(kira; kushüthara)*
South central Bhutan, early twentieth century. 267 cm (including 2.5-cm fringe at each end) x 142 cm. Phillips Collection, Peabody Essex Museum (E74571). Warps of handspun cotton (unbleached and indigo-dyed blue) and colored wild silk. Warp-faced plainweave ground, with discontinuous and continuous supplementary-

weft patterning in wild silk. One row of weft twining at each end. Natural dyes. Handstitched.

Fig. 7.11
Woman's dress *(kira; kushüthara)*
Central Bhutan, 1930s-1940s. 223.5 cm x 143.5 cm. Lent by the Minneapolis Institute of Arts (82.102.1), Gift of Bud Grossman. Cotton warp-faced plainweave ground; discontinuous supplementary-weft patterning (parachute silk?).

Fig. 7.12
Panel of cloth for making into a raincloak *(charkab)*
Sephu, Tongsa District, c. 1984. 446 x 37 cm. Phillips Collection, Peabody Essex Museum (E200265). Wool, twill; natural and synthetic dyes.

Woman's dress *(kira; tarichem)*
Tang Valley, Bumthang District, 1992. 135 (warp) x 250 cm. Phillips Collection, Peabody Essex Museum (E200235). Wool, twill.

Fig. 7.13
Woman's dress *(kira; bumthang mathra)*
Jakar, Bumthang District, 1986. 159 (warp) x 200 cm. Lent by Diana K. Myers. Twill. Handspun local wool; natural dyes. Facing: cotton fabric *(pangtsi* pattern) from Assam.

Woman's dress *(kira; mathra pesar)*
Woven in the household of Sonam Yödon, Dechenchöling, late 1980s. 148.5 (warp) x 260 cm. Phillips Collection, Peabody Essex Museum (E200385). Imported wool twill ground; imported silk discontinuous supplementary-weft patterning. Synthetic dyes.

Two loom lengths for making a man's robe, *bumthang mathra* pattern
Bumthang, 1970s. 1040 x 24 cm and 1046 x 24.5 cm. Lent by Lisina and Frank Hoch. Wool twill. Natural dyes.
Presented by His Royal Highness Namgyal Wangchuck in 1979.

Fig. 7.14
Panel of cloth *(yathra)*
Bumthang, c. 1978. 310 x 44.5 cm. Phillips Collection, Peabody Essex Museum (E74564). Australian wool; twill ground with discontinuous supplementary-weft patterning. Natural and synthetic dyes. One end hemmed; one end cut.

Loom length *(yathra)*
Bumthang, c. 1970. 320 x 51 cm. Lent by Lisina and Frank Hoch. Bhutanese wool; twill ground with discontinuous supplementary-weft patterning. Natural dyes. One end cut; one end warp loops.
Woven by Am Rinchen Penjor from the wool of her sheep and presented in 1971.

EXHIBITED BUT NOT ILLUSTRATED:

Little girl's play loom with partially woven textile
From the household of Kesang, Tangmachu, Lhuntshi District, 1992. Warp: 136 cm; weft: 2 cm. Phillips Collection, Peabody Essex Museum (E200206). Wooden sticks, straw. Cotton warp-faced plainweave ground with discontinuous supplementary-weft patterning in imported cotton and acrylic yarns. One row of weft twining at end.

Basket for wool (*bekhur*)
From the household of Ugen Tshomo, Tang Ugyenchöling, Bumthang, c. 1990. Circ: 78 cm; h: 12 cm. Phillips Collection, Peabody Essex Museum (E200199).

Holding stick with raw carded wool (A) and **spindle with yarn** (B)
From the household of Ugen Tshomo, Tang Ugyenchöling, Bumthang, c. 1990. A: 23 cm long x 5.8 cm wide; B: 28.5 x 4 cm. Phillips Collection, Peabody Essex Museum (E200197 A, B). A: wood. B: sheep wool.

Wild silk cocoons
Mela Bazaar, Samdrup Jongkhar-Assam border, 1992. About 6.5 x 3 cm for a single example. Phillips Collection, Peabody Essex Museum (E200184).

Skein of wild silk yarn, undyed
Mela Bazaar, Samdrup Jongkhar-Assam border, 1992. L: 40 cm; diam: 5 cm. Phillips Collection, Peabody Essex Museum (E200185).

Cotton bolls
From the fields of Sangay Dolma, Thongsa, Pemagatshel District, 1992. Phillips Collection, Peabody Essex Museum (E200191)

Skein of handspun cotton yarn, undyed
Dyed by Sangay Dolma, Thongsa, Pemagatshel District, 1992. L: 60 cm; diam: 9 cm. Phillips Collection, Peabody Essex Museum (E200192).

Hanks of handspun cotton yarn, dyed with madder (A, B) and indigo (C)
Spun by Sangay Dolma, Thongsa, Pemagatshel District, 1992. A: 30 cm long x 8 cm diam. B: 28 cm x 8 cm. C: 29 cm x 7 cm. Phillips Collection, Peabody Essex Museum (E200193 A-C).

Nettle fiber for spinning
From the household of Am Kunzang, wife of Sonam Chögyel, manager of the National Handloom Development Project, Khaling, Tashigang District, 1992. L: 50 cm; diam: 17 cm. Phillips Collection, Peabody Essex Museum (E200194).

Cloth (loom length)
Eastern Bhutan, c. 1978. 226 cm (including 43 cm of unwoven warp) x 48 cm. Lent by Diana K. Myers. Nettle fiber.

Backstrap loom (*pangthag*) with partially woven *lungserma* cloth
From the household of Pema Chöden, Radi Dukpiling, Tashigang District, 1992. Warp: 240 cm: weft: 51 cm. Phillips Collection, Peabody Essex Museum (E200209). Loom pieces: wood, bamboo, metal. Weaving: Assamese wild silk, dyed and redyed in Radi with natural and synthetic dyes; warp-faced plainweave with supplementary-warp patterning. Backstrap: cow hide, wood, leather straps.

Woman's dress (*kira; mensé mathra*)
Eastern Bhutan, mid-twentieth century. 227 cm (including approximately 4-cm fringe at each end) x 123 cm. Lent by the Minneapolis Institute of Arts (82.102.14), Gift of Bud Grossman. Wild silk, warp-faced plainweave with supplementary-warp patterning.

Bag (*kushü phechung*)
Khoma, Lhuntshi District, 1992. 50 x 51 cm. Phillips Collection, Peabody Essex Museum (E200455). Imported cotton yarns, warp-faced plainweave ground; discontinuous and continuous supplementary-weft patterning (*sapma*) in Indian acrylic yarns. Imported Indian cotton, wool, and silk brocade cloth. Card-woven cotton strap; leather; metal studs. Facing: red cotton fabric. Machine stitched.

Card loom with partially woven woman's belt
Chungkar Thongsa, Pemagatshel District, c. 1990. Warp: 278 cm; weft: 5.5 cm. Phillips Collection, Peabody Essex Museum (E200207). Loom pieces: wood, bamboo. Cards: pigskin (?). Weaving: imported wool with discontinuous supplementary-weft patterning in imported silk and metallic yarns. Backstrap: woven bamboo, wood, leather straps.

Backstrap loom with partially woven panel for a woman's dress
Bhutan, before 1981. Warp: 281 cm; weft: 58.5 cm. Phillips Collection, Peabody Essex Museum (E70794). Loom pieces: wood, bamboo. Weaving: several kinds of imported cotton used for warp-faced plainweave ground; discontinuous supplementary-weft patterning (*sapma* and *thrima*) in imported cotton and silk. Backstrap: canvas, wood, Indian rope straps.

Woman's dress (*kira; kushüthara*)
Central Bhutan, early twentieth century. 274 cm (including 5-cm fringe at each end) x 137 cm. Lent by Barbara Adams. Warps of handspun unbleached and indigo-dyed (blue) cotton and of colored wild silk. Warp-faced plainweave ground; discontinuous and continuous supplementary-weft patterning (*sapma* and *thrima*) in wild silk. One row of weft twining at ends. Natural dyes. Handstitched.

Cushion cover (*denkheb*)
Central Bhutan, twentieth century. 154 x 90 cm. Lent by the Museum for Textiles (T80.038). Wool; twill ground with discontinuous supplementary-weft patterning.

Loom length (*yathra*)
Central Bhutan, 1992. 251 cm x 55.5 cm. Anonymous lender. Local and imported wool; twill ground with discontinuous supplementary-weft patterning.

References

Abhayadatta. 1979. *Buddha's lions: The lives of the eighty-four siddhas.* Translated by James B. Robinson. Berkeley.

Adams, Barbara. 1984. *Traditional Bhutanese textiles.* Bangkok: White Orchid Press.

Allione, Tsultrim. 1984. *Women of wisdom.* London: Routledge and Kegan Paul.

Ardussi, J.A. 1977. Brewing and drinking the beer of enlightenment in Tibetan Buddhism. *Journal of the American Oriental Society* 97: 115-24.

Aris, Michael. 1976. "The admonition of the thunderbolt cannon-ball" and its place in the Bhutanese New Year Festival. *Bulletin of the School of Oriental and African Studies* 39, no. 3: 601-35.

___. 1979. *Bhutan: The early history of a Himalayan kingdom.* Warminster, England: Aris & Phillips, Ltd.

___. 1980a. Notes on the history of the Mon-Yul corridor. In Aris and Aung San Suu Kyi 1980, 9-20.

___. 1980b. Sacred dances of Bhutan. *Natural History* 89, no. 3 (March): 38-47.

___. 1982. *Views of medieval Bhutan: The diary and drawings of Samuel Davis, 1783.* London: Serindia Publications, and Washington, D.C.: Smithsonian Institution Press.

___. 1986. Sources for the history of Bhutan. *Wiener Studien zur Tibetologie und Buddhismuskunde* 14: 170-86. Arbeitskreis für Tibetische und Buddhistische Studien, University of Vienna.

___. 1989a. Comment [on radiocarbon dating of Chang Gangkha wall paintings]. In R.E.M. Hedges et al., Radiocarbon dates from the Oxford AMS System: *Archaeometry* Datelist 9. *Archaeometry* 30, no. 2:207-29.

___. 1989b. *Hidden treasures and secret lives: A study of Pemalingpa (1450-1521) and the Sixth Dalai Lama (1683-1706).* London and New York: Kegan Paul International.

___. 1990. Man and nature in the Buddhist Himalayas. In Rustomji and Ramble 1990, 85-101.

Aris, Michael, and Aung San Suu Kyi (eds). 1980. *Tibetan studies in honour of Hugh Richardson* (Proceedings of the International Seminar on Tibetan Studies, Oxford, 1979). Warminster, England: Aris & Phillips, Ltd.

Ashi nangsai namthar (a zhe snang sa'i rnam thar) [*The biography of Nangsa Obum*]. [n.d.] 1984. Thimphu: Department of Education.

Aten Dogyetshang. 1993. *Nyarong tam genma* (nyag rong gtam rgan ma) [*Old stories of Nyarong*]. Dharamsala, India: Amnye Machen Institute.

Aziz, Barbara Nimri, and Matthew Kapstein (eds). 1985. *Soundings in Tibetan civilization: Proceedings of the 1982 seminar of the International Association for Tibetan Studies.* New Delhi: Manohar Publications.

Barker, David K. 1985. Bhutanese handwoven textiles. *Arts of Asia* 15, no. 4 (July-August): 103-11.

___. 1986. *Designs of Bhutan.* Bangkok: White Lotus Co.

Bartholomew, Mark. 1985. *Thunder dragon textiles from Bhutan.* Kyoto: Shikosha Publishing Co.

Baruah, Tapan Kumar M. 1960. *The people of the NEFA [North East Frontier Agency]: The Idu Mishmis.* Shillong, India: On behalf of the Adviser to the Governor of Assam.

Basu, N.K. 1970. *Assam in the Ahom age.* Calcutta: Sanskrit Pustak Bhandar.

Béguin, Gilles. 1991. Techniques of Tibetan painting and sculpture. In Rhie and Thurman 1991, 385-88.

Bell, Sir Charles. 1924. *Tibet: Past and present.* Oxford.

Bell Collection. 1904. *Report on Bhutan west of the Amo Chhu.* MSS EUR F80/5c.1. Oriental and India Office Collections, The British Library (London).

___. 1910. *Secret report on December 1909-January 1910 trip.* MSS EUR F80/5c.3. Oriental and India Office Collections, The British Library (London).

___. 1915a. Letter from the Paro Pönlop to Sir Charles Bell, Political Officer of Sikkim (February 5). MSS EUR F80/5a.19d. Oriental and India Office Collections, The British Library (London).

___. 1915b. Letter from Ugyen Wangchuck, Maharaja of Bhutan, to Sir Charles Bell, Chikyab Lonchen [Political Officer] of Sikkim (annotated March 15). MSS EUR F80/5a.19e. Oriental and India Office Collections, The British Library (London).

Bhattacharjee, Tarun Kumar. 1983. *The Idus of Mathun and Dri Valley.* Shillong, India: Directorate of Research, Government of Arunachal Pradesh.

Bogle, George. 1774. In Markham [1876] 1971 and Collister 1987.

Bögya tsigdzö chenmo (bod rgya tshig mdzod chen mo) [Large Tibetan-Chinese dictionary]. 1985. 3 vols. Beijing.

Bose, Kishan Kant. 1815. In *Political missions to Bootan* [1865] 1972.

Boudot, Eric. 1994. Minority costumes and textiles of southwestern China. *Orientations* 25, no. 2 (February): 59-66.

Butler, Edward A. 1888. *Silkworms.* Paternoster Square [London?]: Swan Sonnenschein, Lowrey, & Co.

Butler, J. 1847. *A sketch of Assam.* Excerpted in Elwin 1959b.

Cacella, Estevão. 1627. *The report which Father Estevão Cacella of the Society of Jesus sent to Father Alberto Laercio, provincial of the province of Malabar of East India, about his journey to Catayo until he came to the kingdom of Potente.* Translated in Aris 1986.

Chandra Das, Rai Sarat. [1902] 1985. *A Tibetan-English dictionary.* Reprint.

Kyoto: Rinsen Book Co.

Cheesman, Patricia. 1982. The antique weaving of the Lao Neua. *Arts of Asia* 12, no. 4 (July-August): 120-25.

___. 1988. *Lao textiles: Ancient symbols, living art*. Bangkok: White Lotus Co.

Chime Wongmo. 1985. Rituals of Bhutanese house construction. In Aziz and Kapstein 1985, 107-14.

Choeki Ongmo. 1991. Vegetable dyeing in Radhi Tsang Khar (Tashi Gang). Typescript. National Handloom Development Project, Khaling.

Choeki Ongmo and Purna Prasad. 1991. A dyer's hand book. Typescript. National Handloom Development Project, Khaling.

Chowdhury, J.N. 1990. *The tribal culture and history of Arunachal Pradesh*. New Delhi: Daya Publishing House.

Collingwood, Peter. 1982. *The techniques of tablet weaving*. New York: Watson-Guptill Publishers.

Collister, Peter. 1987. *Bhutan and the British*. London: Serindia Publications.

Dalton, E.T. 1872. *Descriptive ethnology of Bengal*. Excerpted in Elwin 1959b.

Das, N.C. 1985. Weaving in the folklore of north-east India. In Sen 1985, 228-33.

Davis, Samuel. 1830. Remarks on the religions and social institutions of the Bouteas, or inhabitants of Boutan, from the unpublished journal of the late Samuel Davis, esq. F.R.S. &c. *Transactions of the Royal Asiatic Society of Great Britain and Ireland* 2: 491-517. Reproduced in Aris 1982.

Delog sangye chözom namthar ('das log sangs rgyas chos 'dzom rnam thar) [*Biography of Sangye Chözom who returned from the dead*]. [c. 1800?] 1980. Quoted in Pommaret 1989.

Department of Education. 1992. *A history of Bhutan: Coursebook for class VII*. Thimphu: Ministry for Social Services, Royal Government of Bhutan.

Desgodins, C.H. 1872. *La mission du Thibet de 1855 à 1870*. Verdun, France.

Desideri, Ippolito. 1932. *An account of Tibet*. Edited by Filippo de Filippi. London: Routledge.

Dhar, Bibhas. 1984. The Monpas of Khalegthang area, alias, the Tsanglas: A brief ethnographic account. In Karotemprel and Danda 1984, 295ff.

Driem, George van. 1991. *Guide to official Dzongkha romanization*. Thimphu: Dzongkha Development Commission, Royal Government of Bhutan.

___. 1991 ms. The languages of Bhutan. Paper adapted from the *Report on the first linguistic survey of Bhutan*. Thimphu: Dzongkha Development Commission, Royal Government of Bhutan.

___. 1992. *The grammar of Dzongkha*. Thimphu: Dzongkha Development Commission, Royal Government of Bhutan.

___. 1994. Language policy in Bhutan. In *Bhutan: A traditional order and the forces of change*. Edited by Michael Hutt. London. Forthcoming.

Dunsmore, Susi. 1993. *Nepalese textiles*. London: British Museum Press.

Dutta, Parul. 1990. *The Singphos*. Itanagar, India: Directorate of Research, Government of Arunachal Pradesh.

Elwin, Verrier. 1957. *A philosophy for NEFA*. 2d rev. ed. [1959]. Shillong, India: On behalf of the Adviser to the Governor of Assam.

___. 1959a. *The art of the north-east frontier of India*. Shillong, India: North-East Frontier Agency.

Elwin, Verrier (ed). 1959b. *India's north-east frontier in the nineteenth century*. Madras, India: Oxford University Press.

Emery, Irene. 1980. *The primary structures of fabrics: An illustrated classification*. Washington, D.C.: The Textile Museum.

The Encyclopaedia Britannica. 1911. 11th ed. New York: Encyclopaedia Britannica Co.

Endle, Sidney. [1910?] 1990. *The Kacharis*. Reprint. New Delhi: Low Price Publications.

Fano, Domenico da. 1713. *A short description of the kingdom of Tibet*. In Petech 1952-56.

Feltwell, John. 1990. *The story of silk*. New York: St. Martin's Press.

Ferguson, Douglas C. 1971-72. *The moths of America north of Mexico including Greenland*. Fascicle 20.2, Bombycoidea Saturniidae. London: E.W. Classey Ltd. and R.B.D. Publications Inc.

Ferris, Russell E. 1979. Dyes, natural. In *Encyclopedia of chemical technology*. 3rd ed., vol. 8. New York: John Wiley & Sons.

Fraser-Lu, Sylvia. 1989. *Handwoven textiles of South-East Asia*. Paperback ed. Singapore: Oxford University Press.

Fürer-Haimendorf, Christoph von. 1980. *A Himalayan tribe: From cattle to cash*. Berkeley: University of California Press.

___. 1982. *Highlanders of Arunachal Pradesh: Anthropological research in north-east India*. New Delhi: Vikas Publishing House.

Gait, Sir Edward. [1905] 1967. *A history of Assam*. Reprint. Calcutta: Thacker Spink & Co.

Gittinger, Mattiebelle, and Leedom Lefferts. 1992. *Textiles and the Tai experience in Southeast Asia*. Washington, D.C.: The Textile Museum.

Gorer, Geoffrey. [1938] 1967. *Himalayan village: An account of the Lepchas of Sikkim*. 2d ed. London: Nelson.

Government of Assam, Department of Land Records and Agriculture. 1878-82. *Annual report on the trade between Assam and adjoining foreign countries*. Shillong, India. Published every three years starting in 1884.

Government of Bengal. 1870-1878. *Annual volume of trade and navigation for the Bengal presidency, Calcutta*. Published as *Review of the external land trade of British India, 1878-1880*; *Report on the external trade of Bengal with Nepal, Sikkim and Bhutan, 1881-1891*; and *Report on the external trade of Bengal with Nepal, Tibet, Sikkim and Bhutan*, after 1891.

Griffiths, William. [1838]. Journal of the mission to Bootan in 1837-38. In *Political missions to Bootan* 1865.

Gruning, John F. 1911. *Jalpaiguri district*. Vol. 11, East Bengal district gazetteers. Allahabad, India.

Gyurme Dorje and Matthew Kapstein. 1991. *The Nyingma school of Tibetan Buddhism: Its fundamentals and history*. Vol. 2 reference material. Boston: Wisdom.

Havnevik, Hanne. n.d. [1991?] *Tibetan Buddhist nuns*. Oslo: Norwegian University Press.

Hesselmeyer, C.H. 1867. *A missionary's view of the Akas*. Excerpted in Elwin 1959b.

Hill, Tamara W. 1993. A Himalayan tantric banner. *HALI* 55: 100-109.

Hodson, T.C. [1911] 1989. *The Naga tribes of Manipur*. Reprint. New Delhi: Low Price Publications.

Hooker, J.D. 1855. *Himalayan journals*. 2 vols. London: John Murray.

Hunter, W.W. [1879] n.d. *A statistical account of Assam in two volumes*. Reprint. New Delhi: Low Price Publications.

Huntington, John C. 1986. Notes on the iconography and iconology of the Paro Tsechu festival giant thang-ka. *Orientations* 17, no. 7 (July): 51-57, 74.

Imaeda, Yoshiro. 1987. *La constitution de la théocratie 'brug pa au 17ème siècle et les problèmes de succession du premier zhabs drung*. Ph.D. dissertation. Department of Oriental Languages and Civilizations, University of Paris.

Imaeda, Yoshiro, and Françoise Pommaret. 1990. Note sur la situation linguistique du Bhoutan et étude préliminaire des termes de parenté. *Indo-Tibetan Studies*, Buddhica Brittanica series continua II, Tring: 115-33.

Jackson, David P., and Janice A. Jackson. 1984. *Tibetan thangka painting: Methods and materials*. London: Serindia Publications.

Jacobs, Julian. 1990. *Hill peoples of northeast India: The Nagas*. London: Thames and Hudson.

Karotemprel, Sebastian, and Deepali Danda. 1984. *The tribes of northeast India*. Calcutta: Firma KLM.

Kathrim (bka' khrims) [Bhutan's Legal Code of 1729]. In Aris 1986.

Kennedy, R.S. 1914. *Ethnological report on the Akas, Khoas and Mijis and the Monbas of Tawang*. Quoted in notes to C.H. Hesselmeyer, in Elwin 1959b.

Kolander, Cheryl. 1985. *A silk worker's notebook*. Rev. ed. Loveland, Colorado: Interweave Press.

Kumar, K. 1979a. *The Boris*. Shillong, India: Research Department, Government of Arunachal Pradesh.

___. 1979b. *The Pailibos*. Shillong, India: Research Department, Government of Arunachal Pradesh.

Lahiri, Nayanjot. 1991. *Pre-Ahom Assam*. New Delhi: Munshiram Manoharlal.

Lauf, Detlef. 1976. *Tibetan sacred art*. Berkeley: Shambhala.

Laufer, Berthold. 1918. *Loan-words in Tibetan*. Leiden.

Leeper, Arthur. 1984. Origins of the Tibetan pile rug tradition: Archaeological evidence. In Myers 1984, 21-25.

Lehman, F.K. 1963. *The structure of Chin society*. Illinois Studies in Anthropology, no. 3. Urbana: University of Illinois Press.

Lewis, Paul, and Elaine Lewis. 1984. *Peoples of the Golden Triangle*. London: Thames and Hudson.

Liebenthal, Walter. 1956. The ancient Burma road – a legend? *Journal of the Greater India Society* 16, no. 1: 1-17.

Macgregor, C.R. 1884. *A soldier's view of the Akas*. Excerpted in Elwin 1959b.

Mackenzie, Alexander. [1884] 1989. *The north-east frontier of India*. Reprint. New Delhi: Mittal Publications.

Marak, Julius. 1986. *Garo customary laws and practices*. Calcutta: Firma KLM.

Markham, Sir Clements R. (ed). 1876. *Narrative of the mission of George Bogle to Tibet and of the journey of Thomas Manning to Lhasa*. London: Trübner & Co.

___. [1876] 1971. *Narrative of the mission of George Bogle to Tibet and of the journey of Thomas Manning to Lhasa*. Reprint. New Delhi: Manjusri.

Mehra, Parshotam. 1980. *The north-eastern frontier: A documentary study of the internecine rivalry between India, Tibet and China*. Vol. 2, 1914-54. New Delhi: Oxford University Press.

Mickle, Wendy. 1984. Spinning and sheep. *The Textile Booklist* 9, no. 2 (May): 5-7.

Milne, Leslie. [1910] 1970. *Shans at home*. Reprint. New York: Paragon Book Reprint Corp.

Montmollin, Marceline de. 1982. *Collection du Bhoutan*. Neuchâtel: Musée d'ethnographie.

Myers, Diana K. 1984. *Temple, household, horseback: Rugs of the Tibetan plateau*. Washington, D.C.: The Textile Museum.

___. 1988. Costume and ceremonial textiles of Bhutan. *The Textile Museum Journal (1987)*: 24-53. Washington, D.C.: The Textile Museum.

___. 1989. *Bhutanese textiles*. Exhibition publication. Washington, D.C.: International Monetary Fund Art Society.

___. 1990. Dyeing in the Himalayas. *Brooklyn Botanic Garden Record* 46, no. 2 (Summer): 10-15.

Mynak R. Tulku Rinpoche and Françoise Pommaret. 1989. A rainbow of colors: Notes on the symbolism of colours in Bhutan. *Asian Pacific Cultures*, no. 42: 6-9.

Nado (Lopön; later Lam). 1986. *Druk karpo*; a short name for "'Brug dkar po / 'Brug rgyal khab kyi chos srid gnas stangs" [*The white dragon: The state of religious and secular affairs in the kingdom of Bhutan*]. Bumthang, Bhutan: Tharpaling Monastery.

Nado (Lam). 1987. *The white dragon*. Translated with Diana K. Myers. Typescript. Thimphu.

Nagphel (Dasho). 1967. *Druk chamyig* ('brug 'chams yigs) [*Manual of Bhutanese sacred dance*]. Thimphu.

Nair, P. Thankappan. 1985. *Tribes of Arunachal Pradesh*. Gauhati, India: Spectrum Publications.

Nakao, Sasuke, and Keiji Nishioka. 1984. *Flowers of Bhutan*. Tokyo: Asahi Shimbun Publishing Co.

Nanda, Neeru. 1982. *Tawang, the land of Mon*. New Delhi: Vikas Publishing House.

Nebesky-Wojkowitz, Rene von. 1956. *Where the gods are mountains: Three years among the people of the Himalayas*. Translated by Michael Bullock. London: Wiedenfeld and Nicolson.

Ngawang. 1728. *Gyelrig*; a short name for "Sa skyong rgyal po'i gdung rabs 'byung khungs dang 'bangs kyi mi rabs chad tshul nges par gsal ba'i 'sgron me" [*The lamp which illuminates with certainty generations of kings*]. Blockprint, 54 folios. Quoted in Aris 1986.

___. n.d. *Logyü*; a short name for "Dpal 'brug par lung lha'i gdung brgyud kyis bstan pa'i ring lungs / lho mon kha bzhi las nyi ma shar phyogs su byung zhing rgyas pa'i lo rgyus gsal ba'i me long" [*The mirror which illuminates the story ... *]. Blockprint, 24 folios. Quoted in Aris 1979 and 1986.

North and northeast frontier tribes of India. [1907] 1983. Compiled in the Intelligence Branch, Division of the Chief of the Staff, Army HQ, India. Reprint. New Delhi: Cultural Publishing House.

Olschak, Blanche C. 1966. Bhutanese weaving. *Palette* 24: 2-8.

Pal, Pratapaditya. 1983. *Art of Tibet: A catalogue of the Los Angeles County Museum of Art Collection*. Berkeley: LACMA/University of California Press.

Pallis, Marco. 1960. Do clothes make the man? The significance of human attire. In *The way and the mountain*, 141-59. London: Peter Owen.

Peigler, Richard S. 1993. Wild silks of the world. *American Entomologist* 39, no. 3 (Fall): 151-61.

Pemalingpa. [n.d.] 1976. *Pemalingpa*; a short name for "Bum thang gter ston padma gling pa'i rnam thar 'od zer kun mdzes nor bu'i 'phreng ba zhes bya ba skal ldan spro ba skye ba'i tshul du bris pa" [*The recovered teachings of the great Pemalingpa*]. Blockprint. Appeared as one volume (pha) in the 20-volume reprint of Pemalingpa's collected works, New Delhi.

Pemberton, R.B. [1838] 1966. *Report on the eastern frontier of British India*. Reprint. Gauhati, India. Quoted in Lahiri 1991.

___. [1839] 1976. *Report on Bhutan*. Reprint. New Delhi. Quoted in Collister 1987.

Petech, Luciano. 1990. Duṅ-reṅ. *Acta Orientalia Academiae Scientiarum Hungaricae* 44: 103-11.

___ (ed). 1952-56. *I missionari italiani nel tibet e nel nepal.* 7 vols. Rome.

Pha drukgom shikpai namthar; a short name for "Pha 'drug sgom zhig pa'i rnam par thar pa thugs rje chu rgyun" [*Biography of Pha Drukgom Shikpo*]. n.d. [c. 1580?] Blockprint, 44 folios.

Phukan, J.N. 1981. The first Bhutan mission to Ahom-court in 1801-1802. *Journal of Indian History* 59, nos. 1-3: 225-33.

Political missions to Bootan, comprising the reports of the Hon'ble Ashley Eden, 1864; Capt. R.B. Pemberton, 1837, 1838, with Dr. W. Griffiths's journal [1837-8]; and the account by Baboo Kishen Kant Bose [1815]. (a) 1865. Calcutta: Bengal Secretariat Office. (b) [1865] 1972. Reprint. New Delhi: Manjusri.

Pommaret, Françoise. 1989. *Les revenants de l'au-dela dans le monde tibétain: Sources littéraires et tradition vivante.* Paris: Centre National de la Recherche Scientifique.

___. 1994. Les fêtes aux divinités-montagnes phyva au Bhoutan de l'est. *Proceedings of the VIth Seminar of Tibetan Studies* [1992]. Oslo, Norway. Forthcoming.

Prangwatthanakam, Songsak, and Patricia Cheesman. 1988. *Lan na textiles.* 2d ed. Chiang Mai: Center for the Promotion of Arts and Culture, Chiang Mai University.

Provincial gazetteer of Assam. [1906] 1983. Compiled by Authority, Eastern Bengal and Assam Secretariat. Reprint. New Delhi: Cultural Publishing House.

Rhie, Marilyn M., and Robert A.F. Thurman. 1991. *Wisdom and compassion: The sacred art of Tibet.* New York: Harry N. Abrams.

Rockhill, William Woodville. [1891] 1975. *The land of the lamas.* Reprint. New Delhi.

Rustomji, Nari. 1971. *Enchanted frontiers: Sikkim, Bhutan and India's north-eastern borderlands.* Oxford University Press.

Rustomji, Nari K., and Charles Ramble (eds). 1990. *Himalayan environment and culture.* Shimla: Indian Institute of Advanced Study, and New Delhi: Indus.

Saha, Sudhanshu Bikash (ed). 1987. *Tribes of north east India: Spectrum of changes.* Agartala, India: Rupali Publishing.

Sakya, Jamyang. 1990. *Princess from the land of snow.* Boston: Shambhala.

Schuette, Marie. 1956. Geographical distribution of tablet weaving. *CIBA Review* (Basel, Switzerland) 112: 9-18.

Sen, Souman (ed). 1985. *Folklore in north-east India.* Gauhati and New Delhi: Omsons Publications.

Sharma, Rakesh. 1961. *The people of NEFA: The Sherdukpens.* Shillong, India: North-East Frontier Agency.

Singh, Ramgopal. 1987. The Tang Khuls of Manipur. In Saha 1987, 151-58.

Sonam Tshering. 1990. Some information on vegetable dyes in Bhutan. *Tsenden: A general publication on forestry in Bhutan* 2, no. 1 (Jan.): 11-20. Issued by the Department of Forestry, Royal Government of Bhutan.

Sonam Wangmo. 1990. The Brokpas: A semi-nomadic people in eastern Bhutan. In Rustomji and Ramble 1990, 141-58.

Srivastava, L.R.N. [1962] 1988. *The people of NEFA: The Gallongs.* Itanagar, India: Directorate of Research, Government of Arunachal Pradesh.

Stratton, Carol. 1986. The Paro Tsechu festival and the giant thang-ka. *Orientations* 17, no. 7 (July): 46-50.

Survey of India. 1915. Exploration in Tibet and neighboring regions, 1879-1892. *Records of the Survey of India* 8, pt. 2. Dehra Dun, India: Office of the Trigonometrical Survey.

Taring, Rinchen Drolma. 1986. *Daughter of Tibet.* Boston: Shambhala.

Tendzin Chögyel. 1759. *Lhoi chöjung* (lho'i chos byung) [*Religious history of the south*]. Blockprint, 151 folios. Quoted in Aris 1979.

Tendzin Dorje. n.d. [1986?] ms. *Logyü dordü drizai limbu*; a short name for "'Brug shar phyogs pa'i gnyen lam brtsi stangs dang bkra shis sgang phyogs kyi 'brog pa gnyen sgrigs sbyor bya tshul lo rgyus mdor bsdus dri za'i gling bu" [*A brief account of the manner in which marriages are contracted in eastern Bhutan and the way in which weddings are arranged in the Tashigang region (entitled) the flute of the gandharvas*]. Thimphu.

The Textile Booklist. 1984. Special issues on Bhutan. Nos. 1 (January) and 2 (May).

Todd, Bert Kerr. 1952. Bhutan, land of the thunder dragon. *National Geographic Magazine* 102, no. 6 (December): 714-54.

Trungpa, Chogyam. 1985. *Born in Tibet.* Boston: Shambhala.

Tsybikov, G.T. 1993. *Un pelerin bouddhiste au Tibet.* Paris: Peuples du Monde.

Turner, Samuel. [1800] 1971. *An account of an embassy to the court of the Teshoo Lama in Tibet; containing a narrative of a journey through Bootan and part of Tibet.* Reprint. New Delhi: Manjusri.

Van Springen, Willem. 1992. *Tibetan border worlds: A geo-historical analysis of trade and traders.* Ph.D. dissertation. University of Amsterdam.

Verma, V.S. 1976 ms. *The Tawang Monpas.* Typescript. New Delhi.

Wardle, Thomas. 1881. *Handbook of the collection illustrative of the wild silks of India in the Indian section of the South Kensington Museum.* London: George E. Eyre and William Spottiswoode, Printers to the Queen's Most Excellent Majesty, for Her Majesty's Stationery Office.

Watson, J. Forbes. 1868. *The people of India.* Edited by J. Forbes Watson and John William Kaye. London: India Museum.

Watt, George. [1889] 1972. *A dictionary of the economic products of India.* Reprint. New Delhi.

Welsh, Captain. 1794. *Report on Assam.* In Mackenzie [1884] 1989: 377-94.

White, John Claude. [1909] 1984. *Sikkim and Bhutan: 21 years on the north-east frontier.* Reprint. New Delhi: Cosmo Publications.

___. 1914. Castles in the air: Experiences and journeys in unknown Bhutan. *National Geographic Magazine* 25, no. 4 (April): 365-455.

Wilcox, R. 1832. Memoir of a survey of Assam and the neighboring countries, executed in 1825-6-7-8. *Asiatic Researches* 17. Excerpted in Elwin 1959b, 303-07.

Williamson, Margaret D. 1987. *Memoirs of a political officer's wife in Tibet, Sikkim and Bhutan.* London: Wisdom Publications.

Williamson Collection. Photograph albums. 4 vols. Cambridge University Museum of Archaeology and Anthropology.

Wikan, Unni. 1990. The situation of the girl child in Bhutan. Thimphu: UNICEF.

Yönten Thayé (Je Khenpo). n.d. *Mutig doshel*; a short name for "Chos rgyal chen po shes rab dbang phyug gi dge ba'i cho ga rab tu gsal ba'i gtam mu tig do shal" [*The discourse which illuminates the virtuous rites of the great dharmaraja Sherab Wangchuk (entitled) the necklace of pearls*]. (a) Blockprint, 95 folios. (b) [n.d.] 1970. Reprinted in *Masterpieces of Bhutanese biographical literature,* 431-617. New Delhi: n.p.

Yuthok, Dorje Yudon. 1990. *The house of the turquoise roof.* Ithaca, New York: Snow Lion Publications.

Index